In Times Past

Using Children's Literature to Teach United States History

by Carol Otis Hurst and Rebecca Otis

Innovative Approaches

Strands and Thematic Activities

Chronology of Multicultural Fiction and Nonfiction

Focus Books

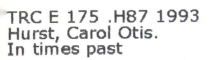

SRA

Macmillan/McGraw–Hill

New York, New York   Columbus, Ohio   Santa Rosa, California   Atlanta, Georgia   Dallas, Texas

With love to Jill Hurst,

in gratitude for and recognition of all she does for teachers.

Acknowledgments

The authors wish to give special thanks to Jacqueline Daley,
Colrain Central School, Colrain, Massachusetts,
and Mary Pat McMahon and Richelle Schiller for the many hours they spent reviewing the book.

Photo Credits
Page 24, Courtesy of Plimoth Plantation, Plymouth, MA.
Pages 167, 174, 175, 182, 188, 189, 194, 214, 233, 238, 242,
    Bettman Archive.

Illustration Credit
Page 268, Scott O. Sheppard

1 2 3 4 5 6 7 8 9 10   99 98 97 96 95 94 93

Table of Contents

Introducing In Times Past

Part 1: Approaches to History Through LIterature

Part 2: Following a Strand

Table of Contents

Part 3: Chronology of History

Focus Books

Appendix

Introducing In Times Past

Integrating Literature and the Social Studies Curriculum

The best teachers and students of history have long known that it is the stories that intrigue and involve us in history. Contrary to what Julius Caesar may have thought, few of us care which phalanx came over which hill in which battle. For most of us, the stories of the people in the phalanx give us a chance to focus on the individuals, and through that focus, we learn to care about the past and the problems people faced. To care about and to begin to understand the past, we need to understand the people and cultures of the time: how people lived and what they wanted and how individual needs and wants conflicted with the needs and wants of others.

For too long, American history textbooks have glossed over the injustices and cruelties to Native Americans, Hispanic Americans, Asian Americans, Black Americans, and other peoples and cultures as the European culture spread throughout the continent. Textbooks have also neglected to highlight the experiences and achievements of women, children, the poor, and people from outside the European cultures. With the use of novels, picture books, and nonfiction trade books, it is possible to provide a more balanced look at this country's not-always-glorious past.

With the increased use of literature in the classroom, we are challenged to use that literature throughout the curriculum. By bringing novels, biographies, and general nonfiction into the social studies curriculum, we can approach the integrated day. We can show students that learning cannot and should not be capsulated and regimented, that one good story leads to another, and that by reading stories about people in our past, we can come to understand where our country has been, what has made it what it is today, and what it might become.

Sometimes books for children oversimplify motivations or deeds. The authors' sources of information are sometimes four or five generations removed from the original. Not all authors for children have subjected themselves to the rigors of accurate historical research. Therefore, both students and teachers should read widely from nonfictional and fictional sources in an attempt to reach something approaching the truth.

Arrangement of In Times Past

☙ Part 1 of *In Times Past*, **Approaches to History Through Literature,** will give you many ideas for presenting history through literature. These approaches, on pages 11–47, include activities that can be applied to almost any historical period. Any or all of these approaches may be used as you and your students read the books suggested in Parts 2 through 4.

> *The Whole Language Approach*
>
> *Truth and Research*
>
> *Living History Museums*
>
> *Time Line Smorgasbord*
>
> *Follow Me*
>
> *Picture This*
>
> *Time Fantasies*
>
> *The Big Picture*

☙ In Part 2, **Following a Strand**, we have shown how to follow a theme through history, studying one facet of history through the books and the years.

Things to Look For in Part 2 Units
- Topic
- Projects and activities
- Nonfiction and fiction books

Discovery and Invention

Activities

- Play What If. Players select any invention or discovery and tell how they think our lives would have been different without that invention or discovery.
- Make a list of the wealthiest families in America or in your community and then try to figure out where their money came from.
- Make a list of fantasy inventions. Be specific about what it will do, how it can be produced, what it will cost to produce, how much it will sell for. Campaign for a patent to a patent committee set up in your classroom.
- Invent Rube Goldberg machines. Design a complicated machine to do a simple task, such as blowing out a match. Make a design for it or even make the machine.
- Investigate the history of the US Patent Office. When did it originate? Who is eligible to receive patents? Obtain statistics about patents: number per year, categories, number of men and women inventors, and so on. Do we still need it? Who decides who receives a patent?
- How has the increasing influence of corporations affected invention? Do individuals get patents now or do they usually belong to the corporation?
- Why are there so few famous women scientists and inventors?
- Through discussion, choose some major inventions, such as the wheel and the plow, and make flow charts showing other important inventions that wouldn't have been possible without that first invention. Do the same with discoveries such as the fact that the earth goes around the sun instead of vice versa. What later discoveries relied on that information?
- Choose a topic, such as the human body, the solar system, medicine, superstition, physics, chemistry, farming, environmental science, or energy. Make a historical chart that shows how our understanding and knowledge of that topic have changed.
- Make a list of the major causes of death during various historical periods. Are all of these diseases under control at present? How do these compare with AIDS?
- Consider the book you are now reading. What inventions and discoveries might the main character care about? Which would he/she think were most uninteresting?
- Choose a book about the past and decide how the story would change if you added a modern invention or discovery.
- How do we as a society determine the focus of research and invention? Has it always been so? Investigate the Manhattan Project. How did government's role in science change after that?
- Look through the biographies of inventors and discoverers throughout history. Do they have anything in common? Are there significant factors in their lives that have a similarity to others? Which of those qualities do you possess?
- Find old catalogues. Which of the inventions shown still exist? Did others evolve into something still used? Which bombed?

In Part 3, Chronology of Events, we have grouped events more or less chronologically so you can turn to almost any period in the history of the United States and find books that broaden and deepen the scope of any history curriculum. In fact this might become your history curriculum.

Things to Look For in Part 3
- Concurrent events
- Influential people
- Popular art, literature, and music
- Nonfiction and fiction books
- Projects and activities

---

202 *Chronology of History*

Exploring and Pioneering: 1850–1890 *The Times at a Glance...*

Movers & Shakers
Cochise
John Brown
Ulysses S. Grant
Horace Greeley
Chief Joseph
Abraham Lincoln
Robert E. Lee
Louis Pasteur
Dredd Scott

Headlines*

1850	California becomes state
1857	Dredd Scott decision
1859	John Brown's raid at Harper's Ferry
1860	South Carolina secedes from the Union
1861	US Civil War begins
1862	Homestead Act to encourage Westward Expansion
1863	Emancipation Proclamation
1866	Fourteenth Amendment grants Blacks full citizenship
1867	Alaska purchased from Russia
1869	Knights of Labor, first successful US labor union
1877	Chief Joseph attempts to lead 800 people to Canada
1883	Brooklyn Bridge completed
1889	First Oklahoma Land Rush

Meanwhile, In Other Parts of the World

1853-1856	Crimean War; Russia defeated
1859	Suez Canal construction begins
1864	Karl Marx presides over First International
1877	Britain annexes South Africa
1879	Chile, Bolivia, and Peru at war
1884	France takes Indochina
1882	Britain consolidates control of Egypt
1887	England dominates center and south of Africa
1888	Kaiser Wilhelm assumes throne of Germany

Inventions & Discoveries

1856	Bessemer invents process for cheap steel
1858	Darwin puts forth theory of evolution
1859	Oil discovered in Pennsylvania
1860	Pasteur uses sterilization to kill bacteria
1863	First subway opens in London
1865	Mendel discovers genetics
1867	Dynamite invented
	First practical typewriter
1876	Telephone patented
	Bacteria identified as cause of disease
1877	Phonograph invented
1879	Incandescent light bulb invented
1884	Photographic film and paper developed
1885	Motor car invented

*Many of the dates are only estimates made by historians and scientists. We tried to verify each date with at least two reliable sources; in cases where we found disagreement, we checked several sources. It is reasonable to expect that in your research you will also find disagreement.

Part 4 is a selection of books that are strong enough to support a wide range of research and activities. We expanded on the books and called them Focus Books and will show you how they can lead to other books and projects.

Things to Look For in Part 4
- Book title and author
- Story summary
- Information about the times
- Things to notice and talk about
- Things to do
- Related books

---

274 *Focus Books*

The Borning Room

The Borning Room
By Paul Fleischman. HarperCollins, 1991.
ISBN 0-06-023785-6

Genre: Historical Fiction

Setting: Ohio, 1820–turn of the century

Summary: One room in the house her grandfather built is the focal point of birth and death in Georgina's life. In that room she was born and she witnesses the birth of a sibling. Eventually, Georgina has her own babies there. There her mother dies giving birth to another baby. The room is also where Georgina's beloved grandfather dies after refusing to change his free-thinking ways.

Background Information
- Superstition played a big role in many people's lives in the nineteenth century.
- There was an Underground Railroad at work in Ohio during the years preceding the Civil War.

Things to Notice and Talk About
- Make a list of the risks every one in that household took.
- Discuss Cory's feelings about being sold away from her children. Was her fear justified? What might have become of Cory?
- Discuss Grandfather's religious beliefs.
- Notice the change in Hattie and Georgina's friendship and when it happened.
- Georgina's family plants trees to commemorate the dead and records births and deaths in the family Bible. What does your family do?

Things to Do
- Read other books about runaway slaves. See page 108.
- Draw a family tree of Georgina's family.

- Find other books in which a building or a part of a building plays an important role, such as *The House of Dies Drear* (below) and *The Root Cellar* (see page 277).
- Compare Georgina to Catherine in *A Gathering of Days* (page 197).
- Find a character from another book, set in another time, who would be a better friend for Georgina than Hattie.
- Find a picture of a house you would use for the location of *The Borning Room* if you were making a movie or television show. Whom would you cast as the characters? Write one scene from the book as a screenplay.

Picture Books
★Dragonwagon, Crescent. **Home Place.** Macmillan, 1990. ISBN 0–02-733190-3
See page 40.

Johnston, Tony. **The Quilt Story.** Putnam, 1985. ISBN 0-399-21008-3
This quilt of memories will witness many more events.

Fiction
Hamilton, Virgina. The House of Dies Drear. Macmillan, 1984. ISBN 0-02-742500-2

Least Sophisticated   Most Sophisticated
An old house on the Ohio River was the scene of drama during the days of the Underground Railroad.

Reiss, Johanna. **The Upstairs Room.** HarperCollins, 1990. ISBN 0-06-4440370-X

During World War II, the upstairs room becomes the hideout and refuge for a Jewish girl.

Book Ratings in In Times Past

In all sections of this book, we have included picture books because of their accessiblity and because the combination of illustrations and well-honed text is so powerful.

We included two rating systems for the books. One is a scale to give you an idea of the sophistication level a young person might need to enjoy the book.

■■■■■■■■■□□□□□□

Least Sophisticated   **Most Sophisticated**

This sophistication level takes into account the student's reading background and experiences. You might want to read aloud some of the more difficult books or ask proficient readers to tape them so more material is available to all learners.

All of the books in this volume are the best we could find on the subjects. Books that we feel are strong enough to support many varied historical and literary activities are called Focus Books. There are, however, many more books that could have been used as Focus Books and that are so good historically and literarily that we recommend purchasing them for your classroom or school library. A ★ indicates an outstanding book and a ◆ indicates a very good book. Books that are not marked offer a good story, interesting information, or will engage certain types of readers, but they are not as strong as the others.

Ideas for Using In Times Past

Here are just a few general suggestions to help you use literature with your students.

- Although *In Times Past* does not concentrate on geography, it is obvious that geography is of great importance in the study of history. Topography, climate, resources, and neighboring cultures should be a part of all historic study.

Starting with Books

- Select an era or theme from Part 2 or Part 3 that you and your students are interested in or one that is covered in your curriculum.

- Locate and read as many of the suggested books as possible. Add your own book discoveries. If you decide to use a Focus Book, you'll want multiple copies. If possible, keep the books you decide to use in the class library.

- After giving your best sales pitch, ask the students to select a book as a starter. If two or more choose the same book, they become a reading group. Don't worry about the grade/reading levels of the books. If the book is too hard, the reader has many choices: struggling through, learning from pictures and spot reading; getting someone else to read it to him/her; reading it with a partner who is more skilled; trying a simpler book. No book is too easy if there is information in it.

- Ask the students to estimate how long it will take them to read the first chapter or two of their books. At the designated time, meet with a student or group of students for a book discussion. What did they notice about the book? What information have they found? What did they find difficult to understand? What did they do about that lack of understanding? What else might they have done? What is the author trying to tell us? Who do they like or dislike in the book? What do they think is going to happen? What do they need more information on? Where might they get that information? Select some of the problems or interests as a basis for mini-lessons. Make these lessons brief (five or ten minutes is ideal) and directed. After these and many other topics have been covered, after you have conducted mini-lessons, ask the students again to estimate the time they think it will take to cover the next section of material. Proceed in this way until the students have absorbed as many books as possible.

- If a student's first book was fiction, suggest that he/she find nonfiction material to support the reading. If the first book was nonfiction, suggest that he/she find a novel set in that time or place or in a time and place with similar conflicts in order to see the events from a more personal point of view.

- Use the students' readings as a basis for discussions and projects that further explore the times and the cultures. Try to help the students avoid common misconceptions. For example, people are often under the impression that the United States was/is the only country in the world in which anything important is occurring.

Whichever literary approach to history that you and your students adopt, textbooks can serve as resource materials and as a means of filling in areas where literary information is sparse or incomplete. Also, textbook reading after, during, and before trade book reading can lead to more fruitful discussions as statements in conflicting sources are being explored.

Using literature-based history enables schools to avoid compartmentalizing learning as history overlaps and, at times absorbs, the language arts block. This helps solve the problems of fitting all the required curriculum into one school year.

Finally, as a teacher, be sure that you model and participate in all the activities you require of the students. As with all learning, better education results when the teacher is an active and participating learner.

Teacher's Resource Books

Atwell, Nancie. **Coming to Know: Writing to Learn in the Intermediate Grades.** Heinemann, 1990. ISBN 0-435-08500-X

This book has four sections: Researching and Reporting, The Power of Learning Logs, Reading and Writing, and Teaching and Learning.

Crafton, Linda. **Whole Language: Getting Started Moving Forward.** Owen, 1991. ISBN 0-913461-19-9

This is a book for those just getting started in whole language. In a clear and engaging style, Crafton examines and explains the philosophy from the ground up and includes specifics.

Gillis, Candida. **The Community As Classroom: Integrating School and Community Through Language Arts.** Boynton, 1991. ISBN 9-0-86709-280-7

We've included this one because of its obvious connection to the social studies curriculum. There is good information about interviewing for information gathering.

Rief, Linda. **Seeking Diversity.** Heinemann, 1992. ISBN 0-435-08724-X

This is the personal experience of a teacher in a middle school, acquiring and adapting the philosophy of whole language into her curriculum.

Stephens, Diane. **Research on Whole Language: Support for a New Curriculum.** Owens, 1991. ISBN 1-878450-13-1

Here is a survey of the available research and a summation of the findings.

Tierney, Robert, Carter, Mark A., and Desai, Laura E. **Portfolio Assessment in the Reading-Writing Classroom.** Gordon, 1991. ISBN 0-926842-08-0

In addition to presenting persuasive arguments and validation for the use of portfolios as a major assessment tool, the authors offer some caveats, the most important of which is that the power of portfolios can be negated if teachers or administrators take over the content, dictating what portfolios should or must contain.

Part 1

Approaches to History Through Literature

Whole Language and History

The Learning Environment and Oral Language Development

- In recent years, educators across the country have become increasingly involved with the philosophy of whole language and the methods that stem from this philosophy. Much of the current research in learning supports whole language educators' contentions that learning occurs most effectively when students are provided with learning experiences that differ markedly from traditional experiences.

- Taking their cue from the way in which oral language is learned, educators began to see that we had been approaching written forms of language in a vastly different and unnecessarily complicated way. In most households, the infant is surrounded by examples of people using oral language to communicate. It is expected that the young child, barring severe mental or physical handicaps, will begin to do likewise. No special materials are used to teach the child to talk. The child first babbles and that pre-speech is welcomed. As the babbling develops toward conventional speech, the child's approximations are accepted and incorporated into bigger hunks of language: "Yes, that's Daddy! Daddy's wearing a funny hat!" Perfection is not expected and the child learns to take greater risks.

- Researchers began to realize that this method of teaching oral language had implications for the teaching of written language as well. If children are immersed in print, if they see people they know and like enjoying reading and writing and being able to communicate that way, children want to try it too. Ask a three-year-old child whether he or she can write and most will cover pages with scribbling to show you how well they can do it. Ask a kindergartner and the answer is seldom so confident, and the writing is often restricted to his or her name or the few words the child has been taught to print correctly. The same is true, unfortunately, of reading. In too many classrooms, reading and writing are thought of as difficult by both teacher and student and approximations are discouraged. "That's not *house*. Read it again. Sound it out. It's *home*."

The Whole Language Approach to Learning

- The whole language classroom encourages responsible learners and risk-taking by

    immersing children in print

    providing continual opportunities to see others using print in meaningful ways

    expecting that children will read and write and encouraging them to do so

    allowing them to assume responsibility for what they will work on in their efforts to learn

    responding to their efforts in positive ways

- A whole language classroom is a community of learners in which teachers function as facilitators and co-learners, not as dispensers of knowledge. Conventional classrooms are transmissional: the teacher and textbook transmit information and the children are expected to absorb it. Whole language classrooms are transactional: the learning community interacts with print, with each other, and with adult models.

- In a whole language classroom, the emphasis is on meaning, not on precise deciphering. Whole language teachers use "real" materials in which language flows naturally and meaningfully, not specially-produced graded books for learners.

- In a whole language classroom, children don't practice writing and reading, they do it. Children don't learn about oral language, writing, and reading, *they use* it and, as they pick up strategies for unlocking meaning, they get better at it.

> *A whole language classroom is a community of learners in which teachers function as facilitators and co-learners, not as dispensers of knowledge.*

Whole Language Across the Curriculum

- Because this philosophy is so successful with the language arts, it is important that we examine its implications in other areas of the curriculum. It soon becomes apparent in a whole language classroom that the lines between subject areas blur. When students are using "real" materials for reading and writing, choosing materials of interest to them, they slip over into other disciplines almost constantly. Readers and writers use science and social studies materials along with art, music, math, and physical education responses and investigations. It makes no sense, then, to have student-directed learning in one field and teacher - textbook-directed learning in another.

- Soon the previously discrete departments of the school curriculum become engulfed by the language arts. We used to call it "reading in the content areas" and we treated this reading differently than we treated the basal reading, at least after third grade. Now kindergarten children are "reading in the content areas" and that change of methodology becomes meaningless. Whole language affects our approach to social studies as it converges with the content areas.

Whole Language and History

- Are there other implications in the whole language philosophy that apply to the study of history in particular? In the whole language classroom, one of your important roles is the creation of the learning environment. In relation to the physical environment of the classroom, this means providing good books, accessible writing materials, and spaces to work individually, in small groups, and as a class. For the emotional environment of the class, it means providing an expectation of success, encouraging approximations, focusing on what is being learned rather than pointing out mistakes. It means creating a climate of inquiry where the awe and excitement of discovery are fostered.

Your involvement in activities as a learner is a vital part of this environment.

- An environment conducive to learning history has these same qualities. It is full of interesting and challenging materials. There is expectation for the success of the studies. Concepts are focused on as each successive approximation of historical perspective is developed.

- Students rebelled at or lost interest in trying to learn to read by mastering a hierarchy of skills that seemed meaningless. Similarly students have long rebelled at memorizing isolated facts and dates of history. Few teachers have encouraged them to find a trickle of interest in the past and pursue it. Yet, history is so diverse and so all-encompassing that most students can do just that. One of the main purposes for this book is to show teachers and students alike that history can be approached by many avenues and that the information gained by pursuing one's interests is as valid and as valuable as any other historical research.

> ⁊
>
> *[The whole language philosophy provides] an expectation of success, encouraging approximations, focusing on what is being learned rather than pointing out mistakes.*

- Your job in a whole language classroom engaged in reading in the content areas is to gather challenging and interesting materials on a variety of levels, to show students what's there, to share some materials with the whole class and some with small groups and individuals, and to demonstrate responses to it.

- It is important to bring the readers together with the right book or nonprint material at the right time. In a whole language classroom, you help students use materials to develop their information base and interpret information in light of previous knowledge and understanding. You, like the rest of the learners, listen and respond to students as they work through concepts, showing them techniques and skills they need to do it better. You group students with common problems, helping them resolve them and listening to their solutions. You establish many opportunities for small and large group discussions in which information and ideas are exchanged and enlarged. A whole language classroom provides many opportunities for cooperative learning and peer teaching.

Whole Language and the History Curriculum

- What if you took the social studies scope-and-sequence in the teacher's manual of your history textbook and analyzed it instead of merely accepting or ignoring it? How can your students develop those stated understandings, concepts, and skills by using primary and secondary nonfiction and fiction materials? What secondary materials are available in your classroom, school library, public library, and personal libraries? What activities might deepen the students' involvement and understanding? What response vehicles are available to evaluate what you and the students have learned and to help you decide what to do next? Is it necessary to stay within the confines of the events discussed in the text to achieve those objectives? Can the study be extended to other times and events, thus capturing the interest of more students?

- Read the student text to see how much emphasis is placed on events and concepts during which times and places. Usually the actual information in an elementary or middle school text is very limited. The developers of such materials have few pages to explain the causes and effects of the Civil War, for instance. Such textbook pages can serve to give students a common place from which to go off in their own direction or to confirm or question what they have found in other sources, but seldom can textbooks serve as complete information sources on an area of history.

- Students are apt to concentrate, at least at first, on gathering isolated facts. Your role in helping students see the bigger picture becomes vital in a whole language classroom. You need to keep asking questions like "But what does this mean?" "How does this information relate to information we already have?" "Does this information have any relationship to what is going on in the world today?" "Have we ever come across this situation in other places in history?" "Isn't this like ...?" As always, you need to demonstrate behavior you want the learners to adopt. Digging below surface information is one of those behaviors.

Evaluation and the Whole Language Approach

- There remains the question of evaluation—always a difficult one in any classroom—and evaluation in a whole language classroom presents its own problems. In a conventional classroom, evaluation in the content areas was often restricted to questions at the end of a chapter, with a larger, but all too similar test, at the end of a unit of study. At best in such situations, all you have is evidence of information or lack thereof, usually fragmentary, that a particular student was able to recall on a specific day and in a specific way.

- Students in a whole language classroom usually do as well as others on such tests, but a larger, more complete assessment is possible in a whole language classroom. Students can and should be encouraged to evaluate their own progress. What did they set out to accomplish and what evidence can they present to show how close to that goal they came? Such evidence could be in the form of a portfolio showing their research and their projects and papers.

- The chart suggested on page 21, constructed by students to show what they know and what they need to know, can be used for group or whole class assessment.

- Peer evaluation is also useful. Students assess the contributions of members of their study group and list ways in which each member contributed.

- It usually falls upon you, however, to evaluate an individual's growth in skills and knowledge, looking for strengths rather than weaknesses, comparing the student as a learner to what he or she was able to do during the last area of study, and helping the student see evidences of growth. (See also Truth and Research for further ideas on assessment and evaluation.)

> *The whole language history classroom is a place where people are engaged in meaningful activities that will help them investigate other times and places and integrate that information into larger concepts and understandings.*

Truth and Research

Getting at the Truth

In the study of history it is important that we see information for what it is: one view of the truth that takes into account some, but never all, of the factors involved. Most likely, we can never have all the data and we must always revise our ideas.

The following are activities and books that help us explore history as an evolving attempt to find the truth.

- Play the gossip game. Write a story and then whisper it to one person who whispers it to the next and so on. After the last person has heard the story, he/she will write it out and compare it to the original story. Make the connection that the farther we're removed from primary sources, the more likely it is that the information has changed.

- Ask students to give detailed accounts of something that happened in the school last year. Ask one witness to tell people who weren't there about the event. Compare accounts and help the students see the relationship between what they discovered about their accounts and the accounts of events such as the Boston Massacre.

- As further proof of the frustrations of figuring out what really happened in the past, have someone from outside the class dash into the classroom and do something startling and unexpected, such as dumping a glass of water on someone (make sure the victim agrees ahead of time) and then rushing away. Ask someone else to come into the classroom to collect eyewitness accounts of what happened, what the perpetrator was wearing, what he/she looked like, and what the victim said or did. Read accounts of similar unexpected events, such as John Brown's raid on Harper's Ferry. Could these events have been similarly distorted?

- Obtain one of the many biographies available of a current leader in our country. Read the book, watching for ways in which the leader's qualities are oversimplified, usually glorified. Then find two biographies of a leader from America's past. Locate one published as closely as possible to that leader's time and another that was written much later. What factors contribute to the changes in our perspective of leaders over time?

What factors contribute to our glorifying of our leaders during their time? What kind of information about our leaders often does not surface until a later time?

- Introduce Ed Young's **Seven Blind Mice** (Philomel, 1992. ISBN 0-399-22261-8), a picture book version of "The Blind Men and the Elephant." Each mouse feels one part of the elephant and interprets the whole truth from that one piece of truth. Students can discuss ways in which the mistakes and perceptions of the mice relate to their own research activities. Each researcher/mouse has brought back truth from his/her research, but each lacks sufficient information to see the big picture. Students can find examples of researchers who had this experience.

- Attitudes and prejudices can also change the perceptions of the researcher and/or the audience. **Through Indian Eyes: The Native Experience in Books for Children** by Beverly Slapin and Doris Seale is an interesting and thought-provoking book for adults. The authors are angry at the portrayal of Native Americans in children's literature and many of their points are well taken. Their truth is not that of the general reader and there is much room for argument in many of their statements. They attack many well-known works as demeaning to their people. Students might be interested to learn of the authors' views on some of the students' favorite books.

- Help students see that there is always more to know, that an understanding or fact may well be the truth as far as it goes or as far as is known today, but that there are always unanswered questions. New information may cast a different light on what we've believed to be the truth. They could write to Jean Fritz and ask her whether she would change any of her nonfiction books because of new information she has encountered or whether there is something about which she wishes she had been able to find more. Have students look at the acknowledgments at the beginning of many books to see some of the sources of information the author used.

Inspiring Research

Research can allow learners to take ownership of their own education, investigating subjects of interest from a variety of sources. Active investigation is an important aspect of life-long learning and training for future academic endeavors. Because information gathering, evaluating, and reporting can be a true engagement of the learner, it can be more effective than passive learning. However, researching topics assigned by someone else often seems to turn students off about research. It often fails to increase their confidence for more involved research activities at a future date.

We often simplify the research process for students in hope of making it less intimidating for them. By assigning simple and well-defined reports, we hope to ease them into what can be a complicated process. In the process we can unintentionally send the message that research is too difficult for them and, perhaps more tragically, we sever the tie between research and the excitement and inspiration that makes research meaningful and makes research skills most easily attained. We need to bring to the idea of research skills the same principle of immersion that is used so successfully with whole language. If we create an environment in the classroom where research ideas and skills and obsessions are apparent everywhere, then students will become more naturally involved.

The subject and object of the research should be determined by real and not manufactured interest. This means that teachers who want students to gain confidence and skills in the field of research must be constantly on the alert for individual and group indications of a desire to know more—about anything!

When you notice that someone wants to know more, you can serve as a support system for nurturing the risk-taking that the most exciting research requires. We do children a disservice when we set them up for research and then send them off to do it on their own. They must see us as colleagues in the process and not get the feeling that the research project is some kind of stunt that we want them to perform for us. Model research skills yourself by identifying and following some of your own questions and sharing your experience with the students.

Your support can consist of locating a book that you think might be helpful and offering it to them, reading it aloud, or suggesting someone they could read it with if it is difficult.

Often what a researcher needs most is someone who will listen to their thoughts and ideas without judgment.

Introduced in the context of something about which students are wondering and about which they would like to know more, research loses some of its intimidating air. Research is simply looking for answers, something children have been doing since that early, incessant, "BUT WHY?"

In any classroom, research activities can break down or can fail to take off in the first place. When this occurs, some self-assessment questions can be of help such as: Are the students getting enough encouragement in the day-to-day aspects of research? Are the adults in the classroom engaged in genuine research as well, thus providing a continuing model of the engaged researcher? Are the connections between the various topics and levels of research obvious to the students? Is the emphasis on the excitement and empowerment of discovery rather than on the skills deemed necessary for research? Are such skills offered as a service to the students in organizing ideas and discoveries and communicating them to others? Is the definition of research broad enough?

To maintain a broad focus for classroom research, some of the following activities may be of use.

- When students are working on a research project, take every opportunity to discuss with them what they're learning, share with them what you are learning and, if possible, discuss how the two areas intersect and overlap.

- Betsy Byars, a noted author of children's books, wrote a brief memoir *The Moon and I* (Messner, 1992. ISBN 0-671-74165-9). With a light and humorous touch, Ms. Byars tells of the way she writes her books. Throughout the account, she also tells of her relationship with a snake, Moon,

> *"We used to think that if we knew one, we knew two, because one and one are two. We are finding that we must learn a great deal more about 'and.' "*
>
> *Sir Arthur Eddington (1892-1944)*

that she found near her cabin. Her need to learn more about snakes in general and Moon in particular became an obsession that, for a brief time, dominated her existence. That obsession, the reasons for it, and the ways in which she conducted her research are so interesting and helpful that you might want to read the brief book aloud at the outset of a research project.

- After reading *The Moon and I,* talk with the students about things that fascinate them. What are they passionate about? What has been happening that seems as opportune as Betsy Byars' meeting with Moon? The students can keep an eye out for the next couple of days for things that interest them. As things occur to them, encourage them to

the questions and brainstorm ways to find the answers. The students can then look for the information and bring it back to the group. When discussing what they learned, you can help the students focus on what they discovered about research. What kind of information was easy to locate? What kind of questions take more in-depth research? Did they uncover any conflicting answers? What types of resources did they find?

- Read a symbolic book or fable such as Leo Lionni's *Little Blue and Little Yellow* (Astor-Honor, 1959. ISBN 0-8392-3018-4) or *Swimmy* (Knopf, 1987. ISBN 0-317-53621-4). Apply the book to the current area of research. Which

---

Information Wanted & Information Found

Help!!!

I need to know George Washington's middle name.

I need information about Native Americans in Connecticut today.

I have letters written by homesteaders in Nebraska.

I know someone who has been to the Mesa Verde pueblos. Has photographs.

---

explore. Make a big deal of it in the same way that Betsy Byars makes a big deal of Moon. This is a great time to set aside a day separate from the regular routine to just follow the leads. Camp out at the library for the day or take a field trip to a larger library, bring tons of books to your classroom, involve other classes and teachers in your obsessions. Students can keep running journals about their obsessions in the manner of Byars'.

- Set up an Information Wanted & Information Found bulletin board in the classroom where students can post notices. This board can also serve as a way to inform others of treasures they've found. In addition to being a way to put finders and seekers together, such boards become one more occasion for "real" writing and reading.

- One or more students can take on the role of note taker in the classroom for a day. Their job is to listen for any unanswered questions. Later another group of students or the whole class can look over

groups or individuals could be represented by the symbols? How is the real situation similar to or different from the symbolism in the story? What else do you need to complete the symbolism or to determine that the symbolism does not fit this situation?

- To become effective researchers, students need to see underlying relationships between and among previously and recently acquired information. Students and teachers should maintain research journals in which observations are recorded daily. Such observations can be brief and factual: "George Washington didn't live in huts with the soldiers at Valley Forge. I wonder how the troops felt?" or attitudinal: "I'm bogging down in my search for information about George Washington's mother. Try the downtown library next, or post a Help Wanted." Journal entries should be acknowledged but not corrected. Students should be encouraged to make statements like, "If this is so, then ... must be true." Such hypotheses always involve risk and students must feel safe to take the risk and they must have opportunities to talk through these hypotheses without fear of ridicule or of being "wrong."

- Use a book that the class really loves. Without any intention of actually researching the answers, brainstorm the questions raised by the book. What did the author need to know in order to write this book? Can we find any of this information ourselves? What else would we need to find out to write the sequel or to write this book from someone else's perspective? Is there anything that we could research that would help us understand this piece of literature better? What kinds of questions does this work raise?

Working Together

Unfortunately little in our society prepares students for effective collaboration. They need the freedom to discover some of this through trial and error, but they also need support in developing listening skills and communication skills along with conflict resolution skills. (See the War and Conflict chapter for information and activities in cooperation and conflict resolution.)

- Set up small group discussions in which students discuss things they're learning. They can make informal charts or diagrams that reflect how their areas of research might be related. It can be a real challenge to try to find relationships between some things, yet thinking that way is a vital part of research. For example

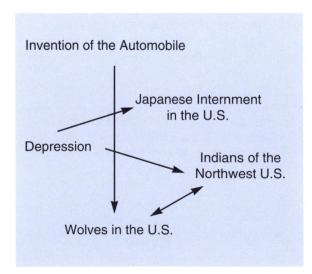

Invention of the Automobile

Japanese Internment in the U.S.

Depression

Indians of the Northwest U.S.

Wolves in the U.S.

- Although the purpose of such an activity is to see relationships and to uncover other avenues of approach, it can take a silly turn. On the board list some topics that are being researched. Have the students tell a little bit of information about what they have discovered. Then a cumulative oral story starts; the sillier the better.

  "Once upon a time there was a Large Wolf. He was on the way to a soup kitchen when he was stopped by border guards. They questioned him about his ancestry. He swore that he was born in the United States, but the authorities thought he might be smuggling secret information to the Japanese military. They put him in an internment camp where he organized a group of Japanese wolves into a study group to find new sources of income for Native Americans."

- Such an activity, while seemingly frivolous, can sometimes free children to see relationships they would otherwise overlook. And in any case, the sense of play is too often absent in the "serious" research done in classrooms.

- During research, students should have opportunities to compare notes and difficulties and to brainstorm for solutions to impasses that open new avenues of approach. Students should be encouraged to look for holes in one another's arguments and conclusions.

- Group discussions also motivate students. It is important for students to know that adult researchers sometimes become disinterested in projects and can get stuck creatively. Talking with others openly about why they might have lost interest and about the parts of the research process that bog them down builds trust and a sense of self-worth. It can also lead to brainstorming for ways to get out of the rut and may lead students back to their original enthusiasm for the research project or on to some new research project that might be more productive.

- Have students choose an area within the current theme that they would like to research. Each student is the "expert" on his/her topic. Now the focus of their research is not a paper or a project but the knowledge itself. Other members of the class can consult the expert as they would any other expert, going to him/her for information and clarification.

Locating and Using Resources

- When students are formulating their questions for research, allow time to discuss possible sources for information. Examine a variety of sources so students discover the arrangement, content, and most efficient way to use each type of book. Ask students to select one of the books at random and then generate a list of questions that that book could probably answer. Perhaps a chart such as the one below would help researchers decide which source would serve their current purposes.

Type of Reference	Content	Possible Uses
Atlas	Table of Contents Maps Glossary/Index	Finding where something happened Getting current information about the area. Locating neighborhoods and borders of an area now and in the past.
Nonfiction Trade Book *The Battle of Lexington and Concord* by Neil Johnson.	Photographs of the reenactment of the battle of Lexington and Concord. Poem by Ralph Waldo Emerson. Backround material on the Revolution. Step-by-step account of the battle.	Finding out about uniforms of both armies. Comparing this battle to others. Finding out why this battle was so important.
Historical Novel *Roll of Thunder, Hear My Cry* by Mildred Taylor.	A story of a poor, Black family in Mississippi in the 1930s. White landowner's viewpoint. An example of the sharecropping system	Getting a sense of the impact of events on individuals and families. Finding examples of personal actions and reactions. Finding out about dress and lifestyle. Looking at various viewpoints. Comparing the experience of these characters to factual information.

- Encourage students to look at an event from as many angles as time permits. This is where the use of trade books is especially valuable. Novels and stories are apt to include divergent views, and this ought to be one of the main topics for discussion. However, an imbalance is often present. For instance, if we are researching the Civil War, we discover that the viewpoint of Southern slave owners is rarely presented in a sympathetic manner. When discussing viewpoints we should consider such things as who else was affected, did all members of a group hold the same viewpoint, did later information strengthen or weaken an argument, and what other factors might have influenced the situation and viewpoint?

- Whenever possible, encourage investigators to chart, map, graph, video /audio tape, and illustrate the information they have gathered. As with any writing, the best way to understand a device used by others is to attempt to use it yourself.

- Librarians can help by tailoring library periods to suit the type of investigation you and your students are conducting. The card catalog (or computer data base) is a reference source and the time to show students how to use it is when they need it. The same is true of encyclopedias, atlases, audio visual aids, fiction, and nonfiction.

- When you and the students find conflicting information, encourage the students to discuss reasons for the disagreement:

Is it a matter of opinion rather than fact?

Is one author unaware of new information?

Can we find verification for either side?

Is one author more qualified than another?

Were the authors influenced by their own backgrounds to interpret the same information differently (back to the **Seven Blind Mice**)?

Will we ever know who's right?

- Magazines can, of course, provide information for research. The very nature of magazines—soft covers with short articles, a visual orientation with many interesting illustrations and captions—makes them less threatening sources than encyclopedias for many researchers. *Cobblestone: The History Magazine for Young People* (Cobblestone Publishing, 30 Grove St., Peterborough, NH 03458) is particularly useful for history students. Not only is it a great source of historical information, it usually devotes an entire issue to many aspects of the same subject. The April 1992 issue about George Washington, for instance, contains the following articles: "Family Matters," "Danger in the Forest," "Farmer Washington," "Washington and Slavery," "A Man for Others, Victory at Trenton," "Martha Washington at Valley Forge," "Journey to the Presidency," "George Washington Live," and "Washington in the Classroom." Interspersed with the articles are pages with cartoons illustrating little-known facts about Washington. The issue concludes with an annotated list of children's books on the subject.

Oral History

- Before students set off to interview people, they should be given time to devise questions and materials that might bring about the most useful responses from their interviewees. Often having two students go together to conduct the interview can be a big help. Before an interview students should also determine the means of recording answers, the best location for the interview, ways to make the interviewee most relaxed or comfortable, the ideal length of time and time of day for the interview, and ways the interviewer can inspire more insightful recollections: photos and keepsakes, period pictures of the town, songs of the period.

- In particular, discovering ways to record the answers can be a real challenge. Have the students begin by interviewing each other about some fun topic. Use different methods of recording, including taking notes and then reading them back to the interviewee to see whether they are an accurate representation, and tape recording, transcribing, and editing. Evaluate the approaches. What factors helped or hindered

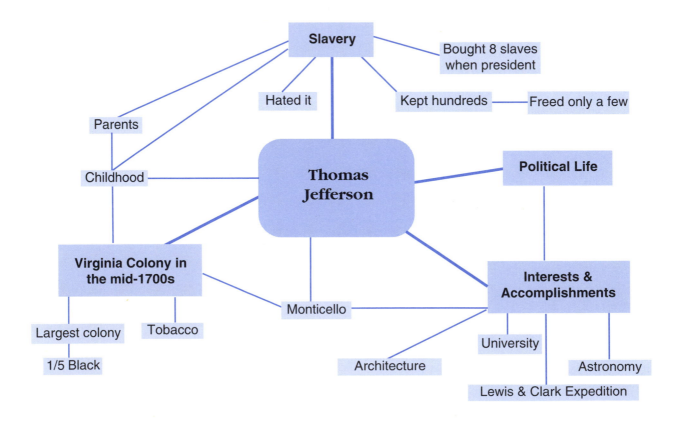

the interview? Which methods produced the most accurate results? What do the interviewers need to work on to perfect their technique?

Organizing Information

- Model an organization technique. Read aloud from a piece of material relevant to the subject. Think aloud as you decide what information is important. Use an overhead to record your notes, thinking aloud about their placement. Use a typical outline format or a less formal webbing to show the interrelationship of facts.

- Ask students to help you visualize the ideas. Make some "therefore" statements in which some information you read aloud is thought out logically or related to facts found elsewhere.

- Think about what you know and what you would like to know. Have students begin a topic study by making a three column chart: "What do we know?" "What questions do we still have?" "What have we found out?" Keep the charts very active. Make the charts flexible so that they can serve as a constant evaluation of the investigation and so that the ownership of the inquiry stays firmly in the hands of the students.

- Encourage students to establish a purpose for reading and then focus the notes they take on how that question or purpose is addressed or answered and on any surprises that turn up. (Unexpected information can change a researcher's direction or inspire further questions and research.) Regardless of the subject or era, encourage students to put information into their own words, focusing on the points they think are most important or the things that are most applicable to the reason for reading the material. Sometimes mapping the information is more useful than outlining (see below).

- To discourage the mindless plagiarism that goes on in much research note-taking, read aloud from a piece of writing: fictional or expository. At the conclusion of the reading, ask children to jot down a few things they learned from the reading. Share the observations and reread to resolve any conflicts. Do the same several times, encouraging children to jot down ideas in their briefest form rather than trying to construct complete sentences.

- While a student is giving information to a group, take notes on an overhead transparency.

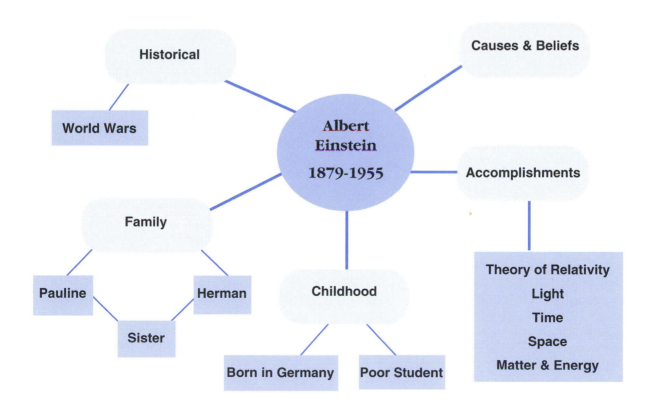

Immediately after the report, show the students the notes you made. Explain what you included and what you omitted in the process. Do the same thing on several such occasions. Later, display the notes again and, with the students, reconstruct the highlights of the presentation.

- If a computer is available, suggest that students enter information and then organize the information so that it is accessible to all researchers. If the students put a one- or two-word title at the beginning of each brief paragraph, most word processors will put those paragraphs in alphabetical order, producing an accessible glossary or mini-encyclopedia. More sophisticated users can use a data base such as *Filemaker* to establish data banks of information. Make copies of the organized information as reference material for other researchers.

- Make sure that during a unit of study, students are exposed to and use charts, graphs, maps, webbing, role-play, brainstorming and guided fantasy, thinking/incubation periods, and journal writing as participants and witnesses. If possible, provide time for the students to use the computer data base, word processing, and outliners. During the unit, or at its completion, encourage each student to evaluate each process: Which processes helped? Which were useless or comparatively so? Which were most efficient and why?

- Many students will need individual and small group instruction and guidance in finding, recording, and organizing research information. Students should be shown ways in which they can find and record information using tapes if writing is difficult or impossible for them. One of the many ways to use volunteers is to have them write information for those having difficulty.

Communicating Findings

Student Lessons

- Teaching is a very good way to learn. Let students teach each other what they learned from their research. Encourage them to use visual and/or audio materials to support and reinforce the information they present. Before, during, and after the presentations, the emphasis should always be on presenting the material in a way that will help other learners, not on presenting it for a single teacher's approval.

Unpublished writing

Students should be encouraged to keep all of the writing they do during a research project: notes, outlines, drafts, and journals. Such material serves as a map of progress, a reviewing device, and a source of loose threads and old ideas not yet used. The notes taken by one student or group of students can help provide others with a new direction for research.

Published writing

- A formal, factual report is only one reporting device for research. There are many other writings to consider.

Formal reports

- In order to show ways of organizing information, ask the students to make statements they believe to be true about an era, topic, or personality before doing any research on the topic. Record their statements without checking for accuracy. With the group treating these statements as fact, organize the statements by category, combining some and eliminating redundancy.

- Use the statements as part of a report, thinking out loud and encouraging input as you organize information. Subtopics within the report can become research topics for individuals or groups. Give each of the students a copy of the report and suggest that they find and eliminate inconsistencies, partial truths, and misstatements as they go about their research.

Picture Book Reports

- Reports can take the form of a picture book. Suggest that some researchers make a picture book, giving information about an area, people, or subject in history that interests them. They might find inspiration in books by Marcia Sewall about the Plymouth Colony and the Native Americans of that time (see page 177).

Using Excerpts

- Students can choose a selection from a book that they think is particularly interesting or relevant to the subject. The person choosing the selection is responsible for supplying any background material that is necessary for comprehension or appreciation of the material. Readers should be encouraged to react to the material personally and in light of other reading they have done. Discussions about the selection should include such things as: What's the point? What aspect of history is the author trying to cover? Was the author's thinking logical? What did the author neglect to mention? Was anything unclear? What questions do you still have?

Magazines and Newspapers

- Let individuals and small groups contribute to a classroom magazine or newspaper that centers around a common theme. **Cobblestone Magazine** (see page 47) can serve as a model for reporting information. With today's computer facilities for desktop publishing, student research material can be organized in a similar manner. A bulletin board could also serve as a newspaper or magazine.

Evaluation

Teacher's Evaluations

- When evaluating students' learning in the area of research, we are looking for two things: First, are they developing more skill as researchers? You can observe whether they are asking questions, obtaining and evaluating information, finding relationships, and communicating their findings to someone else. For each student, make an evaluation sheet listing these elements. As you observe, record the information as a checklist or as anecdotal notes.

- The second thing to evaluate is the acquistion of historical information. What have they discovered in this process and how has their historical understanding developed as a result of this? You can use an evaluation sheet similar to the one above for observing the acquisition of historical understandings.

Student's Evaluations

- Students should have the opportunity to evaluate their learning climate and situations. Do they get more done at home or in the classroom? Do they work better in groups or individually?

- Encourage researchers to look back to their original questions. Have they answered them? Were some questions deemed irrelevant,

distracting, or subordinate to others? What new questions turned up? Did the answers open or close doors in the research? What is the best place to conclude the current study?

- The Information Wanted & Information Found board can also be a way for students to evaluate their work. Did my research aid others in their research? Were my posted answers clear to others or was it necessary for many people to come to me for further clarification? Did I post my sources so that the reader was aware of the reliability of my source? The need for being clear and concise should be apparent in the response to the board inquiries.

- After any information is presented by one group to another, have the audience members fill out exit slips (see below) that evaluate the presentation in a positive way. These exit slips might include simple statements of facts or concepts they learned and suggestions for improving the presentation. Presenters should go over the exit slips together, deciding whether they achieved their goals.

- Formal achievement tests are often mandated and can help you discover some of what a student knows about a particular subject. They are not particularly efficient and not necessarily reliable because all they tell us is what a particular student was able to show he/she knew at a particular time in answer to the questions asked. Students whose research has included some of the activities we suggested should be able to at least equal, if not surpass, those whose learning was of a more passive nature.

- As always in assessment and evaluation, teachers and students working together make the best evaluators. At the conclusion of the project, as well as at appropriate times during the work, you and your students should take time to look at your original goals, make note of skills and insights gained or in progress, and make one another aware of your growth. (See the chapter on Whole Language for additional information about evaluation.)

Exit Slip

Date _____

One thing I learned from this presentation is _____

I still want to know _____

I liked the way you _____

Maybe next time you could _____

Living History Museum

One of the most exciting things that has happened for students of history and the general public in recent years is the creation of living history museums. In these museums, people live and work the way they did in that area in the past, assuming the roles of real settlers. Visitors to a living museum often get a more real sense of the time by observing and interacting with the personnel than they would have by just viewing displays of artifacts or homes. The inhabitants of these villages learn the crafts and speech of the era and work for complete authenticity based on careful research.

It has occurred to us that students might create a living museum, on a much smaller scale of course,

in which they would assume the roles of historical characters. With the living museum as motivation, the students will approach the necessary historical research on a much more personal and immediate level than they would if the assignment were to write a report, answer questions on a test, or even create a display.

Choose a Time and Place

- As a class, choose a year and an area of the country around which you would like to center your studies. All members of the class, including

you, will learn as much as possible about that time and place in order to assume the role of a real person. The research should include finding out about times before and after the year you've chosen. It is important to learn where your characters came from, where they were headed, where their relatives were. It will also be important to know how events in other areas of the country and in other countries affected your characters, even if the characters, as individuals, were unaware of these events. However, the year and place will be the focal point.

Choose Characters

- Help the students choose from an assortment of characters for this extended role playing. Be sure that adults in the classroom choose a role as well. There are advantages to choosing a cast of characters who are not all famous. (Imagine trying to get a sense of what it is like to be a present-day American by interviewing only US senators.) There are also advantages to narrowing the field. For example, choosing many members of one extended family, neighbors on a street, or members of one organization can provide an intimate view of how the historical factors of the time might have affected their interactions.

- Look for names of real people in nonfiction books, other living history museums, local historical societies, and library archives. One of the most interesting sources is the genealogical records of class members. Many families have researched their ancestors and, although this can lead to a peculiar vanity, it can also lead to many real names and characters and locations for a variety of times in history.

- In order to get a more authentic cross-section, or to see history from various perspectives, make sure the cast includes members of many groups: Europeans, Black Americans, Native Americans, Hispanic Americans, Asian Americans, and immigrants of other cultures, if those people were or could have been present at the time. Include members from all socioeconomic classes.

Variations

- Classes can concentrate on one period for an entire year or change periods as the year progresses, starting with early United States history and continuing to the present.

- The class can break into groups, taking characters from different areas of the country during the same year.

- The class can move from one geographical area to others throughout the school year.

- Instead of real people of the time the students can take on roles of characters in a historical fiction book.

- Students can create characters based on what they know about people of the period in general. This might be especially appropriate when trying to include people who were not politically powerful and were not given much coverage in historical nonfiction.

- Students can invite other people to assume roles as characters: aides, librarians, principals, special teachers, school secretaries, volunteers, and any frequent visitors to the classroom.

- It might be possible to have students assume two roles, especially if they all want to be someone famous, or they might pair up, each partner assuming a different role. They can share what they learn so they can alternate roles. In fact, a class that's really involved in the project can rotate character roles among its many members.

Things to Keep in Mind

Keep in mind that many of the "real" living history museums train their interpreters in a few weeks and most of that training is background history of the period in general. It takes very little time to learn the roles of the characters once the research has been assembled.

What takes time is reflecting on how the events and lifestyles of the times might have influenced people's lives. What did they think, feel, fear, hope, and dream? One of the advantages of having each student choose a single character is that students have more time to "get into" their characters.

Anything and everything suggested in this book can add insight to the development of their characters. As the students research by reading fiction and nonfiction, by carefully examining photographs and picture book illustrations, they can ask themselves which facts might have influenced their characters. Are these facts reliable? Is there conflicting evidence? Sharing their information with other classmates will help the students evaluate facts and conflicting evidence.

Ways to Develop Characters

As they develop their characters, researchers might want to try to answer some of the following questions about their characters. There is a form on page 27 that your students might find helpful. You may photocopy it for your students to use. This reference form will provide information to anyone playing the role.

Students might also keep a journal of what they are discovering and how they think the information may influence their character. The journals can include information from books, other students, teachers, films, and other outside sources.

The class might also compile its findings in a large computerized or written reference work.

The Character's Past

- What was life like for the character's grandparents? What was going on then? What stories might the character have heard from grandparents about their past?

- Were the character's parents peasants, workers, upper society, persecuted, or powerful?

- What significant events shaped the character's life and the lives of people around the character?

- If the character immigrated, what was his/her native land like? Where was it? How far away? Is there contact with people still living there? Why did the character leave? What other options did the character have?

The Character's Present

- Where is the character during the time being studied? What are the geological features and how does the terrain affect the character's lifestyle and options?

- What is the economy of the area? What are the political views of the people? Is there more than one cultural group in the area? How do the groups interact?

- How do the people in the area dress?

- What language(s) do they speak? Are they literate?

- What do they eat? How do they cook? How do they get their food?

- How are their homes made? To what inventions do they have access?

- What is the character's job? What other jobs are part of the society?

- What games does the society play? What music does it have? What other entertainment? How are these factors similar to and different from those of nearby cultures?

- What are the society's religious views? How is its religion organized? What other religions have the people been exposed to? How do different religious groups interact? What are the laws about religion? What other beliefs do the groups hold about such things as science and ethics?

- How are families organized? How are responsibilities and authority divided? How are children raised? What are the families' beliefs about marriage? What else do you know about the character's family and friends?

- What is happeningin other areas that influences the country at this time? In what ways (cultural, economic, political, and military) are these influences shown?

- What are the areas of conflict that affect these people? How are they affected? How do they respond? How do their needs affect other groups? What form is the conflict taking?

Concurrent Activities

- Students can stay in character for a given period each day, becoming increasingly authentic as their research continues.

- Students might write diaries for their characters. What were the seasons like? What events were important?

- Develop skits about the characters or present problems for students to solve in character.

- A student might write a manual for future actors to guide them in playing the character.

- Create a time line that includes the life spans of the class's characters. Enter events that might have affected them. Post the time line for easy reference.

- Invite another class to visit. Receive them in character. The next day, visit their classroom in

character, allowing the past to visit the future.

- Have the students write newsy letters in character to someone in a different locality. To get some ideas, read Jean Fritz's *George Washington's Breakfast.* (See page 192.)

- Let the characters take a field trip to the future. (See Time Fantasies on page 36.)

- Write a letter to your character and tell about interesting current events or inventions.

- For further suggestions for successful character activities, look through the books and activities for different time periods, approaches, and strands.

- The final activity might be the reenactment of one day or incident in the lives of the characters. It might be a play, an interactive time during which observers and actors converse in character, or a guided tour of the living museum created by the students.

- The living museum can be the major showcase for a parents' night or a school fair.

Develop a Character

Name	Residence
Family Background	*Personal Information*
Native Country and Time	Birthdate
Ethnic Background	Birthplace
Father's Name	Education
Father's Birthdate	Occupation
Father's Birthplace	Religion
Father's Social Class	Spouse's Name
Father's Religion	Spouse's Birthdate
Mother's Name	Spouse's Birthplace
Mother's Birthdate	Spouse's Education
Mother's Birthplace	Date of Marriage
Mother's Social Class	Children (names, date and place of birth)
Mother's Religion	
Brothers	
Sisters	Death (year and cause)

Time Line Smorgasbord

Unless you are locked into a specific area of history in your curriculum, it really doesn't matter at which point you and the students begin a study. A time line can be the focal point for your history program. Time lines help the students keep track of where they are in history and help them relate information to other events going on during, before, or after the period they're studying.

A time line can be as simple as a long, skinny line on which dates are placed or as complicated as an expanded time line that covers a whole wall of the classroom with book jackets, portraits and photographs, artifacts, graphs and charts, artwork, and other memorabilia. A complicated time line takes a great deal of researching and reading by the students and might, in fact, grow from a simple time line.

Creating Time Lines

- Begin with a simple time line that covers any period you are interested in. As you and the students research the period, add details or additional time lines.

- Students can place names of books, events, personalities, songs, inventions, and much more along the time line as they find information.

- Time lines can be further extended with wanted posters; graphs, charts, and maps of populations, climates, land use, occupations, and family size; poems and lyrics of songs that reflect the era;

letters replicated and fabricated; names of sports figures, statistics and achievements; blueprints and drawings of inventions, and inventors; fabricated newspaper stories and facsimiles of real ones; vignettes and excerpts from books.

- Ribbons or strings can lead from the time line to displays of related materials.

- Suspend mobiles at appropriate spots along the time line. You can make a mobile of pictures or drawings of people. On the flip side of each picture give biographical or historical information about the people. A mobile of an invention, such as the sewing machine, might show sewing machines from the first one to modern ones, pictures of people using the machines, a picture of Elias Howe, and real parts of sewing machines, such as bobbins and needles.

- Challenge the class to include as much information as possible on the time line. When you start the time line, it might consist mostly of idea slips, placed there by researchers to hold the place for their project. These placeholders will tell other students who is doing what on a given topic, and they can go to this expert for advice or information. The result can be an ongoing, hands-on, interactive exhibit area where the landscape of history becomes graphic and tangible and where our understanding of the past is seen as something constantly changing rather than frozen in time by a static set of facts.

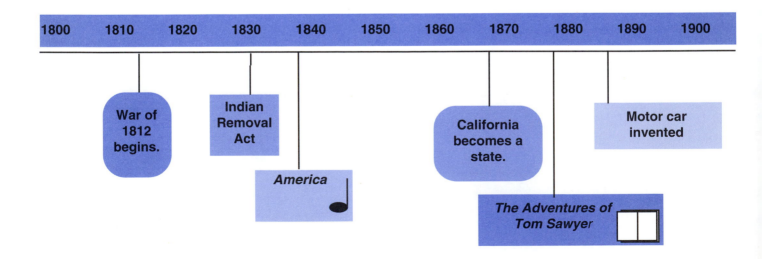

- You can color code time lines to indicate strands.

- Time lines can be generated by computers. One company, Tom Snyder Productions of Cambridge, Massachusetts, offers a program called ***Mac Timeliner*** (see page 47) for making time lines on the Macintosh computer. It lets you develop, edit, and merge time lines of varying lengths.

- Time tables can extend your time lines. How about a time table of timepieces such as hour glasses, watches, alarm clocks, novelty clocks, sundials, and pendulum clocks? Let the students take apart broken clocks to see how they work or maybe even repair them. Arranging such items in chronological order first by guess and then by research is a step in investigating history that can lead to more than just bare facts.

- Additional time tables might include models of cars, planes, or trains.

- How about a What's It For table containing gadgets of times past: an eggbeater, carpet beater, button hook, shoe last, and other items from distant and not-so-distant past? Figuring out what it's for and who would have used it can put you back in time.

- Photo albums from several families, areas, or eras can be history starters; so can toys, dolls, music boxes, books, textbooks, lights, paintings, a stereopticon with slides, or even 35mm slides. Even a single painting can be an entry to the past.

- Sports cards are a consuming interest to many and an investigation of the history of a sport is as valid a part of history as anything else.

- Involve the students' families in the search for historical artifacts. This will lead to stories and reminiscences that will make your classwork more vital and give families an opportunity for sharing. Perhaps some family members will want to be guest speakers and share their experiences directly with the class.

Using Time Lines

- Not only are time lines great ways to organize information, they are also terrific research starters. The class or any individual can stop at any point along the time line and research it thoroughly. Who lived at that time? What was going on in other parts of the world? Which influential people of that time knew each other or affected each other? What did people wear? Listen to? Do for amusement? What did they know about science? Other parts and peoples of the world? What were the conflicts? Could they have been avoided? How did events at that time affect other times?

- Use literature in connection with your time lines. When you read a book, locate the time of its setting on the time line. Find out what was happening in the world at that time. How did that time in history affect the story? How did the past affect the characters? What strands of history are discussed in this book and how were those strands influenced by the past? What is the story behind the story of those strands?

- There are fiction and nonfiction books about almost any period in history that will strengthen the students' perspective. By discussing discoveries made by other readers about other points on the time line, students will be able to grasp the main concepts of history.

Follow Me

- Any story set in a specific time can lead to a historical study. Take characters from the story and find out everything you can about them. If the characters are well constructed, students will be able to suggest reasonable answers to many questions such as these: What do you know about their parents? Their grandparents? Where did they live? What were their attitudes about (almost any topic)? What were their interests and hobbies?

- Then students can move the same characters forward and answer questions such as: Will they stay where they are? What jobs will they have? How will they feel about (almost any topic)? What will their children be like? What about their grandchildren? Which of the students in your class might be their descendants? How could that happen?

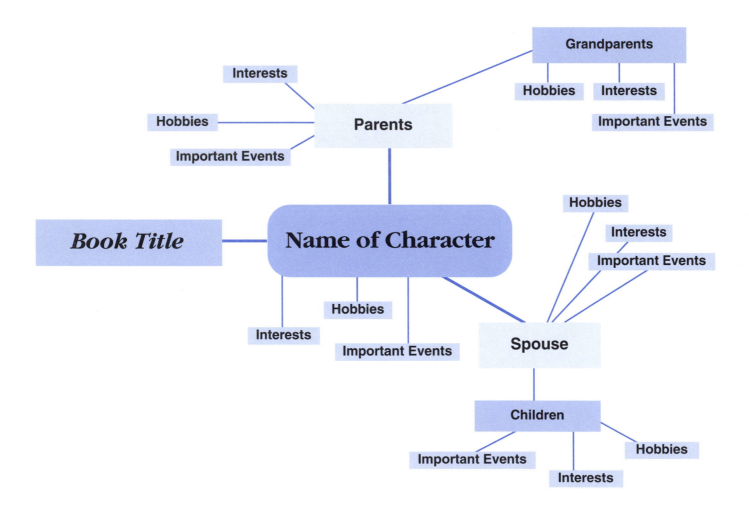

- Any book can be broadened. Instead of going backward or forward in time, go to another area of the country or world at the same time. Research the lives of other people who lived at the same time. Research the lives of other levels of society. How did richer or poorer or more or less powerful people live at the time? What problems did these characters face that others would not have to face?

- You can use books in the Ramona series by Beverly Cleary, for instance, in this manner. In what years did Ramona's parents grow up? What was going on then in the United States and other parts of the world? What music, clothing, and activities would they have enjoyed? Look at the publication date of the first Ramona book. Ramona was six when ***Ramona the Pest/Ramona la chinche*** (Morrow, 1968, and Morrow, 1984) was first published. How old would she be now? If she decides to have a family, when would her children most likely be born? What problems would or did the world have then that Ramona's parents would not have had to deal with? At one point, Ramona's father loses his job. What were the unemployment figures at the time? What are they now? Compare Ramona's problems and concerns with those that might be faced by children in other parts of the world at the time.

- Webbing a book provides a visual map of other activities and related readings. Such webs are visual brainstorming.

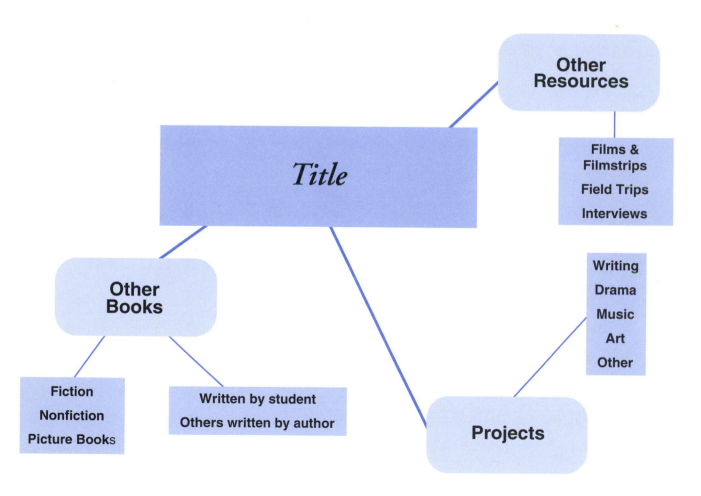

- Web a work of historical fiction yourself. Place your web on the overhead projector and let the students add to it. The Focus Books in Part 4 are webs of a sort, but you can web them further and come up with even more relevant readings and activities.

- Maps will also play a large role in this approach to learning. All kinds of maps are useful: topographical, meteorological, projection, relief, and population. In the same way that the time line charts information and events, a map can serve as a chart into which we can place information, book titles, names of historical figures and events.

- Many historical books include journeys taken by the characters. You can map these journeys, of course. Take it a step further and add pictures of points of interest. Make up picture postcards for the character to send home.

- Mapping will also show you where journeys from more than one book intersect.

- This book, *In Times Past*, can be used by students as a reference for books that relate to and extend their original books.

Picture This

Picture books add a delightful element to any program. Although they are often neglected in our search for information, their accessibility and their beauty and conciseness make them an ideal introduction to almost any topic. They can also provide a great deal of information, even for upper-level students. Picture books can lead students into a wide range of social studies topics and concerns.

• Have the students gather picture books set in the past. Ask them to look at the illustrations and try to put the books in chronological order, using costume and other visual clues. Use illustrated nonfiction books and the text of the picture books to validate or change the order. Make a time line of the books, adding to it as the students discover more books.

This is not an easy task. Take **The Ox-Cart Man** by Donald Hall, for instance. What's the historical setting? The clothing and occupations make us think that it's very early in US history, but look at the city of Portsmouth. Let's assume that it's Portsmouth, New Hampshire. At what time would the city be this developed? Perhaps we can learn more by writing to the Portsmouth Chamber of Commerce or to its historical society. If we receive a list of its oldest buildings, or if we

can find a picture of that city in 1700, 1750, 1800, and 1850, maybe we'll be able to pin down the time of this one book.

• A careful choice of picture books published from the early twentieth century to the present will reveal changing social values. Lois Lenski's books about the Small family, published during the forties, show what was thought to be a "realistic" family. Mama Small does her housework in apron and dress and Papa Small drives his car to work each day. Many other picture books published at about the same time, show animated machinery—**Little Toot, Mike Mulligan and His Steam Shovel, The Little Engine That Could.** Was this to help us accept machinery as friendly elements of our existence?

• A look at picture books that were censored over the past century also shows changing social values and concerns. **Little Black Sambo** is still available from the Putnam Publishing Group and in many libraries; however, usually you must ask for it. Students can learn a great deal about a culture by looking at the history that surrounds such books. How would such a book be greeted today?

• Here are some particularly useful picture books.

Picture Books

★ Cooney, Barbara. **Island Boy.** Viking, 1988. ISBN 0-670-81749-X
A young man settles his family on an island off the coast of Maine. As the years go by, the family grows and members leave and return. Through it all we watch time change life on the island.

★ Dragonwagon, Crescent. **Home Place.** Illustrated by Jerry Pinkney. Macmillan, 1990. ISBN 0-02-733190-3
See page 40.

★ Hall, Donald. **The Ox-Cart Man.** Illustrated by Barbara Cooney. Viking, 1979. ISBN 0-670-53328-9
A farmer loads his wagon with produce and products from his farm and drives to Portsmouth, New Hampshire, where he barters everything including the ox.

★ Johnston, Tony. **Yonder.** Illustrated by Lloyd Bloom. Dial, 1988. ISBN 0-8037-0278-7
A lyrical and compelling text and lovely pictures tell the history of a family that plants trees to celebrate and to remember.

★ Lyon, George Ella. **Cecil's Story.** Illustrated by Peter Catalanotto. Orchard, 1991. ISBN 0-531-08512-0
See page 79.

★ McLerran, Alice. ***Roxaboxen.*** Lothrop, 1991. ISBN 0-688-07593-2

Children from two generations ago live joyfully in the desert of Yuma, Arizona. There they create imaginary towns of rocks and glass. Later, the children revisit Roxaboxen in their minds.

★ Moser, Barry. ***Polly Vaughn.*** Little, 1992. ISBN 0-316-58541-6

Moser has transplanted a traditional English ballad to Appalachia where the children of feuding families fall in love, which, of course, leads to tragedy. The illustrations are exquisite and not only help to tell the story but provide a lot of information about the characters and their personalities.

★ Sewall, Marcia. ***People of the Breaking Day.*** Atheneum, 1990. ISBN 0-689-31407-8
See page 177.

★ ———. ***The Pilgrims of Plimoth.*** Macmillan, 1986. ISBN 0-689-31250-4
See page 177.

★ Yolen, Jane. ***Encounter.*** Illustrated by David Shannon. Harcourt, 1992. ISBN 0-15-225962-7
See page 168.

◆ Andrews, Jan. ***The Auction.*** Illustrated by Karen Reczuch. Macmillan, 1991. ISBN 0-02-705535-3
See page 41.

◆ Baylor, Byrd. ***The Best Town in the World.*** Illustrated by Ronald Himler. Scribners, 1983. ISBN 0-684-18035-9

A back country town in Texas in the early 1900s is idealized by the narrator's father. Illustrations provide a look at an early schoolroom and at earlier pastimes and concerns.

◆ Burleigh, Robert. ***Flight: The Journey of Charles Lindbergh.*** Illustrated by Mike Wimmer. Putnam, 1991. ISBN 0-399-22272-3
See page 227.

◆ Carlstrom, Nancy White. ***Northern Lullaby.*** Illustrated by Leo and Diane Dillon. Philomel, 1992. ISBN 0-399-21806-8
See page 129.

◆ Goble, Paul. ***Death of the Iron Horse.*** Bradbury, 1987. ISBN 0-02-737830-6
See page 124.

◆ Hamanaka, Sheila. ***The Journey.*** Orchard, 1990. ISBN 0-531-08449-3
See page 147.

◆ Harvey, Brett. ***Cassie's Journey: Going West in the 1860s.*** Holiday, 1988. ISBN 0-8234-0684-9
See page 124.

◆ McPhail, David. ***Farm Boy's Year.*** Atheneum, 1992. ISBN 0-689-31679-8

Here is a picture journal of a year in the life of a boy living a century ago in rural Massachusetts.

◆ Medearis, Angela. ***Dancing with the Indians.*** Illustrated by Samuel Byrd. Holiday, 1991. ISBN 0-8234-0893-0

Although the story takes place in the 1930s, there are echoes of slavery and the Civil War. A Black family dances with the Seminole Indians to commemorate the Seminole grandparents who sheltered their grandfather, an escaped slave.

◆   ———. ***The Zebra Riding Cowboy: A Folk Song from the Old West.***
Illustrated by Maria Cristina Brusca. Holt, 1992. ISBN 0-8050-1712-7

See page 205.

◆   Provensen, Alice. ***The Buck Stops Here: The Presidents of the United States.***
HarperCollins, 1990. ISBN 0-06-024787-8

See page 41.

◆   Pryor, Bonnie. ***Lottie's Dream.*** Illustrated by Mark Graham. Simon & Schuster,
1992. ISBN 0-671-74774-6

See page 41.

◆   Rylant, Cynthia. ***Appalachia: The Voices of Sleeping Birds.*** Illustrated by
Barry Moser. Harcourt, 1991. ISBN 0-15-201605-8

*Rylant and Moser grew up in Appalachia and this book beautifully evokes that
time and place in prose and illustration.*

◆   Sanders, Scott Russell. ***Aurora Means Dawn.*** Illustrated by Jill Kastner.
Bradbury, 1989. ISBN 0-02-778270-0

See page 197.

◆   Sis, Peter. ***Follow the Dream: The Story of Christopher Columbus.*** Knopf,
1991. ISBN 0-679-90628-8

See page 169.

◆   Spier, Peter. ***We the People: The Constitution of the United States of
America.*** Doubleday, 1987. ISBN 0-385-23589-5

See page 141.

◆   Stevenson, James. ***Higher on the Door.*** Greenwillow, 1987. ISBN 0-688-06636-4
       ———. ***July.*** Greenwillow, 1990. ISBN 0-688-08822-8
       ———. ***When I Was Nine.*** Greenwillow, 1986. ISBN 0-688-05942-2

See page 227.

◆   Turner, Ann. ***Dakota Dugout.*** Illustrated by Ronald Himler. Macmillan, 1985.
ISBN 0-02-789700-1

See page 205.

◆   ———. ***Nettie's Trip South.*** Illustrated by Ronald Himler. Macmillan, 1987.
ISBN 0-02-789240-9

See page 79.

◆   Van Leeuwen, Jean. ***Going West.*** Illustrated by Thomas B. Allen. Dial, 1992.
ISBN 0-8037-1028-3

*In striking charcoal and pastels, we follow Hannah's journey by covered wagon
and witness her arrival on the lonely prairie.*

◆   Yolen, Jane. ***Letting Swift River Go.*** Illustrated by Barbara Cooney. Little, 1992.
ISBN 0-316-9689-4

*A little girl shares her feelings about her town's being flooded by a reservoir that
will supply water for Boston.*

Time Fantasies

- Time fantasies are literary favorites for many, and as well as being very good reading, they can become a vehicle for learning about history in at least two ways. First, the action of a time fantasy usually involves a trip backward in time. The individual making the time trip often has to use knowledge of history to ascertain the time in which he/she has landed. While in the past, the character and the reader often learn about that historical period through the actions, observations, and dialogues in the story.

- Second, the idea of time fantasy can help students approach history from a more personal perspective. What if you were transported to Ford's Theater on the night of Lincoln's assassination? Would you have tried to stop it? How would history have changed if the assassination had not occurred? What if you were a television reporter suddenly transported with your technology to Ford's Theater directly after the shots were fired? Whom would you interview? What could they tell you?

- Such an approach can become an extensive writing activity in which students, after reading time fantasies, become authors of them, sending characters back in time to a period and place that interests the students. The amount of research necessary to make such stories interesting is considerable and can involve a search for details and an understanding of the period much more complete than that usually gained by students.

- The time fantasy device can become a play involving the whole class in research of the same period and place, as well as in producing the drama for audiences.

- It can also become a guessing game in which one student is transported back in time. Other students create clues to help her/him decide where and when she/he is.

- We have listed several time fantasies below. Many concern English history rather than US history. Not all of them are of equal literary merit, but it is important to have books of several reading levels available, and all of these contain information or ideas for student writing and research.

Picture Books
★ Dragonwagon, Crescent. **Home Place**. Illustrated by Jerry Pinkney. Macmillan, 1990. ISBN02-733190-3
See page 40.

Fiction
★ Babbitt, Natalie. **Tuck Everlasting**. Farrar, 1975. ISBN 0-374-37848-7

————. **Tuck para siempre.** Farrar, 1991.

■■■■■■■■■■□□□□□
Least Sophisticated   Most Sophisticated

Although not a time fantasy in the usual sense, this exquisite novel in which a family unwittingly and quite tragically becomes immortal is included here because of its portrayal of the cycles of life as inevitable and right.

★ Hurmence, Belinda. **A Girl Called Boy.** Houghton, 1982. ISBN 0-395-31022-9

■■■■■■■■■■□□□□□

In one of the rare, good time fantasies with an American setting, Blanche, a young Black girl bored by her father's emphasis on Black pride, is transported back to the days of slavery. Blanche is unimpressed when she is given an African carving passed down from her great-great-great-grandfather, but then it takes her back to the days of slavery where she is mistaken for a runaway. The author uses slave narratives and plantation records for authenticity in this engrossing novel.

★ Lunn, Janet. ***The Root Cellar.*** Scribner, 1983. ISBN 0-684-17855-9

■■■■■■■■□□□□□□□

This is a Focus Book, see page 277.

★ Pearce, Philippa. ***Tom's Midnight Garden***. Dell, 1959. ISBN 0-397-30475-7

■■■■■■■■■■■□□□

This is a British fantasy; however, the book is so well done that to list time fantasies and not include this one would be unfortunate. Also, the time that can be reached through the door in the old house is not too distant from the time in which Tom lives. The climax of the book comes when one of the people of the past is found in the present.

★ Sauer, Julia. ***Fog Magic.*** Puffin, 1986. ISBN 0-14-032163-2

■■■■■■■■□□□□□□□

The time traveler is a girl from Nova Scotia who reaches the fishing village of Blue Cove only through the fog. Unlike some time fantasies, this character can return home at will. It also becomes clear that her father had visited Blue Cove in his youth. The story is haunting and beautifully told.

★ Walsh, Jill Paton. ***A Chance Child.*** Avon, 1980. ISBN 0-380-48561-3

■■■■■■■■■■□□□

More than most time fantasies, this one explores the social and political issues of the past. Creep, an abused child of the present, follows a canal to the period of the Industrial Revolution in England. There his abuse continues as he assumes the role of child laborer and gradually forgets the present. His half-brother, concerned about Creep's disappearance, searches early nineteenth-century documents to find evidence of Creep's life and death.

◆ Boston, Lucy. ***The Children of Green Knowe.*** Harcourt, 1989. ISBN 0-15-217151-7

■■■■■■■■■■□□□□□

Tolly is sent to live with his great-grandmother at Green Knowe. The picture over the fireplace in the mansion shows three children who grew up there in the seventeenth century. At first their lives are reached only through the stories that the old woman tells. Later, the children come into the mansion again.

◆ Cameron, Eleanor. ***The Court of the Stone Children.*** Dutton, 1973. ISBN 0-525-28350-1

————. ***El patio de los niños de piedra.*** Santillana.

■■■■■■■■■■□□□□□

This time fantasy is a well-written mystery. Nina, a child of the present, becomes involved with the story of Dominique, a French woman of the nineteenth century whose father was executed by Napoleon and who needs help clearing her father of murder charges.

◆ Conrad, Pam. ***Stonewords.*** HarperCollins, 1990. ISBN 0-06-021315-9

■■■■■■■■■■□□□□□

Zoe discovers another Zoe (Zoe Louise) who once lived in the same house in 1870. Through a back staircase the modern Zoe travels back and forth in time. She develops a deep friendship with Zoe Louise who can also travel forward into Zoe's time. The modern Zoe fears she has discovered information about Zoe Louise's early death, so she travels back in time to try to save her. Zoe uses information from old newspapers and from gravestones in the local cemetery to piece together information about what happened in the past. The words on the gravestone are the Stonewords.

◆ Cross, Gilbert B. *A Witch Across Time.* Atheneum, 1990. ISBN 0-689-31602-X

■■■■■■■■■■□□□□□

This is a suitably spooky ghost story with historical overtones, as well as the story of a young girl recuperating from anorexia and from a broken romance. You also get a Cook's, or maybe a Cross's, tour of Martha's Vineyard. Hannah Kincaid has been sent to stay with her great-aunt on the island to recuperate and adjust to her father's remarriage. The house is 250 years old and full of history and a most persistent young ghost who draws Hannah into her misery. Hannah's hold on sanity is tenuous, but she draws on strength she didn't know she had to cope with life and even with afterlife.

◆ Wiseman, David. *Jeremy Visick.* Houghton, 1981. ISBN 0-395-30449-0

■■■■■■■■■■■■■□□

*Like **A Chance Child** (page 37), this book explores child labor practices of nineteenth-century England. Matthew, a child researcher, visits a local cemetery and finds evidence of the death of a young boy in the mines of Cornwall. Determined to save the boy, Matthew becomes involved in the mine disaster. Matthew's careful research is what makes the fantasy believable and very useful.*

◆ Woodruff, Elvira. *George Washington's Socks.* Scholastic, 1992. ISBN 0-590-44035-7

■■■■■■■■■□□□□□□

This time a small, insignificant boat is the time travel vehicle. It takes two boys and a girl to another boat that is crossing the Delaware River on a winter's night in 1776. The characterization is strong and the children are quite believable—so is the Hessian soldier whom the children first fear and soon come to like. The realities of war become all too apparent and what seemed to be a war between good and evil becomes a ghastly business with good and bad on both sides.

Estern, Anne Graham. *Letters from Philippa.* Bantam, 1991. ISBN 0-553-15941-0

■■■■■■■■■■□□□□□

Living in current-day Connecticut, Sarah is drawn into the past when she discovers the letters of her great-great-great-aunt Philippa, written around 1852. Following clues that might lead to buried treasure, Sarah and her friends come to believe that Philippa is reaching into the present to clear her name. This book is a natural lead-in to looking through old letters and diaries, scrounging for antiques, and fantasizing about the stories behind them.

McKean, Thomas. *The Secret of the Seven Willows.* Simon, 1991. ISBN 0-671-72997-7

■■■■■■□□□□□□□□□

This is not an unbiased book, but it is easy to read and it addresses some of the problems of time travel. The stereotypes can be used as teaching points; for instance, the Tories in Revolutionary days are shown as rotters. Students can research to show that the Tory argument had its validity, too.

Williams, Ruth L. *The Silver Tree.* HarperCollins, 1992. ISBN 0-06-020296-3

■■■■■■■□□□□□□□□

The book is set in 1991 and 1891. Micki wishes she had never been born and is transported through a dollhouse to 1891 where she develops a friendship with Sarah. Sarah's older brother, Gregory, turns out to be Micki's great-great-grandfather and if she can't figure out certain mysteries, he will die and she will not be born. There is a mysterious egg that is broken in half early in the story and the halves symbolize the good and bad sides of Micki. The mystery involves bringing together the two parts of the egg to form a whole. This time fantasy is fun and adventurous.

The Big Picture

In the lower grades, most curricula suggest that students learn about the past in general ways. It is a general sense of the past, from the big bang through yesterday, that gives us a logical framework into which we can put information. Often, this sense of the past is lacking when we ask upper-grade students to make sense out of or to care about lists of facts in history. To be of long term use, historical studies must be firmly grounded in a sense of time and place as a whole. For instance, understanding the American Revolution as "The" revolution is a less useful concept than understanding the role of revolutions in general throughout time all over the world.

For these reasons we strongly recommend giving students the big picture whenever possible. Upper grades may be confined to a specific area or time because of curriculum demands, but even those confining bonds can be loosened. By so doing, we can create or strengthen an overall sense of the world and our place in it. With any topic chosen for historical study, it is important to constantly refer to the larger framework of history.

In this section, we hit the larger framework of history head-on by listing books and activities especially intended to give a big picture of history. In addition to this section, many of the books and activities in the Following a Strand section are intended to provide a big picture of a particular aspect of history through time. Although this book is limited to US history, we believe that in the classroom this distinction should be eliminated or temporarily suspended whenever possible by looking into what was happening in other places at the time and at occurrences in the past in any country. Time lines that include world history can be especially helpful in expanding our sense of history.

The prospect of engaging with our students in a study of all time all over the world can be overwhelming to say the least. Obviously, when we are already strapped for the time to put one or two centuries of the study of one country into the school day, we cannot expect to attempt a comprehensive study of the history of the world. However, we can, by exposing learners to readings and activities that cover broad and varied spans of time and place, provide a more global view of history.

It is also our experience that, in learning, broadening our study area is often a matter of removing restrictions and not of encompassing more requirements. Again and again in reading US historical literature available, we found ourselves stumbling upon things we were interested in and wanted to know more about, but which we had to steer away from because it was not US history or not the time period being examined.

For instance, what was Asia like that Columbus was so driven to explore it? What was the Muslim world like at that time? What was going on in Polynesia at the time settlers left there to inhabit Hawaii? What was going on in England that brought about the writing of the Magna Carta and set the stage for democracy in America and England? We had the same feelings when we came to periods in American history. Has this sort of thing ever happened anywhere else? And how did the experiences in other places affect these events?

For extended activities that might help to create this sense of our country's history being part of a bigger picture, see Time Line Smorgasbord on pages 28–29, Follow Me on pages 30–32, and Time Fantasies on pages 36–38, or tap into any specific strand on pages 49-157.

The important thing to keep in mind is that, to be understandable and to be functional, the study of history must constantly branch out and move forward and backward.

General Activities

The following activities are designed to help students become aware of the big picture.

- In the Following a Strand section of In Times Past, look through each section for books and activities that approach the strand in a general way. Use these to expand your students' understanding of the past.

- Investigate history through stamps. Photocopy and enlarge stamps representative of each era or used in each era studied. Place them along a time line. Create stamps to commemorate events from the period. How does your design and choice of subject compare to the real ones? Create stamps that would not have been created at the time.

- At a lumberyard or sawmill, get a cross section of the trunk of the largest possible tree. Count the rings to determine the age of the tree. Label the rings to indicate the major events in history during the lifetime of the tree.

- Read Lynne Cherry's *A River Ran Wild* (page 119) or Edith McCall's *Biography of a River* (page 46). Do a similar biography of a natural feature in your area.

- Visit a graveyard to gather a fund of information: names of real people for role playing, an exploration of the changing styles of gravestones, a chance to notice war dead and those that died during epidemics, a chance to find out about infant and child mortality in your area.

- To get a sense of how people affect history, take a major struggle, such as the Civil Rights movement, and pretend that a major figure in it, Martin Luther King, Jr., for instance, had never been born. Ask students to consider the effect of his absence on history.

- To understand how science and invention affect history, think of a major invention, such as the internal combustion engine, and speculate on how history would be changed by the lack of or the postponement of this invention.

- To get an idea of how people's beliefs and values affect history, look at the effect on immigration to the United States if we remove religion as a reason for immigrating. Speculate on the present population of the country.

- Make a brief time line of US history and list important changes in any area (cultures, governmental structures, economic and labor changes, conflicts). Make a similar time line for another country in the same area. Compare and relate the time lines.

- Make a time line of US history from the first human inhabitants or from the first appearance of the continents to the current day. Help the students recognize the relatively small period of time regarded as US history and see how very little is known about so very much of what has happened here. (See Time Line Smorgasbord on page 28.)

- Make a time line or list the big events in history. We usually think of a generation as twenty years. Your parents were born about twenty years before you were. Your great-grandmother was born about sixty years before you. Guess how many "greats" you have to go back to get to a specific event in history.

- Have students create their family tree, filling in the vacancies of unknown people with made-up characters. Around the edges of the tree, place major world events for each generation. If their ancestors were affected by an event, have them indicate this relationship in some graphic way.

Picture Books

★ Cooney, Barbara. *Island Boy*. Viking, 1988. ISBN 0-670-81749-X
See page 33.

★ Dragonwagon, Crescent. *Home Place*. Illustrated by Jerry Pinkney. Macmillan, 1990. ISBN 0-02-733190-3

A present-day family discovers the relics of another family who lived in that spot in the woods long ago. This sensitive picture book shows the present-day family so caught up in imagining what the earlier family must have been like that the earlier family comes to life for a brief time.

★ Hall, Donald. *The Ox-Cart Man.* Viking, 1979. ISBN 0-670-53328-9
See page 33.

★ Johnston, Tony. *Yonder.* Illustrated by Lloyd Bloom. Dial, 1988. ISBN 0-80370278-7.
See page 33.

★ McLerran, Alice. *Roxaboxen.* Lothrop, 1991. ISBN 0-688-07593-2
See page 34.

★ Martin, Jacqueline Briggs. *The Finest Horse in Town.* Illustrated by Susan Gaber. HarperCollins, 1992. ISBN 0-06-024151-9
See page 217.

◆ Andrews, Jan. ***The Auction.*** Illustrated by Karen Reczuch. Macmillan, 1991. ISBN 0-02-705535-3

The old man and his young grandson are justifiably sad as the auction approaches. The old man has already sold off all the animals and now the buildings and equipment must go too, but not before the man and his grandson share their memories of the farm. In a last determination to celebrate the life of the farm, they make scarecrow people all over the land and buildings.

◆ Hamanaka, Sheila. ***The Journey.*** Orchard, 1990. ISBN 0-531-08449-3
See page 147.

◆ Provensen, Alice. ***The Buck Stops Here: The Presidents of the United States.*** HarperCollins, 1990. ISBN 0-06-024787-8

Each president receives a spread in this informative and simple picture book. On the page is his portrait, a rhyming couplet about his life and/or accomplishments, and a tableau of his time. The illustrations look like American primitive paintings with their stiff aspects and, as such, can lead to a discussion on that subject as well. Although the information on each president is necessarily brief, the author has managed to fit an amazing amount of information into this delightful book.

◆ Pryor, Bonnie. ***Lottie's Dream.*** Illustrated by Mark Graham. Simon & Schuster, 1992. ISBN 0-671-74774-6

Lottie, a little girl living in Kentucky, yearns to see the ocean only to find that her family is planning to move even farther from it: to the prairies of Kansas. They travel there by covered wagon, sharing the work of the trip and the work on the farm they build there. Lottie sees the ocean with her young husband, Ben, and wants to stay there, but they don't stay. Many years later, widowed with children grown, Lottie buys a run-down cottage on the shore of Maine where her grandchildren come to vacation with her. Among other things, this picture book shows the passage of time from generation to generation.

Baylor, Byrd. ***The Desert Is Theirs.*** Illustrated by Peter Parnall. Scribner, 1975. ISBN 0-684-14266-X

Desert life, including that of the Papago Indians, is described eloquently with a sense of timelessness.

————. ***The Way to Start a Day.*** Illustrated by Peter Parnall. Scribner, 1978. ISBN 0-684-15651-2

Although this picture book does not confine itself to people in the American past, it does talk about the ceremonies of various cultures in history as the people greeted the new day and how those ceremonies are still celebrated today.

Cornish, Sam. ***Grandmother's Pictures.*** Illustrated by Jeanne Johns. Bradbury, 1974. ISBN 0-87888-092-5
See page 130.

Hiscock, Bruce. ***The Big Tree.*** Atheneum, 1991. ISBN 0-689-31598-8

The tree was a seedling in the time of the Revolution and still stands today. Even before the story begins, we are given a pictorial time line of the tree with modes of transportation representing changing times. Seeing history through the life of a tree is interesting and informative. We pick up science as well as history as the tree grows from seed to maturity.

Scott, Ann Herbert. ***Grandmother's Chair.*** Clarion, 1990. ISBN 0-395-52001-0

A photograph album and the chair are the focal point of a family's history shared by a little girl and her grandmother in this picture book.

Fiction

★ Babbitt, Natalie. ***Tuck Everlasting.*** Farrar, 1975. ISBN 0-374-48009-5
——— . ***Tuck para siempre.*** Farrar, 1991.

Least Sophisticated   **Most Sophisticated**

At first glance, this book appears to have little to do with history, but one finds much information about the cycles of change and the bond of the past with the present. See page 36.

★ Fleischman, Paul. ***The Borning Room***. HarperCollins, 1991.
ISBN 0-06-023785-6

The house in Ohio was built in the late 1700s. In the room just off the kitchen, people were born and died. Outside events reach into the borning room and have their effect on its occupants. The story is much more than a history. This is a Focus Book; see page 274.

◆ Fritz, Jean. ***Brady.*** Puffin, 1987. ISBN 0-14-032258-2

See page 80.

◆ Greenfield, Eloise. ***Sister.*** HarperCollins, 1974. ISBN 0-06-440199-5

Here's a different kind of history. The story is about a present day girl, Doretha, whose older sister is becoming increasingly difficult and distant. In an effort to keep herself in focus, Doretha has kept a journal called "Memories." The journal is written on the leftover pages of a similar book kept by her father. Doretha reads through her entries, which have recorded the good times and the tragedies of her life. In doing so, she is reminded of her rich Black heritage and is reassured that her sister's view and choices in life need not be hers.

◆ Precek, Katharine. ***The Keepsake Chest.*** Macmillan, 1992.
ISBN 0-02-775045-0

Meg hates her new home in Ohio; she liked the big city life she led in Colorado and finds rural Ohio sticky, boring, and completely devoid of shopping malls. It isn't until she, together with her new friend Talley, discovers a chest in the attic and becomes involved with the history of her house and the people who lived there, that Meg can adjust to the present.

General Literature by Jean Fritz

Most of Jean Fritz's books, although concentrating on specific characters and times in history, provide a general sense of how history affects and is affected by the individual. Also, her books do not assign blame or a sense of right or wrong about views, positions, and actions in history. For further information on Jean Fritz, see ***Long Ago and Far Away*** (DLM, 1991. ISBN 1-55924-556-5). Ms. Fritz is an excellent author to examine historically. Here are some of her best.

★ ***And Then What Happened, Paul Revere?*** Coward, 1973. ISBN 0-698-20274-0

■■■■□□□□□□□□□□

See page 72.

★ ***Can't You Make Them Behave, King George?*** Putnam, 1982.
ISBN 0-698-20315-1

■■■■■□□□□□□□□□

See page 72.

★ ***The Double Life of Pocahontas.*** Putnam, 1983. ISBN 0-399-21016-4

■■■■■■■■■□□□□□

See page 180.

★ ***Early Thunder.*** Putnam, 1967. ISBN 0-698-20036-5

■■■■■■■■■□□□□□

This is a Focus Book; see page 264.

★ ***The Great Little Madison.*** Putnam, 1989. ISBN 0-399-21768-1

■■■■■■■■■□□□□□

This is a Focus Book; see page 268.

◆ ***The Cabin Faced West.*** Putnam, 1958. ISBN 0-698-20016-0

■■■■■■■□□□□□□□

See page 185.

◆ ***Make Way for Sam Houston.*** Putnam, 1986. ISBN 0-399-21303-1

■■■■■■■■■■□□□□

See page 211.

◆ ***Shhh! We're Writing the Constitution.*** Putnam, 1987. ISBN 0-399-21403-8

■■■■■□□□□□□□□□

See page 193.

◆ ***Stonewall.*** Putnam, 1979. ISBN 0-399-20698-1

■■■■■■■■■□□□□□

See page 82.

◆ ***Traitor: The Case of Benedict Arnold.*** Putnam, 1981. ISBN 0-399-20834-8

■■■■■■■■■□□□□□

See page 72.

◆ ***What's the Big Idea, Ben Franklin?*** Putnam, 1982. ISBN 0-698-20365-8

■ ■ ■ □ □ □ □ □ □ □ □ □ □ □ □

See page 186.

◆ ***Where Was Patrick Henry on the 29th of May?*** Coward, 1982. ISBN 0-698-20307-0

■ ■ ■ ■ ■ □ □ □ □ □ □ □ □ □ □

See page 72.

◆ ***Who's That Stepping on Plymouth Rock?*** Putnam, 1975. ISBN 0-698-20325-9

■ ■ ■ □ □ □ □ □ □ □ □ □ □ □ □

See page 180.

◆ ***Why Don't You Get a Horse, Sam Adams?*** Putnam, 1974. ISBN 0-698-20292-9

■ ■ ■ ■ ■ □ □ □ □ □ □ □ □ □ □

See page 73.

◆ ***Will You Sign Here, John Hancock?*** Coward, 1982. ISBN 0-698-20308-9

■ ■ ■ ■ ■ □ □ □ □ □ □ □ □ □ □

See page 73.

Bully for You, Teddy Roosevelt. Putnam, 1991. ISBN 0-399-21769-X

■ ■ ■ ■ ■ □ □ □ □ □ □ □ □ □ □

The story of the sickly boy who grew up to be an ebullient war hero and president is told with Fritz's usual blend of humor and humanity.

George Washington's Breakfast. Putnam, 1984. ISBN 0-698-30099-8

■ ■ ■ ■ ■ □ □ □ □ □ □ □ □ □ □

See page 192.

Homesick: My Own Story. Dell, 1984. ISBN 0-440-43683-4

■ ■ ■ ■ ■ ■ ■ ■ ■ ■ □ □ □ □ □

Fritz grew up in China where her parents were missionaries. This is the story of her early years.

Where Do You Think You're Going, Christopher Columbus? Putnam, 1981. ISBN 0-399-20723-6

■ ■ ■ ■ ■ □ □ □ □ □ □ □ □ □ □

See page 171.

Nonfiction

◆ Orlick, Terry. ***The Cooperative Sports and Games Book.*** Pantheon, 1978. ISBN 0-394-73494-7

■ ■ ■ ■ ■ ■ ■ ■ □ □ □ □ □ □ □

See page 56

◆ Shenkman, Richard. ***I Love Paul Revere, Whether He Rode or Not.***
HarperCollins, 1991. ISBN 0-06-016346-1

■■■■■■■■■■□□□□

This is not a children's book, but much of the material in it will be useful to teachers and younger researchers. Shenkman debunks many of the incidents and heroes of history that we've all come to accept as true and wonderful, but he does so through careful researching of the facts. The book has a light touch and many of the incidents are worth reading aloud.

◆ Weitzman, David. ***My Backyard History Book***. Little, 1975. ISBN 0-316-92902-6

■■■■■■■□□□□□□□□

This book is a series of activities that will involve children in history. Starting with finding out about their own names, researching family trees and stories, and proceeding to an exploration of the history of their own towns, the suggested activities are practical and interesting. For instance, the idea of conducting an auction of items in an old Sears catalog would give participants a chance to see the products of the time as well as to get an idea of prices. If you're looking for a way to involve students in the past, this book is a good place to start.

Ashabranner, Brent. ***A Grateful Nation: The Story of Arlington National Cemetery.*** Putnam, 1990. ISBN 0-399-22188-3

■■■■■■□□□□□□□□

With photographs and text, the author tells the story of the founding of Arlington National Cemetery and the history of Arlington House, the mansion that has become part of it. In telling the history of Arlington, the author briefly reviews the wars since the Civil War, tells of the various jobs required to keep the cemetery functioning, and details some of its frequent ceremonies.

————. ***A Memorial for Mr. Lincoln.*** Putnam, 1992. ISBN 0-399-22273-1

■■■■■■□□□□□□□□

The story of the creation of the monument that has so moved visitors is a fascinating one. Although not completed until 1922, the movement to create a suitable monument for Lincoln began on the day of his death. As well as recounting all the triumphs and defeats along the way, the author brings the story up-to-date by reflecting about the newest monument that stands near the Lincoln Memorial: the Vietnam Wall.

Barber, Lynda Graham. ***Gobble! The Complete Book of Thanksgiving Words.***
Illustrated by Betsy Lewin. Bradbury, 1991. ISBN 0-02-708332-2

■■■■■■□□□□□□□□

Concentrating on the history of one celebration, the author gives us some historical information on Puritans, Pilgrims, Indians, various peoples who celebrate the harvest season, and the etymology of words associated with Thanksgiving. Such an approach could be the inspiration for a similar book put together by the children for any other holiday or season.

Grant, Neil. ***The Great Atlas of Discovery***. Knopf, 1992. ISBN 0-679-81660-7

■■■■■■□□□□□□□□

Maps and charts accompany the narration of this book. It covers discoveries from Marco Polo to Buzz Aldrin.

Hauptly, Denis. ***Puerto Rico: An Unfinished Story.*** Atheneum, 1991. ISBN 0-689-31431-0

■■■■■■■■■□□□□□□

The book covers five hundred years of Puerto Rican history, only eleven days of which Puerto Rico was an independent nation. The strategic position of Puerto Rico has made it desirable territory for many larger nations and the island's history has been stormy. The book helps to answer or at least poses the question: Should Puerto Rico be a state, an independent country, or continue in its present status?

Katz, William Loren. ***Black Indians: A Hidden Heritage.*** Atheneum, 1986. ISBN 0-689-31196-6

■■■■■■■■■■■■■□

The author strives to make the point that there is a group of Black Americans who made contributions that have been largely ignored, and in doing so, he is sometimes guilty of drawing conclusions that the evidence doesn't support. These "Black Indians" were African Americans who escaped slavery and were adopted into Indian tribes and people with mixed African and Indian blood. The author also chronicles the relationship between Native Americans and African Americans. This is a weighty book, but the information is difficult to find elsewhere.

Kudlinski, Kathleen. ***Helen Keller: Light for the Blind.*** Viking, 1989. ISBN 0-670-82460-7

■■■■□□□□□□□□□□□

The book covers Helen Keller's life from 1880 to 1968. It describes her learning to communicate, going to college, writing books, performing in vaudeville, and her work for the blind in America and around the world.

McCall, Edith. ***Biography of a River: The Living Mississippi.*** Walker, 1990. ISBN 0-8027-6915-2

■■■■□□□□□□□□□□□

The geology of the river is touched upon, but most of the book recounts the history of the great river, especially during the 1800s. The book is included here, not only for its own content, but for the idea of viewing the history of any river, especially one close to your area, as a way of making history more immediate for young students.

St. George, Judith. ***The White House: Cornerstone of a Nation.*** Putnam, 1990. ISBN 0-399-22186-7

■■■■■■■□□□□□□□□

By telling us the history of the mansion, Ms. St. George gives us glimpses into the lives of the people who have inhabited it since its beginnings in 1792. Starting with George Washington's era and extending to the age of television, the book contains floor plans and photographs of the building and its inhabitants.

Siegel, Beatrice. ***Sam Ellis's Island.*** Four Winds, 1985. ISBN 0-02-782720-8

■■■■■■□□□□□□□□□

The history of the island that became the pass gate for thousands of immigrants to this country is recounted, as is the life of the man whose name it came to bear. Looking at the changes in New York City from the time of Native American inhabitants through the present is an interesting perspective.

Cobblestone Magazine

The following issues of the magazine were devoted to history in general.

Presidential Elections (October 1980)
Genealogy (November 1980)
Connecticut History (January 1981)
Old Time Schools (November 1981)
California History (May 1982)
America's Cowboys (July 1982)
The Circus (August 1982)
Black History Month (February 1983)
Medicine (March 1983)
Archaeology (June 1983)
Folklore (July 1983)
Public Works (August 1983)
Libraries (November 1983)
Soil (December 1983)
Visions of America's Future (January 1984)
The Cherokee Indians (February 1984)
The Olympic Games (August 1984)
Who Came to America (October 1984)
The US Senate (November 1984) |
The Newspaper (January 1985)
The US and the USSR (February 1985)
Veterinary Medicine (June 1985)
Baseball (July 1985)
The Cartoon (August 1985)
The US Mint (September 1985)

American Clothing (October 1985)
Eskimos (November 1985)
Endangered Species (January 1986)
Mexico and the United States (March 1986)
Natural Disasters (April 1986)
American Fads (July 1986)
Children's Toys (December 1986)
Chicago (April 1987)
The Automobile in History (July 1987)
Celebrating Our Constitution (September 1987)
Canada and the United States (March 1988)
The Seafaring Life (April 1988)
Touring the Great Lakes (May 1988)
American Architecture (August 1988)
The Two Party System (November 1988)
Children Who Shaped History (January 1989)
Important Supreme Court Cases (March 1989)
Entrepreneurs of the Past (May 1989)
People with Disabilities (June 1989)
Dine: The People of the Navajo Nation (July 1989)
Environmentalism (August 1989)
What Is History? (January 1990)
The Mississippi River (March 1990)
Taking Stock of Wall Street (April 1990)
Energy: Powering Our Nation (October 1990)
Hawaii (December 1990)
Back issues of the magazine can be obtained from Cobblestone Publishing, 30 Grove St., Peterborough, NH 03458.

Nonprint

Videos

First Ladies. Public Media Video, 1989.

The Smithsonian exhibit of First Ladies' inauguration gowns is the starting point for this look at the personalities and contributions of presidents' wives from Martha Washington to Nancy Reagan.

From My Grandmother's Grandmother Unto Me. Cinema Guild, 1990.

A one-woman show by Clarinda Ross-Clark, filmed in the North Carolina mountains, relates the stories of her family through the generations. The effect is moving and informative.

Lightning on Ice: The History of Hockey. Video Treasures, 1990.

Alan Thicke narrates a history of professional hockey. The film traces the game from its earliest adaptations and includes footage from the first Canadian team in 1875 to the Stanley Cup winners of 1990.

Computer Software

Timeliner and Mac Timeliner. Tom Snyder Productions, 1990.

The user can create time lines varying in length from eons to weeks or even a day with ease, importing graphics, merging with other time lines, printing vertically or horizontally, collapsing and expanding at will. Versions are available for the Apple II, IBM, and Macintosh.

Part
2

Following a Strand

War and Conflict

What Is War?

It is possible and sometimes required to direct students' attention and study to a specific war in some depth. It is also possible to find similarities and differences between and among wars and conflicts and, by doing so, gain some understanding of why wars are fought and what, if anything, is accomplished by war. When this approach is used, you can study some of the factors that cause conflict. You can also study actions and groups that can resolve such conflicts without warfare.

If you use this approach, encourage reading from many sources. By reading both nonfiction, which analyzes and records battles and causes and effects of the wars, and novels and biographies, which attempt to look at conflict through the eyes of one group or character, readers will get a broader picture and more readily empathize with the effects of the war on individuals.

There is an excellent book that you might want to get before you begin this unit. ***Elementary Perspectives 1: Teaching Concepts of Peace and Conflict*** by William Kreidler (Educators for Social Responsibility, 1990. ISBN 0-942349-01-6) is a collection of eighty activities structured to introduce students to peace, human rights, community, conflict resolution, and diversity. These activities are designed to be integrated with the rest of the curriculum to create an ongoing program for strengthening social skills and deepening understanding of international issues. In the development of each concept, the activities begin with personal interactions and expand to international interactions.

Activities

One of our responsibilities to the next generation is to present them with a truly accurate picture of what war is and what it is not. Here are some activities that will help.

- Identify some of the conflicts behind war in general or behind a specific war. Try to go beyond the standard list of causes and list everything you can possibly think of that might have had some bearing on a disagreement or conflict turning into a war.

- How do different factors influence war? Make a chart showing the influences of such things as economics, ethics, human conditions, and political beliefs. Can you find examples of these in history?

- Who are the soldiers in the war and why are they involved? Find statistics on groups of people who were soldiers in the Gulf War. What is the significance of this information?

- Interview military people or people who were on active duty during a war and find out whether they enlisted or were drafted. If they enlisted, find out why. How does this information impact the statistics in the previous activity?

- How should nations decide who should fight in a war? Do governments have a right to require military service of their citizens?

- What is a battle really like? As a class, discuss what you think a specific battle might have been like. How might you feel in these instances: shooting someone, being nearby when someone is wounded or killed, and being wounded yourself? What if your unit were advancing into a battlefield? What if your unit were retreating? What if your unit were surrendering? Under what circumstances might you break ranks and stop fighting? Would it matter to you how deeply you were committed to the cause for which you were fighting?

- Turn the preceding activity into a journal activity.

- After your discussion, read a book such as ***Thunder at Gettysburg*** (see page 52). Then discuss how the real battle compared to Tillie's ideas about war? How did this book compare to what you thought a battle might be like?

- What is the impact of war on the community? Pick a community and research it before, during, and after a war. How does it compare to other communities at the time? What impacts might not be felt for quite a while?

- What is war's impact on the environment? Consider the bombing of Hiroshima and Nagasaki and the War in the Gulf. How long will these areas suffer because of the wars? How many people have been and will be affected?

- Post traumatic stress syndrome. During the Civil War it was called nostalgia, the French called it the sickness of the heart, later it was called shell shock, and now it is called post traumatic stress syndrome. What is it? Interview veterans about this syndrome.

- How does war resolve the issues of a conflict? Does it tend to create win/lose solutions or solutions that meet the needs of both sides? (See Conflict Resolution on pages 54–56 for more information.)

- Who benefits from war? How do the people deal with the conflict between their individual needs and beliefs and those of the world at large? How do wars affect people's careers? How would those who benefit from war be affected if there were no more wars?

- The ethics of war vary from culture to culture. How do ethics influence war? (See The Native American Conflict on pages 59–63 for a few ideas.) What does our culture consider "fair" during war? What does it consider unfair or inhuman? Can you find incidents in our history in which a difference in ethics has worsened a conflict?

- Discover some of the lies that the public has been told during war. What kinds of things are lied about? Why do governments lie? Do you believe that these reasons justify the lies? Is there agreement about when lying is justified?

- Make a chart of the relationship between hard economic times and beginnings of wars.

Picture Books ◆ Zimelman, Nathan. ***Mean Chickens and Wild Cucumbers.*** Illustrated by David Small. Macmillan, 1983. ISBN 0-02-793730-5

There is a hole in the fence dividing the property of two neighbors. One man's mean chicken pecks the other man through the hole in the fence. The second man's cucumber vine tweaks the nose of the first through the same hole. Therefore, we must have a fence-building contest. Eventually, the fences collapse, perhaps aided by the efforts of those mean chickens and wild cucumbers. The lesson is obvious, but the humor and outlandishness make the book a good one.

Dr. Seuss. ***The Butter Battle Book.*** Random, 1984. ISBN 0-394-96580-9

In this fable, a great wall separates the Yooks from the Zooks, but that's not enough to keep matters peaceful. The competition escalates until each side has a bomb and is standing at the wall ready to drop it.

Fiction ★ Paulsen, Gary. ***The Foxman.*** Puffin, 1990. ISBN 0-14-034311-3

■■■■■■■■■■■□□□□

Least Sophisticated   **Most Sophisticated**

See page 88.

★ ———. ***The Monument.*** Delacorte Press, 1991. ISBN 0-385-30518-4

■■■■■■■■■■□□□□

See page 103.

★ Reeder, Carolyn. ***Shades of Gray.*** Macmillan, 1989. ISBN 0-02-77810-9

■■■■■■■■■■■□□□

See page 79.

◆ Avi. ***The Fighting Ground.*** Lippincott, 1984. ISBN 0-397-32074-4

■■■■■■■■■■□□□□

Jonathan is taken by Hessians to a farmhouse where a little boy is the only survivor of his family. When given the opportunity, Jonathan finds it impossible to kill the Hessians. He escapes with the little boy and finds the remnants of the troop he was with in battle. When he realizes that they must have killed the boy's parents, Jonathan smashes his rifle and heads back to the farm, sadder and less certain about the rights and wrongs of war.

◆ Beatty, Patricia. ***Charley Skedaddle.*** Morrow, 1987. ISBN 0-688-06687-9

■■■■■■■■□□□□□□

See page 80.

◆ Collier, James Lincoln and Collier, Christopher. ***My Brother Sam Is Dead.*** Four Winds, 1974. ISBN 0-02-722980-7

■■■■■■■■■■■■■□

See page 70.

◆ Gauch, Patricia Lee. ***Thunder at Gettysburg.*** Putnam, 1990. ISBN 0-399-22201-4

■■■■□□□□□□□□□□

Tillie, a young girl, watches the battle at Gettysburg first from her attic and then from two other houses near the battlefield. In the beginning, watching is exciting, but as torn and wounded soldiers are brought in, the excitement is replaced by horror. The book is short and very easy to read.

Nonfiction   ◆   Meltzer, Milton. ***The American Revolutionaries: A History in Their Own Words: 1750-1800.*** Crowell, 1987. ISBN 0-69004643-X

Here are first-person accounts of men and women who were part of and/or witness to the last half of the eighteenth century, including the French and Indian War and the Revolution.

Rabinowitz, Richard. ***What Is War? What Is Peace? 50 Questions and Answers for Kids.*** Avon, 1991. ISBN 0-380-76704-X

The major focus for this book is the Gulf War, but in answering kids' questions about the reasons for that war the author deals with other wars and with wars in general. The account of the Gulf War is based on the perspective of the United States

War and Conflict

Conflict Resolution and Cooperation

Activities

Studying the history and nature of conflict provides a wonderful opportunity for you to begin the process of teaching and learning conflict-resolution skills and cooperation skills in the classroom. The payoffs are an increase in the class's ability to work together productively and a greater understanding of the issues in our society.

- In a work of literature, identify the areas of personal conflict. What needs are in conflict? Create a chart listing the needs and fears of the various parties. When listing needs, move toward more and more basic, underlying needs. Which of these needs do you think are most basic, most universal?

Some Reasons for the Civil War

The Rebels	The Yankees	President Lincoln
To keep their slaves	To stop slavery	
To operate their plantations	To make things better for Black people	
To maintain their current lifestyles	To create a more just society	
Financial security	To preserve the Union	
To secede	To maintain the authority of national law	
States' rights	To stay within the constitution	
The Confederacy	To preserve current law	
To decide for themselves what to do	To have a secure political system	
To have a say in their fate		
Freedom		

- Do the activity above with a political conflict rather than a personal one.
- One of the underlying tenets of conflict resolution is that in order to create solutions that address everyone's needs, we must be able to listen carefully and accept differences. Identify incidents in a novel that show one side listening carefully to another side. Why was it difficult for the people to listen to each other?
- Identify a conflict and list all the solutions you can think of. Identify who wins and who loses with each solution. Are there any solutions in which everyone loses? Are there any in which everyone wins?
- Take a conflict in history and translate it to a family situation. Identify members of the family with leaders in the historical conflict. If the members of a family behaved the way nations behave, how would society react? What actions do we accept between nations that we would never accept between individuals?
- Play a cooperative game from ***The Cooperative Sports and Games Book,*** (page 56). Compare feelings during and after the competitive game and the cooperative game. How did you feel at the beginning of the game? How did you

feel when you made a mistake? How did you feel toward someone for whom it was a struggle to play well? How did you feel toward someone who seemed to be most effective? How did you feel about your own performance? How satisfied were you at the end of the game? How did you feel toward your friends and classmates after the game?

Fiction

★ Field, Rachel. ***Calico Bush.*** Dell Yearling, 1931. ISBN 0-440-40368-5

Least Sophisticated   Most Sophisticated

When the Indians attack, Marguerite, by necessity, saves the day with a creative nonviolent approach. This is a Focus Book; see page 262

★ Fritz, Jean. ***Early Thunder.*** Putnam, 1967. ISBN 0-698-20036-5

In this book we see an excellent picture of the interactions between individuals within a community on the eve of war. Why were they forced to take sides? How might the conflict have been resolved differently if they had had a mediator and if modern communication had been available between England and the Colonies? This is a Focus Book, see page 264.

★ Hansen, Joyce. ***Out From This Place.*** Avon, 1988. ISBN 0-380-71409-4

The scene is 1862 through 1866 in South Carolina. A group of slaves who escape to Union-occupied islands are told that if they work the land of the plantations for a number of years, they will be given the land. Later the group must decide how to respond when the United States' government reverses its decision and attempts to return the plantations to the white owners. Beginning with armed rebellion, the group struggles to reach a peaceful yet fair resolution. It is painfully clear that there is no easy solution and that the methods of conflict resolution used by the government are pitifully inadequate to address the problem.

★ Spinka, Penina Keen. ***Mother's Blessing.*** Atheneum, 1992. ISBN 0-689-31758-1

Set in Southern California in the middle of the tenth century, this is a story of the journey of a young woman into the land of the Anasazi whose culture was then at its peak. She is destined to become a leader and to bring together three villages that have been locked in conflict. This is also a novel of stubbornness and pride that block the leader's ability to do what is best for the people. See page 163

Nonfiction

◆ Kreidler, William J. ***Creative Conflict Resolution.*** Scott, Foresman, 1984. ISBN 0-673-15642-7

Here are two hundred activities for a K through 6 program on developing cooperation and group skills. With this program, the conflicts in literature become exercises in identifying conflict and finding solutions within the social studies curriculum.

◆ Orlick, Terry. ***The Cooperative Sports and Games Book.*** Pantheon, 1978. ISBN 0-394-73494-7

■■■■■■■□□□□□□□

This book of cooperative activities provides hands-on experiences with problem-solving techniques that focus on everyone's needs and on people's ability to work together for the common good. It also provides a format for introducing conflict negotiation as an alternative to force. Among the games are six played by Inuits of the Canadian Arctic. These games emphasize the collective striving toward a common goal.

Judson, Stephanie. ***A Manual on Nonviolence and Children.*** New Society, 1984. ISBN 0-86571-036-8

■■■■■■■□□□□□□□

This manual includes a section of cooperative games for adults and children.

Schrumpf, Fred, et al. ***Peer Mediation, Conflict Resolution in Schools.*** Research Press, 1991. ISBN 0-87822-331-2

■■■■■■■□□□□□□□

Here is a training manual for students and teachers on peer mediation.

War and Conflict

Nonviolence and War Resistance

Activities

- See the section on the Civil Rights Movement, pages 97–98.

- See the section on the Vietnam War, pages 103–104.

- In *Elementary Perspectives 1: Teaching Concepts of Peace and Conflict* by William Kreidler (Educators for Social Responsibility, 1990. ISBN 0-942349-01-6), there is an activity about violence and fighting on page 99. It suggests that you ask students why they think violence is sometimes used to settle conflicts. Have the students brainstorm a list of positive reasons for using violence to resolve conflicts. Then brainstorm a list of the potentially negative consequences of using violence to resolve conflicts. Which list is longer and why? Which consequences are short term? Which are long term? What are some other ways that we could get the positive effects of fighting without fighting? Where do we get our ideas about fighting?

- Contact the American Friends Service Committee nearest you. Find out all you can about the Quakers' history of war resistance. Which wars have they refused to fight in? What personal sacrifices did they make? What have they done to create alternatives to war? Who have been some of their most famous members?

- Read a biography of a pacifist. Why do pacifists believe that fighting is wrong? What do they do about it? How does society react to their stance? Were they regarded differently in some wars than in others? What similarities and differences are there between their stories and stories of others who believe in personal integrity?

Fiction

★ Sebestyen, Ouida. *Words By Heart*. Little, 1979. ISBN 0-553-27179-2

■■■■■■■□□□□□□□

Least Sophisticated   Most Sophisticated

Lena's family is the only Black family in this town in the Southwest. Lena's father warns her about returning hatred, which is easy to do when the hatred is so overwhelming.

Davis, Ossie. *Just Like Martin.* Simon and Schuster, 1992. ISBN 0-671-73202-1

■■■■■■■■□□□□□□

Isaac's father insists that Martin Luther King, Jr.'s nonviolence will get them nowhere, but Isaac knows his father is wrong, even when their school is bombed.

Nonfiction

◆ Levine, Ellen. *If You Lived at the Time of Martin Luther King.* Scholastic, 1990. ISBN 0-590-42582-X

■■■■■□□□□□□□□□

See page 98.

◆ Stern, Philip Van Doren. ***Henry David Thoreau: Writer and Rebel.*** Crowell, 1972. ISBN 0-690-37715-0

■■■■■■■■■■■□□□□

This biography concentrates on the adult life of this philosopher and nonconformist as a critic and writer, including his refusal to pay war taxes. It is well balanced and presents his thoughts and life in a way that shows their relevance to succeeding generations.

◆ Wheeler, Leslie. ***Jane Addams.*** Silver Burdett, 1990. ISBN 0-382-09968-0

■■■■■■■■■■□□□□

For her extensive work improving living and working conditions, Jane Addams was called, at times, a saint. During the First World War she continued her pacifism, working with the Woman's International League for Peace and Freedom. This difficult decision made her very unpopular at the time.

War and Conflict

The Native American Conflict

Activities

- See also the section on the French and Indian War on page 64.

- When settlers began coming to the North American continent, all of what is now the US was the territory of various Native American nations. At first there was the possiblity of coexistence ,but over the years the conflict about land became a conquest of Native American lands. Would you call this conflict a war? Is there a better term? When did it begin? Did it end? What were some of the problems that both groups faced, how were they addressed, and what were the results?

- Was this a declared war? Who had the power to do so? How is war defined? Was the Korean War a declared war? How about the Vietnamese War? Did we have other undeclared wars? Why? Are there political reasons for undeclared wars?

- Make maps showing land under Indian control at various times in our history. Calculate the land areas.

- Find and read treaties made between Native Americans and the US government.

- Imagine that you are an official in the Bureau of Indian Affairs. It is your job to come to a peaceful agreement with everyone involved in the 1890 Nebraska land question. How would you do this?

- When was the last armed conflict between Native Americans and agents of the US government?

- Write to an authority in a Native American tribe to find out about current problems or disagreements with the US government.

- What if the US government had honored treaties with Indians? Draw a map of what the US might look like today.

- What roles did Native Americans play in the Civil War and more recent wars? Were they required to serve in the military?

- Contrast the ways different cultures view land ownership and use.

- Make a list of leaders on all sides of the conflict among Native American tribes and the immigrants. List such things as accomplishments, beliefs, weapons, and major battles or confrontations and the outcomes.

- List the weapons available to each side during this conflict. How did these affect the outcome of the war?

- Look at art prints of conflict between Native Americans and European settlers. What can you tell about the artists' feelings?

- Find an old US history textbook for children. Read accounts of the conflict. Read a similar account in the most up-to-date US history textbook you can find. Are there differences? Notice the illustrations. What do they show?

- Contrast the ethics and methods of war between the two cultures. Who used which and why? How did they view each other's ethics and warfare methods? How did the differences exacerbate the conflict?

- Break the class into three groups: one European Americans, one Native Americans, and one mediators. Control of the playground is in contention. Must the playground be divided? Can the groups play together? Mediators should familiarize themselves with conflict resolution (page 54). Work toward an equitable solution to playground use.

- Find out about some of the following Indian leaders: Tecumseh, Sequoyah, Chief Joseph, Black Hawk, Crazy Horse, Sitting Bull, and Osceola. To which tribe did each belong? What did they do for their people? What was their fate?

- Find out what each of these leaders thought and did about the battle for Indian lands: George Washington, Abraham Lincoln, Andrew Jackson, Henry Clay, Davy Crockett, and Sam Houston. Make a chart showing this information.

- Trace the Trail of Tears on a map. How many Cherokee began the journey and how many finished it? Write to the tourist bureaus of North Carolina, Georgia, and Oklahoma for photographs of the land. Contrast the new and old homes of the Cherokee.

- Make a chart showing the causes and effects of the Seminole War.

- What role did schools and education play in the conficts? Why were many schools for Native Americans boarding schools? Write to the Bureau of Indian Affairs to find out when and whether changes in policy occurred.

- Form groups to represent Regina's father, from ***I Am Regina*** (page 191), Tecumseh and his tribe, and Weasel from ***Weasel*** (page 192). Discuss opening Oklahoma to non-Indian settlers in the Land Rush. Who had a right to the land?

Picture Books

★ Sewall, Marcia. ***People of the Breaking Day.*** Atheneum, 1990. ISBN 0-689-31407-8
See page 177.

★ Yolen, Jane. ***Encounter.*** Illustrated by David Shannon. Harcourt, 1992. ISBN 0-15-225962-7
See page 168.

◆ Goble, Paul. ***Death of the Iron Horse.*** Bradbury, 1987. ISBN 0-02-737830-6
See page 124.

Locker, Thomas. ***The Land of Gray Wolf.*** Dial, 1990. ISBN 0-8037-0936-6
See page 185.

Fiction

★ Keehn, Sally M. ***I Am Regina.*** Philomel, 1990. ISBN 0-399-21797-5

■■■■■■■■■■□□□□

Least Sophisticated   **Most Sophisticated**

See page 191.

◆ Bohner, Charles. ***Bold Journey: West with Lewis and Clark.*** Houghton, 1985. ISBN 0-395-36691-7

■■■■■■■□□□□□□□

See page 198.

◆ Collier, James Lincoln and Collier, Christopher. ***The Bloody Country.*** Macmillan, 1985. ISBN 0-02-722960-2

■■■■■■■■■■■■■□

See page 191.

◆ Kissinger, Rosemary. ***Quanah Parker: Commanche Chief.*** Pelican, 1991. ISBN 0-88289-785-3

■■■■■■■■□□□□□□

This is a fictionalized biography of the man whose mother was a Caucasian and whose father was a Comanche chief. His mother, Cynthia Parker, was kidnapped by the Comanches as a child and returned to the white culture as an adult, but she was not able to adjust to white society. That background and his mixed racial heritage caused Quanah a great deal of pain. As a leader of his people, he promised to drive the whites from the land but eventually surrendered to them. His leadership continued, however, as he tried to promote peaceful coexistence.

◆ Paulsen, Gary. ***Canyons.*** Delacorte, 1990. ISBN 0-385-30153-7

■■■■■■■■□□□□□□

A modern teenager finds the skull of an American Indian who was shot a hundred years earlier in the desert and decides to find the proper resting place for the bones.

Magorian, Jim. ***Keeper of Fire.*** Council for Indian Education, 1984. ISBN 0-89992-088-8

■■■■■■■□□□□□□□

See page 208.

O'Dell, Scott. ***My Name Is Not Angelica.*** Dell, 1989. ISBN 0-440-40379-0

■■■■■■■■■□□□□□□

See page 185.

Nonfiction ◆ Bealer, Alex W. ***Only the Names Remain: The Cherokees and the Trail of Tears.*** Little, 1972. ISBN 0-316-08520-0

■■■■■■■□□□□□□□

See page 200.

◆ Ehrlich, Amy. ***Wounded Knee: An Indian History of the American West.*** Adapted from Dee Brown's *Bury My Heart at Wounded Knee*. Holt, 1974. ISBN 0-440-95768-0

■■■■■■■■■■□□□□

See page 135.

◆ Fisher, Leonard Everett. ***The Oregon Trail.*** Holiday, 1990. ISBN 0-02-719020-X

■■■■■■■□□□□□□□

See page 200.

◆ Freedman, Russell. ***Indian Chiefs.*** Holiday, 1987. ISBN 0-8234-0625-3

■■■■■■■□□□□□□□

See page 186.

◆ Fritz, Jean. ***Make Way for Sam Houston.*** Putnam, 1986. ISBN 0-399-21303-1

■■■■■■■■■□□□□□

See page 211.

◆ Waldman, Carl. ***Atlas of the North American Indian.*** Facts On File, 1985. ISBN 0-87196-850-9

■■■■■■■■■■■□□□

Although this book is intended for an adult audience, it is appropriate for middle school students and is a good reference for teachers of any grade level. It has articles on many individual tribes that provide background and historical information. Many maps show Indian lands from prehistory through the present. In addition there are military maps of the wars between whites and Indians, of the intertribal conflicts, and of the locations of the various cultural components.

Claro, Nicole. ***The Cherokee Indians.*** Chelsea, 1991. ISBN 0-7910-1652-8

■■■■■■■□□□□□□□

See page 136.

Cobblestone Magazine

The Cherokee Indians (February 1984)
Joseph, a Chief of the Nez Percé (September 1990)

Doherty, Craig and Doherty, Katherine. ***The Apaches and Navajos.*** Watts, 1989. ISBN 0-531-15607-9

■■■■■■■■■□□□□□

See page 136.

Lawson, Don. ***The United States in the Indian Wars.*** HarperCollins, 1988. ISBN 0-690-04713-4

■■■■■■■■■□□□□□

The concentration here is on how different concepts of land ownership were the underlying cause of the bloody conflicts.

Lee, Martin. ***The Seminoles.*** Watts, 1989. ISBN 0-531-15604-4

■■■■■■■■■□□□□□

See page 138.

Nabokov, Peter. ***Native American Testimony: An Anthology of Indian and White Relations, First Encounter to Dispossession.*** HarperCollins, 1972. ISBN 0-690-03840-2

■■■■■■■■■□□□□□

Using excerpts from speeches and oral histories, the Native American point of view of the settling of the continent by European cultures is given. The book is amply illustrated with photographs, art prints, and maps.

Shorto, Russell. ***Tecumseh and the Dream of an American Indian Nation.*** Silver Burdett, 1989. ISBN 0-382-09569-3

■■■■■■■□□□□□□□

See page 201.

Smith, Carter. ***Bridging the Continent.*** Millbrook, 1992. ISBN 1-56294-130-5

————. ***The Conquest of the West.*** Millbrook, 1992. ISBN 1-56294-129-1

————. ***Exploring the Frontier.*** Millbrook, 1992. ISBN 1-56294-128-3

————. ***The Legendary Wild West.*** Millbrook, 1992. ISBN 1-56294-133-X

————. ***Native Americans of the West.*** Millbrook, 1992. ISBN 1-56294-131-3

————. ***The Riches of the West.*** Millbrook, 1992. ISBN 1-56294-132-1

■■■■■■■■□□□□□□

This clearly written, copiously illustrated set of books gives a clear picture of the push of the Europeans to the Pacific coast. Each volume contains a time line of significant events and the text is written in brief passages to accompany the illustrations.

Sonneborn, Liz. ***The Cheyenne Indians.*** Chelsea, 1992. ISBN 0-7910-1654-4

■■■■■■■■□□□□□□

See page 139.

Stein, R. Conrad. ***The Story of the Homestead Act.*** Childrens, 1978. ISBN 0-516-04616-0

■■■■■□□□□□□□□□

See page 213.

————. ***The Story of the Trail of Tears.*** Childrens, 1985. ISBN 0- 516-04683-7

■■■■■□□□□□□□□□

See page 201.

————. ***The Story of Wounded Knee.*** Childrens, 1983. ISBN 0-516-04665-9

■■■■■□□□□□□□□□

See page 223.

War and Conflict

The French and Indian War
1755-1763

Activities

- Divide the group into five teams for research and role-playing: English settlers in America, French settlers and traders in America, Indians of the Northeast region, French soldiers, and English soldiers.

- Make wanted posters for leaders of each of the groups. The posters could be advertisements for a leader or for the capture of an enemy.

- Make models of the styles of housing used by each group.

- Speculate on the consequences of different resolutions of the wars. What if people had honored the treaties they made with each other? What if a different side had won? What if all groups had come out of the conflict with equal power?

- There was a great contrast between life in Montreal and life in Boston during this period. The Boston population was mostly Puritan and the Montreal population was primarily Catholic. Dress dolls as people from each city. Make a list of the things Montrealers did that were forbidden in Boston at the time.

- Find information about Boston and Montreal today. What signs can you find of their founders and of the life established during the time of the French and Indian War?

- Find out about Cajun cooking and culture as it exists today. Cook a Cajun dish.

- Several of the stories below are about people who were held captive by Indians and the struggles they faced to become part of either the Indian or the white settlers' world. Which story was most believable? Why? Can you imagine yourself in such a situation? To which world would it be hardest for you to adapt?

Fiction

★ Field, Rachel. *Calico Bush.* Dell Yearling, 1931. ISBN 0-440-40368-5

■■■■■■■■■■□□□□□

Least Sophisticated   **Most Sophisticated**

Although this novel is set at a slightly later time, the conflict between French and English is apparent. This is a Focus Book; see page 262.

★ Keehn, Sally M. *I Am Regina.* Philomel, 1990. ISBN 0-399-21797-5

■■■■■■■■■■■□□□□

See page 191.

★ Richter, Conrad. *The Light in the Forest.* Banta, 1990. ISBN 0-553-26878-3

■■■■■■■■■□□□□□□

Both this book and **I Am Regina** *(above) concern the return of Indian captives to their white families. In this book, the boy, called True Son by his adopted Lenni-*

Lenape Indian family and John by his natural mother and father, hates the white people who reclaim him. The value systems of the Native Americans and the white settlers are in conflict and the boy vows to remain an Indian no matter what his natural family does to him. The book recounts the savagery on both sides, but it is with the Indian that the author and reader sympathize.

◆ Gilman, Dorothy. ***Girl in Buckskin.*** Ballantine, 1956. ISBN 0-449-70380-0

This story takes place in 1703-1704 in the Northeast wilderness. It is a good, fast moving adventure story. Becky's brother, Ezeck, was captured by Canadian Indians when he was eight and released at fourteen. Their parents were killed at the time of his capture. Becky has been living as a bound servant. She decides to escape with Ezeck into the wilderness. She and her brother become friends with an Indian couple and are adopted by their tribe. This friendship is used to show changes in Becky's attitude toward Indians. During the war in 1704, Ezeck decides to return to his original captors in Canada and Becky decides to return to the whites, however, not as a servant.

◆ Speare, Elizabeth George. ***Calico Captive.*** Houghton, 1985. ISBN 0-395-07112-7

This story is based on a true incident in which Susannah and James Johnson, with their three children and Susannah's younger sister, Miriam Willard, were taken captive by the Indians and held for ransom in Montreal. The story focuses on the effect of Miriam's captivity. Her Puritan views and lifestyle contrast sharply with the life of the French settlers in Montreal, and her loyalties are shaken when she is forced to choose between marriage to a dashing young Frenchman and marriage to a sturdy and studious young English settler.

Edmonds, Walter. ***The Matchlock Gun.*** Dodd, 1941. ISBN 0-399-21911-0

This novel, set in New York, depicts Native Americans as savage and merciless and tells of the resourcefulness of a young boy defending his household during his father's absence.

Longfellow, Henry Wadsworth. ***Evangeline and Other Poems.*** Airmont, 1985. ISBN 0-8049-0094-9

Although Longfellow's poetry is not considered topnotch by many of today's critics, upper-elementary students enjoy it. The title poem, "Evangeline," is a long narrative romance between Evangeline and Gabriel who are separated when the Acadians are forced to leave Canada.

Nonfiction ★ Marrin, Albert. ***Struggle for a Continent: The French and Indian Wars 1690-1760.*** Atheneum, 1987. ISBN 0-689-31313-6

This book is an excellent source book even though it is lengthy and sometimes so thorough in its accounts of battles as to be tedious. We recommend it because of its beginning chapters that concentrate on the vastly different lifestyles and goals

*of the three major groups in conflict at the time: the Indians, British Colonists, and French Colonists. The descriptions of life inside the longhouses of the Iroquois are particularly useful. We recommend that teachers read it for greater understanding themselves and then that they read pertinent parts to or with students. The last chapter about the mandated return of Indian captives is particularly relevant to **I Am Regina** (see page 191).*

◆ Meltzer, Milton. ***The American Revolutionaries: A History in Their Own Words: 1750-1800.*** Crowell, 1987. ISBN 0-690-04643-X

■■■■■■■■□□□□□□□

See page 53.

Anderson, Joan. ***Pioneer Settlers of New France.*** Lodestar, 1990. ISBN 0-525-67291-5

■■■■■■■□□□□□□□□

Photographs of recreated Louisbourg, Nova Scotia, illustrate French-Canadian life during the final years of King George's war.

Cwiklik, Robert. ***King Philip and the War with the Colonists.*** Silver Burdett, 1989. ISBN 0-382-09573-1

■■■■■■■■■■□□□□□

King Philip was not a European ruler, but the leader of Indian tribes in New England during the seventeenth century. King Philip, the son of Massasoit the Wampanoag chief who befriended the Colonists, was sure that if the Indian tribes banded together, they could kill off or frighten away the Colonists who were usurping the land. King Philip's War was a bloody one and this biography examines his life and death.

Smith, Carter. ***Battles in a New Land: A Sourcebook on Colonial America.*** Millbrook, 1991. ISBN 1-56294-034-1

■■■■■■■■■■■□□□□

This fact-filled resource book uses illustrations, paintings, and drawings to show the French and Indian War and skirmishes among Colonists.

War and Conflict

The Revolutionary War
1775–1783

Activities

- In order to understand some of the feelings the American Colonists might have had in the time preceding the Revolution, ask another group of students (preferably a distant one that knows nothing about your situation) to make up rules by which your classroom must operate. For the first two days, make sure they consult with you about the effect of their laws and take your suggestions as, apparently, Britain did with the Colonists. For the next two days, have the other classroom act arbitrarily and without concern for the effect on your classroom, which is what the Colonists experienced just before the Revolution.

  To contrast this experience, ask the students who were in your classroom last year to make up rules by which your students must operate for the next few days.

  During both periods, ask your students to record their feelings and frustrations. After the experience, discuss the contrasting situations and compare them with the feelings of the real Colonists.

- Make a chart such as the one following to show the actions and reactions of the British government and Colonists during the period just prior to the war. Discuss what either side might have done at any point to alter the next event.

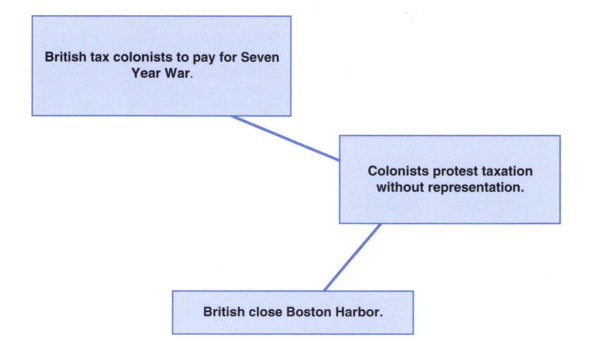

- Develop a token system of rewards for work or good behavior. Tell students that they can use the tokens to buy items during a classroom auction. When most students have a few tokens, begin taxing them to use the bathroom, drinking fountain, paper, and so on. Compare their feelings to those of Colonists.

- Find out what happened at the Boston Massacre. Tell it from the point of view of a British soldier, a Colonist, and an uninvolved third party.

- Re-enact the Boston Massacre or the Tea Party.

- Find out what important people of the times thought or did about the Boston Tea Party.

- Cover one of the events of the Revolution as a reporter who writes for people in the other colonies.

- Talk to people in your area who are upset by current taxation. What are they doing about it? What can they do?

- What taxes do you pay? List all the things that you buy or that someone buys for you in the next week. Record and total the taxes. Who gets the tax money?

- Hold a peace negotiation conference between the Patriots and the British parliament with the assistance of mediators. First, divide the group into three teams. One team will research the Revolution, looking for the viewpoints of parliament and Loyalists. Another team will look for the viewpoints of the Patriots. A third section will research basic mediation approaches and techniques. (See pages 55–56 for books offering mediation techniques.) After the initial research, discuss different viewpoints with assistance from the mediators. Then continue investigating and begin thinking about solutions. Come together again for final problem solving. Evaluate the process. What might have made it more effective?

- Contrast the casualties in the Revolution to those in the Civil War. What are some possible explanations for the differences? Can you find any information about this?

- Create a three-dimensional map showing Boston as it was during the siege of Boston. Show British ships in the harbor and the position of American troops in Cambridge. Trace Henry Knox's trip to Boston from Fort Ticonderoga to break the siege. Compare the ease with which the British isolated Boston to the problems of more current sieges such as those of Iraq or Syria.

- After reading or hearing some selections from Thomas Paine's "Common Sense," write your own "Common Sense" about something that concerns you. Decide whether you will write about just one side in order to make a point or whether you will explore diverse aspects of the issue. How does this reflect your reason for writing?

- Who determines the rules of your classroom? Would it be better if the students made the rules? What about a balance between matters the teacher resolves and those students resolve? Did you consider the possibility of deciding together? Draw up one or more proposals about changes you would like to see.

- Share descriptions of different types of leaders you discovered in your reading and research. How did others view these people's leadership qualities? How do you view them? Compile an anthology of leadership portraits in which you address leadership qualities directly.

- Pretend that you are one of the Colonists. Write a letter explaining your point of view to imaginary relatives who are still in England. Can you do this while also being sensitive to the fact that your relatives might view things differently? What do you think they will find most difficult to understand?

- Write a diary as if you were living at the time of the Revolutionary War. Begin your diary before the war and show how events shape your feelings and opinions.

- Create a time line across one wall of your classroom. As you research, post significant events and facts to create a picture of the many aspects of the conflict. ***The Revolutionary War: A Sourcebook on Colonial America*** (page 74) contains a good time line of events of the war itself and ***The Explorers and Settlers*** (see page 171) from the same series has a good time line of the period just before the war.

- Compare the way the Revolution was viewed by the Patriots, the Loyalists, the middle-of-the-road Colonists, the French, the British, the Germans, the slaves, the poor people, the various Indian tribes, the Canadians, and so on.

- Make a map of Eastern North America indicating the cultural groups present at the time. Code areas of conflict. Make a similar map for a later period.

- Chart the factors that might have affected the viewpoint of the cultural groups present at the time. In addition to their ethnicity, consider the length of time they had been in the country, their reasons for being in America, and their economic classes.

- Put Benedict Arnold on trial for treason. Have a judge, jury, witnesses, and lawyers for both sides, and, of course, someone to play the role of Arnold.

- Rewrite one of the books or stories that you have read that takes the Patriots' side. This time take the side of the Loyalists. Remember that many believed the king was appointed by God. Many of the British and Loyalists thought it was hypocritical for Patriots to ally themselves with France because it was also a monarchy and perhaps a worse one. Some believe, in hindsight, that the upper classes and intellectual elite liked the idea of becoming independent because they thought they would be more powerful in the new government and that the Revolution would sidetrack the political unrest that was occurring among the poor and the slaves.

Picture Books

◆ Gauch, Patricia Lee. ***This Time, Tempe Wick?*** Putnam, 1974. ISBN 0-698-20300-3

Based on legend, this is the story of a young girl who hid her horse from the Continental army by hiding it in her bedroom for three days.

◆ Turner, Ann. ***Katie's Trunk.*** Illustrated by Ron Himler. Macmillan, 1992. ISBN 0-02-789512-2

There aren't many picture books about the Revolution, but this is an especially good one. Katie's Tory family lives in fear of harassment by the rebels. They have been subjected to taunts and isolation already. When a group of rebels comes to Katie's home, intent on robbing and trashing, Katie hides in a trunk. One rebel neighbor, finding her in the trunk, distracts his rebel friends and leaves her undisturbed and unhurt. The point, of course, is that there was real human kindness on both sides.

Gauch, Patricia Lee. ***Aaron and the Green Mountain Boys.*** Illustrated by Margot Tomes. Shoe Tree Press, 1972. ISBN 1-55870-220-2

After taking over Fort Ticonderoga in 1777, British soldiers marched on Bennington, Vermont, intent on seizing supplies stored there. The Green Mountain boys, stretched to the limit of capacity, were summoned quickly. While they were there, they had to be fed and housed. This is the story of one boy and what he might or might not have done to help the situation.

Longfellow, Henry Wadsworth. **Paul Revere's Ride.** Illustrated by Ted Rand. Dutton, 1990. ISBN 0-525-44610-9

Longfellow might have taken some liberties with fact in his epic poem about the ride, but it makes a fine picture book with Ted Rand's illustrations of moonlit landscapes and lamplit street scenes that reflect the atmosphere of the time.

Fiction

★ Fritz, Jean. **Early Thunder.** Putnam, 1967. ISBN 0-698-20036-5

■■■■■■■■■■□□□□□

Least Sophisticated   Most Sophisticated

This is a Focus Book; see page 264.

★ O'Dell, Scott. **Sarah Bishop.** Houghton, 1980. ISBN 0-395-29185-2

■■■■■■■■■■■■■■□

Sarah has good reason to hate war. Her father, a Loyalist, died after being tarred and feathered by the rebels. Her brother died on a British prison ship. Sarah is arrested as part of the harassment and escapes to the Connecticut wilderness where her struggle is with the elements rather than with the war. This is a Focus Book; see page 266.

◆ Avi. **The Fighting Ground.** Lippincott, 1984. ISBN 0-397-32074-4

■■■■■■■■■■■□□□□

This is an account of two days of a boy's life during the American Revolution. After he is captured in battle by three Hessian soldiers, Jonathan realizes that fighting is a complex activity and that informed choices are extremely important. In a farmhouse where a little boy is the only survivor of his family, Jonathan finds it impossible to kill the sleeping Hessians. He escapes with the little boy and finds the remnants of his troop. Realizing that they must have killed the boy's parents, Jonathan smashes his rifle and returns to the farm, less certain about the rights and wrongs of war.

◆ Collier, James Lincoln and Collier, Christopher. **My Brother Sam Is Dead.** Four Winds, 1974. ISBN 0-02-722980-7

■■■■■■■■■■■■■■□

Sam, the only member of his family who is not a Tory, joins the Rebel army. When he is falsely accused of stealing cattle, his family's sympathies work against him, and he is tried and executed as an example of General Putnam's discipline. His death is a matter of political expediency, not a matter of right or wrong. This is a more cynical look at the war than one finds in most children's literature.

◆ Forbes, Esther. **Johnny Tremain.** Houghton, 1943. ISBN 0-395-06766-9

■■■■■■■■■■■■■■□

Johnny Tremain is a silversmith's apprentice in Boston. Another apprentice, jealous of Johnny's skill, causes him to be terribly burned by molten silver. Because of his shriveled hand, Johnny must find other work. As a rider for the Boston Observer, Johnny becomes interested in the Revolution and participates in the Boston Tea Party and other revolutionary acts. He also learns to accept himself, wounds and all. The book is an idealistic look at the Revolution.

◆ Reit, Seymour. ***Guns for General Washington: A Story of the American Revolution.*** Harcourt, 1990. ISBN 0-15-200466-1

■■■■■■■■■■■□□□□

This is a fictionalized account of Henry Knox's trip from Fort Ticonderoga to Boston to break the siege of Boston. The story sticks closely to the facts with some dialogue added. We see the hazardous journey through the eyes of Will Knox, Henry's younger brother. The action goes back and forth between Knox and his men on the trail and the armies and civilians in Boston under siege. Other characters in the story include George Washington, Paul Revere, and General Howe.

◆ Woodruff, Elvira. ***George Washington's Socks.*** Scholastic, 1992. ISBN 0-590-44035-7

■■■■■■■■■□□□□□□

See page 38.

Edwards, Sally. ***George Midgett's War.*** Macmillan, 1985. ISBN 0-684-18315-3

■■■■■■■■■■■□□□□

The people of Ocracoke Island, off the coast of North Carolina, want no part of the war. Then British Raiders kill the deaf-mute woman who tends their pigs and carry off the pigs. The Islanders' revenge entails taking precious salt to the American Army at Valley Forge. The plot focuses on the fact that some choices in war are based on personal feelings rather than on political convictions.

Hoobler, Dorothy and Hoobler, Thomas. ***The Sign Painter's Secret: The Story of a Revolutionary Girl.*** Illustrated by Donna Ayers. Silver Burdett, 1991. ISBN 0-382-24143-6

■■■■■□□□□□□□□□□

This short and easy-to-read story is about a young girl who spies for the Rebels during the Revolutionary War. Although the absolute certainty of every character in the plot is unrealistic, there is a believable and informative sense of family life in occupied Philadelphia in 1777.

Jensen, Dorothea. ***The Riddle of Penncroft Farm.*** Harcourt, 1989. ISBN 0-15-200574-9

■■■■■□□□□□□□□□□

After Lars moves from his home in present-day Minnesota to Pennsylvania, he is contacted by the ghost of one of his ancestors who gives him the inside story on the Revolution, especially the days at Valley Forge.

McKean, Thomas. ***The Secret of the Seven Willows.*** Simon, 1991. ISBN 0-671-72997-7

■■■■■■■□□□□□□□□

See page 38.

Monjo, F. N. ***Poor Richard in France.*** Dell, 1973. ISBN 0-440-46110-3

■■■■■□□□□□□□□□□

This story covers the years from 1776 to 1778. It was supposedly written by Benjamin Franklin's grandson as he accompanied his grandfather in France while Franklin attempted to convince France to sign a treaty with the Colonists. This is a very friendly approach to an understanding of diplomacy and war.

Seabrooke, Brenda. ***The Chester Town Tea Party.*** Illustrated by Nancy Coates Smith. Tidewater, 1990. ISBN 0-87033-422-0

■■■■■□□□□□□□□□□

This is a fictionalized account of an event in 1774 Maryland that supported the Boston Tea Party. Many details of life in Colonial America are embedded in the story.

Wibberly, Leonard. ***John Treegate's Musket.*** Farrar, 1959. ISBN 0-374-43788-2

■■■■■■■■■■■■■■□

John Treegate is a Loyalist who fought for the king at the Battle of Quebec. Changing sides is easier for his son, Peter, who quickly joins the Revolutionary forces. John defects just in time for the Battle of Bunker Hill.

Nonfiction

★ Fritz, Jean. ***And Then What Happened, Paul Revere?*** Coward, 1973. ISBN 00-698-20274-0

■■■■□□□□□□□□□□□

This is a short history of Paul Revere that concentrates on his eventful ride. It makes a good introduction to this period because, like all of Fritz's short biographies, it is historically correct even as she manages to breathe life into the heroes of our past. This book gives us a sense of what Boston must have been like during the Revolution.

★ ———. ***Can't You Make Them Behave, King George?*** Putnam, 1982. ISBN 0-698-20315-1

■■■■■□□□□□□□□□□

Here is the Revolution from the point of view of the reigning British monarch, a man of incredible vanity and misjudgment. The humor is considerable but is based on fact.

◆ ***Cobblestone Magazine***

The following issues were devoted to topics of the Revolution:
Boston Massacre (March 1980)
American Revolution Tales (September 1983)
Alexander Hamilton (March 1987)
British Loyalists (August 1987
Thomas Jefferson (September 1989)
Back copies are available from Cobblestone Publishing
30 Grove Street, Peterborough, NH 03458.

◆ Fritz, Jean. ***Traitor: The Case of Benedict Arnold.*** Putnam, 1981. ISBN 0-399-20834-8

■■■■■■■■■■□□□□□

Here is his flamboyant life from his boyhood to his death, not in battle as he had hoped but in bed in London. We see his acts of bravery as well as those of treachery.

◆ ———. ***Where Was Patrick Henry on the 29th of May?*** Coward, 1982. ISBN 0-698-20307-0

■■■■■□□□□□□□□□□

The great orator is fleshed out and humanized with Fritz's sure touch and we also get a glimpse of eighteenth-century America.

◆ ————. ***Why Don't You Get a Horse, Sam Adams?*** Putnam, 1974. ISBN 0-698-20292-9

■■■■■☐☐☐☐☐☐☐☐☐

In her brief but humanizing biography, Fritz gives us a picture of a funny and believable man who was capable of stirring the Colonists to action.

◆ ————. ***Will You Sign Here, John Hancock?*** Coward, 1982 ISBN 0-698-20308-9

■■■■■☐☐☐☐☐☐☐☐☐

Fritz gives us a close look at the man whose signature dominates the Declaration of Independence. With his wealth, Hancock purchased friendships his selfishness sometimes drove away, but his wealth also helped finance the Revolution.

◆ Johnson, Neil. ***The Battle of Lexington and Concord.*** Four Winds, 1992 ISBN 0-02-747841-6

■■■■☐☐☐☐☐☐☐☐☐☐

Color photographs of a recent re-enactment illustrate this book that gives some background and a step-by-step account of the first battle of the Revolution.

◆ Marrin, Albert. ***The War for Independence.*** Atheneum, 1988. ISBN 0-689-31390-X

■■■■■■■■■☐☐☐☐☐

This is an excellent reference source about the Revolutionary War. The beginning, detailing the causes of the conflict, is the strongest section. The rest details the stories of the battles themselves. This might be a good book for the teacher or the most able and/or interested readers to read and then excerpt for others.

◆ Meltzer, Milton. ***The American Revolutionaries: A History in Their Own Words: 1750-1800.*** Crowell, 1987. ISBN 0-690-04643-X

■■■■■■■■☐☐☐☐☐☐

See page 53.

Carter, Alden R. ***The American Revolution: At the Forge of Liberty.*** Watts, 1988. ISBN 0-531-10569-5

■■■■■■■■■■☐☐☐☐☐

The book begins with the Continental Army's arrival at Philadelphia in 1777 and ends when the Revolution does in 1783.

————. ***The American Revolution: Birth of the Republic.*** Watts, 1988. ISBN 0-531-10572-5

■■■■■■■■■■☐☐☐☐☐

Here are the last days of the Revolution and the forging of a new government.

————. ***The American Revolution: Colonies in Revolt.*** Watts, 1988. ISBN 0- 531-10576-8

■■■■■■■■■■☐☐☐☐☐

Beginning with the death of an eleven-year-old boy in the streets of Boston and leading up to the full-fledged war, this book uses maps, paintings and lithographs, and clear text to tell the story.

———. *The American Revolution: Darkest Hours.* Watts, 1988. ISBN 0-531-10578-4

■■■■■■■■■■□□□□□

This book begins with the call to arms at Concord and ends with the destruction of Burgoyne's army at Saratoga.

Quackenbush, Robert. *Pass the Quill, I'll Write a Draft: A Story of Thomas Jefferson.* Pippin, 1989. ISBN 0-945912-07-2

■■■■■□□□□□□□□□□

This is a brief book with a light touch that covers the life of the great man from 1743 to 1826.

Smith, Carter. *The Revolutionary War: A Sourcebook on Colonial America.* Millbrook, 1991. ISBN 0-56294-039-2

■■■■■■■■□□□□□□□

This book uses prints, maps, and some drawings for illustration. It contains a time line of the events in the Colonies juxtaposed with other major events in the world.

Stein, R. Conrad. *The Story of the Boston Tea Party.* Childrens, 1984. ISBN 0-516 04666-7

■■■■■□□□□□□□□□□

The book starts with the Boston Massacre and other causes of the conflict between the British and Americans and leads up to the actions of the Sons of Liberty. It points out that relations between the two groups had been equitable and that, at the beginning of the Revolution, only thirty percent of the populace wanted independence from Britain. The book also explains Sam Adams's role as orator, master of propaganda, and spearhead of the war movement.

Stevens, Bryna. *Deborah Sampson Goes to War.* Carolrhoda, 1984. ISBN 0-87614-254-4

■■■■■□□□□□□□□□□

Set in New England 1781-1783, this is an easy-to-read biography of Deborah Sampson who posed as a man to fight in the American Revolution. After the war, Deborah Sampson received an honorable discharge and a military pension because of her wounds. She later became the first woman lecturer in the United States.

Swanson, June. *David Bushnell and His Turtle: The Story of America's First Submarine.* Atheneum, 1991. ISBN 0-689-31628-3

■■■■■□□□□□□□□□□

See page 122.

Nonprint

Videos

The Other Boston Tea Party. New England Foundation for the Humanities, 1989.

Samuel Adams and Harrison Gray Otis meet for tea and discuss the issues and events of the time with humor and concern.

War and Conflict

The War of 1812
1812-1815

Activities

- Find out about Dolley Madison and what she did at the White House when the British were coming.
- Find, read, and sing the second, third, and fourth verses of the "Star Spangled Banner."
- Compare Britain's opinion of the United States before and after the War of 1812.
- Find out when relations between the two countries began to improve.
- Have there been times since 1812 when America and England have been on different sides in a dispute or war?

Picture Books

◆ Spier, Peter. ***The Star Spangled Banner.*** Doubleday, 1973. ISBN 0-385-23401-5

Using words from the anthem with intricate illustrations showing the battle and events that led up to the composing of the words, Spier produces a fine sense of the time.

Nonfiction

Greeson, Janet. ***An American Army of Two.*** Carolrhoda, 1992. ISBN 0-87614-547-0

■■■■■■□□□□□□□□□

Least Sophisticated   **Most Sophisticated**

This simple account tells of the time the British Army was in the harbor at Scituate, Massachusetts, taking food and goods from the citizens and only the men of the Home Guard were anywhere near the area to defend it. However, they came to the rescue the first time the townsfolk needed them. When the British heard their fife and drum playing "Yankee Doodle," they fled back to their ships. The next time, however, the Home Guard was too far away to help and two sisters hiding in the bushes frightened the British away by playing first softly and then more loudly on a fife and drum.

Mitchell, Barbara. ***Cornstalks and Cannonballs.*** Carolrhoda, 1980. ISBN 0-87614-472-5

■■■■■■■■■■■□□□□

During the War of 1812, British Navy ships threatened the town of Lewes, Delaware. The men aboard the ships were starving and so their captain ordered the townspeople to supply them with meat. The people refused and eventually the navy was ordered to shell the town. The people responded in kind, using old cannons from the Revolution and picking up spent cannonballs from the beach to fire at the ships. At last they blackened farm tools and cornstalks to look like weapons and the ships left the harbor.

War and Conflict

The Mexican War
1845-1848

Activities

- Make a map showing the territory of the United States before and after the Mexican War.

- Create a series of maps on outlines of what are now the United States and Mexico. Show the national boundaries at several periods during the expansion of the United States. By mapping the years 1802, 1803, and 1850, you will have a vivid picture of the significance of the Mexican War.

- Find out what each of the following leaders did in or about the Mexican War: James Polk, Abraham Lincoln, Henry David Thoreau, Zachary Taylor, Ralph Waldo Emerson, William Lloyd Garrison, and Frederick Douglass.

- Find out what part racism played in the war with Mexico. Congressman Giles of Maryland in the Congressional Globe of February 11, 1847, is quoted as saying "I take it for granted, that we shall gain territory, and must gain territory, before we shut the gates of the temple of Janus. We must march from ocean to ocean. We must march from Texas straight to the Pacific Ocean, and be bounded only by its roaring wave. It is the destiny of the white race, it is the destiny of the Anglo-Saxon race."

- Find out what role slavery played in the war with Mexico. This statement is from an editorial in a Manchester, New Hampshire, newspaper: "We have heretofore held our peace in regard to the annexation of Texas, for the purpose of seeing whether our Nation would attempt so base an action. We call it base, because it would be giving men who live upon the blood of others, an opportunity of dipping their hand still deeper in the sin of slavery. Have we not slaves enough now?"

- Find newspaper articles from this period. What role did newspapers play in the war? Which newspapers supported it and which opposed it?

- What was the population of Mexico during this time? What kind of government did it have? Who ran the country? There were a million Creoles (whites of Spanish blood), two million Mestizos (Indians mixed with Spanish), and three million Indians. The Creoles controlled Mexico. Which group would have most of the power and money at the time? Which group would have been the soldiers? Who would have been officers?

- What are some of the reasons that people enlisted in the US army during the Mexican War? Did they get what they wanted?

- Why did the United States want California so badly?

- Make a chart showing the major battles of the Mexican War and their outcomes.

Name of Battle	Mexican Casualties	American Casualties	Outcome
Vera Cruz *Mexico City* *Matamoros* *Monterey*			

Nonfiction

◆ ***Cobblestone Magazine***

The following issues of the magazine were devoted to this subject.

The Alamo (March 1982)
Mexico and the United States (March 1986)
Hispanic Americans (April 1989)
Back issues of the magazine can be obtained from Cobblestone Publishing 30 Grove St., Peterborough, NH 03458.

◆ Stern, Philip Van Doren. ***Henry David Thoreau: Writer and Rebel.*** Crowell, 1972. ISBN 0-690-37715-0

Least Sophisticated   Most Sophisticated

Thoreau considered the Mexican War unjustified. He was sent to jail because he refused to pay taxes to support it. See page 58.

◆ Pinchot, Jane. ***The Mexicans in America.*** Lerner, 1989. ISBN 0-8225-1022-4

Although this book covers much more than this period, it has information about the war and the causes and effects.

McKissack, Patricia and McKissack, Fredrick. ***Frederick Douglass: The Black Lion.*** Childrens, 1987. ISBN 0-516-03221-6

Douglass used his eloquence to oppose the war.

Richards, Norman. ***The Story of the Alamo.*** Childrens, 1970. ISBN 0-516-04601-2

Although the Battle of the Alamo took place in 1836, the reasons for the battle and the results had a bearing on the Mexican War that followed. The author traces the Alamo from its construction through the famous battle to its recapture by Sam Houston. ***The Alamo*** *by Herma Silverstein (Dillon, 1992. ISBN 0-87518-502-9) is similar to this one.*

Rickerby, Laura Ann. ***Ulysses S. Grant and the Strategy of Victory.*** Silver Burdett, 1990. ISBN 0-382-09944-3

One chapter of this book is devoted to the causes and battles of the Mexican War, especially as Grant experienced them.

War and Conflict

The Civil War
1861-1865

Activities

- Make a map showing the states and territories of the United States in 1861. Color the slave states and free states in different colors. Mark the sites of major battles.

- Find out how far the rifles used at that time could fire. Stand the class in two lines that far apart. How clearly can you see each other? Can you tell hair color? Height? Compare that to the view the American soldiers had of the Iraqis during the Gulf War.

- Look at current state flags. Which still carry symbols used on the Confederate or Union flags?

- What roles did drummer boys have during the Civil War? What do they do now?

- Find out which cities and other pieces of land changed hands from Union to Confederate and vice versa.

- Find the name and regiment of one Civil War soldier. Write to the National Archives and Records Service in Washington, DC, to request application NATF Form 26. Fill out the form and ask for pensions, bounty land warrant applications, and military service records. Research the battles your soldier or sailor was in.

- Bring in any Civil War memorabilia that families in your area may have.

- The Civil War is sometimes called the War Between the States. What's the difference? Why do some people prefer one name over the other?

- What's wrong with states seceding from the Union? Have any tried to secede since the Civil War? What might have been the outcome if they had been allowed to secede?

- Read some civilian accounts of battles. Would you have stayed to watch a battle?

- Role-play a meeting between Generals Grant and Lee in the 1870s. What would they have said to each other? Each respected the other as a general. Would they have been able to be friends?

- Find out what happened to the time's most important people after the war: Jefferson Davis, Robert E. Lee, Ulysses S. Grant, and John Wilkes Booth.

- Compare the assassination of Lincoln to the assassination of John F. Kennedy.

- Make a list of Lincoln's dilemmas during the Civil War. Compare them to Franklin Roosevelt's dilemmas during World War II and George Washington's during the Revolution.

- Is it true that the American Revolution was a successful revolution, but the Civil War was not? Why?

- Are we the only country to have had a civil war? What other countries have had similar conflicts? What were the outcomes?

Picture Books ★ Lyon, George Ella. ***Cecil's Story.*** Illustrated by Peter Catalanotto. Orchard, 1991. ISBN 0-531-08512-0

This thoughtful and sad picture book shows us a young boy who waits for his mother to find his wounded father. The book jacket, an integral part of the book, shows his prewar family: his father wielding an ax, his mother churning butter, and Cecil playing with wooden soldiers, one of which is missing an arm. It's Civil War time and Cecil works and tries to be hopeful, crying only at night. War, as we well know, is hard, especially for those who wait, and wait he must. At last his parents return; his father is minus one arm but able to pick him up with his other.

◆ Turner, Ann. ***Nettie's Trip South.*** Illustrated by Ronald Himler. Macmillan, 1987. ISBN 0-02-789240-9

We go with young Nettie as she travels from Albany, New York, to Richmond, Virginia, in the years just prior to the Civil War. The book is based on a real diary and provides us with a Northern white girl's view of the horrors of slavery, including the degradation of a slave auction. There is reference to the constitutional opinion that slaves were three-fifths of a person, that they were given no last name, and that they were not allowed to learn to read. It's a strong book.

Ackerman, Karen. ***The Tin Heart.*** Atheneum, 1990. ISBN 0-689-31461-2

Two little girls, who represent the conflict between North and South, live on each side of the Ohio River. Mahaley Hutchison rides her father's ferry frequently because it gives her a chance to visit her friend Flora Scotchman on the other side. When the war breaks out, the visits cannot continue and each girl wears half of a tin heart to symbolize that the friendship survives.

Fiction ★ Reeder, Carolyn. ***Shades of Gray.*** Macmillan, 1989. ISBN 0-02-775810-9

Least Sophisticated   Most Sophisticated

Will lost his whole family during the Civil War. Now he lives with a man he believes to have betrayed the cause during the war. There are many allusions to the war, its causes, and its terrible aftermath. See **Long Ago and Far Away** *(DLM, 1991. ISBN 1-55924-556-5) for ideas about using this book.*

★ Steele, William O. ***The Perilous Road.*** Scholastic, 1990. ISBN 0-590-45128-6

This is a Focus Book; see page 275.

◆ Beatty, Patricia. ***Jayhawker.*** Morrow, 1991. ISBN 0-688-09850-9

Before and during the Civil War, there were skirmishes and battles in Missouri and Kansas as Jayhawkers (Abolitionists) raided Missouri, a slave state, to free slaves and to ruin slave owners. The Jayhawkers' opponents, the Bushwhackers, were equally fervent and did a great deal of damage on their raids in Kansas. In this novel, we observe some of the action and explore some of the emotions as Lij, a young boy takes over his father's Jayhawker role. Although most of the Jayhawkers are depicted as kind and most of the Bushwhackers as evil, the author makes an attempt at evenhandedness.

◆ ———. ***Charley Skedaddle.*** Morrow, 1987. ISBN 0-688-06687-9

■■■■■■■■■□□□□□□

The last years of the war are years of growing up for Charley Quinn, a twelve-year-old tough from the streets of New York City. Unhappy at home, Charley is thrilled at the glory of war and for the opportunity to avenge his brother's death at Gettysburg. He is smuggled into the army where he becomes a drummer for the 140th New York division and participates in the first skirmish of the Wilderness battles. Horrified by the battle and his own part in it, Charley "skedaddles" and develops into an integral part of a Virginia mountain woman's household.

◆ Fritz, Jean. ***Brady.*** Puffin, 1987. ISBN 0-14-032258-2

■■■■■■■■■□□□□□□

Set in 1836 in Pennsylvania, this novel shows Jean Fritz's ability to see all sides of a controversy. Here the Underground Railroad is the focus. Brady is a teenager whose father is an Abolitionist preacher. His mother grew up in the South and is not convinced that slavery is wrong. Brady must make decisions about his beliefs and his actions. He finds the strength to keep a secret when he comes to understand the effects his actions have on something larger than himself.

◆ Gauch, Patricia Lee. ***Thunder at Gettysburg.*** Putnam, 1990. 0-399-22201-4

■■■■■□□□□□□□□□□

This is an account of the battle as seen by Tillie, a young girl, first from her own attic and then from two other houses near the battlefield. In the beginning the battle is exciting and then, as torn and wounded soldiers are brought in, the excitement is replaced by horror. The book is short and very easy to read.

◆ Keith, Harold. ***Rifles for Watie.*** HarperCollins, 1987. ISBN 0-06-447030-X

■■■■■■■■■■■□□□□

This Newbery Award winner has been around a long time, but it may be unique in its ability to show the war through the eyes of a soldier who saw the war from both sides. Jefferson Davis Bussey is a Union soldier and spy in the Western campaign who accidently becomes a member of Stand Watie's Cherokee Rebels.

◆ Perez, N. A. ***The Slopes of War.*** Houghton, 1990. ISBN 0-395-54979-5

■■■■■■■■■■■□□□□

Buck Summerhill loses his leg in the fight for Little Round Top at Gettysburg, his home town. His sister Bekah is caring for a wounded Union soldier upstairs while injured Rebels are being cared for on the ground floor of their home. There is considerable information about real officers and battles in this fictional work.

Hoobler, Dorothy and Hoobler, Thomas. ***Next Stop, Freedom: The Story of a Slave Girl.*** Silver Burdett, 1991. ISBN 0-382-24145-2

■■■■■□□□□□□□□□□

This is a short, simple novel of only fifty-four pages. The characters are rather flat, but the story line is uncomplicated and it does furnish insight into the horrors of slavery and the hope that Harriet Tubman and the underground railroad offered the slaves.

Wisler, G. Clifton. ***Red Cap.*** Lodestar, 1990. ISBN 0-525-67337-7

■■■■■■■■■■■□□□□

This is a fictionalized account of the battle years as seen by Ransom J. Powell, a drummer boy in the Union Army.

Nonfiction

★ Lester, Julius. ***To Be a Slave.*** Dial, 1968. ISBN 0-8037-8955-6

■■■■■■■■■■□□□□□

Using writings and interviews of the slaves as primary sources, the author chronicles their capture, transport, and enslavement in the South during and after the Civil War. The book presents a terrible and intimate portrait of slavery. Lester excerpted short passages and explores the experiences of those who lived through them. It's a fascinating book and a source of rare primary material about slavery. Because it includes names, the book is a rich source for role-playing activities and an example of the differences between primary and secondary sources.

★ Murphy, Jim. ***The Long Road to Gettysburg.*** Clarion, 1992. ISBN 0-395-55965-0

■■■■■■■□□□□□□□□

With numerous photographs, the author tells the story of the soldiers and civilians who witnessed the great battle. The author begins with Lincoln ready to deliver the Gettysburg Address and flashes back to the convergence of the two armies in the peaceful Pennsylvania countryside. Murphy is particularly successful in focusing on individuals, using their letters and testimony to take the war to a personal level.

★ Myers, Walter Dean. ***Now Is Your Time: The African-American Struggle for Freedom.*** HarperCollins, 1992. ISBN 0-06-024371-6

■■■■■■■■■■■□□□□

Although the book covers much more than the period of the Civil War, there is a large section devoted to that time.

◆ Chang, Ina. ***A Separate Battle: Women and the Civil War.*** Lodestar, 1991. ISBN 0-525-67365-2

■■■■■■■■■■■■■■□

This is a thorough study of women's experiences during the war. The experiences are vivid because of the photographs and period artwork. Here are photos of some of the women who impersonated men so they could fight and photos of female spies and the Soldiers' Aid Society members. The book includes famous women and ordinary women. Although the book's content is fairly sophisticated, the material is accessible to less able readers because of abundant photographs and explanatory captions.

◆ ***Cobblestone Magazine***
The following issues of the magazine were devoted to the Civil War:
Civil War Highlights (April 1981)
Great Debates (January 1987)
The Civil War Reconstruction (May 1987)
The Battle of Gettysburg (July 1988)
Back issues of the magazine can be obtained from Cobblestone Publishing 30 Grove St., Peterborough, NH 03458.

◆   Fisher, Leonard Everett. ***Tracks Across America: The Story of the American Railroad 1825-1900.*** Holiday, 1992. ISBN 0-8234-0945-7

See page 126.   ■■■■■■■□□□□□□□

◆   Fritz, Jean. ***Stonewall.*** Putnam, 1979. ISBN 0-399-20698-1

■■■■■■■■■□□□□□

Fritz provides a well-rounded picture of the legendary Stonewall Jackson, the Confederate general, showing us his obsession with rules and his neurotic behavior. Fritz also shows us why the strange man was so adored by his troops that he became the epitome of Southern gallantry. The narration deals with the battles of Chancellorville, including the Battle of Manassas and many other skirmishes.

◆   Kent, Zachary. ***The Story of the Battle of Shiloh.*** Childrens Press, 1991. ISBN 0-516-0-4754-X   ■■■■■■■□□□□□□□

This book deals with General Grant and his decisions during one of the bloodiest Civil War battles. Illustrated by photographs and period artwork, this is a very thorough account of the Battle of Shiloh in which 13,000 Union soldiers and 11,000 Confederate soldiers died. The battle established Grant's willingness to take countless casualties to win battles.

◆   McMullan, Kate. ***The Story of Harriet Tubman, Conductor of the Underground Railroad.*** Dell, 1991. ISBN 0-440-40400-2

■■■■■■■□□□□□□□

This moving, well-written biography begins with Harriet's owner hiring her out to another white family, further breaking up an already shattered family. The book describes Harriet's escape, her rescue of her family, and her spy work for the Union Army. She managed a network of spies for the Union and was part of the invasion of Combahee with Colonel Montgomery. After the war, she returned to Auburn, New York. By the end of her life, Harriet had accumulated property that she wanted to leave to needy Black people. Unfortunately, her last wishes were not carried out.

◆   Ray, Delia. ***A Nation Torn: The Story of How the Civil War Began.*** Dutton, 1990. ISBN 0-525-67308-3

■■■■■■■■■■■■□□

The book is a thoughtful one that begins with the contrast between the industrial North and the rural South and continues to the firing on Fort Sumter. The text is clear and well illustrated with photographs and documents, giving a well-rounded account of the causes of the Civil War.

◆   Reit, Seymour. ***Behind Rebel Lines: The Incredible Story of Emma Edmonds.*** Harcourt, 1988. ISBN 0-15-200416-5

■■■■■■■□□□□□□□

Set in 1861 through 1865 on the war front, this is the story of Emma Edmonds who posed as a man to join the army. This short book is full of her escapades as a spy in many disguises. Her favorite disguise was as Cuff, a Southern slave. It is estimated that over four hundred women posed as men in order to fight in the Civil War. The book includes an epilogue about Edmonds receiving a veteran's

*pension through a special act of congress. This book stands on its own as good
reading at the same time that it involves us in a fascinating aspect of the past.*

Ashabranner, Brent. ***A Memorial for Mr. Lincoln.*** Putnam, 1992.
ISBN 0-399-22273-1   ■■■■■□□□□□□□□□□
See page 45.

Collins, James L. ***John Brown and the Fight Against Slavery.*** Millbrook, 1991.
ISBN 1-56294-043-0   ■■■■■■□□□□□□□□□

*Photographs and a straightforward text present the life of this fierce Abolitionist.
The book starts with Brown's last stand at Harper's Ferry and flashes back to his
beginnings in Torrington, Connecticut. It concentrates on his hatred of slavery
and his conviction that God appointed him to abolish it. There are also brief
histories of slavery, the Abolitionist Movement, the Missouri Compromise, and
Harriet Tubman.*

Dubowski, Cathy Ernst. ***Clara Barton: Healing the Wounds.*** Silver Burdett,
1991. ISBN 0-382-09940-0
■■■■■■■■■■□□□□□

*Part of the History of the Civil War series, this book relates the story of the famous
teacher, nurse, and spokesperson who founded the American Red Cross. It
includes time tables of the war and of Clara Barton's life.*

Durwood, Thomas. ***John C. Calhoun and the Roots of War.*** Silver Burdett,
1991. ISBN 0-382-099936-2
■■■■■■■■■■□□□□□

*This book is also part of the History of the Civil War series. It concerns the South
Carolinian who served in many offices of government and articulated the
southern viewpoint. The book covers Calhoun's personal life and his political
skirmishes.*

Johnson, Neil. ***The Battle of Gettysburg.*** Four Winds, 1989. ISBN 0-02-747831-9
■■■■■■■■■■□□□□□

*Using photographs of the reenactment of the battle, this book presents a candid
account of the battle and graphically shows the effects on people and animals.*

Murphy, Jim. ***The Boys' War: Confederate and Union Soldiers Talk about
the Civil War.*** Clarion, 1990. ISBN 0-89919-893-7
■■■■■■■■■■■□□□□

*Actual letters and diaries detail the experiences of boys under sixteen who fought
in the Civil War. The misspellings and poor grammar show the limited education
of most of the boys.*

Ray, Delia. ***Behind the Blue and Gray: The Soldier's Life in the Civil War.***
Lodestar, 1991. ISBN 0-525-67333-4
■■■■■■■■□□□□□□□

*Using the many documents still in existence, the author focuses on the details of
life in both armies.*

Reef, Catherine. ***Gettysburg.*** Dillon, 1992. ISBN 0-87518-503-7

■■■■■□□□□□□□□

Color and black-and-white photographs are used to show the battle and its aftermath and the military park that now serves as the battle's monument.

Rickerby, Laura Ann. ***Ulysses S. Grant and the Strategy of Victory.*** Silver Burdett, 1990. ISBN 0-382-09944-3

■■■■■■■■■■□□□□

Although this book touches on Grant's life before and after two wars, most of it concerns his career, from his service in the Mexican War through his presidency. The time lines are useful and the text is clear, even though some of the maps are not. The campaigns of the Civil War are well done. The book is a valuable reference source.

Shorto, Russell. ***Abraham Lincoln and the End of Slavery.*** Millbrook, 1991. ISBN 01878841-12-2

■■■■■■□□□□□□□

Although Lincoln's life and motives for issuing the Emancipation Proclamation are slightly romanticized, the text does show that he was a consummate politician and that he issued the proclamation in order to keep France and England out of the Civil War. The book ends with a brief account of his assassination.

Shumate, Jane. ***Sojourner Truth and the Voice of Freedom.*** Millbrook, 1991. ISBN 1-56294-041-4

■■■■■■□□□□□□□

Isabella, the woman who was to be known as Sojourner Truth, was born a slave to the Hardenbergh family in New York about 1797. She was sold to the Nealy family when she was nine. Her next master, Dumont, promised to free her but reneged. So, taking her youngest baby with her, she ran to the Van Wageners, a Quaker family. She sued a white master for selling her son, Peter, after Emancipation was declared in New York, and she won, becoming the first Black in that state to win a suit against a white man. Soon afterward, she became a traveling preacher, thrilling listeners with her rich voice. She spoke out frequently against slavery. It was then that she changed her name. She met many famous people and the book has sidebars about some of them.

Shura, Mary Francis. ***Gentle Annie: The True Story of a Civil War Nurse.*** Scholastic, 1991. ISBN 0-590-44367-4

■■■■■■□□□□□□□

At sixteen, Anna Etheridge was a volunteer in the Second Michigan Volunteer Regiment of the Union Army. Although some conversations and actions in the book are certainly fictionalized, the story stays close to the facts most of the time and provides a look at a real woman of her time.

Nonprint

Filmstrips

People of the American Civil War. National Geographic, 1991

Using direct quotations, good narration, and interesting graphics this series of three filmstrips ("Crying for Freedom," "Riding the Political Storm," and "Witnessing the Conflict") depicts common people and soldiers as well as well-known figures such as Clay, Calhoun, and Webster.

War and Conflict

The Spanish-American War
1898

Activities

- List the major American industries, such as coal and iron, and find out why they might have welcomed the war.
- Why did American industries of the time believe they needed foreign markets?
- What was the role of the Navy after 1814, when we were no longer being threatened by foreign countries?
- Locate information about the Robber Barons. How did the Spanish-American War change their personal wealth?
- What is imperialism and how did it effect the Spanish-American War? What groups in the US were supportive of imperialism and why? What groups opposed it?
- On a world map, show countries the United States possessed before and after the Spanish-American War. Chart the possessions and show when they came under US influence, why, and their relationship to the US government.
- Follow our relationships with the Philippines, Hawaii, Puerto Rico, Cuba, and Guam to the present day.
- Find out what happened in February 1899 in the Philippines.
- Senator Albert Beveridge said on January 9, 1890,

  Mr. President, the times call for candor. The Philippines are ours forever. . . . And just beyond the Philippines are China's illimitable markets. We will not retreat from either . . . We will not renounce our part in the mission of our race. . . . trustee, under God, of the civilization of the world. . . . The Pacific is our ocean. . . . Where shall we turn for consumers of our surplus? Geography answers the question. China is our natural customer. . . . The Philippines give us a base at the door of all the east. . . No land surpasses in fertility the plains and valleys of Luzon. Rice and coffee, sugar and coconuts, hemp and tobacco. . . . The wood of the Philippines can supply the furniture of the world for a century to come. At Cebu the best informed man on the island told me that 40 miles of Cebu's mountain chain are practically mountains of coal. . . . I have a nugget of pure gold picked up in its present form on the banks of a Philippine creek. . . . My own belief is that there are not 100 men among them who comprehend what Anglo-Saxon self-government even means, and there are over 5 million people to be governed. It has been charged that our conduct of the war has been cruel. Senators, it has been the reverse. . . . Senators must remember that we are not dealing with Americans or Europeans. We are dealing with Orientals.

  Granted, Senator Beveridge is just one man giving a speech, but what does this speech show about his rationale for the war? Do you think many shared his views?

Nonfiction

Bachrach, Deborah. ***The Spanish-American War.*** Lucent, 1991.
ISBN 1-56006-405-6

■■■■■■■■■■■□□□□
Least Sophisticated   **Most Sophisticated**

This overview of the war that helped to establish the United States as a world power shows the role played by "yellow journalism" and propaganda in manufacturing a war in spite of President McKinley's aversion to the war. The text is clear and highlights many focal points for discussion.

Kent, Zachary. ***The Story of the Rough Riders.*** Childrens, 1991.
ISBN 0-516-04756-6

■■■■■■□□□□□□□□□

The Rough Riders, under the leadership of Lieutenant Colonel Theodore Roosevelt, were a motley crew. "Western cowboys ran in step alongside New York millionaires. Full-blooded, sharpshooting Indians fought beside blue-blooded Ivy League athletes." Because the story of this troop is the story of the Spanish-American War, we gain insights into William Randolph Hearst's and Joseph Pulitzer's roles in promoting a Cuban revolution into a full-scale war. We also get a glimpse of Roosevelt's personality. The text is clear and understandable and there are many photographs.

War and Conflict

World War I
1914–1918

Activities

- Tell the class to pretend that they are now eighteen years old. Present the class with the following information in the form of an announcement:

  An archduke and his wife from Austria-Hungary have just been assassinated in Serbia by a Serbian teenager, so Austria-Hungary has declared war on Serbia. Germany and Italy had a treaty with Austria-Hungary that stated they would be allies if war broke out, so Germany and Italy have entered the war. Russia is a friend of Serbia and Britain and France have an alliance with Russia, and they have begun fighting Germany, Italy, and Austria-Hungary. The United States is a friend of Britain and France and so may enter the war. Will you fight? Will you enlist?

  After some discussion, show some propaganda posters from the World War I effort.

- Sing or play a recording of "Over There." Explain to the class that these and other methods of building support for the war effort and for promoting the draft worked in 1917. Suggest that students brainstorm and perhaps produce posters, leaflets, poems, and songs that might work for them.

- Figure out how old Adolph Hitler was during this war. How might his life at the time have influenced his later feelings? How about others who became leaders during World War II, such as Churchill, Stalin, and Roosevelt?

- Ten million people died on the battlefield. Twenty million died of hunger and disease related to the war. What did the war accomplish?

- Make a chart listing each country that participated in the war. Show what each country wanted and what it got.

- How long did the United States stay neutral in the war? How neutral was it?

- In 1907, Woodrow Wilson said: "Concessions obtained by financiers must be safeguarded by ministers of state, even if the sovereignty of unwilling nations be outraged in the process . . . the doors of the nations which are closed must be battered down." How does this statement compare to his strong feelings about the League of Nations?

- How did the military build-up and the forming of national alliances in Europe contribute to the outbreak of war? Has military build-up ever provided national security? Did it prevent nuclear war or did it increase the risk?

- Find reproductions of posters used to promote the war. To what or whom do they appeal?

- Find out about the use of mustard gas in World War I. Who used it? What were its effects? Was it the first and/or the last time poisonous gas was used in warfare?

- Many historians feel that the Treaty of Versailles that ended World War I was one of the major causes of World War II. Find out why they feel that way.

Fiction

★ Kinsey-Warnock, Natalie. ***The Night the Bells Rang.*** Dutton, 1991. ISBN 0-525-65074-1

■■■■■■■□□□□□□□□

Least Sophisticated   Most Sophisticated

In this small but very nice novel, we see life in rural Vermont while World War I rages in Europe. In spite of its isolation, the family is touched by the war. The school bully, Aden Cutler, torments Mason, who wishes him dead. Later, Aden performs an act of heroism that only Mason sees and Mason tells no one about it. When Aden is killed in the battle of Argonne Forest, Mason is the only one with a kind thought for him. After the bells ring out to celebrate the end of the war, Mason comforts Mrs. Cutler. Although the setting is not the war, the insights on rural life are considerable.

★ Paulsen, Gary. ***The Foxman.*** Puffin, 1990. ISBN 0-14-034311-3

■■■■■■■■■■□□□□□

While exploring the wilds of northern Minnesota, Carl and his cousin, the narrator of the story, come upon The Foxman, a badly disfigured, kind, and tragic figure who lives in isolation in the wilderness. This wise man was maimed by mustard gas during World War I, and his stories of the war are in direct contrast to the stories the boys heard from their uncles who also fought in the war. The uncles' stories, which strike the narrator as cruel, are told with a somewhat awful humor. The Foxman explains that the uncles are "making roses out of manure" in an effort to come to grips with the horrors of war. The book is an eloquent and subtle anti-war book.

Fine, Anne. ***The Book of the Banshee.*** Little, 1992. ISBN 0-316-28315-0

■■■■■■■■□□□□□□□

This is a contemporary novel, but the main character is engrossed in a memoir of life in the World War I trenches and relates to it personally. He feels his home is in the midst of a war, which at times seems almost as overwhelming.

Houston, Gloria. ***Littlejim.*** Philomel, 1990. ISBN 0-399-2220-0

■■■■■■■□□□□□□□□

Although the time is World War I and there are references to it, the war is not the focus of this novel. Littlejim's father and uncle have a lumber business that is thriving because of the war, but otherwise the Appalachian setting is peaceful. The drama concerns the attempts, often futile, of scholarly, talented Littlejim to earn his father's respect and love. It's not action-packed, but there is gentleness here.

Kudlinski, Kathleen. ***Hero Over Here.*** Viking, 1990. ISBN 0-670-83050-X

■■■■■□□□□□□□□□□

The influenza that struck during World War I killed more people around the world than the war itself. This is one boy's battle as the flu strikes his family and his town during the last days of World War I.

Nonfiction

Lewis, Claudia L. ***Long Ago in Oregon.*** HarperCollins, 1987. ISBN 0-06-023839-9

■■■■■☐☐☐☐☐☐☐☐☐☐

In this book of poems, set during World War I, there are hints of the war, but mostly life goes on in Oregon much as it did all across America in that simpler time. Some of the images are graphic but always childlike. "I could not have told which froze me most, the crawling snakes or sight of them flung to bonfire death."

Maynard, Christopher. ***The Aces: Pilots and Planes of World War I.*** Watts, 1987. ISBN 0-531-10367-6

■■■■■☐☐☐☐☐☐☐☐☐☐

Just as the title says, this book contains many photographs of early aircraft and the people who flew them in battle.

War and Conflict

World War II 1939-1945

Activities

NOTE: Because this is a book that concentrates on US history, we have restricted most of the books and activities to those that have a strong United States focus. However, this is a good area of study for bridging US and world history. A study of the Holocaust through literature could obviously take a whole year.

- Make a flow chart similar to the one on page 67, showing the events that led up to World War II in Europe.

- Make another flow chart to show the events that led up to the war in the Pacific.

- On either chart, identify events that might have been prevented by a different action or reaction. At what point do you think war was inevitable?

- Many math activities can grow out of a study of this war because of the abundance of figures and statistics available. Find figures showing casualties for this war. Compare them to those of other wars. Compare them to such catastrophies as the current rate of death due to AIDS, auto accidents, and natural disasters. Find out what proportion of each country's population was killed during the war. How were the casualties distributed over age and gender groups?

- Find out about the decision by the United States to drop two atomic bombs on Japan. Many people believe it was necessary and that it ended the war and, therefore, the killing more quickly. Others believe it was unnecessary and caused needless suffering. Find the arguments to defend both points of view. Debate the subject, bringing in as much evidence as possible.

- Read *Sadako and the Thousand Paper Cranes* (page 92) and then find out more about the casualties and other effects of the atomic bombs dropped on Nagasaki and Hiroshima. What were the immediate results? What were the long term results? What are the current effects?

- Make a chart showing the leaders of World War II: Churchill, Roosevelt, Stalin, Mussolini, Tojo, Hitler, DeGaulle. What did they want? What were their strategies?

- On a world map, show the possessions and borders of the major participants of the war before 1938. On a similar map, show the possessions and borders after 1945. Using the two maps, talk about the feelings a Japanese person might have had about the changes, what it might have been like to live in Berlin then, and so on.

- Use the information in Theodore Taylor's *Air Raid—Pearl Harbor* (page 95) with a book such as the Focus Book *Stepping on the Cracks* by Mary Hahn (page 295). After reading the second book, speculate on how the events described in the first work, a nonfictional account of the events leading to war in the Pacific, affected the lives of Margaret and Elizabeth in *Stepping on the Cracks.*

- Read *Number the Stars/¿Quien Cuenta las Estrellas?* by Lois Lowry (Houghton, 1989. ISBN 0-395-51060-0 and Hispanic Book Distributors) or another novel set in this time. The setting of *Number the Stars* is Europe during the war. List the choices made by the main characters regarding the war or the effects of war. What choices did they have? Find out about other decisions that placed people in danger, such as hiding refugees, resisting the war, black marketeering, enlisting in the service, emigrating, hiding themselves, engaging in sabotage and underground activities, and hoarding.

- Sing songs of the war. How does it make you feel to sing them? Talk to someone who was alive during the war about how they felt about those songs then and now.

- Read one of the novels set in America during this time. Make a list of the effects of the war on the characters.

- Women played a more active part in the armed services during World War II than in previous wars. Write to the Department of the Armed Forces in Washington, DC, for statistics and other information about women in war before, during, and after World War II.

- Visit a local cemetery and the war memorial in your town. Identify the oldest soldier buried or memorialized there. Look for more than one member of a family killed in wars. Look for familiar names of people who were killed in World War II. Note the age at death. Look for epitaphs. Can you find out whether members of the armed services from your town were buried abroad or at Arlington National Cemetery. Local veterans groups might be able to give you this kind of information.

- Visit or call a veteran's hospital to see whether you can interview people there about their memories of World War II.

- During World War II, the English broke the secret code of the Germans, giving them information about proposed attacks and maneuvers. Churchill knew that the Germans were about to launch a bombing of Coventry. If he told the citizens of Coventry that they were about to be bombed, the Germans would know he had broken the code. What did he do? What could he do? What would you have done?

- How did the agreements at the end of World War II set the scene for the cold war? Were there alternatives? What role did the United Nations assume?

- Read books about the Holocaust (a few are listed below). Talk about genocide: Did it happen before World War II? Has it happened since? What are people doing about it?

Abells, Chana B. ***Children We Remember.*** Greenwillow, 1986. ISBN 0-688-06372-1

This book of photographs and memories of children of the Holocaust will haunt anyone who opens it.

Adler, David A. ***We Remember the Holocaust.*** Holt, 1989. ISBN 0-8050-0434-3

The survivors tell their stories of this tragic period of time in this abundantly illustrated book for children.

Tames, Richard. ***Anne Frank.*** Watts, 1990. ISBN 0-531-10763-9

Intended for a younger audience than **The Diary of Anne Frank,** *this book gives us background, diagrams, and pictures of the tragic life of Anne Frank.*

Wild, Margaret. ***Let the Celebrations Begin!*** Orchard, 1991. ISBN 0-531-08537-6

In this picture book, people in a concentration camp keep one another's spirits alive and eventually celebrate their liberation.

Yolen, Jane. ***The Devil's Arithmetic.*** Viking, 1988. ISBN 0-670-81027-4

A present-day Jewish child is transported in time to the days of the Holocaust.

- Who helped the Jews during this time? Find out about the role of countries such as Denmark and the US. Find out about the "Ship of Fools." Did it create the same problems as those created by the "boat people" from Haiti and other lands?

Picture Books

◆ Cech, John. ***My Grandmother's Journey.*** Illustrated by Sharon McGinley-Nally. Bradbury, 1991. ISBN 0-02-718135-9

In the case of the woman whose life is the basis for this picture book, the Russian Revolution and World War II, with all its hardships, were the way out of poverty and deprivation because she came to America after the liberation of Germany.

◆ Morimoto, Junko. ***My Hiroshima.*** Viking, 1990. ISBN 0-670-83181-6

Morimoto remembers how on August 6, 1945, she remained home from school because of a stomachache. Crawling through the rubble that had once been her school, she saw the immediate aftermath of the bomb. Later, she found the bones of many of her friends in the rubble. Many years later, she returns to the site to see students pursuing a peaceful existence in the same spot where she had seen such horror. The picture book is extremely powerful and unwincing.

Hest, Amy. ***The Ring and the Window Seat.*** Scholastic, 1990. ISBN 0-590-41350-3

The carpenter building Stella's window seat is saving his money to bring his daughter to America from war-torn Europe. Stella puts the money she was saving for a special ring into his tool box.

Fiction

★ Levitin, Sonia. ***Journey to America.*** Aladdin, 1987. ISBN 0-689-71130-1

■■■■■■■■■■■□□□□

Least Sophisticated   Most Sophisticated

Although most of the action of this story takes place in pre-war Germany, the plight of the Platt family is similar to that of many Jews in Germany at the time. Lisa's father is already in America, working to save enough money to get the family to America. Things in Germany worsen rapidly, so the family must live in Switzerland. There the danger from the Nazis is removed, but life is difficult with no money. To survive, the partial family must separate.

◆ Aaron, Chester. ***Alex, Who Won His War.*** Walker, 1991. ISBN 0-8027-8098-9

■■■■■■■■■■□□□□□

The fears of many have come true: Spies land in Connecticut and fourteen-year-old Alex is under great tension. They invade the home of Alex's defenseless neighbors and Alex takes a dead man's wallet. The suspenseful plot contains quite a bit of information about the fears and tensions of civilian life during the war.

◆ Coerr, Eleanor. ***Sadako and the Thousand Paper Cranes.*** Putnam, 1977. ISBN 0-399-20520-9

■■■■■■□□□□□□□□□

This book is based on the true story of a Japanese child who died of leukemia twelve years after being exposed to the intense radiation of the atom bomb that was dropped on Hiroshima. This brief novel shows how Sadako's hope infected all around her. Sadako was convinced that if she could fold one thousand paper cranes, she would live. Sadako had folded only six hundred forty-four before she died. There is a film of the same title from Informed Democracy Videos, narrated by Liv Ullman.

◆ Greene, Bette. ***The Summer of My German Soldier.*** Dial, 1973.
ISBN 0-8037-8321-3

■■■■■■■■■■□□□

Few are aware that we had prisoner of war camps on American soil during World War II. One of them was in Arkansas, and this is the story of how a young Jewish girl befriends a German prisoner.

◆ Hahn, Mary Downing. ***Stepping on the Cracks.*** Clarion, 1991.
ISBN 0-395-58507-4

■■■■■■■□□□□□□□□

This is a Focus Book. See page 295.

◆ Hest, Amy. ***Love You, Soldier.*** Four Winds, 1991. ISBN 0-02-743635-7

■■■□□□□□□□□□□□□

Kate's father goes off to war and she and her mother cope with the loneliness, helped by their neighbors in the New York City apartment building. After Kate's father is killed in action, Kate's mother falls in love again, and Kate learns to accept Sam. The novel is brief, but there is a great deal of insight into life on the home front.

◆ Little, Jean. ***Listen for the Singing.*** HarperCollins, 1991. ISBN 0-06-023910-7

■■■■■■■■■■■□□□□

See page 235.

◆ Lowry, Lois. ***Autumn Street.*** Houghton, 1980. ISBN 0-395-27812-0

■■■■■■■■■■□□□□□

Elizabeth is a kindergartner when Pearl Harbor is bombed. Her father goes to war and she and her family move to her grandparents' home in Pennsylvania. Here she struggles to make sense of the world around her in a well-to-do home with black servants. Elizabeth's tragic experiences at home reflect the horror of her father's experiences in the war. We get a glimpse of life on the home front during the war, mostly a world without men. The racism is readily apparent.

◆ Uchida, Yoshiko. ***The Journey Home.*** Macmillan, 1978. ISBN 0-689-50126-9
◆ ————.***Journey to Topaz.*** Creative Arts, 1985. ISBN 0-916870-85-5

■■■■■■■■■□□□□□

These two perceptive novels tell the story of Yuki and her family in a Utah prison camp during World War II. This Japanese-American family had been prosperous in California. After the war and their release, they return to find that their home and the father's job are gone. The prejudice is not gone, however, and they continue to fall victim to it.

Chaikin, Miriam. ***Lower! Higher! You're a Liar.*** HarperCollins, 1984. ISBN 0-06-021186-5

■■■■■■■■■■□□□□□

This is a distant view of what's happening to the Jews in Europe as seen through a family of Jews living in Borough Park, Brooklyn, during World War II. Molly's family learns of Hitler's deeds from the radio news as broadcast by Gabriel Heatter. Meanwhile, Molly is involved with an enemy at school.

Choi, Sook Nyul. ***Year of Impossible Goodbyes.*** Houghton, 1991. ISBN 0-395-57419-6

■■■■■■■■■■■■■□

Although this book is not set in America, reading it should add to an understanding of the time. Ten-year-old Sookan's narrative of survival during the Japanese occupation of North Korea and the Communists' takeover in 1945 is frank and compelling.

Davies, Andrew. ***Conrad's War.*** Crown, 1980. ISBN 0-679-80434-X

■■■■■■■■■■■□□□□

Conrad is in love with war and convinced that he could have whipped the Nazis single-handed. Fantasy gives Conrad his chance. Everything goes just the way he had imagined it would until he becomes a Nazi with orders to shoot at and destroy a French ambulance. Suddenly war seems less desirable.

Glassman, Judy. ***The Morning Glory War.*** Dutton, 1990. ISBN 0-525-44637-0

■■■■■■■■■■□□□□□

When Jeannie's class writes to servicemen stationed overseas, her feud with a popular classmate takes a back seat and she becomes totally involved in her writing.

Hoobler, Dorothy and Thomas. ***Aloha Means Come Back: The Story of a World War II Girl.*** Silver Burdett, 1991. ISBN 0-382-24156-8

■■■□□□□□□□□□□□

This book is a short, easy-to-read novel suited for less capable readers. Although the characters lack dimension, the plot line covers the attack on Pearl Harbor and the racial prejudice that had such devastating effects on Japanese-Americans .

Hotze, Sollace. ***Summer Endings.*** Clarion, 1991. ISBN 0-395-56197-3

■■■■■■■■□□□□□□

It's the summer of 1945; the war in Europe has just ended. Her father, who has been a prisoner in Poland, is coming home, and Christine Kosinski has to adjust to all the changes. Details of life in Chicago add to the color of the novel.

Smith, Doris Buchanan. ***Salted Lemons.*** Macmillan, 1980.

■■■■■□□□□□□□□□

Darby and her family move to Atlanta, Georgia, during the Second World War and Darby has great difficulty adjusting to the kids there. When her only friend, Yoko, born and bred right there, is relocated with her Japanese-American family to a relocation camp and the friendly German grocer is called a spy, it's almost too much for Darby.

Nonfiction

◆ Hamanaka, Sheila. ***The Journey: Japanese Americans, Racism and Renewal.*** Orchard, 1990. ISBN 0-531-08449-3

■■■■■■□□□□□□□□

See page 147.

◆ Houston, Jeanne Wakatsuki and Houston, James D. ***Farewell to Manzanar.*** Bantam, 1989. ISBN 0-553-23692-X

■■■■■■■■■■□□□□□

See page 236.

◆ Sullivan, George. ***The Day Pearl Harbor Was Bombed: A Photo History of World War II.*** Scholastic, 1991. ISBN 0-590- 43449-7

■■■■■■□□□□□□□□

This book uses many startling photographs and covers more of the war than the title implies. It also talks about the Holocaust and the dropping of the atom bomb.

◆ Taylor, Theodore. ***Air Raid—Pearl Harbor! The Story of December 7, 1941.*** HarperCollins, 1971. ISBN 0-690-05373-8

■■■■■■■□□□□□□□

Taylor recounts the bombing of Pearl Harbor and the events leading up to it from a predominantly Japanese point of view. His style is straightforward, letting the details supply the drama. For students who like accounts of battles, especially air battles, this easy-to-read book may be the one to hook them on history.

Dolan, Edward F. ***America in World War II: 1941.*** Millbrook, 1991. ISBN 1-878841-05-X

■■■■■■■□□□□□□□

This book covers the year that marked America's entry into World War II, opening with the bombing of Pearl Harbor, the motivations behind the attack, and ending with the digging in of American and Filipino troops at Bataan.

————. ***America in World War II: 1942.*** Millbrook, 1991. ISBN 1-56294-007-4

■■■■■■■□□□□□□□

The book begins with the fighting in the Philippines and ends with Eisenhower's troops poised for battle in North Africa. As in the first book, Dolan documents his text with photographs, some in color, maps, and drawings.

Hopkinson, Deborah. ***Pearl Harbor.*** Dillon Press 1991. ISBN 0-87518-475-8

■■■■■■■□□□□□

The USS Arizona Memorial at Pearl Harbor stands over the water above the spot where the USS Arizona lies at the bottom of the harbor. Here is the story of the Memorial along with a brief history of Hawaii up through the war years. The author stresses how much the country pulled together to win the war.

War and Conflict

The Korean War

- We have not forgotten the Korean War; however, at this time we can find no fiction or nonfiction for young people that addresses this war.

War and Conflict

The Civil Rights Movement

Activities

- See also Slavery on page 106, Politics and Government on page 140, and Racism, Sexism, and Equality on page 146.

- Make a list of the rights that the Civil Rights Movement targeted. Which of these do you think would be most important to you and your family? Which of these directly concerned people your age?

- Interview someone who participated in a Civil Rights protest.

- Who influenced Martin Luther King, Jr.'s philosophy of nonviolent protest? How had Gandhi used nonviolence?

- How does nonviolence work? (See page 57 in the War and Conflict section.) What were the pros and cons of using nonviolence as the major strategy of the Civil Rights Movement? What groups currently employ nonviolence?

- Make a time line of Civil Rights legislation.

- Take the characters from one of the books in this section and place them on the time line above. Then move them to a different time. How would their lives change?

- Watch sections of the PBS television program "Eyes on the Prize."

- Find and sing some of the songs used by the movement.

- Compare and discuss the goals and deeds of Martin Luther King, Jr., John Kennedy, Robert Kennedy, George Wallace, Ross Barnett, Lester Maddox, Sheriff Clark, Malcolm X, James Meredith, and Rosa Parks.

- Concentrate on one point of conflict in the struggle, such as the bus boycott. Divide the class into sections: one section for each side of the conflict and a separate section to investigate mediation skills. After giving time for research, generate ways to settle the conflict.

- Make a list of politicians whose careers and lives were affected by the Civil Rights struggle. Which side were they on? What did they do? How effective were they?

- What role did churches play in the struggle? Why were they successful? What stands did they take? What roles in social change have been or are being taken by your church or one that you know about?

- What choices did some of the characters in the books in this section have to make? What factors or people influenced their choices? What were the effects of the choices they made?

- During school desegregation in the South, Norman Rockwell painted a particularly poignant illustration of a young African-American girl being escorted to school by US marshals. Finding and showing the illustration will help create some feeling for the time and an understanding of the power of an illustration to affect people's opinions.

Picture Books

Greenfield, Eloise. **Rosa Parks.** Illustrated by Eric Marlow. HarperCollins, 1973. ISBN 0-690-71211-1

This fictionalized biography of the life of Rosa Parks is set against a background of the Civil Rights' abuses of the past.

Fiction

◆ Moore, Yvette. **Freedom Songs.** Orchard, 1990. ISBN 0-531-08412-4

■■■■■■■■■■■□□□
Least Sophisticated　　**Most Sophisticated**

Sheryl and her African-American family go from Brooklyn to her grandmother's in North Carolina. There she experiences the warmth of the family reunion and the cold reality of Jim Crowism. This is Sheryl's journey to find a role for herself in the struggle for Civil Rights.

◆ Taylor, Mildred D. **Roll of Thunder, Hear My Cry.** Dial, 1976. ISBN 0-8037-7473-7　■■■■■■■■■■□□□□□

This is a Focus Book; see page 297.

———. **The Friendship and The Gold Cadillac.** Bantam, 1989. ISBN 0-553-15765-5　■■■■■■■■□□□□□□□

These are two short stories based on the Black experience. The second, "The Gold Cadillac," tells of a Black family's trip to the South in 1950.

Nonfiction

★ Myers, Walter Dean. **Now Is Your Time: The African-American Struggle for Freedom.** HarperCollins, 1992. ISBN 0-06-024370-8

■■■■■■■■■■■□□□□

This book provides the valuable service of tracing the history of African Americans from the first slave ship through the Civil Rights Movement. Although at times the author uses hyperbole, the view of United States history as Black history is invaluable. In addition to the familar people, such as Martin Luther King, Jr., Malcolm X, and Frederick Douglass, we learn about the lives and contributions of less well-known people, such as Lewis Lattimer and Meta Warrick. Even if the reading level of this book is too difficult for some students, it is an excellent teacher resource.

◆ Adoff, Arnold. **Malcolm X.** Crowell, 1970. ISBN 0-066-446015-0

■■■■■■■□□□□□□□□

From his beginnings, through the prison years, to his emergence as a leader in the African-American community, this book presents a balanced view of a controversial man.

◆ Levine, Ellen. **If You Lived at the Time of Martin Luther King.** Scholastic, 1990. ISBN 0- 590-42582-X

■■■■■□□□□□□□□□□

This little book is surprisingly informative. Concentrating on the subject of the Civil Rights struggle of the 1950s and 1960s, rather than on the life of King himself, the book tells about the segregation laws, their overturn, the Freedom Riders, the bus boycott, and the roles of many people involved in the Civil Rights Movement.

◆ Parks, Rosa. ***Rosa Parks: My Story.*** Dial Books, 1992. ISBN 0-8037-0673-1

■■■■■■■■■□□□□□

Rosa Parks's autobiography resounds with the honesty and wisdom of someone who's been there and who seeks simply to tell the truth. It is like a good oral history—as if she were seated beside you, talking naturally to you about her life. She begins with her memories of her great-grandparents and traces their stories through slavery and sharecropping. Some of her ancestors tried to please the whites and others rebelled. Rosa Parks, an activist for civil rights, refused to give up her seat on a bus in Montgomery in 1955. This sparked the first large direct action of the Civil Rights Movement. Parks reflects on what it has meant to be seen as a symbol of the movement. She shares with us the years since then—the struggles, the victories, the losses, the changes still needed. Here is a woman of great compassion and firm convictions.

◆ Rubel, David. ***Fanny Lou Hamer: From Share Cropping to Politics.*** Silver Burdett, 1990. ISBN 0-38209923-0

■■■■■■■■■■□□□□

Fanny Lou Hamer was a sharecropper in Mississippi in the 1950s. There she heard about voter registration and got in touch with Student Nonviolent Coordinating Committee as the first step into the Civil Rights Movement. Because the Democratic party in Mississippi discouraged Black voter registration, she helped organize the Mississippi Freedom Democratic Party that nominated delegates for the national convention in 1964. The group's demand to be seated as the real democratic party resulted in a compromise that earned Fanny Lou Hamer a seat as a fully-accredited delegate to the 1968 convention. Her work led to opening the Democratic party to Blacks in the South. She went on to form a cooperative for Black sharecroppers before she died in 1977. The book gives a good description of that part of the Civil Rights Movement and the times in which it occurred.

Collins, David. ***Black Rage: Malcolm X.*** Macmillan, 1992. ISBN 0-87518-498-7

■■■■■■□□□□□□□

This is a very sympathetic look at Malcolm Little who became Malcolm X. It presents his conversion to Islam while in prison as his arrival at the truth that gave him a focus for his rage. The book concentrates on his youth and prison years with only a brief chapter on his later political work and his assassination.

Haskins, James. ***Thurgood Marshall: A Life for Justice.*** Holt, 1992. ISBN 0-8050-2095-0

■■■■■■■■■■□□□□

The Supreme Court justice who significantly shaped judicial history began his fight for justice by challenging and changing laws that were supposed to maintain a "separate but equal" system for Black people in the South. His landmark victory was in Brown vs. the Board of Education, which began the desegregation of public schools in 1954. The writing is clear and supported by numerous photographs.

Harrison, Barbara and Terris, Daniel. ***A Twilight Struggle: The Life of John Fitzgerald Kennedy.*** Lothrop, 1992. ISBN 0-688-08830-9

■■■■■■■■■□□□□□

Although this book deals with the entire life of President Kennedy, the Civil Rights struggle occupies a large section of the book and is well done. See page 144.

Turner, Glennette Tilley. ***Take a Walk in Their Shoes.*** Cobblehill, 1989.
ISBN 0-525-65006-7

■■■■■■■■□□□□□□□

Short but telling accounts of the lives and accomplishments of such Civil Rights leaders as Frederick Douglass, Rosa Parks, and Ida Wells.

Nonprint

Videos

Brown vs the Board of Education. Coronet.

The film is a dramatization of the events leading up to and following the Supreme Court decision that was the beginning of the desegregation of the South.

Free at Last. Encyclopedia Britannica.

Using dramatizations, newsreel clips, and excerpts from his speeches, the film deals with Martin Luther King, Jr.'s life and contributions at an upper-elementary school level.

War and Conflict

The Cold War

Activities

- Using the World Almanac, letters to government and other officials, and other sources, get as many statistics as possible that pertain to the Cold War. What information can you get from these statistics? What surprises you?

- How were the events in the Cold War like real war? What were the casualties? Expenditures? Results? Options for resolutions? Was it ever a declared war? Was there a definite end? Were there heroes? Declared wars have battles. What would you consider to be the battles of the Cold War?

- Who benefited from the Cold War? Who lost money or power when tensions eased?

- Find information about the military industrial complex and its growth during the Cold War.

- Find newspaper articles about the Russians in the 1960s and in 1990s. Can you tell how we viewed each other? What were people's concerns? Values?

- What individuals and groups were working to end the Cold War? How successful were they?

- Find pen pals in any country that was part of the Soviet Union. Survey your parents about what they were told about the Soviets when they were growing up. Ask your pen pals to do the same with their parents about Americans.

- For forty years the Bulletin of Atomic Scientists has published a clock that displays how close some scientists think we are to nuclear holocaust based on the number of "minutes before midnight." Write to them at 6042 S. Kimbark, Chicago, IL 60637, about the history of the clock, the times when its setting was changed, and the reasons.

Fiction

Ransom, Candice F. ***Ladies and Jellybeans.*** Bradbury, 1991. ISBN 0-02-775665-3

■■■■■■■□□□□□□□□

Least Sophisticated   Most Sophisticated

Wendy's nervous about starting third grade; she hopes her work won't include current events that her sixth-grade sister studies. Wendy knows nothing about the Cold War and very little about Eisenhower and that worries her. She's frightened about the threats of war but feels helpless to do anything about it.

Nonfiction

Epler, Doris. ***The Berlin Wall: How It Rose and Why It Fell.*** Millbrook, 1992. ISBN 1-56294-114-3

■■■■■■■■■■□□□□□

This is not an easy book, but the information is stated clearly. The author does particularly well outlining the postwar tensions that led to the wall. Accompanying photos add drama and make some of the information accessible to less able readers.

Harrison, Barbara and Terris, Daniel. ***A Twilight Struggle: The Life of John Fitzgerald Kennedy.*** Lothrop, 1992. ISBN 0-688-08830-9

■■■■■■■■■■□□□□□

Although this book deals with the entire life of Kennedy, there is material about the Bay of Pigs, the Cuban missile crisis, and the Berlin Wall. See page 144.

Smith, Samantha. ***Samantha Smith: Journey to the Soviet Union.*** Little, 1985. ISBN 0-316-80175-5

■■■■■■■□□□□□□□□

This ten-year-old American wrote a letter to Yuri Andropov, then leader of the Soviet Union, about her concerns about a nuclear war. His answer included an invitation for her to visit his country. The book furnishes both letters and accounts of her visit.

War and Conflict

The Vietnam War

- On a world map, show the countries that were involved in the Vietnam War.
- Make a chart showing the participants, when their participation started and ended, and their casualties.
- Find out what Vietnam was like before the war. What kind of government did it have? What did people do for a living? What did the countryside look like? Then find out what Vietnam was like when the war ended.
- Chart the opposition to the war from our first involvement to the end. Who were the protesters? How did they protest? How many protesters were there?
- How did television affect the war? How did that change the rules about television coverage of the Gulf War?
- How did the war affect Presidents Kennedy, Johnson, and Nixon?
- Talk to veterans of the Vietnam War through veterans groups or through a VA hospital. Ask them how they felt about the war then and now and how it affected their lives.
- Why is the Vietnam War Memorial, the Wall, so effective and affecting?
- Why was this war more controversial than other wars? What were the feelings and opinions on many sides?
- Get in touch with Vietnamese organizations in this country. Find out about the problems of Vietnamese immigrants. Is there anything you can do to help? Talk to a Vietnamese immigrant about life in Vietnam before, during, and after the war.

Picture Books ★ Bunting, Eve. ***The Wall.*** Illustrated by Ronald Himler. Clarion, 1990. ISBN 0-395-51588-2

A picture book that captures a moment and an era, this is one that should not be missed. A boy and his father search the Wall for his grandfather's name. Carefully they take a rubbing and then leave a picture weighted down with stones. Other people are there, too, and their stories are implied in this touching book.

Fiction ★ Paulsen, Gary. ***The Monument.*** Delacorte Press, 1991. ISBN 0-385-30518-4

■■■■■■■■■■■□□□□

Least Sophisticated   **Most Sophisticated**

There have only been eighteen casualties of war from Bolton, Kansas, through the years, but when one of the town's citizens announces that Bolton ought to have a monument, Mick is commissioned to do the job. At the end of the book, Mick moves on. The town has its monument, although it's not what anyone had in mind. Everyone is changed, and we're all richer for having been in Mick's presence for a while.

◆ Boyd, Candy D. ***Charlie Pippin.*** Macmillan, 1987. ISBN 0-02-726350-9

■■■■■■■■■■□□□□□

Charlie's father, who fought in Vietnam, refuses to discuss it with her or with anyone else. His anger is palpable and often matched by hers. For a class project, Charlie takes on the war and her father and tries to understand both, even making a clandestine trip to Washington to look at the Wall.

◆ Paterson, Katherine. ***Park's Quest.*** Lodestar, 1988. ISBN 0-525-67258-3

■■■■■■■■■■■□□□□

Unable to come to terms with his father's death in the war, Park visits his grandfather in Virginia. There he becomes friends with a Vietnamese-American girl who helps him work through his grief.

◆ Pettit, Jayne. ***My Name Is San Ho.*** Scholastic, 1992. ISBN 0-590-44172-8

■■■■■■■■■■■□□□□

San Ho was separated from his mother during the Vietnam War, and it is years before they find each other. By that time his mother has married an American, and San Ho's troubles are not over. He must adapt to his new country and his new family. Beginning with a chapter explaining the effect of the war on the Vietnamese people, this is a sad book but a good one.

Nonfiction

◆ Ashabranner, Brent. ***Always to Remember: The Story of the Vietnam Veterans Memorial.*** Putnam, 1988. ISBN 0-399-22031-3

■■■■■■■□□□□□□□□

In addition to describing the monument and the effect it has had on thousands of visitors, the book details its evolution from a dream. Jan C. Scruggs, a veteran of Vietnam, wanted to build a memorial that would help the American people resolve their conflicts over the war while honoring its victims. The memorial was designed by Maya Ying Lin, a twenty-one-year-old architectural student at Yale.

Hoobler, Dorothy and Hoobler, Thomas. ***Vietnam: Why We Fought.*** Knopf, 1990. ISBN 0-394-91943-2

■■■■■■■□□□□□□□□

This is a surprisingly even-handed account of the many causes of the war in Asia.

Marrin, Albert. ***America and Vietnam: The Elephant and the Tiger.*** Viking, 1992. ISBN 0-670-84063-7

■■■■■■■■■■■■□□□

With customary thoroughness, Marrin provides background for the conflict. His report on the conflict itself is less critical and less evenhanded than in some of his previous books. However, his portraits of Ho Chi Minh and Lyndon Johnson are well developed.

Nickelson, Harry. ***Vietnam.*** Lucent, 1989. ISBN 0-56006-110-3

■■■■■■■■■■□□□□□

It's hard to pin the Vietnam War to any decade because it started at least as far back as the 1950s and continued to 1972. This book covers that period and traces the conflict from its start to its quasi-resolution.

War and Conflict

The Gulf War

Activities

- Because this war is recent, the perspective of time is still absent from the literature. Many adoring and exulting books came out about the major figures on the United States' side of the war and, currently, such nonfiction books make up the bulk of available material. However, this very fact can make a study of the war and its literature interesting to your students. Would books published for young people right after other wars have had the same tone? Have they changed? Can we find some of the earlier ones? Careful searches can uncover some that were published during World War II in which the racism and nationalism were apparent and, from today's perspective, appalling. This can lead to discussions and research on propaganda and the role of emotion in recounting "fact."

Fiction

★ Giff, Patricia Reilly. ***The War Began at Supper: Letters to Miss Loria.*** Dell, 1991. ISBN 0-440-40572-6

■■■■■□□□□□□□□□□

Least Sophisticated   Most Sophisticated

Using letters supposedly written by a third-grade class to a former student teacher, Giff has given us a chance to discuss how war in general, and the Gulf War in particular, affects children. The children's letters show their denial, their often exaggerated fears, and finally their acceptance of the fact that many of their fathers, mothers, and neighbors are directly involved in the war. The children's letters show these stages and the more trivial concerns that vie for attention amidst the talk of war.

Nonfiction

Everston, Jonathan. ***Colin Powell.*** Bantam, 1991. ISBN 0-553-15966-6

■■■■■■■□□□□□□□

This is, as you would expect, an adulatory biography of the son of Jamaican immigrants who became a four-star general and chairman of the Joint Chiefs of Staff. The book is an interesting account of the military career of the man whose face and voice became so familiar to us during the Gulf War.

King, John. ***The Gulf War.*** Dillon, 1991. ISBN 0-87518-514-2

■■■■■■■■■□□□□□

This book is not easy to read but does give a fairly balanced account of the conflict by recounting the history of relations between Kuwait and Iraq and pointing out the mixed messages Saddam Hussein was receiving from the United States. In addition to relating the factors specifically contributing to the conflict, the author traces the history of the Arab countries. All of this leads to an excellent source of information about the Gulf War and the Israeli-Palestinian conflicts.

Work and Workers

Slavery

Activities

- Find out about as many kinds and conditions of slavery as you can: house slaves, field slaves, living conditions, abuse, paternalistic treatment, humane treatment, and opportunities for freedom.

- Find out about as many different conditions of near-slavery from any time period as you can: bondservants, sharecroppers, sub-minimum wage workers, servants, migrant workers, apprentices, dead-end jobs, and some homemakers.

- Find commonalties and differences among the workers in the two activities above. Chart numbers, races, lengths of service, conditions of release, health conditions, education, prospects for the future, and family life for each job or condition.

- Create two characters from the first two activities. Have them meet, plan an escape, discuss who is better off, work on the same enterprise, move forward or backward in time, or go to another country.

- Write diaries and role-play any of the characters above.

- Find the arguments used to defend each type of slavery. Appoint one class member to assume the role of a person who believed or believes that to be true. Attack and defend his/her position.

- Go back to the first two research topics and make cause-and-effect charts for each, giving economic and historic reasons.

- Find the names of well-known historic figures, especially the US presidents, who were slave owners. Make a bulletin board display with portraits of these people. Under each portrait, list the person's accomplishments as well as his/her role in slavery.

- Research the role of the North in slavery. For instance, the cotton mills of the North needed the cotton produced by the slaves in the South. Compare that to current American use of goods made in other countries by cheaper labor.

- Make a chart like the following:

What the Slaves Wanted	What the Slave Owners Wanted	What the Northern Factories and Consumers Wanted	What the Abolitionists Wanted

- Using the information on the chart on the previous page, decide how the Civil War and the Emancipation addressed each desire or need.

- Brainstorm other solutions that might have met as many or more of those needs expressed in the chart.

- Brainstorm possible solutions for people who felt they had no choice but to keep slaves.

- Contrast the role of a slave owner with his/her slaves and the role of a modern-day parent with his/her children.

- Look at the time preceding the Civil War and brainstorm other avenues that could have been used to bring an end to slavery.

- Imagine yourself as a slave on a Southern plantation. You have received word that you are now free. Most likely you have no money and can neither read nor write. What are your options? Where can you go? The country is in the middle of the war. Most of the plantations near you have been robbed and ruined. Role-play getting together with some of the other slaves to discuss what you will do tomorrow, next week, next month, and next year.

- Locate the Big Dipper. Find out how and why it was used by escaping slaves. Sing "Follow the Drinking Gourd."

- Sing some of the songs from slave times. What role did music play in the lives of the slaves?

- Find out about the Quakers who played important roles in the Underground Railroad. Find out about the origin of their religion and its beliefs. Because Quakers are often pacifists, they must have opposed the Civil War that was bringing about an end to slavery. How might they have coped with this conflict of beliefs?

- Find out how much risk the people in the Underground Railroad were taking. Would you be willing to participate? How does the risk compare to that taken by people helping Jews escape Nazi Germany? How does it compare to people helping illegal aliens now?

- If you had to hide people in your house, where would you hide them? Who would you trust with the information? How long do you think you could keep them hidden? Who would be most likely to discover your secret? Would they help or hurt?

- After reading several books about escaping slaves, plot on a map the routes they took to safety. Find their eventual destinations. Was it their nearest and most direct refuge?

- Using Julius Lester's book ***To Be a Slave*** (page 81), which contains information from real people, find a quote that would apply to and could have been used by one of the characters from a novel you read.

- Contrast the living conditions of the various slaves in the literature.

- Make a storyboard for a sequel to any of the books you read about slaves. A storyboard is a linear flow chart that outlines the story and allows room for adding details. Writers of television dramas and books often start with a storyboard.

- Jump ahead a generation and make a storyboard about the lives of the children of one of the characters in a book you read.

- Find out about slavery in the world today. Write to the United Nations Human Rights Department and to Amnesty International to find out which countries allow slavery. Read the article on slavery today in Newsweek magazine (May 4, 1992).

- Mauritania is one country in which slavery is still prevalent. Write to our embassy there to find out what the United States and the government of Mauritania are doing about it.

Picture Books

Turner, Ann. **Nettie's Trip South.** Illustrated by Ronald Himler. Macmillan, 1987. ISBN 0-02-789240-9
See page 79.

Marie, D. **Tears for Ashan.** Creative Press Works, 1989. ISBN 0-9621681-0-6
This picture book tells of an African boy witnessing his friend's capture by European slavers.

Fiction

★ Baker, Betty. **Walk the World's Rim**. HarperCollins, 1965. ISBN 0-06-020381-1

■■■■■■■□□□□□□□

Least Sophisticated   Most Sophisticated

See page 163.

★ Hansen, Joyce. **Out From This Place.** Avon Camelot, 1988. ISBN 0-380-71409-4

■■■■■■■■■■□□□□□

See page 55

★ Hurmence, Belinda. **A Girl Called Boy.** Houghton, 1982. ISBN 0-395-31022-9

■■■■■■■□□□□□□□

See page 36.

◆ Armstrong, Jennifer. **Steal Away.** Orchard, 1992. ISBN 0-531-05983-9

When the young orphan, Susannah, moves in with relatives in Virginia in 1855, she is presented with a personal slave, Bethlehem. Slave life is repellent to Susannah and life with her relatives becomes untenable so Susannah and Bethlehem escape on the Underground Railroad. The book contains a great deal about plantation life and the Quakers' role in the Underground Railroad.

◆ Collier, James Lincoln and Collier, Christopher. **Jump Ship to Freedom.** Dell, 1987. ISBN 0-440-44323-7

■■■■■■■■■■■■□□

See page 192.

◆ Beatty, Patricia. **Jayhawker.** Morrow, 1991. ISBN 0-688-09850-9

■■■■■■■■■□□□□□□

See page 79.

◆ Fox, Paula. **The Slave Dancer.** Bradbury, 1982. ISBN 0-02-735560-8

■■■■■■■■■■□□□□□

Jessie is kidnapped by a slaving crew to play the flute for the slaves being moved from Africa. The ship is wrecked and Jessie and a Black child swim ashore where they are befriended by an elderly escaped slave. The book details the horrors of the slave trade and slave passage, forbidden by US law, and provides a different look at slavery.

◆ Gilman, Dorothy. ***Girl in Buckskin.*** Ballantine Books, 1956.
ISBN 0-449-70380-0108

■■■■■■■■■■□□□□□

See page 65.

◆ Rinaldi, Ann. ***Wolf by the Ears.*** Scholastic, 1991. ISBN 0-590-43413-6

■■■■■■■■■■■■□□□

See page 198.

◆ Sanfield, Steve. ***The Adventures of High John the Conqueror.*** Orchard, 1989.
ISBN 0-531-08407-8

■■■■■■■■■□□□□□□□

This is a collection of short stories about a trickster folk character, High John. High John was first a slave and later a sharecropper who used his wits and wiles to get the best of the white masters. There is a good deal of information about slave life in the tales and in the explanatory material.

Nonfiction

★ Jacobs, Francine. ***The Tainos: The People Who Welcomed Columbus.*** Putnam, 1992. ISBN 0-399-22116-6

■■■■■■■■■■■■□□□

This book details the enslavement of Indians and the beginning of the importation of African slaves to Haiti, the Dominican Republic, Cuba, Jamaica, and Puerto Rico.

★ Lester, Julius. ***To Be a Slave.*** Dial, 1968. ISBN 0-8037-8955-6

■■■■■■■■■■□□□□□

See page 81.

★ Myers, Walter Dean. ***Now Is Your Time: The African-American Struggle for Freedom.*** HarperCollins, 1992. ISBN 0-06-024371-6

■■■■■■■■■■■□□□□

See pages 81 and 98.

◆ ***Cobblestone Magazine***

The following issues of the magazine were devoted to slavery topics:
Harriet Tubman (February 1981)
Black History Month (February 1983)
The Civil War: Reconstruction (May 1987)
Frederick Douglass: Fighter for Freedom (February 1989)

◆ McMullan, Kate. ***The Story of Harriet Tubman, Conductor of the Underground Railroad.*** Dell, 1991. ISBN 0-440-40400-2

■■■■■■■□□□□□□□□

See page 82.

Bryan, Ashley. ***Walk Together Children: Black American Spirituals.*** Atheneum, 1974. ISBN 0-689-70485-2

■■■■■■■□□□□□□□

Twenty-four spirituals provide a musical story of the American slaves.

Collins, James L. ***John Brown and the Fight Against Slavery.*** Millbrook, 1991. ISBN 1-56294-043-0

■■■■■■■□□□□□□□

See page 83.

Hamilton, Virginia. ***Anthony Burns: The Defeat and Triumph of a Fugitive Slave.*** Knopf, 1988. ISBN 0-394-98185-5

■■■■■■■■■■□□□□□

Burns escaped slavery and ran to Boston where he was arrested and brought to trial. His trial pitted Abolitionists against those in favor of the Fugitive Slave Act. This biography is well done and helps sketch in the man behind the furor.

Levine, Ellen. ***If You Traveled on the Underground Railroad.*** Scholastic, 1988. ISBN 0-590-40556-X

■■■■■■■□□□□□□□

This book uses a question and answer format to provide information about its subject.

Rappaport, Doreen. ***Escape from Slavery: Five Journeys to Freedom.*** HarperCollins, 1991. ISBN 0-06-021632-8

■■■■■■■□□□□□□□

Rappaport gives a brief history of the Fugitive Slave Act of 1793 and then tells fascinating tales of real-life heroism and daring.

Shorto, Russell. ***Abraham Lincoln and the End of Slavery.*** Millbrook, 1991. ISBN 0-1878841-12-2

■■■■■■■□□□□□□□

See page 84.

Shumate, Jane. ***Sojourner Truth and the Voice of Freedom.*** Millbrook, 1991. ISBN 1-56294-041-4

■■■■■■■□□□□□□□

See page 84.

Yates, Elizabeth. ***Amos Fortune, Free Man.*** Dutton, 1967. ISBN 0-525-25570-2

■■■■■■■■□□□□□□

Born free but sold into slavery as a young man, Amos Fortune purchased his freedom and that of several others. His life is movingly presented in this Newbery Award winner.

Nonprint

Videos

Follow the Drinking Gourd. American School Publishers, 1990.

The musical score is supplied by banjo, guitar, and ocarina in this video from the book by the same title.

Work and Workers

Workers and Their Rights

Activities

- See page 128 for more information on immigrant cultures.

- See *Immigrants* by Carol Otis Hurst (DLM, 1992. ISBN 0-7829-0064-X) for more ideas and activities about immigrants.

- Have each class member design and make a card such as a valentine. Choose one design to produce on an assembly line. Subdivide the tasks so that a group of students performs one tiny task over and over as their part in the production of the card. Compare the individually-produced and the mass-produced valentines and the feelings of the students who produced them.

- Make a monthly budget for a person earning minimum wage with a family of three.

- List the jobs that you would like to have as an adult. Find out what preparation and skills are necessary for that job. Can you get that training and acquire those skills? Can anyone?

- Read about the Triangle Shirt Fire and compare conditions at the factory before the fire with those in a factory near you.

- Talk to a person who has worked in a factory for a long time about the changes in working conditions over the years. Talk to a person in management of the same or a similar factory about the same subject. Chart their responses about wages, safety, benefits, work space, and morale. See whether you can account for any differences.

- Find out what work a person your age could do in 1860, 1900, 1940, and 1980. Find out the same information about someone five years younger than yourself. Why were children particularly suited to some types of work? What price did the children pay? Read *Lyddie* (see page 113).

- Find out about the rise of labor unions and their status. What do you think about the necessity of unions?

- Take an opinion poll of the adults in your household about unions. Are they necessary? Useful? What's wrong with them? What's good about them? Are you a union member? Could you be? Will you be?

- Investigate the local and national history of a union in your area.

- Almost every community has had a strike at one time or another. Find out about the latest or current strike in your area. What was the outcome? What was the cause? Who benefitted from the strike?

- Talk to the management of a plant that doesn't have a union. Why is there none? Was there ever? Has there been an attempt to organize the workers? Does the manager think the workers would like to unionize now? Does management want a union? How would a union change things?

- With your classmates, form a student union. What issues will you address? How can you address them more effectively as a group than as individuals? If the teacher is management, how much power does he/she have to change working conditions?

- Find as many statistics as you can about immigrants to this country. Look for patterns of increased immigration at various periods. When did many Germans come? Irish? Cambodians? See whether you can figure out the cause for each increase and decrease in immigration.

- Examine your own community's history for the role immigrants played in it. Where did most recent immigrants work? What were their working and living conditions? Have things changed in recent years?

- Go through three pages of your phone book and see whether you can tell by looking at the names which country the people might have come from. Chart the percentages of each nationality represented in your community today.

Picture Books

◆ Bunting, Eve. ***How Many Days to America: A Thanksgiving Story.*** Clarion, 1988. ISBN 0-89919-521-0

In this picture book the action and feelings of modern immigrants echo those of the original Pilgrims.

◆ Hendershot, Judith. ***In Coal Country.*** Knopf, 1987. ISBN 0-394-98190-1

With charcoal and chalk, the artist re-creates the dusty look and feel of life in a coal mine town.

◆ Rappaport, Doreen. ***Trouble at the Mines.*** Crowell, 1987. ISBN 0-690-0446-1

This is a true story of the coal miners' strike at Arnot, Pennsylvania, as seen through the eyes of Rosie, who will march with Mother Jones.

Dionetti, Michelle. ***Coal Mine Peaches.*** Illustrated by Anita Riggio. Orchard, 1991. ISBN 0-531-05948-1

Three generations of an Italian family are represented in this picture book. Grandfather's work was first in the coal mines and later he labored on the Brooklyn Bridge. He first told his stories to his co-workers and then to his family.

Smucker, Anna Egan. ***No Star Nights.*** Knopf, 1990. ISBN 0-394-89925-3
There are no stars because of the pollution from the furnaces in the steel town.

Fiction

★ Hesse, Karen. ***Letters from Rifka.*** Holt, 1992. ISBN 0-8050-1964-2

■■■■■■□□□□□□□
Least Sophisticated   **Most Sophisticated**

This is a Focus Book; see page 286.

◆ Collier, James Lincoln and Collier, Christopher. ***The Clock.*** Delacorte, 1992. ISBN 0-385-30037-9

■■■■■■■■■■■■□□

Annie's father is a spendthrift; he can't resist buying the things he wants even when his family suffers for it. The year is 1806 and Annie has to abandon her plans to be a teacher to work at the woolen mill to help pay her father's debts. There is a great deal of information about working in the mills and the book goes well with Lyddie (see below). The characters express concerns about the effect of factories on the economy, and in an afterword, the authors talk about the facts behind the novel and pose the question of whether the industrial revolution was progress.

◆ Kidd, Diana. ***Onion Tears.*** Orchard, 1991. ISBN 0-531-08470-1

Nam, a Vietnamese immigrant, seldom speaks and tries not to cry, but her overwhelming sense of isolation becomes worse when the only teacher who understands her becomes ill.

◆ Paterson, Katherine. ***Lyddie.*** Lodestar, 1991. ISBN 0-525-67338-5

Illiterate and impoverished Lyddie goes to work in the mills of Lowell, Massachusetts, in the mid-eighteen hundreds in order to pay off her family's indebtedness. She regretfully signs up her younger sister to work as a doffer in the dangerous mills. Living in the company's boarding house, putting up with the slave hours and wages, even fending off the unwanted attentions of the mill supervisor, only make Lyddie stronger. At the end of the book, she's refusing the safety of a marriage, at least temporarily, to go to college.

Paulsen, Gary. ***The Crossing.*** Orchard, 1987. ISBN 0-531-08309-8

Manny's only hope appears to be crossing the border into the United States and leaving the poverty of his Mexican border town behind. Crossing the border takes skill and determination and a strange friendship with an American soldier.

Van Raven, Pieter. ***A Time of Troubles.*** Scribner, 1990. ISBN 0-684-19212-8

Fourteen-year-old Roy and his father leave their shack on Chesapeake Bay during the 1930s Great Depression to go to California where they've been assured of a job. Crossing the desolate Dust Bowl, they arrive in California's migrant labor camps only to find that they've been tricked and that only starvation wages are available. The exploitation of the workers is apparent.

Yep, Laurence. ***Dragonwings.*** HarperCollins, 1975. ISBN 0-06-026738-0

Eight-year-old Moonshadow goes to San Francisco at the bidding of his father during the Gold Rush. There he becomes part of the rapidly expanding Chinese-American community.

Nonfiction   ◆ ***Cobblestone Magazine***

The following issues of the magazine were devoted to topics concerning work and workers:
Transcontinental Railroad (May 1980)
Industrial Revolution (September 1981)
Wheat Farming (April 1982)

America's Cowboys (July 1982)
The Circus (August 1982)
The Erie Canal (October 1982)
Immigrants: Part 1 (December 1982)
Immigrants: Part 2 (January 1983)
Black History Month (February 1983)
Shakers (April 1983)
Public Works (August 1983)
Soil (December 1983)
The Great Depression (March 1984)
Whaling (April 1984)
Computers (June 1984)
Susan B. Anthony and the Women's Movement (March 1985)
World War II: The Homefront (December 1985)
The Automobile in History (July 1987)
The Seafaring Life (April 1988)
Hispanic Americans (April 1989)
People with Disabilities (June 1989)
Environmentalism (August 1989)
Taking Stock of Wall Street (April 1990)
Energy: Powering Our Nation (October 1990)
Back issues of the magazine can be obtained from Cobblestone Publishing
30 Grove Street, Peterborough, NH 03458.

Ashabranner, Brent. ***The New Americans: Changing Patterns in U. S. Immigration.*** Putnam, 1983. ISBN 0-396-08140-1

■■■■■■■■■□□□□□

This book uses first-hand accounts from immigrants of many cultures to tell of recent immigration policies and their effect on immigrants.

McKissack, Patricia and McKissack, Fredrick. ***A Long, Hard Journey: The Story of the Pullman Porter.*** Walker, 1990. ISBN 0-8027-6885-7

■■■■■■■■■■■□□□

The biography of A. Philip Randolph, the organizer of Pullman porters in the 1920s, is linked to the exploitation of African Americans since Reconstruction days.

Mitchell, Barbara. ***Shoes for Everyone: A Story about Jan Matzeliger.*** Carolrhoda, 1986. ISBN 0-87614-290-0

■■■■■■■■□□□□□□□

A biography of a fascinating man, this book recounts the life of a half-Dutch, half-Surinamese inventor of a shoe-lasting machine that revolutionized the shoe industry.

Nonprint

Videos

In Coal Country. *American School Publishers, 1990.*

The author's hometown of Willow Grove, Ohio, in the 1930s is shown directly from the picture book by the same title. The musical accompaniment is typical mountain music.

Work and Workers

Agriculture

Activities

- Find old maps of your town. See what areas were farmed over the years. Figure out the percentage of land devoted to agriculture. Find out what crops were raised and why. Has the predominant crop changed over the years? What is it now?

- What foods do you eat that are imported from another state? Another country? Take your family's itemized grocery bill and estimate how much of the food is raised within your state. Contrast that to food produced on a subsistence farm of today or of long ago.

- Read Edith McCall's book **Pioneering on the Plains** (Childrens, 1980. ISBN 0-516-03358-1) in which she talks about the equipment needed to homestead a quarter section. Talk to a person who farms a similar area today. What money and equipment does he/she feel are necessary? Would an Amish farmer agree?

- Read the picture book **The Auction** (page 41) in which a farm is being auctioned. Talk to a person who has had or who knows someone who has had a similar experience. What could have been done to change the situation?

- Talk to a person who has farmed for a long time. Talk to a younger farmer. How are their opinions about farming different? Why do you think this is so?

- Select a few common processed foods. From the list of ingredients, determine how much of the price of the food goes to the farmers.

- Investigate insecticides and fertilizers. What are their pluses and minuses? What happened to DDT? Have there been improvements in efficiency and safety? Call the local County Cooperative Extension Service to see what is being done in your area to lessen the dependence on chemicals.

- How is the water in your area? How pure is it? What are the contaminates? Could contamination have been prevented? What is being done to improve things? What are the alternatives?

- Look at picture books showing farms of long ago and those showing farms of today. Compare the differences in farm structures.

- Compare the daily life of people on a small family farm to the life of people on a large agribusiness farm.

Picture Books

★ Sewall, Marcia. **Pilgrims of Plimoth.** Macmillan, 1986. ISBN 0-689-31250-4
See page 177.

◆ Andrews, Jan. **The Auction.** Illustrated by Karen Reczuch. Macmillan, 1991. ISBN 0-02-705535-3
See page 41.

◆ McPhail, David. ***Farm Boy's Year.*** Atheneum, 1992. ISBN 0-689-31679-8
See page 34.

Aylesworth, Jim. ***Country Crossing.*** Illustrated by Ted Rand. Atheneum, 1991.
ISBN 0-689-31580-5
See page 124.

Allen, Thomas. ***On Granddaddy's Farm.*** Knopf, 1989. ISBN 0-394-89613-0
See page 227.

Fiction

★ Hamilton, Virginia. ***Willie Bea and the Time the Martians Landed.***
Greenwillow, 1983. ISBN 0-688-02390-8

Least Sophisticated   **Most Sophisticated**

This is a Focus Book; see page 291.

◆ Armstrong, William H. ***Sounder.*** HarperCollins, 1969. ISBN 0-06-020144-4

See page 148.

◆ Taylor, Mildred D. ***Roll of Thunder, Hear My Cry.*** Dial, 1976.
ISBN 0-8037-7473-7

This is a Focus Book; see page 297.

◆ Weitzman, David. ***Thrashin' Time: Harvest Days in the Dakotas.*** Godine,
1991. ISBN 0-87923-910-7

*This oversize book is deceptive: it looks like a picture book, yet it contains
relatively few pictures; the title implies a nonfiction book, but there is a story line.
It contains a great deal of information about the mechanization of farming in
the early 1900s. Included are detailed diagrams of the first steam-driven tractor
and the narrative contains many details about how the machine worked. The
story is told in the present tense by a young boy on one of the cooperative farms
formed to get the most use of the tractor and labor.*

Nonfiction

◆ ***Cobblestone Magazine***
The following issues of the magazine were devoted to this subject:
Wheat Farming (April 1982)
Soil (December 1983)
The Amish (November 1987)
*Back issues of the magazine can be obtained from Cobblestone Publishing, 30
Grove Street, Peterborough, NH 03458.*

Nonprint

Videos

Roll of Thunder, Hear My Cry. American School Publishers, 1990.

Audios

Roll of Thunder, Hear My Cry. American School Publishers, 1990.
Sounder. American School Publishers, 1990.

Discovery and Invention

Activities

- Play What If. Players select any invention or discovery and tell how they think our lives would have been different without that invention or discovery.

- Make a list of the wealthiest families in America or in your community and then try to figure out where their money came from.

- Make a list of fantasy inventions. Be specific about what the inventions will do, how it can be produced, what it will cost to produce, how much it will sell for. Campaign for a patent to a patent committee set up in your classroom.

- Invent Rube Goldberg machines. Design a complicated machine to do a simple task, such as blowing out a match. Make a design for it or even make the machine.

- Investigate the history of the US Patent Office. When did it originate? Who is eligible to receive patents? Obtain statistics about patents: number per year, categories, number of men and women inventors, and so on. Do we still need it? Who decides who receives a patent?

- How has the increasing influence of corporations affected invention? Do individuals get patents now or do they usually belong to the corporation?

- Why are there so few famous women scientists and inventors?

- Through discussion, choose some major inventions, such as the wheel and the plow, and make flow charts showing other important inventions that wouldn't have been possible without that first invention. Do the same with discoveries such as the fact that the earth goes around the sun instead of vice versa. What later discoveries relied on that information?

- Choose a topic, such as the human body, the solar system, medicine, superstition, physics, chemistry, farming, environmental science, or energy. Make a historical chart that shows how our understanding and knowledge of that topic have changed.

- Make a list of the major causes of death during various historical periods. Are all of these diseases under control at present? How do these compare with AIDS?

- Consider the book you are now reading. What inventions and discoveries might the main character care about? Which would he/she think were most uninteresting?

- Choose a book about the past and decide how the story would change if you added a modern invention or discovery.

- How do we as a society determine the focus of research and invention? Has it always been so? Investigate the Manhattan Project. How did government's role in science change after that?

- Look through the biographies of inventors and discoverers throughout history. Do they have anything in common? Are there significant factors in their lives that have a similarity to others? Which of those qualities do you possess?

- Find old catalogues. Which of the inventions shown still exist? Did others evolve into something still used? Which bombed?

- Do the same activity with a current catalogue. Which inventions do you think are winners and which will bomb?

- Suppose your classroom receives a million dollars to invest in research. Which of society's current problems will you support? Will any money go for space? For pure research? For medical cures? For pollution-free cars?

- Choose any invention such as the telephone. For what period of time did Alexander Graham Bell work on that invention? Convert the figure into number of days. Speculate about what he did on those days. Would he probably have spent time relaxing? Playing with his children? Talking to Watson? Sleeping? Eating? Goofing off? What would he do while actively working in his lab?

- Select an invention and see whether you can figure out what people thought its effects would be and contrast them with what the effects truly are. Don't forget the repercussions of the invention on the environment and on other inventions.

- Research the ways in which military needs have influenced technology. Discuss the pros and cons of that alliance.

- Chart the motivations behind inventions.

- Divide the class in half. On each side of the classroom there are three people who have the money to invest in a factory that will produce economical, pollution-free automobiles with long-distance capability. On one side of the classroom, these three people have the responsibility and the power to set up the factory, hire people to do the necessary jobs, and pay them accordingly. On the other side of the classroom, all members of the group share in the decision making. After the decisions are made, discuss how each member feels. Do some feel okay about getting less pay because they have fewer responsibilities? How committed are they to the quality of their product? How satisfied are they in their jobs? What are their grievances?

- After the previous activity, discuss what other approaches an industry could use in setting up a workplace. (See the section on Work and Workers for further activities.)

- Alexander Graham Bell said, "The inventor is a man who looks around upon the world and is not contented with things as they are. He wants to improve whatever he sees; he wants to benefit the world; he is haunted by an idea, the spirit of inventiveness possesses him." Have you found evidence in your research of the truth of that statement? Which inventors and discoverers seemed to feel that way?

- Alexander Graham Bell also said that he had a Rule of Three: "Observe! Remember! Compare!" What do you suppose he meant?

Picture Books

- Burleigh, Robert. ***Flight: The Journey of Charles Lindbergh.*** Illustrated by Mike Wimmer. Putnam, 1991. ISBN 0-399-22272-3

  See page 227.

- Cherry, Lynne. ***A River Ran Wild.*** Harcourt, 1992. ISBN 0-15-200542-0

  The focus of this book is the Nashua River in New Hampshire from 1400 to 1990. The book shows how the river went from clean to polluted and back to clean. Each spread also shows the wildlife that originally surrounded the river and then, after manufacturing pollution takes over, we see the many tools and other items produced by the factories.

Fiction

★ Hamilton, Virginia. *Willie Bea and the Time the Martians Landed.* Greenwillow, 1983. ISBN 0-688-02390-8

■■■■■■■□□□□□□□

Least Sophisticated   Most Sophisticated

This is a Focus Book; see page 291.

◆ Collier, James Lincoln and Collier, Christopher. *The Clock.* Delacorte, 1992. ISBN 0-385-30037-9

■■■■■■■■■■■■□□

See page 112.

◆ Weitzman, David. *Thrashin' Time: Harvest Days in the Dakotas.* Godine, 1991. ISBN 0-87923-910-7

■■■■■■■□□□□□□□

See page 116.

Nonfiction

◆ *Cobblestone Magazine*

Thomas Edison (February 1980)

Back copies are available from Cobblestone Publishing, 30 Grove Street, Peterborough, NH 03458

◆ Freedman, Russell. *The Wright Brothers: How They Invented the Airplane.* Holiday, 1991. ISBN 0-8234-0875-2

■■■■■■■□□□□□□□

Using photographs taken by Orville and Wilbur Wright, the author presents their lives and accomplishments. The focus of the book is on their considerable accomplishments. Brothers of extraordinary closeness, Orville and Wilbur set about to make flying machines possible and accessible and they accomplished this in a remarkably short period of time, setting in motion the Age of Flight.

◆ Mitchell, Barbara. *We'll Race You, Henry: A Story about Henry Ford.* Carolrhoda, 1987. ISBN 0-8234-0875-2

■■■■■■■□□□□□□□

The facts of Ford's life are here, but even more interesting are the explanations of the technology behind his Model T Ford.

◆ Randolph, Sallie and Bolick, Nancy O'Keefe. *Shaker Inventions.* Walker, 1990. ISBN 0-8027-6934-9

■■■■■■■■■□□□□□

The Shaker communities settled in New England in the late 1700s and continued through the 1800s. With high standards of cleanliness and a celebration of the joy of work, the Shakers wasted nothing and used their creative minds to make work more efficient. They developed the first washing machine, clothespins, sulfur matches, rolling pins, and the Dorothy cloak. They also refined many already existing inventions and discoveries. This book includes many fine illustrations of their furniture and inventions and reflects the Shaker life.

◆ St. George, Judith. ***Dear Dr. Bell . . . Your Friend, Helen Keller.*** Putnam, 1992. ISBN 399-223337-1

This is a dual biography. Most of the book deals with the friendship between Alexander Graham Bell and Helen Keller and the ways in which they helped each other. In the process, we learn about the times and about the drive behind both people to achieve and excel. The book is not long and is very easy to read.

Epstein, Sam and Epstein, Beryl. ***George Washington Carver: Agricultural Scientist.*** Dell, 1991. ISBN 0-440-40404-5

This is a straightforward account of Carver's life and achievements. It's easy-to-read story format makes it excellent for younger readers.

Glassman, Bruce. ***The Crash of '29 and the New Deal.*** Silver Burdett, 1986. ISBN 0-382-06978-1

See page 230.

Haskins, Jim. ***Outward Dreams: Black Inventors and Their Inventions.*** Walker, 1991. ISBN 0-8027-6993-4

This book is strong in its coverage of the historical backdrop for Black inventors. Here we find the inventors of the machine lubrication device that was the origin of the phrase "the real McCoy," the ironing board, a telephone, an inexpensive source of cortisone, a communication system for trains, and many others.

Jones, Charlotte Foltz. ***Mistakes That Worked.*** Doubleday, 1991. ISBN 0-385-26246-9

From the ice-cream peddler who ran out of dishes and invented the ice-cream cone to the nuisance of cockleburs leading to the invention of Velcro, we see many oddball discoveries in an entertaining book.

Kent, Zachary. ***The Story of Henry Ford and the Automobile.*** Childrens, 1990. ISBN 0- 516-04751-5

They called him "Crazy Henry" because of his determination to build a horseless carriage; but from that rainy night in June of 1896 when he first drove his "Quadricycle" to the Cadillac Hotel in Detroit, they changed their minds. Going quickly through his childhood and young adult years, the book concentrates on the time from the beginning of the Detroit Automobile Company, which marked the end of a horse-drawn society. He insisted on building affordable cars rather than luxurious models. When he developed the Model T, he had made the simplest and most advanced automobile yet devised. In 1913, he began to streamline its production, developing the first commercial assembly line. The book is easy to understand and contains many photographs and a time line of Fords in the frontispiece.

Lomask, Milton. *Great Lives: Invention and Technology.* Macmillan, 1991. ISBN 0-684-19106-7

■■■■■■■□□□□□□□

This book is a collection of twenty-five biographies of inventors and researchers from all over the world. There are references to the controversies surrounding each person and the opinions of different biographers. This apparently well-researched book makes a good reference. There is a comprehensive chronological listing of important dates in the history of invention and technology that begins at the end of the B.C. period.

Smith, Carter. *The Arts and Sciences: A Sourcebook on Colonial America.* Millbrook, 1991. ISBN 0-56294-037-6

■■■■■■■■■□□□□□

Using prints, photographs, and drawings, the book presents information about medicine and science in the Colonial period.

Stevens, Bryna. *Ben Franklin's Glass Armonica.* Illustrated by Priscilla Kiedrowski. Dell, 1983. ISBN 0-440-40584-X

■■■■■■□□□□□□□□

Here is a short, easy-to-read book about Benjamin Franklin's invention of a musical instrument. It made beautiful music and was very popular at the time (even Mozart wrote music for it). Eventually, however, it caused nerve damage in some of the people who played it and so fell out of use.

Swanson, June. *David Bushnell and His Turtle: The Story of America's First Submarine.* Atheneum, 1991. ISBN 0-689-31628-3

■■■■■□□□□□□□□□

In the mid-seventeen hundreds, David Bushnell invented a submarine that looked very much like two turtle shells joined together. With it, he attempted to bomb British warships during the Revolution but was unsuccessful. Humiliated by his failure, he spent the remaining years of his life in hiding.

Weidt, Maryann and Anderson, Lydia M. *Mr. Blue Jeans: A Story about Levi Strauss.* Carolrhoda, 1990. ISBN 0-87614-421-0

Starting in Bavaria during the 1800s and moving to the days of the Gold Rush, the book not only details events in the life of Levi Strauss but also gives us a look at much of our country during those years.

Nonprint

Videos

Going Up: The Story of the Otis Elevator Company. Pyramid Film & Video.
David Macaulay narrates the story of the Otis family's invention and marketing techniques. The film shows the first primitive elevators and some modern versions.

Henry Ford Museum and Greenfield Village. Select Video Publishing.
A tour of the museum gives us glimpses of the recreated Menlo Park laboratory of Thomas Edison, a 1940s diner, and Henry Ford's cars.

Transportation and Communication

Activities

- Go to a car dealership and get pictorial information they might have on older models. Ask parents, grandparents, and others which is most like their first car.

- Make models of aircraft. Arrange them chronologically.

- Make a pictorial time line of telephones.

- Find old letters from your family treasures, town library, or books. Compare the length, subject, writers, and recipients to your mail yesterday. How has mail changed? How does your family convey news to others now? Who writes letters? Why?

- Read **Letters from Phillipa** by Anne Graham Estern (page 38) and **Dear Mr. Henshaw/Querido Señor Henshaw** by Beverly Cleary and other books in which letters play an important part. What if the information were conveyed by fax machine? How would the plot change? The characters? The mood of the book?

- Pretend that it's 1849 and your father, who went west to pan for gold, has just sent word to you and your family to leave Atlanta and join him immediately in San Francisco. He'll meet you at the dock. How can you get there? What will it cost you? How will you let him know when you're arriving? How long does he have to wait on the dock?

- Pretend that your father, who went to help rebuild Saudi Arabia in 1992, has sent word to you and your family living in Kansas City, Missouri, to join him immediately in Jidda. He'll meet you at the airport. How can you get there? What will it cost you? How will you let him know when you're arriving? How long does he have to wait at the airport?

- Find or create a poster advertising for mail-order brides. How did current transportation and communication affect that phenomenon?

- Sign on as a Pony Express rider. What skills do you already have? What skills will you need to brush up on? What are you most apprehensive about?

- Choose a character from one of the historical books you're reading. Write a letter to the character describing how communication and transportation have changed since his/her time. Would the character believe you?

- Make a quill pen and some ink. Copy a letter or group of letters from an earlier correspondence. How did you do?

- Chart different modes of transportation and their energy uses per person or per weight of cargo moved. Note the environmental impacts.

- Find out how the demands of war change transportation and communication.

- What demands have accelerated communication and transportation placed on society? How have we met or failed to meet these demands?

- Find out about communication with blind and/or deaf people. Learn to sing a song using sign language. Use ear plugs or some other means of eliminating or decreasing your hearing for a period of time. Try a little Braille reading.

- See the Focus Book **The Root Cellar** on page 277.

Picture Books

◆ Goble, Paul. **Death of the Iron Horse.** Bradbury, 1987. ISBN 0-02-737830-6

Told from the viewpoint of the American Indians, this picture book is based on an actual incident in 1867 when the Cheyenne Indians wrecked a Union Pacific freight train. As always with Goble's books, the illustrations are stunning and contain many of the patterns and rhythms of Native American design. The coming of the train fulfilled the dire prophecy of a Cheyenne prophet named Sweet Medicine and, through the brief account, you get some feeling for the threat the railroad represented to the Native Americans who lived on the Plains.

◆ Harvey, Brett. **Cassie's Journey: Going West in the 1860s.** Holiday, 1988. ISBN 0- 8234-0684-9

This is a picture book based on the actual accounts of journeys by covered wagon to the Midwest.

◆ Quackenbush, Robert. **Clear the Cow Pasture, I'm Coming in for a Landing! A Story of Amelia Earhart.** Simon & Schuster, 1990. ISBN 0-671-68548-1

This light-hearted but surprisingly factual account of some of the highpoints of the life of the flyer is presented in three sections. One section provides an explanation of flight by a mother bird.

◆ Spier, Peter. **The Erie Canal.** Doubleday, 1990. ISBN 0-385-05234-0

Spier illustrates an old folk song and, in so doing, gives us many details of the life on and around the great canal.

◆ ———. **Tin Lizzie.** Doubleday, 1990. ISBN 0-385-13342-1

With wonderful and amusing water colors, Peter Spier tells us the tale of the life of one Model T Ford.

Aylesworth, Jim. **Country Crossing.** Illustrated by Ted Rand. Atheneum, 1991. ISBN 0-689-31580-5

A country crossing, a man, a boy, and a train show us life sixty years ago.

Brandt, Betty. **Special Delivery.** Carolrhoda, 1988. ISBN 0-87614-312-5

This easy-to-read book is a brief history of the United States Postal Service.

Dicerto, Joseph J. **The Pony Express: Hoofbeats in the Wilderness.** Watts, 1989. ISBN 0-531-10751-5

The service is traced from its beginning to end in a brief book with many illustrations.

Gibbons, Gail. **The Great St. Lawrence Seaway.** Morrow, 1992. ISBN 0-688-06984-3

In this simple picture book, Gibbons traces the history of the St. Lawrence as a river and as a means of connecting the cities and resources of the Great Lakes to the Atlantic. There are also clear diagrams of the way locks work.

Hiscock, Bruce. **The Big Tree.** Atheneum, 1991. ISBN 0-689-31598-8

See page 41.

Quackenbush, Robert. **She'll Be Comin' Round the Mountain.** HarperCollins, 1988. ISBN 0-397-32266-6

The words of the old song are illustrated with a takeoff on Buffalo Bill's Wild West Show.

Fiction

◆ Curry, Jane. **What the Dickens!** McElderry, 1991. ISBN 0-689-50524-8

Least Sophisticated **Most Sophisticated**

An adventure story set in Pennsylvania during the 1840s, this book provides a raft of information about transportation on the Juaniata Canal that went from Harrisburg to Hollidaysburg where it connected with the Portage railroad over the Allegheny Mountains to Johnstown. The action centers around Charles Dickens who is making an American tour and two dastardly and illiterate villains who are out to steal his manuscript. Their attempt is foiled by two enterprising canal boat children.

◆ Leonard, Laura. **Finding Papa.** Atheneum, 1991. ISBN 0-689-31526-0

Mama is dead and the three children set out to find their irresponsible father by journeying West on the train in 1905. The children suffer many of the trials and tribulations of train travel before reaching their very surprised stepmother-to-be in San Francisco, only to find that their father is in Nevada.

◆ Taylor, Mildred. **Mississippi Bridge.** Dial, 1990. ISBN 0-8037-0427-5

See page 149.

Gondosch, Linda. **The Best Bet Gazette.** Lodestar, 1989. ISBN 0-525-67287-7

See page 241.

Hamilton, Virginia. **The Bells of Christmas.** Harcourt, 1989. ISBN 0-15-206450-8

See page 220.

Nonfiction

◆ **Cobblestone Magazine**

The following issues of the magazine are devoted to transportation and communication topics:
Transcontinental Railroad (May 1980)
America's Lighthouses (June 1981)
Pony Express (October 1981)
Submarines (January 1982)
The Erie Canal (October 1982)
The Wright Brothers (December 1984)
The Newspaper (January 1985)

The US Postal Service (May 1985)
The Automobile in History (July 1987)
Salem and the East Indies Trade (September 1988)
The Magic of Radio (October 1988)
Tuning In to Television (October 1989)
The Mississippi River: Father of Waters (March 1990)
Amelia Earhart: Heroine of the Skies (July 1990)
Energy: Powering Our Nation (October 1990)
Back issues of the magazine can be obtained from Cobblestone Publishing
30 Grove Street, Peterborough, NH 03458.

◆   Fisher, Leonard Everett. ***Tracks Across America: The Story of the American Railroad, 1825-1900.*** Holiday, 1992. ISBN 0-8234-0945-7

■■■■■■■■□□□□□□

Using primary sources for photographs and quotes, Fisher provides us with the definitive children's book on the railroads, especially those of the nineteenth century. There is information on the role the railroads played in the Civil War, as well as the scandals and accidents involving railroads. Technical information about the engineering and physical science of railroads is clearly described and diagrammed.

◆   Freedman, Russell. ***The Wright Brothers: How They Invented the Airplane.*** Holiday, 1991. ISBN 0-8234-0875-2

■■■■■■■■□□□□□□

See page 120.

◆   Mitchell, Barbara. ***We'll Race You, Henry: A Story about Henry Ford.*** Carolrhoda, 1986. ISBN 0-87614-291-9

■■■■■■■□□□□□□□

See page 120.

◆   Reit, Seymour. ***Behind Rebel Lines: The Incredible Story of Emma Edmonds.*** Harcourt, 1988. ISBN 0-15-200424-6

■■■■■■■□□□□□□□

See page 82.

◆   St. George, Judith. ***The Brooklyn Bridge: They Said It Couldn't Be Done.*** Putnam, 1992. ISBN 0-399-61282-3

■■■■■■■■■■□□□□□

Conceived by John Augustus Roebling, a German immigrant, and carried to completion under the leadership of his son and daughter-in-law, the bridge was the greatest engineering feat of its day and succeeded in binding together the boroughs of Brooklyn and Manhattan but not without tremendous cost in lives and money. Although the book goes into great detail about the engineering and construction of the bridge, the text is surprisingly interesting and the drawings help explain the text.

◆ ———. *Dear Dr. Bell . . . Your Friend, Helen Keller.* Putnam, 1992. ISBN 399-223337-1

■■■■■■□□□□□□□□

While dealing with the lives and friendship of these two amazing people, the book reveals considerable information about the telephone, telegraph, lip-reading, manual alphabets, and teaching the deaf to speak.

Kent, Zachary. *The Story of Henry Ford and the Automobile.* Childrens, 1990. ISBN 0- 516-04751-5

■■■■■■■□□□□□□□

See page 121.

Kudlinski, Kathleen. *Helen Keller: Light for the Blind.* Viking, 1989. ISBN 0-14-032902-1

■■■■□□□□□□□□□□

See page 46.

McCall, Edith. *Biography of a River: The Living Mississippi.* Walker, 1990. ISBN 0-8027-6914-4

■■■■■□□□□□□□□□

See page 46.

St. George, Judith. *Panama Canal: Gateway to the World.* Putnam, 1989. ISBN 0-399-21637-5

■■■■■■■□□□□□□□

See page 223.

Stein, R. Conrad. *The Story of the Erie Canal.* Childrens, 1985. ISBN 0-516-0482-9

■■■■■■■□□□□□□□

See page 201.

Tessendorf, K. C. *Wings Around the World: The American World Flight of 1924.* Atheneum, 1991. ISBN 0-689-31550-3

■■■■■□□□□□□□□□

In 1924 eight members of the US Army Air Service used what little flight technology was available to circle the world in one hundred seventy-two days. Photographs accompany the text.

Nonprint

Videos

Golden Gate Bridge: The History and People of the World's Greatest Bridge. California Video.

The video uses interviews, art work, and film footage to show the four-year construction period of the bridge and then shows its fiftieth-anniversary celebration.

Cultures

Activities

- See Work and Workers on pages 106–117 for more activities and books about immigrants and cultures.

- List the cultures represented in your class.

- Discuss novels in which a major part of the plot is a character caught between cultures; for example, ***Julie of the Wolves*** (see page 132), ***Light in the Forest*** (page 64), ***I Am Regina*** (page191), ***Walk the World's Rim*** (page 108), and ***Squanto*** (page 256). What is each author's message?

- Make a calendar showing important days from diverse cultures.

- On a map of the United States, show places where various cultures have first made an impact. Find place names that reflect those cultures.

- Learn to say a simple phrase or conduct a simple conversation in at least three languages that are new to you.

- Find out whether your family or your ancestors ever experienced prejudice because of their nationality, religion, race, or culture. Is your family a victim of such prejudice now? Why?

- Contact any cultural organizations for public relations people to speak to your class and for any catalogs or promotional material.

- Celebrate diversity: play music from different cultures to begin the day, hold a multicultural banquet, learn songs and dances from various cultures, find dolls dressed in costumes of various cultures, display art from other countries, find books that reveal the cultures.

- Visit places of worship of as many religions as possible. Talk to the religious leaders about their beliefs and practices.

- Interview people from different religions. Ask them about the major tenets and practices of their religion. Make a chart showing ways in which the religions are alike. Can you construct at least one ethical statement that each person you talked to would agree with?

- List the different cultures represented in your area and then find out how many major cultures are represented. How might you make contact with them? How can you learn more about them.

- Develop skits and role-playing situations about people in cultures other than yours.

- Place the major immigrations into the US on a time line. Beneath it, place a time line showing major events in US history. Discuss how those events might have affected and concerned these groups.

- Find Cinderella stories from many cultures. Compare them and see whether they reveal what that culture admired.

- Make a contrast chart about cultures. Include art, food, religion, music, stories, family structure, ethics, and customs
- Find out about strong regional cultures that exist in America today. Which of them appear to have developed in the United States? Why and how did it happen?
- Which of your family's or culture's traditions do you most admire? Which do you hope your own children will continue? Which of another culture's values or traditions would you like to adopt?
- What in your home shows your culture?
- After reading and enjoying Byrd Baylor's *The Way to Start a Day* (see page 41) and *I'm in Charge of Celebrations* (Macmillan, 1986. ISBN 0-684-18579-2) list other celebrations. Choose one and work together on a picture book similar to Baylor's about the way different cultures might celebrate that ritual.

Picture Books

★ Anno, Mitsumasa. *Anno's USA.* Putnam, 1988. ISBN 0-399-21595-6

In this wordless book, a traveler begins at our West Coast and travels across the country, discovering our culture and our history.

★ Dragonwagon, Crescent. *Home Place.* Macmillan, 1990. ISBN 0-02-733190-3

See page 40.

★ Yolen, Jane. *Encounter.* Illustrated by David Shannon. Harcourt, 1992. ISBN 0-15-225962-7

See page 168.

◆ Baylor, Byrd. *The Best Town in the World.* Illustrated by Ronald Himler. Scribners, 1982. ISBN 0-684-18035-9

See page 34.

◆ Bruchac, Joseph, London, Jonathan, and Locker, Thomas. *Thirteen Moons on Turtle's Back: A Native American Year of Moons.* Philomel, 1992. ISBN 0-399-22141-7

This beautiful picture book depicts the thirteen moons of a Native American year. Each illustration is accompanied by a tale from a different tribe. While enjoying the stories and pictures, we get a glimpse of the Native Americans' reverence for the earth.

◆ Carlstrom, Nancy White. *Northern Lullaby.* Illustrated by Leo and Diane Dillon. Philomel, 1992. ISBN 0-399-21806-8

Breath-taking artwork celebrates an Alaskan night. We see figures in the mountains, rivers, trees, and lights of the far North and get a feeling for the things important to the people who live there.

◆ Hamanaka, Sheila. *The Journey.* Orchard, 1990. ISBN 0-531-08449-3

See page 147.

◆ Kendall, Russ. ***Eskimo Boy: Life in an Inupiaq Eskimo Village.*** Scholastic, 1992. ISBN 0-590-43695-3

This photographic essay concentrates on one young boy in the village and shows his daily life and dreams, giving us a closer look at an isolated culture that is impacted less by white cultures than most. As good as the bulk of the book is, there is even more useful information in the afterword that briefly chronicles the history of the native Alaskan cultures.

◆ Rylant, Cynthia. ***Appalachia: The Voices of Sleeping Birds.*** Illustrated by Barry Moser. Harcourt, 1991. ISBN 0-15-201605-8
See page 35.

◆ Say, Allen. ***El Chino.*** Houghton, 1990. ISBN 0-395-52023-1

The hero of this picture book biography, Billy Wong, the Chinese-American son of a grocer, has been told over and over that he can be anything he wants to be. He tries playing basketball but has neither the height nor the talent. After a visit to a bullring in Spain, however, he knows. He needs to be a bullfighter. At first he tries to hide his Chinese identity. It isn't until he takes pride in what he is—a Chinese-American bullfighter—that he succeeds.

◆ Spier, Peter. ***People.*** Doubleday, 1980. ISBN 0-385-13181-X

Although this book does contain some unfortunate stereotypes, it gives a global and pictorial look at cultures around the world. The stereotypes themselves can provide a point for discussion.

◆ ———. ***We the People: The Constitution of the United States of America.*** Doubleday, 1987. ISBN 0-385-23589-5

Careful examination of the pictures clarifies the meaning of the Preamble to the Constitution. The illustrations provide an excellent starting point for a study of cultures in the United States.

Aylesworth, Jim. ***The Folks in the Valley: A Pennsylvania Dutch ABC.*** Illustrated by Stefano Vitale. HarperCollins, 1992. ISBN 0-06-021929-7
This alphabet book is based on the Pennsylvania Dutch culture and furnishes some information about the Pennsylvania Dutch people.

Baylor, Byrd. ***The Way to Start a Day.*** Illustrated by Peter Parnall. Scribner, 1978. ISBN 0-689-71054-2
See page 41.

Cornish, Sam. ***Grandmother's Pictures.*** Illustrated by Jeanne Johns. Bradbury, 1974. ISBN 0-87888-092-5
A young Black child visits his grandmother who lives alone. She shows him her photograph album and tells the stories—not all pleasant—behind the pictures

Croll, Carolyn. ***The Three Brothers.*** Putnam, 1991. ISBN 0-399-22195-6
In a Pennsylvania Dutch setting, the author tells a traditional tale from Germany and in the process gives us a glimpse of the Pennsylvania Dutch culture.

Ernst, Lisa Campbell. ***Sam Johnson and the Blue Ribbon Quilt.*** Mulberry, 1992. ISBN 0-688-11505-5

Sam Johnson, rejected by his wife's quilting club because of his gender, forms a men's quilting club. Both clubs compete for best quilt in a local contest. After both quilts are soiled, the two clubs combine the unsoiled sections of each quilt to make a new pattern. The custom of quilting, the folk quilt patterns that frame each page, and the steps in quilting are all described in the book.

Faber, Doris. ***The Amish.*** Doubleday, 1991. ISBN 0-385-26130-6

Starting with the emigration of the Amish from Europe in the 1700s and proceeding through the complicated legal issues since 1950, the author uses a picture book format with realistic scenes of Amish life.

Friedman, Ina R. ***How My Parents Learned to Eat.*** Illustrated by Allen Say. Houghton, 1984. ISBN 0-395-44235-4

An American sailor meets and falls in love with a young Japanese woman and somehow they adjust to each other's culture—at least as far as eating is concerned—in this picture book narrated by the couple's daughter.

Kesey, Ken. ***The Sea Lion: A Story of the Sea Cliff People.*** Viking, 1991. ISBN 0-670-83916-7

A pourquoi tale, this story tells of a crippled Indian boy in the Pacific Northwest who sets himself against an evil sea spirit to win the respect of his tribe. The tale reveals many of the values and traditions of the Native American people.

Kuklin, Susan. ***How My Family Lives in America.*** Bradbury, 1992. ISBN 0-02-751239-8

The book deals with the lives of three children: an African American, a Hispanic American, and a Chinese American. A parent of each child was born in another country and the families want to preserve their heritage.

Mendez, Phil. ***The Black Snowman.*** Illustrated by Carole Byard. Scholastic, 1989. ISBN 0-590-40552-7

This story begins in Africa with an aged storyteller of the Ashanti tribe and his magic kente cloth. After the village is invaded and slaves are taken to America, the kente makes its way to America. Now only a rag, it is discovered by two boys in contemporary America who use it for their snowman. The snowman comes to life and brings the older boy a vital demonstration of his vast and proud heritage.

Fiction

★ Baker, Betty. ***Walk the World's Rim.*** HarperCollins, 1965. ISBN 0-06-020381-1

■■■■■■■□□□□□□□

Least Sophisticated   Most Sophisticated

See page 163.

★ Hurmence, Belinda. ***A Girl Called Boy.*** Houghton, 1982. ISBN 0-395-31022-9

■■■■■■■■■□□□□□

See page 36.

★ O'Dell, Scott. *Island of the Blue Dolphins.* Houghton-Mifflin, 1960. ISBN 0-395-06962-9

■■■■■■■■□□□□□□

Karana lives with her family in a village on the Island of the Blue Dolphins. Aleuts, led by a Russian captain, come to hunt sea otters and betray the villagers, killing many of the men, including Karana's father. The new chief decides to relocate the village on the far-away mainland, and so the island is evacuated. Karana's younger brother, Ramo, is left behind and Karana jumps overboard to be with him, convinced that the ship will return for them soon. Ramo is killed by wild dogs and Karana is left to survive alone. She first wounds and then befriends the leader of a wild dog pack. For more ideas about this book, see **Long Ago and Far Away** *(DLM, 1991. ISBN 1-55924-556-5).*

★ Spinka, Penina Keen. *Mother's Blessing.* Atheneum, 1992. ISBN 0-689-31758-1

■■■■■■■■■■■□□□□

See page 55.

★ Wunderli, Stephen. *The Blue Between the Clouds.* Holt, 1992. ISBN 0-800-1772-0

■■■■■■■□□□□□□□

This is a Focus Book about a friendship between an Indian boy and a white boy growing up in Utah in the 1940s. The treatment of the Indian ceremonies and beliefs is quite respectful and informative. This is a Focus Book; see page 293.

◆ Gilman, Dorothy. *Girl in Buckskin.* Ballantine, 1956. ISBN 0-449-70380-0

■■■■■■■■■■□□□□□

See page 65.

◆ George, Jean Craighead. *Julie of the Wolves.* HarperCollins, 1972. ISBN 0-06-021944-0

————. *Julie y los lobos.* Hispanic Book Distributors.

■■■■■■■■■■□□□□□

Julie has run from her new and much older husband's unwanted attentions to get to a pen pal's home in San Francisco. She gets lost on the Alaskan tundra without food or shelter. Julie studies the behavior of a wolf pack and gains acceptance in order to survive. In the process, she turns toward the more traditional Eskimo ways. For more ideas about this book see **Long Ago and Far Away** *(DLM, 1991. ISBN 1-55924-556-5).*

◆ Greenfield, Eloise. *Sister.* HarperCollins, 1974. ISBN 0-06-440199-5

■■■■■■□□□□□□□□

See page 42.

◆ Little, Jean. *Listen for the Singing.* HarperCollins, 1991. ISBN 0-06-023910-7
See page 235.

◆ Pettit, Jayne. *My Name Is San Ho.* Scholastic, 1992. ISBN 0-590-44172-8

■■■■■■■■■■□□□□

San Ho's mother came to America and married before she and San Ho were reunited. San Ho's acculturation process is well told.

◆ Rogers, Jean. ***Goodbye My Island.*** Greenwillow, 1983. ISBN 0-688-01965-X

■■■■■■■□□□□□□□

This is a first person account of Eskimo life on a small island ninety miles from Nome. Because of the Eskimos' dwindling numbers, the Bureau of Indian Affairs has decided to close the school. Without a school, everyone knows that the last hold-out families cannot stay on the island. In the process of telling about the last year on the island, the author tells us much about Eskimo culture.

◆ Uchida, Yoshiko. ***The Best Bad Thing.*** Aladdin, 1983. ISBN 0-689-50290-7

■■■■■■■■■■□□□□

The story takes place in the Bay Area of California during the thirties. Much against her will, Rinko is sent to help out Mrs. Hata, a widow with three children trying to eke out a living raising and selling cucumbers. There is much information about Japanese-American culture. The tensions between cultures is touched upon as well. This is the sequel to ***A Jar of Dreams*** *(see page 149).*

Barrie, Barbara. ***Lone Star.*** Delacorte, 1990. ISBN 0-385-30156-1

■■■■■■■■■■□□□□

See page 236.

De Trevino, Elizabeth Borton. ***El Guero.*** Sunburst, 1989. ISBN 0-374-31995-2

■■■■■■■□□□□□□□

This fact-based story about a turn-of-the-century Mexican youth's daring attempt to free his father from an unjust imprisonment contains substantial information about the Mexican culture and beliefs of the time. See page 219.

Feelings, Tom. ***Tommy Traveller in the World of Black History.*** Black Butterfly, 1991. ISBN 0-86316-202-9

■■■■■■□□□□□□□□

In comic strip format, this book concentrates on six Black people whose roles in history vary from major to minor. The author's aim is to instill pride in the accomplishments of the past. Although the book is often simplistic, it fulfills a need.

Hamilton, Virginia. ***The Bells of Christmas.*** Harcourt, 1989. ISBN 0-15-206450-8

■■■■■■□□□□□□□□

See page 220.

Joseph, Lynn. ***A Wave in Her Pocket: Stories from Trinidad.*** Clarion, 1991. ISBN 0-395-54432-7

■■■■■□□□□□□□□□

Although this is an island culture's stories, the book is cited here because of the relationship between Amber and her grand-aunt who tells the stories of her past and of the island on which they live.

Robinson, Margaret. *A Woman of Her Tribe.* Scribner, 1990. ISBN 0-684-19223-3

■■■■■■■■■■■■■□

Annette Broadhead is half-English and half-Nootka Indian and has lived all her life in the Nootka village. When she is offered a scholarship to the academy, her mother is pleased that Annette will learn about the other half of her heritage. Soon Annette faces difficult choices as the white culture overwhelms her. At the same time, she is training for the women's initiation rites of her tribe. The theme of conflicting cultures and loyalties is well handled in this coming-of-age novel.

Tate, Eleanora E. *Thank You, Dr. Martin Luther King!* Watts, 1990.
ISBN 0-551-15151-4

■■■■■■■■□□□□□□□

This novel recounts the search for her African-American identity by fourth grader, Mary Elouise, a most unwilling searcher. Throughout most of the story, Mary Elouise negates her African heritage and is embarrassed when teachers mention the subject. There is some reason for her discomfort because some of the teachers in this South Carolina school, although probably well-meaning, are themselves ignorant of many of the facts about Black heritage. Although the book at times becomes didactic, there is a great deal of information about African cultures and about the ample reasons for Black pride.

Nonfiction

◆ ***Cobblestone Magazine***

The following issues of the magazine were devoted to this subject:
Philadelphia Mummers (January 1980)
Genealogy (November 1980)
Old Time Schools (November 1981)
Old Sturbridge Village (February 1982)
California History (May 1982)
Immigrants: Part 1 (December 1982)
Immigrants: Part 2 (January 1983)
Black History Month (February 1983)
Shakers (April 1983)
Archaeology (June 1983)
Folklore (July 1983)
Jazz (October 1983)
Libraries (November 1983)
The Cherokee Indians (February 1984)
Chautauqua (July 1984)
The Olympic Games (August 1984)
Who Came to America (October 1984)
Baseball (July 1985)
American Clothing (October 1985)
Eskimos (November 1985)
Mexico and the United States (March 1986)
American Fads (July 1986)
Music from the 1950s (August 1986)

Witchcraft (October 1986)
Children's Toys (December 1986)
The Amish (November 1987)
The American Theater (December 1987)
Canada and the United States (March 1988)
American Architecture (August 1988)
The Magic of Radio (October 1988)
Hispanic Americans (April 1989)
People with Disabilities (June 1989)
Dine: The People of the Navajo Nation (July 1989)
Pilgrims to a New World (November 1989)
Norman Rockwell (December 1989)
The People of Williamsburg (February 1990)
America's Zoos (August 1990)
Joseph, a Chief of the Nez Percé (September 1990)
Hawaii (December 1990)
Back issues of the magazine can be obtained from Cobblestone Publishing, 30 Grove Street, Peterborough, NH 03458.

◆ Ehrlich, Amy. ***Wounded Knee: An Indian History of the American West.*** Adapted from Dee Brown's *Bury My Heart at Wounded Knee*. Holt, 1974. ISBN 0-440-95768-0

This well-edited text tells of the Navajo, Apache, Cheyenne, and Sioux Indians' struggle against the settlers of the West from 1860 to 1890.

◆ Ferris, Jeri. ***Native American Doctor: The Story of Susan LaFlesche Picotte.*** Carolrhoda, 1991. ISBN 0-887614-443-1

Susan LaFlesche Picotte was born in Nebraska in 1865, the daughter of Chief Iron Eye, a bi-racial Omaha Indian. Susan went East to school and then entered a women's medical school in Philadelphia. She served as the unofficial chief of her reservation and fought political battles in Washington, winning, among other things, the Indians' right to control their own money and property. She fought the abuse of alcohol and worked towards her dream of a hospital on the reservation. This book allows us a more personal view of the Native Americans' efforts to cope with the devastation brought by Western society. In contrast to Indians who wanted to preserve the Indian way of life, Susan wanted her people to adopt Christianity and farming.

◆ Freedman, Russell. ***Immigrant Kids.*** Dutton, 1980. ISBN 0-525-32538-7

Early twentieth-century New York City is brought to life by period photographs and first person accounts of immigrant children of the time.

◆ Houston, Jeanne Wakatsuki and Houston, James D. ***Farewell to Manzanar.*** Bantam, 1989. ISBN 0-553-23692-X

See page 236.

◆ Pinchot, Jane. ***The Mexicans in America.*** Lerner, 1989. ISBN 0-8225-022-4

■■■■■■■■■□□□□□□

This book contains a great deal of well-illustrated historical information and traces the history of Mexico and the United States from pre-Mayan days to the present. Of course, it also celebrates the culture of the Mexican-American people and stresses their contributions to the American language and culture. The last chapter provides photographs and brief biographies of many sports, political, and artistic figures from the Mexican-American population.

◆ Randolph, Sallie and Bolick, Nancy. ***Shaker Inventions.*** Walker, 1990. ISBN 0-8027-6934-9

■■■■■■■■■■□□□□□

See page 120.

◆ Uchida, Yoshiko. ***The Invisible Thread.*** Messner, 1992. ISBN 0-671-74164-0

■■■■■■■■■■■■□□□

Uchida has written several fiction books about the Japanese-American culture (see pages 133, 149, 235). In this book she tells her story: growing up in Berkeley, experiencing suspicion, prejudice, and imprisonment during World War II, and then visiting Japan in the 1930s where she was also in conflict with the culture. At last she comes to grips with her cultural background. The book is well illustrated and provides an interesting author study.

Beyer, Don E. ***The Totem Pole Indians of the Northwest.*** Watts, 1989. ISBN 0-531-10750-7

■■■■■■■■■■□□□□□

This book describes the seven primary Indian tribes of the Northwest. It also covers the Indians' first contact with whites, the world of humans and spirits, life in the village, and living with white people.

Claro, Nicole. ***The Cherokee Indians.*** Chelsea, 1991. ISBN 0-7910-1652-8

■■■■■■■□□□□□□□□

The changing ways of the Cherokee, especially since the arrival of Europeans, is outlined with a straightforward although not compelling text.

Doherty, Craig and Doherty, Katherine. ***The Apaches and Navajos.*** Watts, 1989. ISBN 0-531-15607-9

■■■■■■■■■■□□□□□

Illustrated with photographs of artifacts, handwork, drawings, and maps, this rather dry text describes the two tribes that are part of the Athapaskan Pueblo culture from their early history to their present-day existence. Although the material lacks color, it could be a useful information source.

Finkelstein, Norman. ***The Other Fourteen Ninety-Two: Jewish Settlement in the New World.*** Scribner, 1989. ISBN 0-684-18913-1

■■■■■■■■■■□□□□□

Although the book does cover the immigration and contributions of Jews to America, it also recounts much of their previous history. Because a history of the

Jews is, to a large extent, a history of the world, this book covers an amazing amount of time and events in a fairly small space. The text is clear with many illustrations. Although much of the history will be familiar to Jews with a strong traditional and religious background, for those who are not Jewish, there is new and interesting information.

Herda, D. J. ***Ethnic America: The North Central States.*** Millbrook, 1991. ISBN 1-56294-016-3

————. ***Ethnic America: The Northeastern States.*** Millbrook, 1991. ISBN 1-56294-014-7

————. ***Ethnic America: The Northwestern States.*** Millbrook, 1991. ISBN 1-56294-018-X

————. ***Ethnic America: The South Central States.*** Millbrook, 1991. ISBN 1-56294-017-1

————. ***Ethnic America: The Southeastern States.*** Millbrook, 1991. ISBN 1-56294-015-5

————. ***Ethnic America: The Southwestern States.*** Millbrook, 1991. ISBN 1-56294-019-8

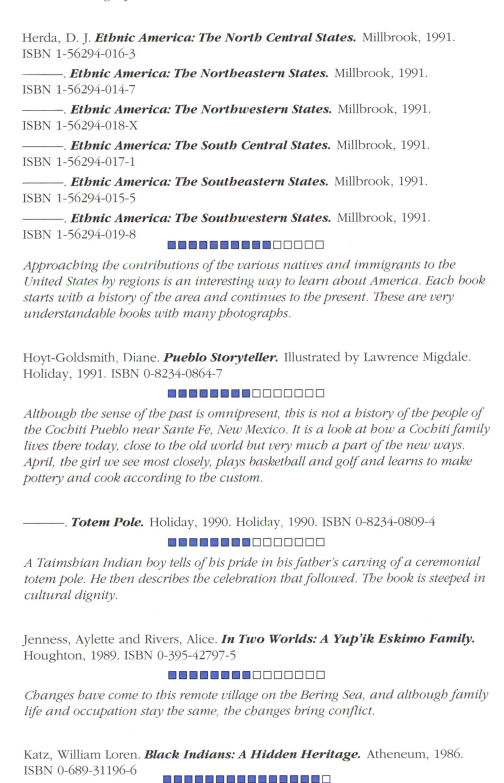

■■■■■■■■■□□□□□

Approaching the contributions of the various natives and immigrants to the United States by regions is an interesting way to learn about America. Each book starts with a history of the area and continues to the present. These are very understandable books with many photographs.

Hoyt-Goldsmith, Diane. ***Pueblo Storyteller.*** Illustrated by Lawrence Migdale. Holiday, 1991. ISBN 0-8234-0864-7

■■■■■■■■□□□□□□

Although the sense of the past is omnipresent, this is not a history of the people of the Cochiti Pueblo near Sante Fe, New Mexico. It is a look at how a Cochiti family lives there today, close to the old world but very much a part of the new ways. April, the girl we see most closely, plays basketball and golf and learns to make pottery and cook according to the custom.

————. ***Totem Pole.*** Holiday, 1990. Holiday, 1990. ISBN 0-8234-0809-4

■■■■■■■■□□□□□□

A Taimshian Indian boy tells of his pride in his father's carving of a ceremonial totem pole. He then describes the celebration that followed. The book is steeped in cultural dignity.

Jenness, Aylette and Rivers, Alice. ***In Two Worlds: A Yup'ik Eskimo Family.*** Houghton, 1989. ISBN 0-395-42797-5

■■■■■■■■□□□□□□

Changes have come to this remote village on the Bering Sea, and although family life and occupation stay the same, the changes bring conflict.

Katz, William Loren. ***Black Indians: A Hidden Heritage.*** Atheneum, 1986. ISBN 0-689-31196-6

■■■■■■■■■■■■■■□

See page 46.

Lankford, Mary D. *Hopscotch Around the World.* Morrow, 1992.
ISBN 0-688-08420-6 ■■■■■■□□□□□□□□

Although this is not strictly a history book, we've included it because it's fascinating and because it reminds us that a history of games is a useful strand to follow.

Larsen, Ronald J. *The Puerto Ricans in America.* Lerner, 1989.
ISBN 0-8225-0238-0 ■■■■■■□□□□□□□□

Beginning with the devastation of the native Arawaks by Ponce de León, this book concisely chronicles the history of the island and of the people who immigrated to the mainland from the island. The book does not glorify their lives here; there is coverage of the poverty and exploitation as well as the drugs, crime, and gang warfare that continue to wreak havoc on the people. Its final chapter talks about the contributions made by some of the immigrants.

Lee, Martin. *The Seminoles.* Watts, 1989. ISBN 0-531-15604-4
■■■■■■■■■■□□□□□

The constant relocation of the Seminoles is covered in this book that includes chapters on war, life on the hammocks, the Seminole way, and some information on modern Seminole life. This book is a bit less dry than others in the series.

McGovern, Ann. *If You Lived with the Sioux Indians.* Scholastic, 1972. ISBN 0- 590-41683-9 ■■■■■□□□□□□□□□

This book details daily life for the Sioux in the Dakotas before 1850. It addresses many misconceptions about Indian life. There is a brief section on Sioux life today.

Porter, A. P. *Kwanzaa.* Carolrhoda, 1991. ISBN 0-87614-668-X

■■■■■□□□□□□□□□

This is an explanation of the African-American holiday conceived by Maulana Karenga to remind his people of their rich heritage. The book includes an explanation of the symbols and rituals of the holiday.

Rutledge, Paul. *The Vietnamese in America.* Lerner, 1987. ISBN 0-8225-0235-6
■■■■■■■□□□□□□□

The author traces the ethnic background of the people currently called Vietnamese, briefly summarizes the history of their country, including the Vietnam War, and then concentrates on the lives of the Vietnamese who came to the United States.

Shorto, Russell. *Tecumseh and the Dream of an American Indian Nation.*
Silver Burdett, 1989. ISBN 0-382-09569-3

■■■■■■■■□□□□□□
See page 201.

Smith, Carter. *Native Americans of the West.* Millbrook, 1992.
ISBN 1-56294-131-3 ■■■■■■■■□□□□□□
See page 63.

Sonneborn, Liz. ***The Cheyenne Indians.*** Chelsea, 1992. ISBN 0-7910-1654-4

■■■■■■■■□□□□□□

Part of a series, this book is weak on current Cheyenne life but very strong on life of that tribe during the 1800s. It begins in 1740 and the arrival of horses on the plains, which changed the Indian way of life. The book describes customs and the history of the Cheyenne people, chronicling their interactions with other Indian nations and with the whites and the United States government. The book includes a time line of Cheyenne history.

Wolfson, Evelyn. ***From Abenaki to Zuni: A Dictionary of Native American Tribes.*** Walker, 1988. ISBN 0-8027-6789-3

■■■■■■■■□□□□□□

The information is clear and, although inclined to be superficial, there is a fund of information here and an ample source of ideas for further research.

Yates, Janelle. ***Zora Neale Hurston.*** Ward Hill Press, 1991. ISBN 0-9623380-7-9

■■■■■■■■□□□□□□

Rising out of tragedy and poverty, Zora Neale Hurston used her academic skills to carve a life for herself. Born and raised in central Florida, she moved to Harlem and became a figure in the Harlem Renaissance of 1919 through 1930. Her career included collecting African-American folklore, writing plays and novels, and storytelling.

Nonprint

Videos

American Patchwork: Songs and Stories about America: Cajun Country. PBS Video, 1990.

Folklorist Alan Lomax hosts this video about the Cajun culture, which includes a Mardi Gras celebration. Old photographs and engravings are used to show the lives of the Acadians in Canada before their forced exile to Louisiana. Their music shows their traditions and their spirit.

Chicano Park. Cinema Guild, 1989.

The park is beneath the Coronado Bridge in San Diego. With the park as a central point, we see the changes in a Chicano community from the Great Depression to 1970. Barrio Logan is shown as a thriving community, and the film focuses on Chicano achievements and pride.

From My Grandmother's Grandmother Unto Me. Cinema Guild, 1990.

See page 47.

Audios

Listening for the Crack of Dawn. August House Audio, 1991.

Storyteller Donald Davis tells four stories about Appalachia in the 1950s. The tapes are entertaining and are also good examples of oral history gathering.

Politics and Government

Activities

- The period from 1751 to 1800 was a time of formation for many governments. See 1751-1800 in the Chronology section for activities that explore and contrast those governments (page 188).

- What rules govern your classroom? Who made them? Which are essential? Which could you most easily do without? What would happen if there were no rules? Could someone else make up new rules? Do all classrooms need the same rules?

- Investigate what it costs to run for political office at the local, state, and federal levels. Can anyone in your family afford it? Where would the money come from? What is it used for?

- Interview local politicians about their job, their election, and what they recommend changing about the way the political system works. Do they think their last campaigns were fair?

- Interview politicians about what they expected to achieve and what they actually achieved. Are there factors involved that they didn't know about before they began?

- Talk to politicians in your community. Ask them whether they were elected or appointed and for how long. Ask them who they are responsible to and what their duties are. Use large cards on a moveable surface to show that organizational set-up. Do the same for all the jobs in your local government. Interrelate the organizational set-ups until you have a chart of the organization of government within your community, as described by the people you interviewed. Check to see how accurate your chart is.

- Make a list of some organizations in your area, such as the PTA, the school board, the Grange, a cooperative bank, or an arts council. Find out about their governing structures.

- Find out what other ways of structuring democracy were investigated by the founding fathers before they decided on the current structure. See Jean Fritz's ***The Great Little Madison*** (page 268), Natalie Bober's ***Thomas Jefferson: Man on a Mountain*** (page 193), and other books listed in The New Nation (page 188).

- Chart the distinct powers of the three branches of our federal government. What would be the consequences of moving some of the powers to a different branch?

- Read biographies of members of the Supreme Court, including an early justice such as John Marshall, a more recent one such as Earl Warren and a current one such as Sandra Day O'Connor. Have the qualifications for the position or the stature of the justices changed over the years?

- Find out how the government serves as a protective body. Investigate such groups as the Food and Drug Administration, OSHA, and the National Park Service. How and why were they organized? Do they currently have the power they had when they were created? How effective have they been? To whom are they responsible?

- How does a law change? Who decides? What is the process?

- Consider an action the government has taken recently. How does your family feel about it? What can they do about it?

- Write a letter to someone in government about a matter you feel strongly about. Is there something you want done about it? Ask for a reply and information.

- Investigate the career of a social activist such as Henry Thoreau, Martin Luther King, Jr., Ralph Nader, Rachel Carson, or Phyllis Schaffly. What was each person's most effective action? What passions drove them? What vehicles and methods did they use? What organizations supported them?

- Create a puppet show of one of the early governmental organization meetings.

- Compare the corruption described in Gail B. Stewart's book **What Happened to Judge Crater?** (see page 143) with that involving other public figures in the past and present? Why is government so vulnerable to corruption and what kinds of things are people doing to prevent it?

- Select any political period and, using a web, show how the various political figures during that time interacted with each other, how they felt about each other, which had common goals, and which were working in opposite directions.

Picture Books

◆ Spier, Peter. **We the People: The Constitution of the United States of America.** Doubleday, 1987. ISBN 0-385-23589-5

Starting with a map of the United States in 1787, including insets for Boston, Savannah, Philadelphia, and New York City, the book goes on to crowd a treasure of usable and accessible information into a few pages. The history of the Constitutional Convention is presented in a few pages and the Preamble to the Constitution is illustrated with Spier's minute watercolors, presenting a contrast between civilization then and now. He goes on to show cultures and activities in present-day United States. Careful examination of the pictures clarifies the meaning of the Preamble.

◆ Provensen, Alice. **The Buck Stops Here: The Presidents of the United States.** HarperCollins, 1990. ISBN 0-06-024787-8

See page 41.

Fiction

★ Avi. **Nothing But the Truth.** Orchard, 1991. ISBN 0-531-08559-7

Least Sophisticated   Most Sophisticated

Subtitled "A Documentary Novel," this book is almost guaranteed to provoke discussion; certainly the incident around which the book revolves did so. We follow the plot through a series of documents—memos, journal entries, newspapers, talk show stories, and written conversations—as a simple incident grows. The truth is that a ninth-grade student, annoyed by a teacher's perceived inflexibility, decides to annoy her in turn by humming the National Anthem when it is played over the loud speaker during opening exercises even though the rule states that students should "stand at respectful silent attention." The teacher, a sincere and dedicated woman, rises to the bait and throws the kid out of her class. From then on things just grow vastly out of proportion. Has the right of free speech been violated or abused? The results are calamitous for both teacher and student. Who's wrong?

★ Spinka, Penina Keen. ***Mother's Blessing.*** Atheneum, 1992. ISBN 0-689-31758-1

■■■■■■■■■■□□□□

See page 55.

◆ Reeder, Carolyn. ***Grandpa's Mountain.*** Macmillan, 1991. ISBN 0-02-775811-7

■■■■■■■□□□□□□□

See page 228.

◆ Uchida, Yoshiko. ***The Journey Home.*** Macmillan, 1978. ISBN 0-689-50126-9

■■■■■■■■■■□□□□□

See page 235.

Oneal, Zibby. ***A Long Way to Go.*** Viking, 1990. ISBN 0-670-82532-8

■■■■■□□□□□□□□□

See page 229.

Nonfiction

◆ ***Cobblestone Magazine***

The following issues of the magazine were devoted to this subject:
Presidential Elections (October 1980)
The Constitution (September 1982)
Public Works (August 1983)
Visions of America's Future (January 1984)
The Cherokee Indians (February 1984)
Starting a Nation (September 1984)
The US Senate (November 1984)
The US and the USSR (February 1985)
Susan B. Anthony and the Women's Movement (March 1985)
The US Postal Service (May 1985)
The US Mint (September 1985)
Mexico and the United States (March 1986)
Eleanor Roosevelt (November 1986)
Great Debates (January 1987)
Alexander Hamilton (March 1987)
The Civil War: Reconstruction (May 1987)
Celebrating Our Constitution (September 1987)
Canada and the United States (March 1988)
The Two Party System (November 1988)
Frederick Douglass: Fighter for Freedom (February 1989)
Important Supreme Court Cases (March 1989)
Environmentalism (August 1989)
Thomas Jefferson (September 1989
Energy: Powering Our Nation (October 1990)
Hawaii (December 1990)
George Washington (April 1992)

◆   Force, Eden. ***John Muir.*** Silver Burdett, 1990. ISBN 0-382-09965-6

■■■■■■■■■■■□□□□

See page 211.

◆   Fritz, Jean. ***Shhh! We're Writing the Constitution.*** Putnam, 1987.
ISBN 0-399-21403-8

■■■■■□□□□□□□□□□

See page 192.

◆   Levine, Ellen. ***If You Lived at the Time of Martin Luther King.*** Scholastic,
1990. ISBN 0-590-42582-X

■■■■■□□□□□□□□□□

See page 98.

◆   Rubel, David. ***Fanny Lou Hamer: From Share Cropping to Politics.*** Silver
Burdett, 1990. ISBN 0-382-09923-0

■■■■■■■■■■■□□□□

See page 99.

◆   Stern, Philip Van Doren. ***Henry David Thoreau: Writer and Rebel.*** Crowell,
1972. ISBN 0-690-37715-0

■■■■■■■■■■□□□□

See pages 58 and 77.

◆   Stewart, Gail B. ***What Happened to Judge Crater?*** Crestwood, 1992.
ISBN 0-89686-617-3

■■■■■■□□□□□□□□□

*This book explores the disappearance of Judge Crater, a state Supreme Court
justice in New York in 1930. Speculations about his disappearance included
charges of corruption and the idea that he might have been killed because he
knew too much. Investigating the mysteries of history is an effective way of
involving some students.*

◆   Wheeler, Leslie. ***Jane Addams.*** Silver Burdett, 1990. ISBN 0-382-09968-0

■■■■■■■■■■□□□□

See page 58.

Bober, Natalie S. ***Thomas Jefferson: Man on a Mountain.*** Atheneum, 1988.
ISBN 0-689-31154-0

■■■■■■■■■■■■■□

See page 193.

Durwood, Thomas. ***John C. Calhoun and the Roots of War.*** Silver Burdett,
1991. ISBN 0-382-24045-6

■■■■■■■■■□□□□□

See page 83.

Evans, J. Edward. **Freedom of Speech.** Lerner, 1990. ISBN 0-8225-1753-1

■■■■■■■■□□□□□□□

After tracing the history of censorship, the author goes on to show the development of the article in the Bill of Rights that protects free speech. He then tells of the times in our history that freedom of speech has been curtailed.

Foster, Leila. **The Story of the Great Society.** Childrens, 1991. ISBN 0-516-04755-8

■■■■■■□□□□□□□□□

See page 246.

Freedman, Russell. **Franklin Delano Roosevelt.** Clarion, 1990. ISBN 0-89919-379-X

■■■■■■■■■■□□□□□

See page 237.

Harrison, Barbara and Terris, Daniel. **A Twilight Struggle: The Life of John Fitzgerald Kennedy.** Lothrop, 1992. ISBN 0-688-08830-9

■■■■■■■■■■□□□□□

Unlike many biographies of political figures, this book is not an adulatory one. It presents a balanced figure of the man, including his dilemmas, his shortcomings, his political compromises, his charm, and his accomplishments. We also see that he lacked a clear commitment to desegregation until it was politically expedient.

Jacobs, William Jay. **Abraham Lincoln.** Scribner, 1991. ISBN 0-684-19274-8

■■■■■■□□□□□□□□□

Focusing on Lincoln's great resolve and ambition, this accessible biography shows how Lincoln's ideals controlled his actions in governing the country. The details are manageable for some less able readers, without being unnecessarily simplistic.

———. **George Washington.** Scribner, 1991. ISBN 0-684-19275-6

■■■■■■□□□□□□□□□

This is a book from which less able readers can extract a good deal of information. The book does not glorify Washington, but does show how he could have chosen to remain a wealthy gentleman farmer instead of devoting his life to leading a new nation.

Kent, Zachary. **John Quincy Adams, Sixth President of the United States.** Childrens, 1987. ISBN 0-516-01386-6

■■■■■□□□□□□□□□□

See page 193.

———. **The Story of the Peace Corps.** Childrens, 1990. ISBN 0-516-04752-3

■■■■■■□□□□□□□□□

See page 246.

Larsen, Anita. **The Rosenbergs.** Crestwood, 1992. ISBN 0-89686-612-2

■■■■■■□□□□□□□□□

See page 241.

McKissack, Patricia. ***Jesse Jackson: A Biography.*** Scholastic, 1989. ISBN 0-590-43181-1

■■■■■■■■■□□□□□

The tone is sometimes a bit too worshipful; however, the facts are here and the life of the Civil Rights worker who became the first African American to run for president is simple and interesting.

Pious, Richard M. ***Richard Nixon: A Political Life.*** Messner, 1991. ISBN 0-671-72852-0

■■■■■■□□□□□□□

See page 252.

Quackenbush, Robert. ***Pass the Quill, I'll Write a Draft: A Story of Thomas Jefferson.*** Pippin, 1989. ISBN 0-945912-07-2

■■■■■□□□□□□□□

See page 74.

Sandak, Cass R. ***The Franklin Roosevelts.*** Crestwood, 1992. ISBN 0-89686-639-4

■■■■■■■□□□□□□

See page 231.

———. ***The Jacksons.*** Crestwood, 1992. ISBN 0-89686-636-X

■■■■■■■□□□□□□

See page 201.

———. ***The Nixons.*** Crestwood, 1992. ISBN 0-89686-638-6

■■■■■■■□□□□□□

See page 253.

Shorto, Russell. ***Tecumseh and the Dream of an American Indian Nation.*** Silver Burdett, 1989. ISBN 0-382-09569-3

■■■■■■■■□□□□□

See page 201.

Nonprint

Videos

Bill of Rights. Coronet.

A sudden gust of wind interrupts a professor's boring lecture and brings in a lively introduction to the writers of the Bill of Rights in 1787. The video gives background about the effect of the amendments on American lives then and now.

Congress: What It Is, How It Works and How It Affects You. Center for Humanities.

This video tape includes historic artwork and explains how Congress works and covers the history of "minor disputes and outright battles" among the branches of the government.

Racism, Sexism, and Equality

Activities

- See also Work and Workers, Civil Rights Movement, and specific time periods.

- Design a survey about the changes that people perceive to have occurred in racism and sexism over time. Conduct the survey. Tabulate your results.

- Prepare a time line showing how and when changes in racism and sexism occurred. Include such matters as suffrage, career opportunities, desegregation, Jim Crow laws, and property rights.

- Research the history of the Ku Klux Klan. How is it perceived today? Has our perception changed over the years? Is the Klan active in your community today? Why?

- Research the history of the Nazi movement. How is it perceived today? Has our perception changed over the years? Is the Nazi movement active in your community today? Why?

- Research the history of the NAACP. How is it perceived today? Has our perception changed over the years? Is the NAACP active in your community today? Why?

- Chart the information from the three preceding activities and similar ones for other organizations into the following categories: Current Goals, Current Activities, Long Range Goals, and Community Effect.

- Think about a cultural or racial group that is currently under attack. Find out all you can about that group: its heritage, population, culture, values, or anything else that will help you understand them. Find similarities to your own culture.

- Consider a group against whom you feel some prejudice. Find out all you can about that group: its heritage, population, culture, values, or anything else that will help you understand them. Find similarities to your own culture. What contributed to your prejudice?

- Read a novel published during the 1950s, such as **Henry and Beezus** by Beverly Cleary (Morrow, 1952. ISBN 0-688-31383-3). Jot down examples of Mrs. Huggins's role in the family. Do the same for a book like **Anastasia Krupnik** by Lois Lowry (Houghton-Mifflin, 1979. ISBN 0-395-28629-8). Are the attitudes reflected in these two books parallel to the attitude changes in our society?

- Find statistics to show how women's roles have changed since 1900.

- Read the picture book **Piggybook** by Anthony Browne (Knopf, 1986. ISBN 0-394-98416-1) to people of a variety of ages and both genders. Does the reception vary? Why? Who gets angry or uncomfortable? What do you think of the book's message?

- In any of the novels listed in this section, how does the race or gender of characters affect their options, resources, self-perception, and goals?

- What kinds of forces have changed racism and sexism over time? What can you do about it?

- Role-play a classroom in which racial or sexual prejudice affected children in classrooms at some other period of time: segregation of Black and white students, different curriculum and expectations for each gender. Divide the classroom into groups of brown-eyed and blue-eyed students. Assign the roles: Black or white and male or female to each group for a period. Students can keep journals of their experiences and reactions.

- How does racial background affect the ability of a culture to assimilate if it chooses to? Read **Farewell to Manzanar** (see page 236) in which a Japanese-American girl reflects on how being Asian causes others to see her as foreign.

- Some Native Americans live on reservations. Find out how they decide whether to stay or leave? Are they the only group of people in this situation?

- Make a list of basic human rights that should apply to all people regardless of race, religion, life style, or physical ability. (See the quote from Senator Beveridge in the Spanish-American War section on page 85.)

- Read the story **Sneetches** by Dr. Seuss (Random, 1961. ISBN 0-394-80089-3). In **Elementary Perspectives** (see page 50), the author suggests these discussion questions to follow reading the book: "The Sneetches were not born prejudiced. How did they learn prejudice? How did it hurt the Plain-Belly Sneetches? How did it hurt the Star-Belly Sneetches?"

Picture Books

- Brenner, Barbara. **Wagon Wheels.** HarperCollins, 1978. ISBN 0-06-020669-1

  Johnny, one of three motherless Black boys, moves with his father from Kentucky to Kansas in the 1870s. There they join the Black community in Nicodemus, Kansas. Johnny is left there to care for his younger brothers while their father goes in search of better land. Then the three boys undertake a 150-mile trip to the permanent homestead their father establishes further west.

- Golenbock, Peter. **Teammates.** Harcourt, 1990. ISBN 0-15-200603-6

  This picture book relates the prejudice and racism that confronted but seldom confounded Jackie Robinson in his baseball career. It concentrates on the friendship between Robinson and the equally famous Peewee Reese.

- Hamanaka, Sheila. **The Journey.** Orchard, 1990. ISBN 0-531-08449-3

  The illustrations and text of this picture book tell the often tragic story of Japanese Americans through the story of the author's own family. The book is powerful and the images are haunting.

- Hoffman, Mary. **Amazing Grace.** Illustrated by Caroline Binch. Dial, 1991. ISBN 0-8037-1040-2

  Grace is full of life and ambition. Gap-toothed, Black, and vibrant, she sees no reason that she can't bring her exuberance and love of stories to the role of Peter Pan in the class production. When the kids tell her she can't because she's a girl and because she's Black, she gets support from her mother and her grandmother. She sweeps the audition, just as we knew she would.

- Lionni, Leo. **Little Blue and Little Yellow.** Astor-Honor, 1959. ISBN 0-8392-3018-4

  In this nearly classic fable, illustrated with torn colored-paper, Little Blue and Little Yellow accidentally become green.

◆ Medearis, Angela. ***Dancing with the Indians.*** Illustrated by Samuel Byrd. Holiday, 1991. ISBN 0-8234-0893-0

See page 34.

Greenfield, Eloise. ***Rosa Parks.*** Illustrated by Eric Marlow. HarperCollins, 1973. ISBN 0-690-71211-1

This fictionalized biography of the life of Rosa Parks is set against a background of the Civil Rights' abuses of the past.

Fiction

★ Spinka, Penina Keen. ***Mother's Blessing.*** Atheneum, 1992. ISBN 0-689-31758-1

■■■■■■■■■■■□□□□

Least Sophisticated   Most Sophisticated

See page 55.

◆ Armstrong, William H. ***Sounder.*** HarperCollins, 1969. ISBN 0-06-020144-4

■■■■■■■■■■□□□□□

Set in the South in the late 1800's, ***Sounder*** *is based on the true story of a family of Black sharecroppers and their beloved hunting hound, Sounder. When there is not enough game in the woods to sustain them, the father steals a pig for meat and is sent to jail and then to do hard labor. When his owner is arrested, Sounder attempts to follow the wagon and suffers a crippling bullet wound. The oldest son, who is still a child, narrates this story of love and faith, cruelty and death. This book is good one for exploring the South after slavery was abolished.*

◆ Hooks, William. ***Circle of Fire.*** Atheneum, 1982. ISBN 0-689-50241-9

■■■■■■■□□□□□□□

The effects of the Ku Klux Klan and its activities are felt by almost every one, especially these three young people who befriend a tinker boy. Convinced that his father is a member of the Klan, Harrison has to make a difficult decision when he learns that the Klan is about to raid the tinker camp.

◆ Lowry, Lois. ***Autumn Street.*** Houghton, 1980. ISBN 0-395-27812-0

■■■■■■■□□□□□□□

See page 93.

◆ Moore, Yvette. ***Freedom Songs.*** Orchard, 1990. ISBN 0-531-0-8412-4

■■■■■■■■■■■■□□□

See page 98.

◆ O'Dell, Scott. ***My Name Is Not Angelica.*** Dell, 1989. ISBN 0-440-40379-0

■■■■■■■■□□□□□□□

See page 185.

◆ Taylor, Mildred D. ***Roll of Thunder, Hear My Cry.*** Dial, 1976.
ISBN 0-8037-7473-7

■■■■■■■■■□□□□□

Life in rural Mississippi in the 1930s, as seen by Cassie Logan, is pretty grim. There are night riders, boycotts, retribution, lynch mobs, and violence, except in her home, which is full of love and concern. This is a Focus Book; see page 297.

◆ ———. ***Mississippi Bridge.*** Dial, 1990. ISBN 0-8037-0426-7

■■■■■■■□□□□□□□

The climax of this book is a bus accident in which many people are killed. The fact that all of the passengers on the bus are white is particularly ironic because Black people had been forced off the bus in order to make room for the whites. The book is a reflection on Jim Crow laws and on the prejudice and fear they produced.

◆ Uchida, Yoshiko. ***A Jar of Dreams.*** Atheneum, 1981. ISBN 0-689-50210-9

■■■■■■■■■□□□□□

Rinko and her Japanese-American family are harassed almost daily by Wilbur Starr and must counter that threat while coping with the Depression. They rediscover their own tradition when Aunt Waka comes to the states from Japan for the summer. She pushes them to challenge the discrimination. Together they establish a flourishing laundry business against all odds. The characterization in all of Uchida's novels is very strong.

Marino, Jan. ***The Day That Elvis Came to Town.*** Little, 1990.
ISBN 0-316-54618-6

Wanda's life changes when the new boarder offers a meeting with Elvis Presley. Although the meeting never takes place, Wanda's attitudes do change for the better. The setting of the American South helps the author explore the racism of the time.

Taylor, Mildred D. ***The Friendship and The Gold Cadillac.*** Bantam, 1989.
ISBN 0-553-15765-5

■■■■■■■□□□□□□□

These are two short stories based on the Black experience. The second story, "The Gold Cadillac," tells of a Black family's trip back to the South in 1950.

Nonfiction ★ Myers, Walter Dean. ***Now Is Your Time: The African-American Struggle for Freedom.*** HarperCollins, 1992. ISBN 0-06-024370-8

See page 98.

◆ Adoff, Arnold. ***Malcolm X.*** Crowell, 1970. ISBN 0-06-446015-0

■■■■■■■□□□□□□□

See page 98.

◆ Archer, James. ***Breaking Barriers: The Feminist Revolution from Susan B. Anthony to Margaret Sanger to Betty Friedan.*** Viking, 1991. ISBN 0-670-83104-2

■■■■■■■■■■■□□□

In addition to being the well-written, well-researched biographies of three strong women, this book provides a bridge for three independent lives to a powerful movement toward women's rights. It includes the difficult moments as well as the triumphs. This is a challenging book for young people who are ready to be challenged. Many of the unresolved questions and unfinished tasks outlined in the book should provide material for discussion.

◆ Chang, Ina. ***A Separate Battle: Women and the Civil War.*** Lodestar, 1991. ISBN 0-525-67365-2

■■■■■■■■■■■■□

See page 81.

◆ Ferris, Jeri. ***Native American Doctor: The Story of Susan LaFlesche Picotte.*** Carolrhoda, 1991. ISBN 0-887614-443-1

■■■■■■■□□□□□□□

See page 135.

◆ Houston, Jeanne Wakatsuki and Houston, James D. ***Farewell to Manzanar.*** Bantam, 1989. ISBN 0-553-23692-X

■■■■■■■■■□□□□□

See page 236.

◆ Levine, Ellen. ***If You Lived at the Time of Martin Luther King.*** Scholastic, 1990. ISBN 0- 590-42582-X

■■■■■□□□□□□□□□

See page 98.

◆ Parks, Rosa. ***Rosa Parks: My Story.*** Dial, 1992. ISBN 0-8037-0673-1

■■■■■■■■■□□□□□

See page 99.

◆ Reit, Seymour. ***Behind Rebel Lines: The Incredible Story of Emma Edmonds.*** Harcourt, 1988. ISBN 0-15-200424-6

■■■■■■■■□□□□□□

See page 82.

◆ Rubel, David. ***Fanny Lou Hamer: From Share Cropping to Politics.*** Silver Burdett, 1990. ISBN 0-382-09923-0

■■■■■■■■■■□□□□

See page 99.

◆ Schniedewind, Nancy and Davidson, Ellen. ***Open Minds to Equality: A Sourcebook of Learning Activities to Promote Race, Sex, Class, and Age Equity.*** Allyn and Bacon, 1983. ISBN 0-13-637264-3

■■■■■■■■■■□□□□□

This guide for teachers and students contains imaginative and useful activities for integrating language arts, history, and math. Objectives are clearly stated and there are references to many related source books.

◆ Wheeler, Leslie. ***Jane Addams.*** Silver Burdett, 1990. ISBN 0-382-09968-0

■■■■■■■■■■■□□□□

See page 58.

Ayer, Eleanor. ***Margaret Bourke-White.*** Dillon, 1992. ISBN 0-87518-513-4

■■■■■■■□□□□□□□□

See page 155.

Collins, David. ***Black Rage: Malcolm X.*** Macmillan, 1992. ISBN 0-87518-498-7

■■■■■■■□□□□□□□□

See page 99.

Haskins, James. ***Thurgood Marshall: A Life for Justice.*** Holt, 1992. ISBN 0-8050-2095-0

■■■■■■■■■■■□□□□

See page 99.

Jackson, Jesse. ***Make a Joyful Noise Unto the Lord: The Life of Mahalia Jackson.*** Crowell, 1974. ISBN 0-690-43344-1

■■■■■■■■■■■■□□□

See page 156.

Katz, William Loren. ***Black Indians: A Hidden Heritage.*** Atheneum, 1986. ISBN 0-689-31196-6

■■■■■■■■■■■■■■□

See page 46.

McKissack, Patricia and McKissack, Fredrick. ***Frederick Douglass: The Black Lion.*** Childrens, 1987. ISBN 0-516-03221-6

■■■■■■■■■■■□□□□

From his birth as a slave to his accomplishments as writer and orator, this biography is well told.

————. ***James Weldon Johnson: Lift Every Voice and Sing.*** Childrens, 1990. ISBN 0-516-04174-6

■■■■■□□□□□□□□□□

Although the facts of Johnson's life are certainly here, the strength of the book lies in its account of the prejudices, bigotry, and violence of the time during which he lived.

Meltzer, Milton. ***Betty Friedan: A Voice for Women's Rights.*** Viking, 1985. ISBN 0-670-80786-9

■■■■■■■□□□□□□□

Betty Friedan's role in the Women's Liberation Movement is covered briefly, but the book concentrates on her early years as an activist.

Rickerby, Laura Ann. ***Ulysses S. Grant and the Strategy of Victory.*** Silver Burdett, 1991. ISBN 0-382-09944-3

■■■■■■■■■■■□□□□

Although not the focus of this book, information on slavery and the abolitionist movement are included.

Turner, Glennette Tilley. ***Take a Walk in Their Shoes.*** Cobblehill, 1989. ISBN 0-525-65006-7

■■■■■■■□□□□□□□

See page 100.

Nonprint

Videos

Brown vs the Board of Education. Coronet.

The film is a dramatization of the events leading up to and resulting from the Supreme Court decision that was the beginning of the desegregation of the South.

Free at Last. Encyclopedia Britannica.

Using dramatizations, newsreel clips, and excerpts from his speeches, the film deals with Martin Luther King, Jr.'s life and his contributions. It is written on an upper-elementary school level.

There Was Always Sun Shining Someplace: Life in the Negro Baseball Leagues. Refocus Films.

This film covers the period from the late 1890s to the disbanding of the league in the 1940s. James Earl Jones narrates the film that shows the triumphs and trials of the players in the league through old photographs, personal reminiscences, and footage from home movies.

Art and Artists

Activities

- Find art to illustrate any event or period of history in which you are interested. If you had the ability, what would you change in that piece of art? Why?

- Find similarities among artists' lives that might account for their achievements.

- Make a chart showing the various roles of art during U.S. history. Consider Native American art, art as religious inspiration, folk art, artists' colonies, and art as investment. Reflect on how the needs and conditions of the cultures determined the roles art would play.

- Make individual lists that show what you consider art. Combine individual lists into a group list. Identify those ideas that all or most of you share.

- Consider photography. What roles have photographers played throughout history? What would it be like to be a photographer like Solomon Butcher (see page 210) or like Margaret Bourke-White (see page 155)? What demands did society place on them? What were their options? What were their rewards?

- Form groups to investigate an art form in America. Make displays to show the art form at its best.

- Take a piece of visual art and find suitable music and poetry to accompany it. Look at **Songs of the Wild West** (see page 210) for inspiration.

- Gather all the art you can find that represents the historical period you're studying. Use visual art, poetry, music, handicrafts, and literature.

- Gather books on quilting. See **Once Upon a Time** (DLM, 1990. ISBN 1-55924-4) for additional activities and books on quilting. Make a quilt book that shows quilt patterns. For each quilt, make up a story that reflects the area and time it might have come from.

- Find utilitarian antiques that were created with some form of art to make them more pleasing to look at.

- Make a video tape to show the history of film in America.

- Create a video tape or other audio-visual presentation to show the history of children's literature in America.

- Create a work of art to show your reaction to a historical event, person, or era. Use a variety of art forms, such as collage, poster, montage, video, and painting.

- Make up lyrics and instrumentation that evoke an era you are studying. Then find other works of music that evoke the same era.

- Find posters or reproductions that reveal an era or event in time.

- Collect picture books that evoke an era. Talk about what the art does for the books that the words cannot do (see pages 33-35).

- Find prints of paintings created in early America and in several periods since that time. What has changed? Do things look more or less real? What are the artists trying to do?

- At and before the turn of this century, theater groups and actors often traveled to small towns to give performances of Shakespeare and other great plays. Does it still happen? Why? How has local theater changed?

- Find one work of art that intrigues or delights you. Find out as much as you can about its history. Sometimes art books will tell you when and where a piece of art was created. Sometimes an art museum will help you. Try the art department of the nearest college or university for more information. If you can't find out much about the art itself, find out about the person who created it. Find a way to share what you have found out.

Picture Books

Baylor, Byrd. ***When Clay Sings.*** Macmillan, 1972. ISBN 0-684-18829-5
See page 163.

Fiction

★ Yates, Elizabeth. ***The Journeyman.*** Bob Jones University Press, 1990. ISBN 0-89084-535-2

■■■■■■■■■■□□□□□
Least Sophisticated   Most Sophisticated

This is a Focus Book. See page 272.

Avi. ***The Man Who Was Poe.*** Orchard, 1989. ISBN 0-531-05833-6

■■■■■■■■■■■■■□□

See page 207.

Henry, Marguerite. ***Benjamin West and His Cat Grimalkin.*** Macmillan, 1947. ISBN 0-02-743660-8

■■■■■■■□□□□□□□

This is a fictionalized account of the early life of Benjamin West, a painter from eighteenth-century Pennsylvania who painted frontier life in the new country. The book also furnishes insight into the culture of Pennsylvania, in particular the Quaker culture. Artistic images were considered frivolous and ungodly by the Quakers and Benjamin's family was torn between pride in his talent and their religious views.

Weaver, Lydia. ***Child Star: When Talkies Came to Hollywood.*** Viking, 1992. ISBN 0-670-84039-4

■■■■■□□□□□□□□□

See page 230.

Nonfiction

★ Peet, Bill. ***Bill Peet: An Autobiography.*** Houghton, 1989. ISBN 0-395-50932-7

■■■■■■■□□□□□□□

This Caldecott honor book is liberally illustrated with Peet's drawings of himself and the people and places important in his life. It is lengthy but can be appreciated on many levels.

★ ***Cobblestone Magazine***

The following issues were devoted to arts and artists:
John Aububon (April 1980)
Willa Cather (December 1980)
Frederic Remington (November 1982)
Shakers (April 1983)
Jazz (October 1983)
Mark Twain (May 1984)
Chautauqua (July 1984)
The Art of Photography (April 1985)
The Cartoon (August 1985)
American Clothing (October 1985)
Laura Ingalls Wilder (February 1986)
Walt Whitman (May 1986)
Music from the 1950s (August 1986)
The Hudson River School (February 1987)
The Transcendentalists (June 1987)
The American Theater (December 1987)
The South as Perceived by Its Artists (February 1988)
American Architecture (August 1988)
The Magic of Radio (October 1988)
Louisa May Alcott (December 1988)
Tuning In to Television (October 1989)
Norman Rockwell (December 1989)
Colonial Craftsmen (June 1990)

★ Collier, James Lincoln. ***Louis Armstrong: An American Success Story.***
Macmillan, 1985. ISBN 0-02-722830-4

Collier, an author of excellent historical fiction, turns his talents toward the real life of the indomitable jazz great, Louis Armstrong, showing us Armstrong's roots in New Orleans and his place in music history.

★ Turner, Robyn Montana. ***Georgia O'Keeffe.*** Little, 1991. ISBN 0-316-85649-5

With a liberal use of photographs and beautiful reproductions of her work, the book is a concise and straightforward account of this amazing American artist who found her own voice to speak through the colors and shapes on her canvases. It's a winner.

Ayer, Eleanor. ***Margaret Bourke-White.*** Dillon, 1992. ISBN 0-87518-513-4

Concentrating on the career of this world-renowned photographer, the book uses Bourke-White's photographs and those taken of her on her travels throughout the world. There is a great deal about the gender roles of the time and the expectation that she should be content to shoot tire commercials instead of daring to go into places seemingly inappropriate for a woman of her time.

Bober, Natalie. *A Restless Spirit: The Story of Robert Frost.* Holt, 1991. ISBN 0-8050-1672-4

■■■■■■■■■□□□□□

Frost's life, with an accent on his great love for his long-suffering wife Elinor, is told clearly and sometimes lyrically, interweaving excerpts from his work with photographs of him, his friends, and his family. We also see the man's torment and guilt; the death and unhappiness of so many of those he loved took their toll. The number of houses and locales to which he led his family boggles the mind, but his restless spirit and determination to succeed as a poet took precedence over everything else, and Elinor lent her will to his.

Brenner, Barbara. *On the Frontier with Mr. Audubon.* Coward, 1977. ISBN 0-698-30756-9

■■■■■■■□□□□□□□□

See page 199.

Byars, Betsy. *The Moon and I.* Julian Messner, 1992. ISBN 0-671-74165-9

■■■■■■■■□□□□□□□

See page 16.

Collier, James Lincoln. *Duke Ellington.* Macmillan, 1991. ISBN 0-02-722985-8

■■■■■■■■■■■□□□

Here's the life of the self-taught musician who overcame racial prejudices to become the master artist of his time.

Gherman, Beverly. *Agnes de Mille: Dancing off the Earth.* Macmillan, 1990. ISBN 0-689-31441-8

■■■■■■■■■■■□□□

The biography of the dancer and choreographer whose accomplishments included the choreography for "Oklahoma" and the works of Aaron Copeland is told here with liberal quotes from de Mille herself.

Greene, Katherine. *The Man Behind the Magic: The Story of Walt Disney.* Viking, 1991. ISBN 0-670-82259-0

■■■■■■■■■■■□□□

The book contains the main facts of Disney's life; however, the author also spends considerable time on the thefts of ideas that plagued his studio and the rules of working at Disneyland.

Jackson, Jesse. *Make a Joyful Noise Unto the Lord: The Life of Mahalia Jackson.* Crowell, 1974. ISBN 0-690-43344-1

■■■■■■■■■■■□□□

This is an interesting and often lyrical telling of the life of the famous gospel singer. It starts with her birth in 1911 and covers her involvement in the Civil Rights Movement and her many contributions to African-American music.

McKissack, Patricia and McKissack, Fredrick. ***James Weldon Johnson: Lift Every Voice and Sing.*** Childrens, 1990. ISBN 0-516-04174-6

■■■■■□□□□□□□□□□

See page 151.

Meryman, Richard. ***Andrew Wyeth.*** Abrams, 1991. ISBN 0-8109-3956-8

■■■■■■■□□□□□□□□

One of America's best-known artists came by his profession naturally. His father was N. C. Wyeth, a great artist and illustrator who had a strong influence on children's literature illustration. According to this biography, N. C. Wyeth was not an easy man to live with. The author explains the work of Andrew Wyeth.

Probosz, Kathilyn Solomon. ***Alvin Ailey, Jr.*** Bantam, 1991. ISBN 0-553-15930-5

■■■■■■■□□□□□□□□

See page 253.

Smith, Carter. ***The Arts and Sciences: A Sourcebook on Colonial America.*** Millbrook, 1991. ISBN 0-56294-037-6

■■■■■■■■■■□□□□□

Using prints, photographs, and drawings, the book contains information about the art and music created by the early colonists.

Stevens, Bryna. ***Ben Franklin's Glass Armonica.*** Illustrated by Priscilla Kiedrowski. Dell, 1983. ISBN 0-440-40584-X

■■■■■■□□□□□□□□□

See page 122.

Part 3

Chronology of History

Before Columbus: Pre-1492 *The Times at a Glance...*

Movers & Shakers

Anasazi Indians

Mayans

Aztecs

Mississippians

Woodland Peoples

Leif Ericson

Headlines*

c. 3800 BC	Cultivation of corn in New Mexico
c. 3200 BC	Pictographs drawn on cave in Montana
c. 2800 BC	Copper implements used near Lake Superior
c. 2600 BC	Pottery made in Georgia
c. 1150 BC	Woodland hunters develop canoe for river travel
c. 800 BC	Cultivation of maize in the Ohio River Valley
c. 500 BC	Drought-resistant maize grown in New Mexico
c. 420 BC	Mammoth Cave explored
c. 380 BC	Permanent settlement in Louisiana; continues until arrival of Europeans
c. 140 BC	Hopewell culture at height in Ohio
c. AD 100	Pyramid of the sun begun in Mexico
c. 340	Anasazi Indians occupy Canyon de Chelly in Arizona
c. 370	Old Stone Fort built on Little Duck River in Tennessee
c. 450	Bows and arrows used
c. 490	Anasazi pit houses built near Mesa Verde
c. 550	Burial mounds constructed in Great Lakes area
c. 700	Pueblos built at Mesa Verde
c. 760	Mississippian Culture flourishes
c. 850	Mayans complete migration to Yucatan peninsula
c. 880	Cahokia mound built in Illinois
c. 1000	Leif Ericson visits Vinland
c. 1050	Elaborate underground water system devised in Mexico
c. 1100	Pueblo established at Kinishba, Arizona
c. 1295	Emerald Mound built in Mississippi to serve as cultural center
c. 1325	Aztec empire founded
c. 1413	Salado people move into valley of Gila River
c. 1420	Itzcoatl leads Aztecs to conquer Mexico and Guatemala
c. 1430	Angel Mound built on Ohio River
c. 1466	Pachacuti gains control of Peru for Incas
c. 1480	Aztec calendar stone completed

*Many of the dates are only estimates made by historians and scientists. We tried to verify each date with at least two reliable sources; in cases where we found disagreement, we checked several sources. It is reasonable to expect that in your research you will also find disagreement.

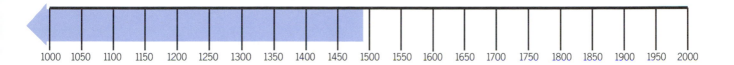

| 1000 | 1050 | 1100 | 1150 | 1200 | 1250 | 1300 | 1350 | 1400 | 1450 | 1500 | 1550 | 1600 | 1650 | 1700 | 1750 | 1800 | 1850 | 1900 | 1950 | 2000 |

Meanwhile, In Other Parts of the World

c. 5000 BC	Farming settlements in Mesopotamia
c. 3300 BC	Upper and Lower Egypt established as kingdoms
c. 1050 BC	City States established in Greece
c. 776 BC	First recorded Olympic Games
c. 753 BC	Founding of Rome
c. 336 BC	Rise of Alexander the Great
c. 214 BC	Great Wall of China completed
c. AD 30	Jesus crucified
c. 476	End of Roman empire
c. 770	Charlemagne rules
c. 1000	Norse invade Europe
1066	Norman conquest of England
1096	First Crusade begins
c. 1211	Genghis Khan invades China
1215	King John forced to sign Magna Carta
1337	Hundred Years War begins between England and France
1347-1352	Black Death devastates Europe
1403	China begins naval expeditions to India and Africa
c. 1419	Henry the Navigator explores African coast
1455-1485	Wars of the Roses

Books

c.	1350	*Gesta Romanorum* (Deeds of the Romans), fables that were told to children
	1484	Caxton's *Aesop's Fables*

Inventions & Discoveries

c. 3800 BC	Sledges used for transport
c. 2800 BC	Fork-branched plow used in Egypt
c. 2700 BC	365-day calendar developed in Egypt
c. 2500 BC	Great Pyramid of Khufu finished
c. 2300 BC	Horizontal looms developed
c. 2000 BC	Flush toilet invented in Crete
c. 1600 BC	Writing introduced in China
c. 620 BC	First known map of world
c. 200 BC	Crossbow invented
c. 100 BC	Paper invented in China
c. AD 700	Windmill invented
730	Gunpowder invented
760	Block printing invented in Japan
1250	Cannons invented
1280	Spinning wheel invented
1370	System of locks for river travel devised
1448	Movable type invented
1470	Invention of rifle

Before Columbus: Pre-1492

Activities

- See Cultures on page 128.

- Before reading about this period, gather as a class to talk about and record what you think it was like on this continent before Columbus. How many different cultures were here? How "advanced" were the civilizations and in what ways? How did the communities get along with each other? What were the political structures? How long had people been living on this continent? How widely had people traveled?

- The previous activity can lead to nonfiction research to validate or repudiate ideas or it can lead to the reading of any of the suggested fiction.

- Find illustrations of Native Americans from fiction and nonfiction. Look particularly at expressions, posture, and actions. Try to figure out why they were portrayed as they were in each illustration. For instance, in ***All Pigs on Deck*** (Delacorte, 1991. ISBN 0-383-30440-4), the Indians look sweet, helpless, innocent, and friendly. Could this be a reaction to years of portraying Indians in an unfavorable light?

- Make black ceremonial paint from animal grease and charcoal; whitish paint from clay and animal grease; other colors from edible berries and grease.

- Some Indian tribes moved their villages with the seasons. Role-play a discussion about moving from your area now. What factors would you need to consider?

- Make a model of a wigwam, a long house, a hogan, and a teepee. Indian children sometimes made such playhouses. Make one big enough to use in this way.

- Hold a Native American celebration. What would the Indians in your area have celebrated? What activities would have been a part of their celebration?

- In the Wampanoag culture, a guardian spirit, or Manitou, was chosen for each member. What might that have meant to them? Choose a Manitou for yourself. What can you find out about your Manitou? If it lives near you, can you track it or observe it for a day?

- Some Indians had a ritual in which something precious was burned as a gesture of gratitude. If you were to burn something precious to send to the spirit world, what would it be? Read Tomie dePaola's ***Legend of the Indian Paintbrush*** (Putnam, 1988. ISBN 0-399-21534-4) in which a similar sacrifice is made.

- Ask someone to hold a workshop about edible plants. Try a local nature center. Do not do this yourself without absolute knowledge of the safety of plants.

- Plant a patch of corn and beans surrounded by pumpkins.

- Find examples of pottery from various cultures of this period. Choose one culture's designs and shapes and make your own work of art. For example, make a collage using the shapes of the pottery from one culture. Use various textures, colors, and opacity. It's important that it not be an amalgam of some generic "Indian" look, but that it be inspired by the art of one culture.

- Find a way to show which civilizations existed simultaneously or contiguously in this time period throughout the new world. For example, you might construct a chart showing time periods, with symbols for each civilization, and then overlap them with a time line.

- Make up a quiz game, patterned after the Jeopardy program, with information you have gathered for this time period.

- Make a web showing the civilizations that existed before Columbus. Connect any that had contact with each other. Trace as many paths as possible from one civilization to more distant ones.

- Make a display of artifact replicas from various civilizations existing before Columbus: dwellings, boats, currency, pottery, jewelry, clothing, and mounds.

Picture Books

◆ Baylor, Byrd. ***One Small Blue Bead.*** Scribner, 1992. ISBN 0-684-19334-5

This is a republication of one of Byrd Baylor's earliest books. It tells of an early tribe of cave dwellers in the American Southwest who are unaware that other groups exist until an old man seeks them out. A boy does the physical work for the old man until he returns with a boy from another tribe who hands the first boy a small blue bead. He accepts it as a symbol of brotherhood.

◆ Carrick, Carol. ***Big Old Bones.*** Illustrated by Donald Carrick. Clarion, 1989. ISBN 0-89919-734-5

With humor and delight, the Carricks tell the tale of nineteenth-century Professor Potts and his family who discover dinosaur bones while on a train trip to the Old West. After carefully transporting the bones to his laboratory back East, Professor Potts and his family put the bones together in many ways, each time coming up with erroneous conclusions about the dinosaurs. The book concludes with an explanation of some of the many mistakes archeologists have made in reconstructing dinosaurs, including an error that wasn't corrected until 1979.

Baylor, Byrd. ***When Clay Sings.*** Macmillan, 1972. ISBN 0-684-18829-5

This is a tribute to the art of the prehistoric Indian tribes that inhabited the desert areas of North America.

Yolen, Jane. ***Sky Dogs.*** Illustrated by Barry Moser. Harcourt, 1990. ISBN 0-15-275480-6

An old Blackfoot Indian tells how he came to be called He-who-loves-horses back in the time before the Plains Indians had horses. Using old Native American tales and legends, Yolen shows how the horses might have come to the Indian.

Fiction

★ Spinka, Penina Keen. ***Mother's Blessing.*** Atheneum, 1992. ISBN 0-689-31758-1

■■■■■■■□□□□□□□□

Least Sophisticated   Most Sophisticated

This delightful book, set in Southern California in the tenth century, is a story loosely based on several Chumash myths. It tells of the journey of one young woman into the land of the Anasazi, whose culture was then at its peak. At her birth there is a prophesy that the child will grow up to be a leader of the people who will bring together warring villages. When her father, the leader of the village, discovers that the baby is a girl, he disowns her and divorces her mother. The child eventually fulfills the prophesy and is a wise and compassionate leader. This is a novel of conflict and of stubbornness and pride that get in the way of a leader's ability to do what is best for the people. It is rich in the diversity of peoples living in the area at the time, and we see many styles of leadership and experience the shortcomings of each.

Denzel, Justin. ***Hunt for the Last Cat.*** Philomel, 1991. ISBN 0-399-22101-8

■■■■■■■■■■■■□□□□

Set eight thousand years ago in prehistoric Florida, this story is based on bones of paleo-Indians, saber-toothed tigers, and giant sloths discovered in sinkholes. Using the latest scientific knowledge, the author crafts a story of a boy, a girl, and a clan living at the time of the last saber tooths. The girl is the last survivor of her clan, which was killed off by disease. She lives alone in the woods because some people in the boy's clan believe she is a spirit-changeling of a saber-toothed cat. In spite of this a friendship grows between the boy and girl while the clan attempts to save itself from another saber tooth currently stalking the village. The book explores a part of American history seldom mentioned.

Nonfiction

★ Jacobs, Francine. ***The Tainos: The People Who Welcomed Columbus.*** Putnam, 1992. ISBN 0-399-22116-6

■■■■■■■■■■■□□□□□

See page 109.

Batherman, Muriel. ***Before Columbus.*** Houghton, 1981. ISBN 0-395-54954-X

■■■■□□□□□□□□□□

A brief and simple introduction to the Indian cultures in America before Columbus, this book includes descriptions of hunters, basket makers, and farmers.

Freedman, Russell. ***Buffalo Hunt.*** Holiday, 1988. ISBN 0-8234-0702-0

■■■■■■■■□□□□□□

Using paintings by many of the great Western artists as illustrations, Freedman's book shows the ways buffalo were used by the Indian and how the destruction of the buffalo herds helped lead to the destruction of the Indian cultures.

Trimble, Stephen. ***The Village of Blue Stone.*** Macmillan, 1990. ISBN 0-02-789501-7

■■■■■■■■■□□□□□

Although this book is a picture book, its text is quite lengthy and rather complicated. However, it's worth the trip through the pages to learn about one year in the life of an Anasazi community in about the year 1000. The cliff dwellers, in the corner where Utah, Colorado, New Mexico and Arizona meet, lived in a world in which art, the land, work, and religion were inseparable.

Wheeler, M. J. ***First Came the Indians.*** Atheneum, 1983. ISBN 0-689-50258-3

■■■■■□□□□□□□□□

Using a poetic text, the author briefly outlines the beliefs and social structure of six North American Indian tribes: the Creek, Chippewa, Iroquois, Sioux, Makah, and Hopi. It could serve as an introduction to a more extensive examination of Indian cultures or as an overview of the cultures that existed before the white settlers arrived.

Columbus and After: 1492–1600 *The Times at a Glance...*

Movers & Shakers

Juan Rodriquez Cabrillo
Jacques Cartier
Samuel de Champlain
Christopher Columbus
Francisco Vásquez de Coronado
Hernando Cortés
Hernando De Soto
Sir Francis Drake
Batholomew Ferillo
Bartholomew Gosnold
Henry Hudson
Louis Jolliet
Juan Ponce de León
Prince Henry
Queen Isabella
Sir Walter Raleigh
Jean Ribaut
Giovanni da Verrazano
Amerigo Vespucci

Headlines*

1492	Columbus makes first widely known European landing in Western Hemisphere
1497	Amerigo Vespucci claims he discovered the American mainland in 1491; makes second voyage in 1501 and declares that the new lands are not part of Asia
1497	John Cabot explores Eastern Canada
1508	Cuba explored by Sebastian de Ocampo to establish settlements
1508	Puerto Rico colony established by Ponce de León
1513	Florida explored by Ponce de León
1530	Sugar becomes as important as gold as an import to Europe from Western Hemisphere
1532	Horses introduced into South America
1533	Inca empire ends with strangulation of Atahualpa by Pizarro
1535	Lower California is explored by Hernando Cortés
1541	Mississippi River discovered by Hernando De Soto
1570	Five North American Indian tribes confederate under the name Iroquois
1564	Aztecs decimated by disease
1565	St. Augustine, the first permanent European settlement in North America, established in Florida
1565	470 slaves taken from Africa to be sold in Spanish colonies in America by Sir John Hawkins
1579	Sir Francis Drake lands in California and claims area near present-day San Francisco for England
1584	Roanoke Island colony established by Sir Walter Raleigh
1586	Sir Francis Drake destroys Spanish settlement at St. Augustine
1598	Pueblo territory in Southwest colonized by Spanish
1599	Over 900,000 Black slaves in New World
1600	France gains monopoly of fur trade in New World

*Many of the dates are only estimates made by historians and scientists. We tried to verify each date with at least two reliable sources; in cases where we found disagreement, we checked several sources. It is reasonable to expect that in your research you will also find disagreement.

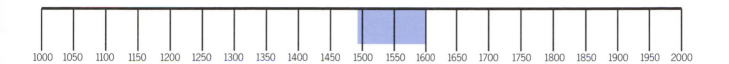

1000	1050	1100	1150	1200	1250	1300	1350	1400	1450	1500	1550	1600	1650	1700	1750	1800	1850	1900	1950	2000

Meanwhile, In Other Parts of the World

1492	Ferdinand and Isabella expel Jews from Spain while continuing Inquisition
1509	Henry VIII becomes King of England
1512	Spanish colonists import black slaves into Hispaniola to replace decimated Indians
1516	Hapsburg dynasty founded in Spain
1518	Martin Luther's Reformation grows
1521	Magellan killed after discovering Philippines
1542	Universal Inquisition established by Pope Paul III
1558	Elizabeth I assumes throne of England
1562	Series of civil wars begin in France
1563	Separatists' movement begins in England
1563	Rice riots in Japan
1578	China's population reaches 60 million
1580	Sir Francis Drake circumnavigates the world
1588	England defeats Spanish Armada
1591	North Africa's Black culture destroyed by Spanish

Inventions & Discoveries

1511	Watch invented
1568	Mercator map published
1589	Knitting machine invented
1597	Sector invented by Galileo Galilei

Fads & Customs

1610	Tobacco becomes the rage in London

Art

1497	DaVinci completes *Last Supper*
1501	Michelangelo begins *David*
1560	Pieter Bruegel the Elder's *Children's Games*
1590	Shakespeare's first play, *King Henry VI*

Books

1400s	Horn Books
1485	Malory's *Le Morte d'Arthur*
1514	*Book of Hours*
1548	King Henry's Primers
1500s	Chapbooks

Columbus and After: 1492–1600

Activities

Note: As you look at the settlement of North America by Europeans, you'll read about the discovery and occupation of new lands and about the massacre and exploitation of the native people. It's important, while teaching and learning about the explorers and settlers, not to turn them into superheroes. These people, like most of the other conquerors throughout history, treated the inhabitants as less than human. Many of the suggested books show how the actions of the powerful affected the powerless.

- See The Native American Conflict on page 59, Slavery on page 106, and Before Columbus on page 160.

- Pretend you're an explorer and take a field trip. Take notes about the trip and create a map for a king and queen at home to see.

- Discover the schoolyard and make a map of it.

- Turn about. Role-play Native Americans discovering Europe or Asia or Africa.

- Construct models of ships used by early explorers and settlers.

- Re-enact a moment of discovery. Note how two people see the same event differently.

- Marco Polo's book inspired Christopher Columbus. Has any book inspired you to do something? Talk to others about things in their reading that inspired them.

- What were the motivations of the different explorers: money, fame, politics, adventure, freedom, religion? How did their motivations influence their interactions?

- If you were an East coast Indian, what European things would you like to acquire? What would you barter for them? Find out what kinds of trades people made?

- Who and what would you bring to a new place to set up a fort or outpost? Re-enact establishing a fort. How would conflicts be settled?

- Find out what farm animals currently in North America are from the Old World. What animals did Native Americans have?

- Prove that the world is round. Patricia Lauber's book ***How We Learned the Earth Is Round*** (HarperCollins, 1990. ISBN 0-690-04862-9) outlines several experiments.

- Pretend you are one of the explorers. Write a letter to your backers, telling of your discoveries and triumphs.

Picture Books

★ Yolen, Jane. ***Encounter.*** Illustrated by David Shannon. Harcourt, 1992. ISBN 0-15-225962-7

This beautiful picture book tells of the arrival of the Columbus expedition as experienced by a native Taino boy. Wary and distrustful of the strangers, he warns others not to have anything to do with them, but his people are open and guileless, making their exploitation easy.

Adler, David A. ***Christopher Columbus: Great Explorer.*** Illustrated by Lyle Miller. Holiday House, 1991. ISBN 0-8234-0895-7

This black-and-white picture book shows Columbus's life in surprising detail. Although the book ends with the statement, "His bravery at sea and his discoveries encouraged others to sail to unknown lands," the book also mentions some of the cruel effects that Columbus had on the natives, even stating that many killed themselves rather than submit to the explorer's cruelty.

Fischetto, Laura. ***All Pigs on Deck: Christopher Columbus's Second Marvelous Voyage.*** Illustrated by Letizia Galli. Delacorte, 1991. ISBN 0-385-30439-0

This very simple book is useful because it shows Columbus's attempt to colonize the areas he had discovered on his first voyage. Not only did he bring pigs, he also brought tailors, writers, carpenters, and doctors to the New World.

Maestro, Betsy and Maestro, Giulio. ***The Discovery of the Americas.*** Lothrop, 1991. ISBN 0-688-06837-5

A beautiful picture book examines the voyages of discovery from the facts to the suppositions and possibilities.

Sis, Peter. ***Follow the Dream: The Story of Christopher Columbus.*** Knopf, 1991. ISBN 0-679-80628-8

Starting with Columbus's childhood dreams, the book summarizes Columbus's life and accomplishments and is illustrated with fascinating maps and pictures.

Fiction

★ Baker, Betty. ***Walk the World's Rim.*** HarperCollins, 1965. ISBN 0-06-020381-1

■■■■■■■■□□□□□□□
Least Sophisticated   Most Sophisticated

Set in 1534 in Texas, New Mexico, Arizona, and Mexico, this book is based on historical figures and incidents. This is the story of an Indian youth, Chakoh, and a Black slave, Esteban. When three Spaniards and Esteban come to Chakoh's village in the midst of famine, Chakoh decides to travel with Esteban to Mexico City to learn more about the white man's god. Their friendship suffers a severe blow when Chakoh learns that Esteban is a slave. Chakoh must reexamine his hatred of slaves and his adulation of all that is from the white culture.

Boegehold, Betty D. ***A Horse Called Starfire.*** Bantam, 1990. ISBN 0-553-05861-4

■■■□□□□□□□□□□□□

The horse went with her Spanish master to the New World and there her master died. She stayed with the body until a young Indian found and claimed her.

Conrad, Pam. ***Pedro's Journal: A Voyage with Christopher Columbus, August 3, 1492–February 14, 1493.*** Caroline House, 1991. ISBN 1-878093-17-7

■■■■■■■■□□□□□□□

This journal covers Columbus's first voyage to the New World through the eyes of a literate and sensitive cabin boy who is frightened to be so far from home, honored to be singled out by Columbus as his personal favorite, and, later, horrified by the taking of slaves and the lack of compassion on the part of Columbus and his men. Supposedly, it is Pedro who, taking his turn at the helm, a forbidden treat, drives the Santa Maria aground on a reef and causes it to sink.

Hooks, William H. ***The Legend of White Doe.*** Macmillan, 1988.
ISBN 0-02-744350-7

■■■■■■■□□□□□□□

Although this short novel tells the legend of what happened to Virginia Dare, the first white child born in the New World, its setting is mostly in the Indian culture of the late 1500s. The few facts that are known about the first settlers of Roanoke and about Virginia Dare are covered in the preface.

Lawson, Robert. ***I Discover Columbus: A True Chronicle of the Great Admiral and His Finding of the New World, Narrated by the Venerable Parrot Aurelius, Who Shared in the Glorious Venture.*** Little, 1941.
ISBN 0-316-51760-7

■■■■■■■□□□□□□□

Apparently Columbus was a vain and rather foolish man who, but for the direction provided by Aurelius, a parrot, would have remained a buffoon in a monastery in Spain. According to Aurelius, even the famous voyage was in his hands because Columbus, who really wanted to remain in Spain, spent most of his time in bed seasick. Although this is not Lawson's most successful pseudo-biography (Ben and Me retains that title), it provides a humorous look at history and encourages a search for the underlying facts.

Litowinsky, Olga. ***The High Voyage: The Final Crossing of Christopher Columbus.*** Delacorte, 1977. ISBN 0-385-30304-1

■■■■■■■■□□□□□□

This book, set in 1502, is based on a book written by Columbus's son Fernando in the 1530s. When he was thirteen, Fernando accompanied his father on the last expedition. This is a challenging book but full of the lore and lure of the open sea.

Spinka, Penina Keen. ***White Hare's Horses.*** Atheneum, 1990.
ISBN 0-689-31654-2

■■■■■■■■■■■□□□

In the California of the 1500s, White Hare, a Native-American girl, uses her courage and skills to save her people from Aztec conquerors.

★ Jacobs, Francine. ***The Tainos: The People Who Welcomed Columbus.*** Putnam, 1992. ISBN 0-399-22116-6

■■■■■■■■■■■□□□

See page 109.

◆ ***Cobblestone Magazine***

The following issues of the magazine were devoted to this era:
Spanish Conquest (March 1981)
The Buffalo (August 1981)
The Beaver Trade (June 1982)
The Cherokee Indians (February 1984)
Who Came to America? (October 1984)

◆ Fritz, Jean. ***Where Do You Think You're Going, Christopher Columbus?***
Putnam, 1980. ISBN 0-399-20723-6

■■■■□□□□□□□□□□

Fritz uses a light touch in her faithful rendering of the facts. Here is one of the most successful, easy reading books about Columbus's voyages and visions.

◆ Lauber, Patricia. ***Who Discovered America: Mysteries and Puzzles of the New World.*** HarperCollins, 1992. ISBN 0-06-023728-7

■■■■■■■□□□□□□□

After a brief view of Columbus's voyage, Lauber undertakes other mysteries, such as who were these "Indians"? We learn about civilizations in the New World and find out how modern science views the migration across the land bridge and about the theory that early Irish priests and Vikings visited the New World long before Columbus.

◆ Lowe, Steve. ***The Log of Christopher Columbus.*** Philomel, 1992.
ISBN 0-399-22139-5

■■■■■■■□□□□□□□

Excerpts from Columbus's log produce a more immediate sense of the man than some children's biographies do. It is also useful as a sample of journals or diaries.

◆ Smith, Carter. ***The Explorers and Settlers: A Sourcebook on Colonial America.*** Millbrook, 1991. ISBN 0-56294-035-X

■■■■■■■■■□□□□□

This is one in a series of six books that are excellent resource books for a study of the American Colonial Period and the events that preceded it.

Anderson, Joan. ***Spanish Pioneers in the Southwest.*** Lodestar, 1989.
ISBN 0-525-67264-8

■■■□□□□□□□□□□□

The author and illustrator recreate a Spanish outpost in New Mexico.

Ash, Maureen. ***Vasco Nuñez de Balboa: Expedition to the Pacific Ocean.***
Childrens, 1990. ISBN 0-516-03057-4

■■■■■■■■□□□□□□

This biography of the first European to see the Pacific is factual and well written.

Brown, Warren. ***The Search for the Northwest Passage.*** Chelsea, 1990.
ISBN 0-7910-1297-2

■■■■■■■■■■■□□□

This account of the numerous attempts to discover the mythical passage does not gloss over the cruelties and negative aspects of the explorers' actions.

Burch, Joann. ***Isabella of Castile: Queen on Horseback.*** Watts, 1991.
ISBN 0-531-20033-7

■■■■■■■■■■■■■□

Queen Isabella is included because of her influence on development in the New World. Her biography is straightforward; however, her role in the Inquisition is passed off as the villainy of Torquemada.

Fisher, Leonard Everett. **Prince Henry the Navigator.** Macmillan, 1990. ISBN 0-02-735231-5   ■■■■■□□□□□□□□□□□

Many of the books about later explorers cite the influences of Prince Henry and his discoveries on later voyages. Here Fisher gives us a picture biography of the Portuguese explorer. The strength of the book is the informative illustrations.

Fradin, Dennis. **Amerigo Vespucci.** Watts, 1991. ISBN 0-531-20035-3

■■■■■■■■□□□□□□□

This book outlines Vespucci's achievements while moralizing a bit too heavily perhaps on the evils he committed. However, the author does talk about the changing values of the time and the belief that the captured Indian slaves would gain more by becoming Christians than they would lose by becoming slaves.

Fritz, Jean. **Brendan the Navigator: A History Mystery about the Discovery of America.** Putnam, 1979. ISBN 0-698-20473-5

■■■■□□□□□□□□□□□

There is a great deal of evidence that Columbus was far from the first to land on Western shores. Here Fritz uses her wit and wisdom to tell us what little is known about the Irish monk who might have been the first European in North America.

Hills, Ken. **The Voyages of Columbus.** Random, 1991. ISBN 0-679-82185-6

■■■■■■■■□□□□□□□

Using old prints and drawings to illustrate the text, the book begins with Columbus's childhood but concentrates on his triumphs and travails. There is little information about his effect on the natives he discovered.

Krensky, Stephen. **Christopher Columbus.** Random, 1991. ISBN 0-679-90369-0

■■■□□□□□□□□□□□□

This very simple book tells of Columbus's first voyage and his triumphal return.

Leon, George deLucenay. **Explorers of the Americas Before Columbus.** Watts, 1989. ISBN 0-531-10667-5

■■■■■■■■□□□□□□□

This book is an investigation into the lives of various early explorers.

Osborne, Mary Pope. **The Story of Christopher Columbus: Admiral of the Ocean Sea.** Dell, 1987. ISBN 0-440-41275-7

■■■■■■■□□□□□□□□

This brief biography presents the background and struggle of Columbus's first voyage. It also describes his later voyages and his attempts to settle the islands he found. For the most part, it does not gloss over his treatment of the natives and includes an epilogue that describes the author's research and questionable sources.

Simon, Charnan. **Leif Eriksson and the Vikings.** Childrens, 1991. ISBN 0-516-03060-4   ■■■■■□□□□□□□□□□□

This is a simple treatment of Eriksson and other Viking explorers.

Triggs, Tony D. ***Viking Warriors.*** Bookwright, 1990. ISBN 0-531-18356-4

■■■□□□□□□□□□□□□

Although this book does not concern itself with Viking explorers, the facts that it does contain about the Vikings' way of life are presented simply and are accompanied by clear and informative illustrations.

Weiner, Eric. ***The Story of Henry Hudson: Master Explorer.*** Dell, 1991. ISBN 0-440-40513-0

■■■■■■■■□□□□□□□

Little is known about Hudson's early years and the author spends little time on them. Most of the book tells of his daring voyages in the North as he tried again and again to find a water route through the North American continent to Asia. His determination eventually caused a mutiny, and he was last seen cast adrift in the waters of Hudson's bay.

Whitman, Sylvia. ***Hernando de Soto and the Explorers of the American South.*** Chelsea, 1990. ISBN 0-7910-1301-4

■■■■■■■■■■■■□□□

A book in the World Explorers series, this book is one of the few accounts that is specific about the massacres and horrid treatment of the Native American tribes with whom the explorers came in contact.

Nonprint

Videos

The Age of Exploration Series. Encyclopedia Britannica, 1991.

A five-part series with colorful visuals, such as animated maps and art prints, recounts the accomplishments of the European explorers from their positive aspects. Little time is spent on the effect of the voyages on native peoples.

The Discovery of the Americas. Spoken Arts.

The video uses the book by Betsy and Giulio Maestro of the same title, which starts with the immigration of early civilizations across the land bridge from Asia and ends with the more familiar travels of Cabot, Balboa, Magellan, and Columbus.

Filmstrips

Columbus and the Age of Discovery. SVE, 1991.

This is a set of three tapes and filmstrips: "The World before Columbus," "Columbus Finds a New World," and "Columbus Changes the World." Maps, artwork, and photographs create a factual and accessible fund of information.

The Time of the Pilgrims and Early Settlers: 1600–1700 *The Times at a Glance...*

Movers & Shakers

John Endicott

Sir Ferdinando Gorges

Thomas Hooker

Anne Hutchinson

Massasoit

Peter Minuit

Pocahontas

Powhatan

Miles Standish

John Smith

Peter Stuyvesant

Thomas West

John White

Roger Williams

Edward Winslow

John Winthrop

*Headlines**

1621	Massasoit makes treaty not to harm Pilgrims if Pilgrims respect Indian land and rights
1664	English take New Amsterdam from Dutch; name it New York
1669	Massachusetts Bay Colony takes over Maine
1673	Marquette and Jolliet explore Mississippi River
1675-1676	King Philip's War ravages New England
1682	William Penn arrives in Pennsylvania; its Frame of Government grants religious tolerance
1689-1697	King William's War outcome inconclusive
1692	Salem witch trials

*Many of the dates are only estimates made by historians and scientists. We tried to verify each date with at least two reliable sources; in cases where we found disagreement, we checked several sources. It is reasonable to expect that in your research you will also find disagreement.

1000 1050 1100 1150 1200 1250 1300 1350 1400 1450 1500 1550 1600 1650 1700 1750 1800 1850 1900 1950 2000

Meanwhile, In Other Parts of the World

1663	French take control of Canada from private company
1685	King Louis XIV revokes freedom of worship for Huguenots; many emigrate

Inventions & Discoveries

1642	Pascal invents adding machine
1657	Pendulum clock
1670	Minute hands on watches

Music

1650	Minuet popular at French Court
1666	Stradivarius violin created
1692	*Adeste Fideles*

Books

1656	Cotton's *Spiritual Milk for Boston Babes*
1658	Comenius's *Orbis Pictus*
1678	Bunyan's *Pilgrim's Progress*
1683	*New England Primer*
1667	Milton's *Paradise Lost*
1686	Bunyan's *A Book for Boys and Girls or Country Rhymes for Children*

The Time of the Pilgrims and Early Settlers: 1600–1700

Activities

- See The Native American Conflict on page 59, Cultures on page 128, Before Columbus on page 160, and ***The Salem Witchcraft Trials*** on page 258.

- The early Pilgrims built their houses using wattle and daub. Build wattle and daub models with clay, sand, and straw plastered on stick forms. It will crack, but so did the wattle and daub.

- List some ways of preserving food before canning and freezing were available. Find out what foods were preserved in those ways. Try it.

- Dry apples. Core the apples, leaving the skin on. Slice the apples across, making apple rings. Pass a string through the holes, leaving a space between slices. Hang them to dry.

- Make a list of the things you think the early settlers would have brought with them from Europe. Find actual lists and compare them.

- Pick herbs such as thyme, basil, or rosemary. Taste them as fresh herbs and then dry them. Prepare a dish using one or all of your dried herbs.

- Plant or design an authentic kitchen garden. Write to Plimouth Plantation for directions.

- Using descriptions from books or information from the historic museums, diagram or make a model of an early village.

- Write to curators of a history museum or living history museum and ask questions that have come up during your research.

- Make a list of the things the Pilgrims and other early settlers agreed to do in the Colony for their sponsors. Mark which of the items they accomplished in the agreed upon time.

- Find examples of words and expressions that were part of early American English. What words do we use today instead of those early words? Find some words that are currently in the process of change.

- Find inventive or multiple spellings of the same word in the early settlers' writings. When did spelling become standardized?

- Write a journal entry about your daily life, using the language and spelling the early settlers might have used.

- Find early songs and categorize them according to their type and the need they filled: story, work, spiritual, release, humor. Find current songs that fill each of these needs.

- The Pilgrims drew up the Mayflower Compact as a constitution. Compare the individual rights issues in the Mayflower Compact to those in the US Constitution. Create a constitution for your classroom. How does it compare with the Pilgrims' constitution?

- Make one of these dishes taught to the early Colonists of New England by Native Americans: succotash, johnnycake, Indian pudding, corn oysters, red flannel hash, or apple pandowdy. (Recipes for these dishes are in ***Slumps, Grunts and Snickerdoodles.*** See page 187.)

- Explore the reasons settlers came to Colonial America. Make a chart showing this information.

- Show how the local landscape affected the settlers' choices by drawing a map of the area. Identify important land features and their uses.

- How would your current locality be used by similar settlers? Is there fresh water nearby? How about a food source? What materials could they use for shelter? On a map of your area, indicate the best spot for their village.

- How did Native Americans and Pilgrims interact? How are two cultures interacting in your area? Use Marcia Sewall's two books on the same area, **People of the Breaking Day** and **The Pilgrims of Plimoth,** for information on the two cultures.

- To show the difficulties of communication between settlers and Native Americans, divide your classroom down the middle for a day. People can only talk to people on their own side. They can use only non-verbal communication with the other side. Have both groups work together to complete a class project.

- Create your own examples of rustic art. Use toys made from natural substances and decorate them. Decorate clothing using only materials available to the early settlers.

- Invent games that need no equipment or create equipment out of available materials. What games do you play that the early settlers could have played?

- Most of the Pilgrims and many of the other early settlers were illiterate. Spend a day at school without reading anything. How much of the world is cut off for you?

- Write a story about how members of your household would behave if they were forced to live in one room the way the early settlers did. Could any of their problems be solved?

- How much food does a person need for a year? How did the early settlers store it? Use empty boxes to approximate the volume of food for one year for one person. Label the boxes by type: meat, vegetables, grains, sweets, fruit, and dairy products.

- Compare the uses of oil today with those of the early settlers. What did they use instead of oil? Try some of the simpler substitutions.

- Imagine not being able to be open about your religious beliefs and having to pretend to agree with someone else's. Compare your own religious views with those of the Pilgrims or Puritans. Which ones would you have to change or pretend to change? Write a letter to someone sympathetic to your plight.

- Find out about about hornbooks. Make one for today. What would you put on a single page for beginning readers?

- Compare the tasks of Wampanoag women with those of English peasant women. Who performed those tasks in other ages, areas, and cultures?

Picture Books ★ Sewall, Marcia. **People of the Breaking Day.** Atheneum, 1990. ISBN 0-689-31407-8

A member of the Wampanoag tribe, who occupied the area that became Plymouth, tells of the ceremonies and customs that mark the passages of life of these people who lived in harmony with nature under the guidance and wisdom of Massasoit.

★ ————. **The Pilgrims of Plimoth.** Macmillan, 1986. ISBN 0-689-31250-4

This beautiful picture book gives us a historically accurate look at the life of the Pilgrims about 1630. Told from the points of view of several Pilgrims, the book does much to erase many of the misconceptions about those early settlers.

Costabel, Eva Deutsch. ***The Jews of New Amsterdam.*** Atheneum, 1988. ISBN 0-689-31351-9

The first Jewish venture into North America was in 1654 when twenty-three Jews bound for Amsterdam, Holland, in flight from persecution in Brazil, landed in New Amsterdam. Although hardly received with open arms, they stayed in the colony and, in 1657, Asser Levy became the first Jewish citizen of North America. Although it is oversimplified, this book gives quite a bit of information about the Jews' effect on the Dutch of New Amsterdam and the Dutch culture's influence on the Jews.

Dalgliesh, Alice. ***The Thanksgiving Story.*** Illustrated by Helen Sewell. Aladdin, 1954. ISBN 0-689-71053-4

*Although this is a book intended for younger readers, it does contain accurate information about the Mayflower, its passengers, and their first year in a new land. Because it also mentions Constance Hopkins and her family, it ties in well with Patricia Clapp's book, **Constance** (at the bottom of this page).*

Lobel, Arnold. ***On the Day Peter Stuyvesant Sailed into Town.*** Harper, 1971. ISBN 0-06-443144-4

Obviously this book is not about the Pilgrims but about the Dutch Colony of New Amsterdam in 1647 when Stuyvesant arrived. After giving us an initial summary of the facts about Stuyvesant, this charming picture book tells, in rhyme, of Stuyvesant's dismay at the dirt and lack of pride exhibited by the settlers there. Not known for his patience, Stuyvesant was soon issuing orders to clean up and get organized. After a few years of hard work, even Peter Stuyvesant's tender sensibilities were satisfied and the whole town celebrated. The story ends with a picture of Manhattan now as part of Stuyvesant's dream. The story line is simple, but there is a great deal of information and concept development here.

McGovern, Ann. ***If You Sailed on the Mayflower in 1620.*** Illustrated by Anna DiVito. Scholastic, 1991. ISBN 0-590-45161-8

This book is based around short, informative answers to questions about life on the Mayflower and in the Colony during that first year. There's a cutaway diagram of the Mayflower showing people crowded inside it. The text is simple, but the book quite successfully involves the reader in the problems and concerns of the early settlers.

Fiction

♦ Clapp, Patricia. ***Constance: A Story of Early Plymouth.*** Morrow, 1991. ISBN 0-688-10976-4

■■■■■■□□□□□□□□

Least Sophisticated   Most Sophisticated

This is the imaginary journal kept by a real person from the time she arrives in North America on the Mayflower until her wedding five years later. Although a work of fiction, the book sticks quite closely to the facts and provides some insight into the hardships and triumphs of the first few years in the new land.

♦ ———. ***Witches' Children: A Story of Salem.*** Puffin, 1987. ISBN 0-14-032407-0

■■■■■■■■■■■□□□

Mary Warren tells us of the Salem witch trials in a first person narrative that is historically correct and terrifyingly compelling. Mary admits that she started raving about witches just for sport and soon got caught up in the hysteria. When she tries to explain, she is herself tried as a witch. This book works well with **Tituba of Salem Village** *. See page 258 for* **The Salem Witchcraft Trials** *, a Focus Book closely related to this novel.*

◆   Cohen, Barbara. **Molly's Pilgrim.** Bantam, 1983. ISBN 0-5532-15833-3

■■■■■□□□□□□□□□□

This book actually takes place during the early 1900s but concerns the early Pilgrims and later immigrants, so we've placed it here. Molly is often teased by her classmates for her imperfect English and foreign ways. When her class studies the Pilgrims, Molly takes pride in her mother's journey across the ocean to find religious freedom.

◆   Monjo, F. N. **The House on Stink Alley.** Dell, 1977. ISBN 0-440-43376-2

■■■■■■■■■■□□□□□

Historical fiction based on primary documents, this is the story of the Pilgrims' years in Holland. The book is narrated by Love Brewster, the son of the church elder. Born in Holland, he is fascinated by the tales of the church's persecution in England and brings us a firsthand account of his father's involvement in the fight against King James' attempts to subvert the democratic structures in some churches. The book ends when the Mayflower sets sail for America. This is a good example of a short piece of literature that is very appropriate for more sophisticated readers. Here we find questions about monarchies, democracy within a spiritual community, the effects of political struggles on families, civil disobedience, church and state, motives, honor, and secrecy.

◆   Petry, Ann. **Tituba of Salem Village.** HarperCollins, 1964. ISBN 0-06-440403-X

■■■■■■■■■□□□□□□

This novel begins in Barbados in 1688 and moves through Boston to Salem, Massachusetts, during the Salem witch trials and the eventual pardoning of all witchcraft prisoners in 1693. Tituba Indian and her husband, John Indian, are slaves of a wealthy widow in Barbados who sells them to pay off gambling debts. They are sold to Reverend Samuel Parris on his way to Boston with his sickly wife, young daughter, and niece Abigail. The minister is an arrogant man who finally moves his family to Salem where he has been hired. From the beginning, there is friction between the minister and his parish. The book explores some of the contributing factors to the witch trials and brings us a close-up look at the effects of those trials on one household. The characters are believable and the story is a gripping one. Many of the participants are indentured boys and girls. We become involved in the structure of the society and the beliefs of the time. See page 258 for **The Salem Witchcraft Trials,** *a Focus Book closely related to this novel.*

◆   Speare, Elizabeth. **The Witch of Blackbird Pond.** Houghton, 1978. ISBN 0-440-49586-2

■■■■■■■■■■□□□□□

Kit is a misfit in a Puritan household. Raised in colorful Barbados, Kit feels peace only in the meadows near Blackbird Pond. There she meets Quaker Hannah, who is considered a witch by the Puritans of Wethersfield. Gradually, suspicion gathers and eventually things come to a head during a witchcraft trial. See page 258 for **The Salem Witchcraft Trials** *, a Focus Book closely related to this novel.*

Bulla, Clyde Robert. ***A Lion to Guard Us.*** Crowell, 1981. ISBN 0-690-04097-0

■■■■■■■□□□□□□□□

Three motherless children set sail for Jamestown to find their father who went ahead to the new land the previous year. Their ship is wrecked near Bermuda, and the children save only the lion's head door knocker from their home in England.

Christian, Mary Blount. ***Goody Sherman's Pig.*** Macmillan, 1990. ISBN 0-02-718251-7

■■■■□□□□□□□□□□□

Her pig kept running away and Goody Sherman was a feisty woman who would not give up the legal battle in 1636 Massachusetts. Taking her case first to the church elders and then to the inferior court, she succeeded in 1642 in appealing to the general court. Eventually, her situation forced the creation of two legislative branches in the Colony. The story is based on fact.

Nonfiction

★ Fritz, Jean. ***The Double Life of Pocahontas.*** Putnam, 1983. ISBN 0-399-21016-4

■■■■■■■■■■■□□□□□

Fritz's touch is as sure as ever as she relates the facts about the Indian princess who, as much as any one person could, exemplified the clash of two cultures. The daughter of Powhatan, Pocahontas was the adopted sister of Captain John Smith. Although for a while she was allowed to move back and forth between the cultures, she soon found herself forced to live in the white man's world, even leaving her beloved wilderness to die in England.

◆ Bradford, William, et al. ***Homes in the Wilderness: A Pilgrim's Journal of Plymouth Plantation in 1620.*** Linnet, 1988. ISBN 0-208-02269-4

■■■■■■■■□□□□□□□

This edited and slightly simplified edition of "Mourt's Relation," the only journal extant written by the Pilgrims themselves during that first year in the New World, is a valuable primary source. Although the language has been simplified, it retains the formal quality of the original.

◆ Fritz, Jean. ***Who's That Stepping on Plymouth Rock?*** Putnam, 1975. ISBN 0-698-20325-9

■■■□□□□□□□□□□□□

This may be the only biography of a real rock. This book tells us less about the Pilgrims (who probably never stepped on it) than it does about the people in the next three hundred years. The rock, laid in the harbor by a glacier, was a very large one and was surely there when the Pilgrims landed, but they'd have to have been crazy to steer their ship toward a big rock when the sandy harbor was safer and handier. Nevertheless, descendents of the original settlers and other people of the town of Plymouth focused on the rock as a symbol. They moved it three times, each time damaging it, but now it stands in a Grecian portico to remind us all of the First Comers, as they called themselves.

Hubbard-Brown, Janet. ***The Secret of Roanoke Island.*** Avon, 1991.
ISBN 0-380-76223-4

■■■■■■□□□□□□□

In a brief and unthreatening format, this is an account of the mysterious disappearance of the first settlers of Roanoke Island. Some background material is included through the experiences of Governor John White. At the conclusion of the book, the author offers some possible and plausible solutions to the mystery.

Penner, Lucille Recht. ***Eating the Plates: A Pilgrim Book of Food and Manners.*** Macmillan, 1991. ISBN 0-02-770901-9

■■■■■■□□□□□□□

Although the book focuses on food, it also contains a great deal of information about other aspects of Pilgrim life, both aboard the Mayflower and after the landing. The book includes recipes for a Pilgrim menu.

San Souci, Robert. ***N. C. Wyeth's Pilgrims.*** Chronicle Books, 1991. ISBN 0-87701-806-5

■■■■□□□□□□□□□

Using a variety of sources, this carefully researched text uses Wyeth's paintings, which were commissioned by the Metropolitan Life Insurance Company in 1940, to tell of the first year in Plymouth Colony.

Nonprint

Videos

Early Colonists. United Learning, 1992.

Pope's Creek Plantation, Jamestown Plantation in Virginia, and St. Mary's City in Maryland are used as material for this film. The film gives background on the people who colonized those areas and tells about their lives after they arrived in America.

The First Thanksgiving. Barr Films, 1991.

A historical re-enactment of the event from the point of view of Love Brewster, who has his own part in setting up the festivities. The film is an opportunity to see the Pilgrims as something other than the dour, colorless people of the stereotypes.

The Pilgrims of Plimoth. Weston Woods Studios, 1988.

Based on Marcia Sewall's picture book, the video is so informative that even children who have already read the book will gain from another look.

The Pilgrims at Plymouth. Barr Films, 1991.

The immigrants are shown in their village, but there is also coverage of the reasons for their move to the New World, the signing of the Mayflower Compact, and the building of their village.

Early Colonial Period: 1700–1750 *The Times at a Glance...*

Movers & Shakers

John Adams
Jeffrey Amherst
Daniel Boone
Joseph Brant
George Calvert
Benjamin Franklin
Patrick Henry
Thomas Jefferson
Father Marquette
Cotton Mather
James Oglethorpe
William Penn
Pontiac
Roger Sherman
George Washington
Eleazar Wheelock
Roger Williams
John Winthrop

Headlines*

1702	War of Spanish Succession begins; Colonists call it Queen Anne's War
1709	Mass emigration of Germans to America begins
1714-1720	Many Scotch-Irish immigrate to Pennsylvania
1718	New Orleans founded
1720-1724	French forts built along Mississippi north from New Orleans
1721	South Carolina becomes a Royal Colony
1728	North Carolina becomes a Royal Colony
1732	Georgia chartered
1735	John Peter Zenger acquitted of libel; appointed public printer for New York and New Jersey
1741	Bering reaches Alaska

*Many of the dates are only estimates made by historians and scientists. We tried to verify each date with at least two reliable sources; in cases where we found disagreement, we checked several sources. It is reasonable to expect that in your research you will also find disagreement.

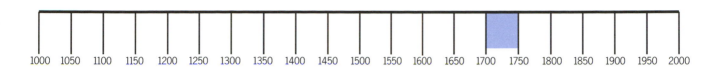

Meanwhile, In Other Parts of the World

1702	French win control of Asiento contract allowing them to transport black slaves to the Spanish colonies
1702-1713	War of Spanish Succession; ends with France losing Canada territory to Britain
1713	Treaty of Utrecht gives Britain control of Asiento slave trade
1733	England prohibits trade between American and West Indian colonies
1739-1748	War of Jenkin's Ear; brings rivalry in America between England and Spain
1740	Frederick the Great of Prussia introduces religious toleration and agricultural reform

Inventions & Discoveries

1721	First smallpox innoculations given in America

Architecture & Music

1732	Independence Hall started
1741	*Rule Britania*
1744	*God Save the King* Quadrille dance popular in France

Books

1697	Perrault's *Little Red Riding Hood*
1715	Watts's *Divine and Moral Songs*
1719	Defoe's *The Life and Strange Surprising Adventures of Robinson Crusoe*
1732	Franklin's *Poor Richard's Almanack*
1744	Cooper's *Tommy Thumb's Pretty Song Book*

Fads & Customs

1734	Great Awakening-spiritual revival in Colonies spearheaded by Jonathan Edwards

Early Colonial Period: 1700–1750

Activities

- See The Native American Conflict on page 59, Slavery on page 106, and Cultures on page 128.

- On a map of the Colonies indicate which Colonies allowed slavery at this time. Further activities about slavery are on pages 106–10.

- Divide the class into teams to represent each Colony. Begin with an arbitrary date, such as 1720, and have each group find out about their Colony at that time. For example, what settlements existed? How big were they? What jobs did the people have? Who did they trade with? What kind of government did the Colony use? What diseases were a problem?

- What events during this time had the most effect on later times? Defend your ideas.

- Find out about clothing of the period. What discoveries, inventions, or new areas of trade made such clothing possible or desirable? Further activities on inventions and discoveries are on pages 118–22.

- Look at the big picture of this time: the Indian wars, the new settlements and immigration, and other major events and movements. Find a way to show how these factors interacted. You might use a play, flow charts, murals, or a web

- Find music and dances from the era. Perform them, listen to them, watch them in films.

- On a map show the principal population centers of the time. Include the locations of Native American groups.

- Look at the make-up of the household in one of the suggested novels. Was this a typical family? How was it different?

- What religions were prevalent in the Colonies at that time? Was religious tolerance on the increase or decrease? On what do you base that opinion?

- What were the values of the time? Who were the heroes?

- How was the drive for expansion reflected in the values of the time?

- What might you assume about the settlers' impact on the environment of this time? Use the figures on population centers to figure out how the countryside must have changed after their arrival.

- How did the arrival of settlers impact the Native American cultures? What happened when they were forced to live in smaller areas and nearer to other tribes and white settlers? How were the relationships of the tribes changed? How did Indians communicate with each other and with white settlers? What were leaders like Pontiac and Joseph Brant doing? What agreements might they have worked out together?

- What were immigrant and Native American cultures doing to preserve their cultures at this time?

- Can you picture yourself living in this era? What would you like about it? Write a diary entry for yourself.

Picture Books

Locker, Thomas. ***The Land of Gray Wolf.*** Dial, 1990. ISBN 0-8037-0936-6

We watch with Running Deer, a young Indian, as the wilderness becomes small farms, villages, and roads until there is no wilderness left.

Fiction

★ Field, Rachel. ***Calico Bush.*** Dell, 1931. ISBN 0-440-40368-5

■■■■■■■■□□□□□□□

Least Sophisticated   Most Sophisticated

This is a Focus Book; see page 262.

◆ Dalgliesh, Alice. ***The Courage of Sarah Noble.*** Aladdin, 1954. ISBN 0-689-71057-7

■■■■□□□□□□□□□□□

This is a Focus Book; see page 260.

◆ Fritz, Jean. ***The Cabin Faced West.*** Putnam, 1958. ISBN 0-14-03225-6

■■■■■■■□□□□□□□□

Ten-year-old Anna Hamilton lives with her family in Western Pennsylvania. Her father built the cabin facing west because he wanted the family to look to the future, not the past. Life as the only little girl in that area is not what Anna wants. She resents the lack of books, windows, and other niceties. Then George Washington comes to dinner. This book is based on the true experiences of the author's grandmother.

◆ Gilman, Dorothy. ***Girl in Buckskin.*** Ballantine, 1956. ISBN 0-449-70380-0

■■■■■■■■■■□□□□□

See page 65.

Avi. ***Night Journeys.*** Pantheon, 1979. ISBN 0-394-94116-0

■■■■■■■■■■□□□□□

Peter York, an orphan, is taken in by Quaker farmer Everett Shinn who, although kind, is frustratingly uncommunicative. When Peter and Everett find two escaped bond servants, Everett, a Justice of the Peace, is unwilling to turn them in. So is Peter as he becomes sympathetic to their plight.

O'Dell, Scott. ***My Name Is Not Angelica.*** Dell, 1989. ISBN 0-440-40379-0

■■■■■■■■■■□□□□□

This is a tale of slavery on the islands of St. Thomas and St. John as told by a young female slave. The slaves' decision to jump into the sea, committing mass suicide, is similar to the one made by many Arawaki Indians rather than face slavery and mistreatment from Columbus and his men.

Nonfiction

◆ Fradin, Dennis. ***The Connecticut Colony.*** Childrens, 1990. ISBN 0-516-00393-3

———. ***The Georgia Colony.*** Childrens, 1990. ISBN 0-516-00392-5

———. ***The Maryland Colony.*** Childrens, 1990. ISBN 0-516-00394-1

———. ***The Massachusetts Colony.*** Childrens, 1990. ISBN 0-516-00386-0

———. ***The New Hampshire Colony.*** Childrens, 1990. ISBN 0-516-00388-7

———. ***The New Jersey Colony.*** Childrens, 1990. ISBN 0-516-00395-X

———. ***The New York Colony.*** Childrens, 1990. ISBN 0-516-00389-5

———. ***The North Carolina Colony.*** Childrens, 1990. ISBN 0-516-00396-8

———. ***The Pennsylvania Colony.*** Childrens, 1990. ISBN 0-516-00390-9

———. ***The Rhode Island Colony.*** Childrens, 1990. ISBN 0-516-00391-7

———. ***The Virginia Colony.*** Childrens, 1990. ISBN 0-516-00387-9

■■■■■■■□□□□□□□□

Each of these books covers more than the Colonial period. Each begins with the Indian cultures that were there before the arrival of the Europeans, proceeds through the first settlements and encounters, and continues through the Revolution. Each includes many photographs and drawings, facsimiles of relevant documents, a time line of the Colony's history, and brief biographies of the important figures in the area.

◆ Freedman, Russell. ***Indian Chiefs.*** Holiday, 1987. ISBN 0-8234-0625-3

■■■■■■■□□□□□□□□

This well-written book covers the lives of six great Western Indian chiefs who led their people into and out of conflict with the white settlers and gives us insight into the motivations and actions of these men.

◆ Fritz, Jean. ***George Washington's Mother.*** Grosset, 1992. ISBN 0-448-40384-6

■■■□□□□□□□□□□□□

This is a very easy-to-read biography of the mother of the Father of Our Country. If you expect nobility and high mindedness of such a woman, you're in for a surprise. According to Jean Fritz, Mary Washington was a nag, a slob, and an extremely self-centered woman. Somehow, George seems more human after reading this one.

◆ ———. ***What's the Big Idea, Ben Franklin?*** Coward, 1976. ISBN 0-698-20543-X

■■■□□□□□□□□□□□□

The fascinating life of one of the best-known signers of the Declaration of Independence is told with Fritz's usual blend of humorous foibles and serious accomplishments. The biography concentrates on Franklin's "big ideas": that lightning and electricity are the same and that the United States should be a free and independent nation. The book is easily accessible to young readers and provides insight into the man and his time.

◆ Perl, Lila. ***Slumps, Grunts, and Snickerdoodles: What Colonial America Ate and Why.*** Clarion, 1975. ISBN 0-395-28923-8

Perl tells how the major ingredients for cooking were cultivated or imported to the Colonies, how they were changed to suit the climate and needs of the Colonists, and then how they were combined to make some regionally popular dishes such as johnnycake, Indian pudding, corn oysters, red flannel hash, apple pandowdy, snickerdoodles, shoo fly pie, hush puppies, spoon bread, and shortnin' bread. Perl also gives the probable origins for these improbable names.

◆ Smith, Carter. ***The Arts and Sciences: A Sourcebook on Colonial America.*** Millbrook, 1991. ISBN 1-56294-037-6

———. ***Battles in a New Land: A Sourcebook on Colonial America.*** Millbrook, 1991. ISBN 1-56294-034-1

———. ***Daily Life: A Sourcebook on Colonial America.*** Millbrook, 1991. ISBN 0-1-56294-038-4

———. ***Governing and Teaching: A Sourcebook on Colonial America.*** Millbrook, 1991. ISBN 0-56294-036-8

*Together with **The Explorers and Settlers** (page 171) and **The Revolutionary War** (page 74) this series of six books makes a handy reference source. Each book contains a detailed time line, showing events in the Colonies and the rest of the world and includes copies of prints and maps to illustrate a clear text.*

Fleming, Alice. ***George Washington Wasn't Always Old.*** Simon, 1991. ISBN 0-671-69557-6

The days of Washington up to his twenty-first birthday are recounted in a way that gives you some insight into his character: his over-protective mother, his relationships with his father and half-brother, and his family's frequent moves. Fleming tells us about a privileged life in eighteenth-century America. By accepting this lifestle as though it applied to everyone of the time, the author is guilty of misinformation, but that very fact makes the book a good starting point for a discussion of class and lifestyle.

Osborne, Mary Pope. ***George Washington: Leader of a New Nation.*** Dial, 1991. ISBN 0-8037-0947-1

This is an interesting, well-rounded biography covering Washington's early years as well as his years of service to the country. Unlike many biographies of Washington, this one includes the fact that he kept slaves and showed no inclination to free them.

The New Nation: 1750–1800 *The Times at a Glance...*

Movers & Shakers

John Burgoyne

George Clark

William Clark

Thomas Jefferson

Meriwether Lewis

Sacajawea

George Washington

Headlines*

1754	George Washington's troops at Fort Duquesne open French and Indian War
1763	Ottawa Chief Pontiac leads Native American uprising against British
1764	British Parliament passes Sugar Act
1765	British Parliament passes Stamp Act
1766	Special congress protests Stamp Act; Act repealed
1769	Colonies begin westward expansion with Tennessee
1770	Five Colonists die at Boston Massacre
1773	Boston Tea Party
1774	Meeting of First Continental Congress
1775	Revolution begins at Lexington and Concord
1776	US Declaration of Independence signed
1781	British surrender at Yorktown
1784	US begins China trade
1787	Northwest Ordinance provides plan of government for Western lands
1788	US Constitution ratified
1791	Bill of Rights adopted
1794	Whiskey Rebellion in Pennsylvania
1797	XYZ affair: conflict over French interference in American shipping

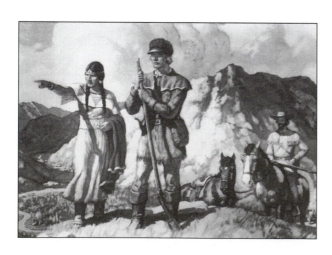

*Many of the dates are only estimates made by historians and scientists. We tried to verify each date with at least two reliable sources; in cases where we found disagreement, we checked several sources. It is reasonable to expect that in your research you will also find disagreement.

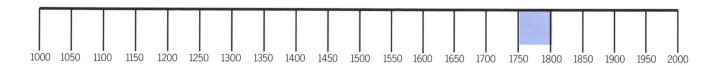

1000 1050 1100 1150 1200 1250 1300 1350 1400 1450 1500 1550 1600 1650 1700 1750 1800 1850 1900 1950 2000

Meanwhile, In Other Parts of the World

1756-1763 Seven Years War—Austria defeated by Prussia

1757 Robert Clive establishes English authority over southern India

1760 Most of Canada under British control

1763 France cedes Canada to England

1766 Mozart's career begins

1768 James Cook explores Australia

1772 Catherine the Great reforms Russian provinces

1783 Sudden growth in English cotton industry marks beginning of English Industrial Revolution

1788 England establishes convict settlements in Australia

1789 French Revolution begins

1793 France becomes a republic
      Reign of Terror begins

1795 Slaves freed in French West Indies

1796 Napoleon defeats Austria

1798 Napoleon defeated by Nelson

1799 Napoleon establishes dictatorship in France

Music

1778 *Oh Dear, What Can the Matter Be*

Books

1766 Newbery's *History of Little Goody Two Shoes*

1776 Paine's *Common Sense*

1783 Webster's *Blue Backed Speller*

1786 Trimmer's *Fabulous Histories*

Inventions & Discoveries

1762 Sandwich invented

1778 Copying machine invented

1783 Self-winding clock invented

1787 Alarm clock invented

1789 Uranium discovered

1790 First US patent on spinning and weaving machine

1793 Cotton gin invented

1796 Smallpox vaccine discovered

1797 Parachute invented

The New Nation: 1750–1800

Activities

- See The Native American Conflict on page 59, The French and Indian War on page 64, The Revolutionary War on page 67, Slavery on page 106, and Cultures on page 128.

- The proclamation issued by the British in 1763 saved all land west of the Appalachians for Native Americans. Colonists could not settle there. Divide the class into three groups: the British, the Colonists, and the Native Americans. Argue for and against the proclamation.

- Find out about the Iroquois Nation. What were its rules for joining different tribes as one nation? Were any of the rules the same as those in our Constitution? Should they have been?

- Find out about the Cherokee Nation. Compare the Cherokee government to the United States government after the Revolution. Why was the Cherokee Nation's government like the US government?

- What type of government did Canada and England set up for Canada? Is this the type of government the United States might have had if the United States had remained part of the British Empire?

- During what stage in the development of England's government did the American Revolution occur? How did the representational aspects of England's government influence the formation of the US government?

- What happened in France after France's revolution. When did they set up a government and what type was it?

- Use flow charts, organizational charts, or graphs to show how each of the above governments was organized. Compare the powers and responsibilities of the king or president, representatives, judiciary, and citizens; election procedures; and statements of individual rights.

- Work with the librarian to create a time line of this era. Talk about which events and people you'll include and why. Show relationships among events with colored string. While reading biographies of the time, work in pairs to see which items on the time line relate to the character. For each item, make a reference card that lists the event, the name of the character, and a statement of how the character might have felt or what he/she might have done about that event.

- Establish a Hall of Fame for this period. Who are the players in this period? How will you determine which of them made the kind of contributions that would qualify them for the Hall of Fame?

- Dramatize any event from one of the fiction or nonfiction books suggested.

- Introduce Matt from ***Sign of the Beaver*** (page 191) to the hero of Gary Paulsen's ***Hatchet*** (Penguin, 1988. ISBN 0-14-032724-X). Would they like each other? What could they teach each other about survival then and now? How would each person's skills be helpful to the other person?

- The book ***Jump Ship to Freedom*** is part of a series of books. Write the plot for a sequel to ***Jump Ship to Freedom.*** What would you need to know about the time?

- Look at the main characters from the suggested fiction books. What factors made them the kind of people they were? What factors do they have in common? Which of them were most affected by political events of this period? Which of them were most affected by their physical environment?

- Do an author study of Jean Fritz. See pages 42–44 for a list of some of her books.

Picture Books

Lindbergh, Reeve. ***Johnny Appleseed.*** Paintings by Kathy Jakobsen. Little, 1990. ISBN 0-316-52618-5

The story of John Chapman is told in rhyme and opulent illustrations that capture the essence of the period and the man.

Fiction

★ Fleischman, Paul. ***The Borning Room.*** HarperCollins, 1991. ISBN 0-06-023785-6

■■■■■■■■■□□□□□□

Least Sophisticated   Most Sophisticated

This is a Focus Book; see page 274.

★ Keehn, Sally M. ***I Am Regina.*** Philomel, 1990. ISBN 0-399-21797-5

■■■■■■■■■■■□□□□

This is a fictionalized biography of Regina Leininger who was captured by Indians in 1755 when she was ten and returned to her mother eight years later. The book provides insight into the fears of the Colonists and the Native Americans. The cruel killing and scalping of her father and brother is Regina's first encounter with the Indians, and she hates and fears them long after her capture and adoption by a group of Allegheny Indians. However, she also witnesses the cruelty and treachery of the settlers. This is a good approach to a study of a clash of cultures.

★ Speare, Elizabeth George. ***The Sign of the Beaver.*** Dell, 1984. ISBN 0-440-47900-2

■■■■■■■□□□□□□□□

In 1768, Matt Hallowell and his father build a house in the Maine woods while the rest of the family is in Massachusetts. In early summer, when the cabin is finished, Mr. Hallowell leaves Matt with a rifle, a field of planted corn, and some minimal survival skills. After a fur trapper steals the rifle and Matt is almost fatally injured, an Indian chief offers to help Matt survive in return for teaching the chief's grandson, Attean, how to read. Attean proves an unwilling pupil, at least at first, but teaches Matt valuable survival techniques and at last a friendship emerges.

◆ Collier, James Lincoln and Collier, Christopher. ***The Bloody Country.*** Macmillan, 1985. ISBN 0-02-722960-2

After the Revolution, the families of Ben Buck and Joe Mountain become part of the Susquehanna Company that is settling Pennsylvania. The Bucks begin operating a mill there. After Indian uprisings and a devastating flood, many of the settlers decide to return to Connecticut. After a quarrel with Joe, who is black and considered a slave by some, Ben leads the settlers to Connecticut, but Ben returns to make the permanent settlement in Pennsylvania near what is now Wilkes-Barre.

◆   ———. *The Clock.* Delacorte, 1992. ISBN 0-385-30037-9

■■■■■■■■■■■■□□

See page 112.

◆   ———. *Jump Ship to Freedom.* Dell, 1987. ISBN 0-440-44323-7

■■■■■■■□□□□□□□

This post-revolution adventure novel takes place in 1787 in Connecticut. It's based on fact and tells the story of a fourteen-year-old slave's struggle to buy his and his mother's freedom. There's a good exploration of Northern slavery and of the Constitutional Convention's influence on slavery. The ending is a little weak, but the characters have depth and feelings.

◆   De Felice, Cynthia. *Weasel.* Macmillan, 1990. ISBN 0-02-726457-2

■■■■■■■■■■□□□□□

Nathan Fowler and his sister are alone in the cabin when Ezra arrives and wordlessly beckons them to follow him into the night wilderness. Their mother is dead and their father left several days before to hunt for food. With trepidation they follow and find their wounded father, and Nathan is brought face to face with an evil killer, Weasel, an ex-Indian fighter. Later, when Nathan has a chance and even a cause to kill Weasel, he does not and this decision returns to haunt him.

Edmonds, Walter. *The Matchlock Gun.* Dodd, 1941. ISBN 0-399-21911-0

■■■□□□□□□□□□□□

Based upon the adventures of a Dutch family in the Hudson River Valley in 1756, this account focuses on the terror and the courage of settlers who were victims of Indian raids. The book portrays Indians as blood-thirsty savages and, as such, should lead to discussion on the subject.

Fritz, Jean. *George Washington's Breakfast.* Putnam, 1984. ISBN 0-698-30099-8

■■■■■■■■■□□□□□

A modern young boy speculates on what George Washington had for breakfast. He is told that, if he can find out, his grandmother will cook it for him. The research takes him through many books and even to Mount Vernon. He gets his breakfast and we get a lot of information about Washington.

Hudson, Jan. *Dawn Rider.* Putnam, 1990. ISBN 0-399-22178-6

■■■■■□□□□□□□□□

Kit Fox is a sixteen-year-old Blackfoot Indian in the mid-1700s. Most of her tribe are leery of horses and the women are forbidden to ride them. Her tribe's one horse becomes Kit's friend and obsession, and she disobeys the taboo. When her camp is attacked, Kit's equestrian skill is necessary and redeeming.

Shub, Elizabeth. *Cutlass in the Snow.* Greenwillow, 1986. ISBN 0-688-05927-9

■■■■■□□□□□□□□□

This slight book is based on a legend passed down in the Campbell family for centuries and tells of a boy and his grandfather who, during the winter of 1797 on Fire Island, discover a cutlass in the snow pointing to buried pirates' treasure.

Nonfiction

◆   Fritz, Jean. ***Shh! We're Writing the Constitution.*** Putnam, 1987.
ISBN 0-399-21403-8

■■■■■□□□□□□□□□□

The trouble didn't end with the Revolution. A document had to be written that would satisfy every representative from every state. As usual, Fritz's text is historically accurate and she includes the human details that let us care. The book includes a copy of the US Constitution.

◆   ————. ***What's the Big Idea, Ben Franklin?*** Putnam, 1982. ISBN 0-698-20543-X

■■■□□□□□□□□□□□□

See page 186.

Bober, Natalie S. ***Thomas Jefferson, Man on a Mountain.*** Atheneum, 1988.
ISBN 0-689-31154-0

■■■■■■■■■■■■■□

A 250-page detailed and scholarly biography, this book starts with a chronology of Jefferson's life, listing major events from his birth in 1743 to his death in 1826. Through the text, we get an intimate view of the circle of young aristocrats in which Jefferson came of age. This is a valuable resource for the Jeffersonian enthusiast and a thorough insight into the conventional view of his life. Use it in concert with material that explores other viewpoints of the man and the period.

Fleming, Alice. ***George Washington Wasn't Always Old.*** Simon, 1991.
ISBN 0-671-69557-6

■■■□□□□□□□□□□□

See page 187.

Kent, Zachary. ***John Quincy Adams, Sixth President of the United States.***
Childrens, 1987. ISBN 0-516-01386-6

■■■■■□□□□□□□□□

Here is a simple biography about the son of a president who became a president.

Loeper, John J. ***Going to School in 1776.*** Macmillan, 1973. ISBN 0-689-30089-1

■■■■■■■□□□□□□□

Using old wood-cuts for illustrations, the author tells of school life in a time of great conflict, but the accent here is on the students, their teachers, their materials of instruction, and the conditions in schools at the time.

Quackenbush, Robert. ***Quit Pulling My Leg: A Story of Davy Crockett.***
Prentice, 1987. ISBN 0-671-66516-2

■■■□□□□□□□□□□□□

This brief biography separates fantasy from fact in the life of this frontiersman.

Nonprint

Videos

Meet the Newbery Authors: James Lincoln Collier and Christopher Collier.
American School Publishers.

Sign of the Beaver. American School Publishers, 1990.

First Steps for a New Nation: 1800–1850 *The Times at a Glance...*

Movers & Shakers

Cochise
John Brown
Dewitt Clinton
Horace Greeley
Andrew Jackson
Chief Joseph
Lewis and Clark
Louis Pasteur
Sequoya
Dred Scott
Tecumseh
Martin Van Buren

Headlines*

1801-1805	Conflict with Barbary pirates who interfere with US shipping
1803	Louisiana Purchase for $15,000,000 gives US territory between Rocky Mountains and Mississippi River
1806	Lewis and Clark Expedition completed
1807	Embargo Act forbids importation of slaves
1812	War of 1812 begins
1813	Creek Indian War (Creek War of 1813)
1817	American Colonization Society formed to return free Blacks to Africa for settlement
1819	Spain cedes control of Florida to US
1819	Financial panic hurts economy
1820	Missouri Compromise prohibits slavery north of latitude 36°30'
1823	Monroe Doctrine declares American continent free of European colonization
1825	Erie Canal completed
1830	Indian Removal Act
1831	Nat Turner leads slave uprising resulting in more than fifty white and more than a hundred slave deaths
1832	Black Hawk War begins
1836	Siege of the Alamo by Mexicans under Santa Anna
1839	Baseball devised
1845	Texas admitted to Union as part of Manifest Destiny
1845-1849	Potato famine in Ireland causes mass immigration to US
1846-1848	Mexican War; US acquires New Mexico, Texas, California, Arizona, Utah, and Nevada
1847	US invades Mexico
1848	Gold discovered in California starting Gold Rush of 1849

*Many of the dates are only estimates made by historians and scientists. We tried to verify each date with at least two reliable sources; in cases where we found disagreement, we checked several sources. It is reasonable to expect that in your research you will also find disagreement.

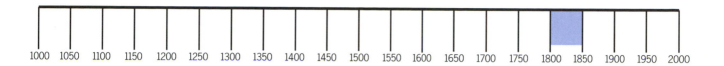

1000 1050 1100 1150 1200 1250 1300 1350 1400 1450 1500 1550 1600 1650 1700 1750 1800 1850 1900 1950 2000

Meanwhile, In Other Parts of the World

1804	Napoleon becomes emperor
1807	Slave trade abolished in British Empire
1814	Napoleon abdicates
1818	US/Canadian border established
1819	British establish Singapore as center for trade with Far East
1837	Queen Victoria takes British throne
1839	China and Britain begin Opium Wars

Inventions & Discoveries

1816	Bicycle invented
1819	First steamship crosses Atlantic
1825	First public steam railroad in England
1830	Screw threads standardized making mass production possible
1834	Electric telegraph patented in England
	Threshing machine invented
1835	Colt pistol, first repeating firearm patented
1838	Morse code invented
1839	Vulcanization of rubber by Goodyear
1842	Anesthesia used in surgery
1847	Semmelweis discovers cause of childbed fever

Music

1802	Beethoven's career begins
1808	*Believe Me If All Those Endearing Young Charms*
1813	Waltz becomes popular in United States
1814	*Star Spangled Banner* composed
1818	*Silent Night*
1822	*Old Oaken Bucket*
1832	*America*
1834	*Turkey in the Straw*
1838	*Flow Gently, Sweet Afton*
1843	*Columbia, the Gem of the Ocean*
1844	Polka becomes popular
1848	*Oh, Susannah*
	Sweet Alice Ben Bolt

Books

1814	Wyss's *The Swiss Family Robinson*
1826	Cooper's *The Last of the Mohicans*
1827	Goodrich's *Tales of Peter Parley about America*
1836	McGuffey's *Eclectic Readers*

First Steps for a New Nation: 1800–1850

Activities

- See The Native American Conflict on page 59, The War of 1812 on page 75, The Mexican War on page 76, Slavery on page 106, Cultures on page 128, and Politics and Government on page 140.

- Which United States' presidents had the best relationships with Native Americans? Defend your answer.

- Map the routes of the Erie Canal and other canals of the period. Find other places where canals would probably work.

- Obtain a topographical map of the area around the Erie Canal. Map the canal to show sights along the canal as they would have been in the late 1800s. Write a brochure inviting people to take a trip along the canal and describe the sights. Find out how long a trip on the canal took at this time. What kind of boat might have been used? How was it powered? Include this information in your brochure.

- Make a time line showing construction and use of canals and railroads. Make a graph that will show the peak activity of each method of transportation.

- Find and sing songs about the Erie Canal.

- Look at a map of Lewis and Clark's trip. As a group list natural landmarks, such as waterfalls, strange land formations, mountains, geysers, glaciers, and rivers. Make a list of the wildlife that Lewis and Clark probably encountered. Pretend that you are with them on their journey. Knowing that people back in Washington, DC, have never seen these animals or landmarks, write a journal entry that you can use to refresh your memory when you return to tell others about the land. Find entries from Lewis and Clark's journals that describe such phenomena. Compare your entry with theirs.

- Do an activity similar to the one above, describing the native people that Lewis and Clark encountered.

- If you were Sacajawea and were confronted by your tribe, how would you defend what you had done to help Lewis and Clark. Suppose that she knew how the whites and Indians would clash and how the encounters would end. How might that knowledge have influenced her decision to help the whites?

- Find the price of gold during the California Gold Rush, the Alaskan Gold Rush, and today. What could you do during each period with the money from the sale of one ounce of gold?

- Find folk songs of the time and determine what events and conditions generated the songs. Use musical instruments of the time to accompany the songs and sing them.

- What, if anything, was different for Americans after the War of 1812?

- Read *A Gathering of Days.* Make a diagram showing how Catherine was affected by events going on in the country and what she learned from each of them. What if she had lived in Louisiana at the time? California? New Mexico? What race would she probably be? How would her lifestyle be different? Which of these events might have affected her no matter where she lived? What other events would have affected her?

- Find the statement about Jefferson that John Kennedy used at a White House banquet for Nobel Prize winners. Do you agree with his assessment of Jefferson? What can you find to support Kennedy's statement? Can you find anything that might contradict it?

- Which political leaders of this time had slaves? Which freed them? What factors influenced their decisions?

- Look into inventions and developments of the time. What can you find that foreshadowed the developments to come? Design a "car" for this time period. Remember that there were no internal combustion engines. You'll have to devise a different kind of power source such as horses, mules, water power, people power, gravity, or pulleys.

Picture Books

◆ Levinson, Nancy. ***Snowshoe Thompson.*** Illustrated by Joan Sandin. HarperCollins, 1992. ISBN 0-06-023801-1

This is the story of a little boy whose father is on the other side of the Sierra Nevadas mining for gold. Snowshoe Thompson, a real person, carries letters from the boy to his father.

◆ Sanders, Scott Russell. ***Aurora Means Dawn.*** Illustrated by Jill Kastner. Bradbury, 1989. ISBN 0-02-778270-0

With striking illustrations, this book tells about the Sheldon family who are bound for Aurora, Ohio, in the early 1800s. They are caught in a terrible storm and have to take shelter under their wagon. According to their information, Aurora is a bustling frontier town, but they find only a surveyor's post. Readers will get a sense of the travails and deceptions to which the first settlers were subjected.

◆ Spier, Peter. ***The Erie Canal.*** Doubleday, 1990. ISBN 0-385-06777-1

See page 124.

Fiction

★ Blos, Joan. ***A Gathering of Days: A New England Girl's Journal, 1830-1832.*** Scribner, 1979. ISBN 0-689-71419-X

Least Sophisticated   Most Sophisticated

*Told through a journal kept from 1830 to 1832, this is the story of a fourteen-year-old girl's acceptance of life and death on a farm in New Hampshire. During those two years, Catherine befriends a runaway slave, risking the wrath of her family and community, and faces and then accepts the death of her dearest friend. See **Long Ago and Far Away** (DLM, 1991. ISBN 1-55924-556-5) for an in-depth look at this book.*

★ Twain, Mark. ***The Adventures of Tom Sawyer.*** Many versions available.

*Twain re-creates, with embellishments, his life in Hannibal, Missouri, in 1840 through the adventures of Tom and his friend Huck Finn. Tom's energetic guileful nature has been the prototype for many characters, including J. D. Fitzgerald's tales of **The Great Brain** (page 220). The adventures are replete with thieves, kidnappers, and murderers. Tom's actions are guided by the Bible-quoting and sincere morality of Aunt Polly and the enviably independent life of Huck Finn.*

◆ Bohner, Charles. ***Bold Journey: West with Lewis and Clark.*** Houghton, 1985. ISBN 0-395-36691-7
■■■■■■■□□□□□□□

This fictional account of the journey is supposedly supplied by Hugh McNeal, a private in the Corps of Discovery.

◆ Carrick, Carol. ***The Elephant in the Dark.*** Scholastic, 1988. ISBN 0-590-42995-7
■■■■■■■□□□□□□□

Set in the early 1800s in Cadbury, Massachusetts, this story concerns Will, a twelve-year-old boy living with his eccentric mother who is quite ill. His father abandoned his mother before Will was born. They are poor and hungry. Will is teased by children and adults because of his mother. He is forced to provide for himself and is helped by Mr. and Mrs. Sanderson who own the general store. When his mother dies, Will is taken in by the Sandersons. Mr. Peacock then comes to town with an elephant. After using the elephant as a commercial enterprise, he leaves the elephant in Cadbury for the winter. Will becomes attached to it, and in the spring he leaves the Sandersons to follow the elephant. The book provides some sense of small town life during that period. The characters are compelling.

◆ ———. ***Stay Away from Simon.*** Clarion, 1985. ISBN 0-89919-343-9
■■■■■□□□□□□□□□

Simon is different and he frightens the villagers of Martha's Vineyard. He has trouble learning and sometimes gets overexcited. Children tell each other terrifying stories about the things he has done. When school is dismissed early because of heavy snow, Lucy and her younger brother, Josiah, take a short cut through the woods. Not only are they lost and in real danger of freezing to death, but Simon is after them. One of the strong points of the book comes from the realization that we haven't learned much in a hundred and sixty years about fearing people who are different.

◆ Curry, Jane. ***What the Dickens!*** McElderry, 1991. ISBN 0-689-50524-8
■■■■■■■□□□□□□□
See page 125.

◆ Henry, Joanne. ***A Clearing in the Forest: A Story about a Real Settler Boy.*** Four Winds, 1992. ISBN 0-274-3671-3
■■■■■□□□□□□□□□

Upper-class life in 1830s Indianapolis is drawn from the writing of Elijah and Calvin Fletcher. Although the book is fictionalized, there is an authentic flavor here. The weather plays an important role, as do the crops, the schools, and the characters in this large family.

◆ Rinaldi, Ann. ***Wolf by the Ears.*** Scholastic, 1991. ISBN 0-590-43413-6
■■■■■■■■■■■□□□

It has long been rumored that Thomas Jefferson had children by one of his slaves, Sally Heming. This novel deals with those children, especially the young and beautiful Harriet Heming. Secure and slightly pampered in spite of and sometimes because of her unique position in her life at Monticello, Harriet is loathe to leave it, even for the freedom others insist will be worth deserting her family for. If Harriet leaves Monticello, she must go far away because free Blacks are not allowed to stay in Virginia. Furthermore, no matter where she goes, there is always the chance that she will be resold into slavery. Therefore, Harriet, with her mother's complicity and the tacit knowledge of Jefferson himself, elects to "pass" as a free white.

Brenner, Barbara. **On the Frontier with Mr. Audubon.** Coward, 1977. ISBN 0-698-30756-9 ■■■■■■■□□□□□□□□

Basing her work on the journal of John James Audubon, Brenner has produced his assistant's journal and perspective on the journey made in 1820 down the Ohio and Mississippi Rivers to paint portraits of birds. Because much of the travel was by boat, we get an upclose look at flatboats, skiffs, and keelboats of the time.

Henry, Marguerite. **Justin Morgan Had a Horse.** Macmillan 1954. ISBN 0-528-82255-1 ■■■■■■■■■□□□□□□

Most of the action here takes place in Randolph, Vermont, between 1790 and 1815. Joel Goss's teacher is Justin Morgan. When Joel sees the schoolmaster's untrained colt, he falls in love with it and agrees to train the colt. Joel is apprenticed to a sawmill operator and saves his money to buy the colt. After the colt is abducted, Joel joins the cavalry in the War of 1812 and becomes a veterinarian's assistant with the hope of finding Morgan's horse. Later the horse and Joel are reunited and the horse goes on to establish a breed: the Morgan horse. This is a book that may be just the thing to bring horse-loving readers into the history program.

Hoobler, Dorothy and Thomas. **Treasure in the Stream: The Story of a Gold Rush Girl.** Silver Burdett, 1991. ISBN 0-382-24144-4 ■■■■□□□□□□□□□□

This short novel is one of a series of books called Her Story. It tells the simple story of the effect of the Gold Rush on one family. Although the characterization is not very strong and the story line is simplistic, it does provide a glimpse of California during the Gold Rush days. Levi Strauss is one of the characters and the effects of Gold Rush fever are apparent.

Monjo, F. N. **Grand Papa and Ellen Aroon.** Dell, 1974. ISBN 0-440-43004-6 ■■■■□□□□□□□□□□

This story, set in 1805, chronicles some of the family life of Thomas Jefferson as seen through the affectionate eyes of his nine-year-old granddaughter. The very simple book mentions only the children and grandchildren that he had through his marriage and not the children rumored to have been born through his relationship with one of his slaves.

O'Dell, Scott. **Streams to the River, River to the Sea.** Houghton, 1986. ISBN 0-449-70244-8 ■■■■■■■□□□□□□□

This is a fictionalized biography of Sacajawea, the Shoshone woman who served as a guide for the Lewis and Clark expedition. Her growing affection for Clark caused her to undertake the dangerous job, carrying her young baby with her. The book sticks quite closely to the facts while giving us some understanding of the Indian cultures the expedition encountered and the Shoshone culture from which Sacajawea came.

Taylor, Theodore. ***Walking Up a Rainbow.*** Delacorte, 1986. ISBN 0-385-29435-2

■■■■■■■■■■□□□□□

After his death, Susan must take her father's sheep from Iowa to California. Aided by some strange and wonderful people, she makes it.

Nonfiction

★ Fisher, Leonard Everett. ***The Oregon Trail.*** Holiday, 1990. ISBN 0-02-719020-X

■■■■■■■□□□□□□□

Maps and photographs combine with clear and often emotional text to tell of the wagon trains that carried some 300,000 people westward during the 1840s and 1850s. The Indians are seen from the travelers' point of view and as such they are referred to as "marauders" whose "treacherous" ways could not be trusted. These views, though jarring to our consciousness, reflect the prejudices of the time.

★ Otfinoski, Steven. ***Lewis and Clark, Leading America West.*** Fawcett, 1992. ISBN 0-449-90398-2

■■■■■■■□□□□□□□

This is a Focus Book; see page 270.

◆ Bealer, Alex W. ***Only the Names Remain: The Cherokees and the Trail of Tears.*** Little, 1972. ISBN 0-316-08520-0

■■■■■■■□□□□□□□

The history of the Cherokee Nation is carefully described in this book. The toll of the forced movement of these people to less hospitable and less desirable lands was part of the US government's effort to subjugate or annihilate the Native Americans.

◆ McNeer, May. ***The California Gold Rush.*** Random, 1950. ISBN 0-394-89177-5

■■■■■■■■□□□□□□

Starting with the discovery of gold at Sutter's Mill, the author tells how the thirst for gold produced a great increase in the number of people rushing West. It tells about the three main ways of getting to California: around the Horn by boat, across the vast land, or by boat south to Panama with a trek across the isthmus and another boat trip up the west coast. No route was easy and many lives were lost. After arriving in San Francisco, there were overcrowded conditions, the difficulties of getting outfitted, finding gold, and staking claims. Many people made money on the gold seekers, most of whom never found gold, and California was changed forever.

Rowland, Della. ***Sacajawea, Guide to Lewis and Clark.*** Dell, 1989. ISBN 0-440-40215-8

■■■■■■■□□□□□□□

Covering the years from 1800 to 1806, this book chronicles what is known of Sacajawea who was a guide for the famous expedition. Through her story we learn about relationships between the American Indian tribes and the explorers.

Sandak, Cass R. ***The Jacksons.*** Crestwood, 1992. ISBN 0-89686-636-X

■■■■■■■□□□□□□□□

As with other books in this series, First Families, this is a brief and generally flattering biography of Rachel and Andrew Jackson. Rachel never served as first lady because she died between the election and the inauguration. There are many paintings and cartoons, and the coverage of this rough and feisty couple is quite complete for such a small book.

Shorto, Russell. ***Tecumseh and the Dream of an American Indian Nation.*** Silver Burdett, 1989. ISBN 0-382-09569-3

■■■■■■■■□□□□□□□

The great Native American chief and orator attempted to bring the tribes together to form a confederacy to save the culture from the advancing pioneers. His life is told simply and with a minimum of adulation.

Stein, R. Conrad. ***The Story of the Erie Canal.*** Childrens, 1985. ISBN 0-516-0482-9

■■■■■■■■□□□□□□□

The determination and dedication of Dewitt Clinton to build a canal through New York state, connecting land and people east of the Appalachians with those west of the mountains, dominates the book. Fortunately, the need for labor on the canal developed at about the same time that hundreds of Irish immigrants arrived in the United States. The working conditions on the canal seem rugged and harsh by today's standards. The book also traces the canal to its present conditions, telling of its effects on society for the past hundred and fifty years.

————. ***The Story of the Trail of Tears.*** Childrens, 1985. ISBN 0-516-04683-7

■■■■■□□□□□□□□□□

Like Bealer's book (page 200), this book covers the story of the Cherokee Nation from its proud accomplishments in Southeastern United States to its shameful treatment at the hands of the United States government. Although this book is less eloquent than Bealer's, it is easier for less able readers to understand.

Nonprint

Videos
A Gathering of Days. American School Publishers.

Audios
A Gathering of Days. American School Publishers.
Justin Morgan Had a Horse. American School Publishers.

Exploring and Pioneering: 1850–1890 *The Times at a Glance...*

Movers & Shakers

Cochise

John Brown

Ulysses S. Grant

Horace Greeley

Chief Joseph

Abraham Lincoln

Robert E. Lee

Louis Pasteur

Dred Scott

Meanwhile, In Other Parts of the World

1853-1856	Crimean War; Russia defeated
1859	Suez Canal construction begins
1864	Karl Marx presides over First International
1877	Britain annexes South Africa
1879	Chile, Bolivia, and Peru at war
1884	France takes Indochina
1882	Britain consolidates control of Egypt
1887	England dominates center and south of Africa
1888	Kaiser Wilhelm assumes throne of Germany

Headlines*

1850	California becomes state
1857	Dred Scott decision
1859	John Brown's raid at Harper's Ferry
1860	South Carolina secedes from the Union
1861	US Civil War begins
1862	Homestead Act to encourage Westward Expansion
1863	Emancipation Proclamation
1866	Fourteenth Amendment grants Blacks full citizenship
1867	Alaska purchased from Russia
1869	Knights of Labor, first successful US labor union
1877	Chief Joseph attempts to lead 800 people to Canada
1883	Brooklyn Bridge completed
1889	First Oklahoma Land Rush

Inventions & Discoveries

1856	Bessemer invents process for cheap steel
1858	Darwin puts forth theory of evolution
1859	Oil discovered in Pennsylvania
1860	Pasteur uses sterilization to kill bacteria
1863	First subway opens in London
1865	Mendel discovers genetics
1867	Dynamite invented
	First practical typewriter
1876	Telephone patented
	Bacteria identified as cause of disease
1877	Phonograph invented
1879	Incandescent light bulb invented
1884	Photographic film and paper developed
1885	Motor car invented

*Many of the dates are only estimates made by historians and scientists. We tried to verify each date with at least two reliable sources; in cases where we found disagreement, we checked several sources. It is reasonable to expect that in your research you will also find disagreement.

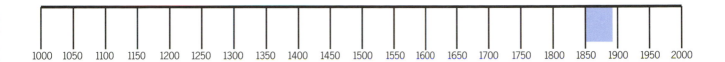

| 1000 | 1050 | 1100 | 1150 | 1200 | 1250 | 1300 | 1350 | 1400 | 1450 | 1500 | 1550 | 1600 | 1650 | 1700 | 1750 | 1800 | 1850 | 1900 | 1950 | 2000 |

Music

1850	*De Camptown Races*
1851	*Old Folks at Home*
1853	*My Old Kentucky Home*
1854	*I Dream of Jeannie*
1855	*Listen to the Mockingbird*
1856	*Darling Nellie Gray*
1857	*Jingle Bells*
1858	*Yellow Rose of Texas*
1866	*When You and I Were Young, Maggie*
1869	*Sweet Genevieve*
	Shoo Fly, Don't Bother Me
1873	*Silver Threads Among the Gold*
	Home on the Range
1876	*I'll Take You Home Again, Kathleen*
	Grandfather's Clock
1878	*Carry Me Back to Old Virginia*
1879	*In the Evening by the Moonlight*
1884	*Love's Old Sweet Song*

Books

1865	Carroll's *Alice's Adventures in Wonderland*
1865	Dodge's *Hans Brinker or the Silver Skates*
1867	Alger's *Ragged Dick*
1868	Alcott's *Little Women*
1876	Twain's *The Adventures of Tom Sawyer*
1877	Sewell's *Black Beauty*
1880	Spyri's *Heidi*
1881	Harris's *Uncle Remus: His Songs and Sayings*
1883	Collodi's *Adventures of Pinocchio*
1884	Twain's *The Adventures of Huckleberry Finn*
1885	Stevenson's *A Child's Garden of Verses*
1886	Burnett's *Little Lord Fauntleroy*

Art That Depicts the Time

"Trappers Saluting the Rocky Mountains" by A. J. Miller

"The Great West" by Currier and Ives

"The Rocky Mountains, Lander's Peak" by Albert Bierstadt

"Merced River, Yosemite Valley" by Albert Bierstadt

"A Home in the Wilderness" by Currier and Ives

"A Herd of Bison Crossing the Missouri River" by William Jacob Hays

"The Pioneer" by Winslow Homer

"Cavalry Charge on the Southern Plains" by Frederic Remington

"Last of the Buffalo" by Albert Bierstadt

"Colonel William F. Cody" by Rosa Bonheur

"A Rainy Day in Camp" by Winslow Homer

"D & R G Locomotive" by Edward Hopper

"My Bunkie" by Charles Schreyvogel

"Above the Sea of Round, Shiny Backs the Thin Loops Swirled and Shot into Volumes of Dust" by N. C. Wyeth

"Singing Vaquero" by Emanual Wyttenbach

"Bronco Buster" by Charles M. Russell

"Last of the Wild Horses" by Frank Albert Mechau

"The Virginia City Bodie Stage" by Edward Borein

"Jesse James" by Thomas Hart Benton

"Miss Annie Oakley" poster

"Across the Continent" by Frances Lora Bond Palmer

"The Mountain Man" by Frederic Remington

"The Cheyenne" by Frederic Remington

Fads & Customs

Sunbonnets

Playing harmonicas & fiddles

Exploring and Pioneering: 1850–1890

Activities

- See The Native American Conflict on page 59, The Civil War on page 78, Slavery on page 106, Cultures on page 128, Discovery and Invention on page 118, and Politics and Government on page 140.

- By reading widely in books set in the late 1800s, students may get a more balanced look at the conflicts. Even books that present only one side can be used for discussion as long as the prejudice is identified.

- Make maps of the United States showing the country at the beginning and end of this period. On the final map show when each section became a part of the United States and how much it cost in lives. Is it possible to estimate the cost in Native American lives?

- Imagine that each member of your class is the head of a family interested in settling in Oregon. What decisions will you need to make? If you decide to travel as a group, what kind of leadership will you need and how will you decide who will fill those roles? What will it cost each family to buy and equip a wagon? (See *The Oregon Trail* on page 200.) This is a wonderful topic for the kind of involved role plays described in Living History Museum (see page 24).

- Read about the Oklahoma land rush. What were the rules for filing claims? Pretend you were President Harrison. You and Congress have decided to let white settlers take over Indian lands. Defend your action and the resulting violence to the citizens of the United States. In hindsight, would you have done anything differently? Why were the United States' citizens not outraged?

- What changes occurred in the Eastern states as a result of the Westward movement? What happened to the land and jobs vacated by people who left for the West?

- According to a report to the United States government in 1878 by John Wesley Powell, land west of the 96th meridian is arid; only a few areas get as much as twenty inches of rain a year. Dry land farming depends on irrigation, and water rights in the West were more valuable than land titles. Knowing this and knowing what we now know about conservation and pollution, what rules for acquiring land and for land use would you establish for the West?

- Map land use in the West at the beginning and the end of this period. Remember that the rules of the Homestead Act required that a percentage of the land be cleared.

- Play the soundtrack from the musical Oklahoma. What political statements does it make?

- Research land swindles during this time. For instance, see page 469 of Trager's *The People's Chronology* (Holt, 1979. ISBN 0-03-017811-8), which tells of a swindler who acquired 14.5 million acres of the richest land in California and Oregon by a variety of amusing devices. Come to class as one of these swindlers and tell the group what you did and how it worked.

- Barbed wire, sometimes called Devil's Rope, was invented in 1873. Between 1873 and 1947, 80.5 million pounds were manufactured. Figure out how the invention of barbed wire changed life west of the Mississippi.

- Read ***Prairie Songs*** (page 206) and ***Prairie Visions*** (page 210). Pam Conrad wrote a nonfiction book about a character from her fiction. Find real life characters who could conceivably step into the plots of any of the suggested fiction. How would they affect the action? Who could they help and how?

- Look at the photographs in ***Prairie Visions.*** Which of the families shown there could be the families in one of the other books?

- Look at the picture book ***Dakota Dugout.*** Does the information in it support or conflict with any of the other books describing life on the prairie?

- For the suggested fiction, make a chart showing the reasons each of the families moved West. Were their reasons typical?

Picture Books

◆ Brenner, Barbara. ***Wagon Wheels.*** HarperCollins, 1978. ISBN 0-06-020669-1

Johnny, one of three motherless Black boys, goes with his father from Kentucky to Kansas in the 1870s. There they join the Black community of Nicodemus, where Johnny is left to care for his younger brothers while their father searches for better land. Then the three boys take a 150-mile trip to the permanent homestead their father established further west.

◆ Goble, Paul. ***Death of the Iron Horse.*** Bradbury, 1987. ISBN 0-02-737830-6

Told from the point of view of the Indians, this picture book is based on an actual incident in 1867, when the Cheyenne Indians wrecked a Union Pacific freight train. As always with Goble's books, the illustrations are stunning and contain many of the patterns and rhythms of Native American design. The coming of the train fulfilled the dire prophecy of a Cheyenne prophet named Sweet Medicine and, through the brief account, you get some feeling of the threat the railroad represented to the people who lived on the Plains.

◆ Harvey, Brett. ***Cassie's Journey: Going West in the 1860s.*** Holiday, 1988. ISBN 0-8234-0684-9

This is a picture book based on the actual accounts of journeys by covered wagon to the Midwest.

◆ Medearis, Angela Shelf. ***The Zebra Riding Cowboy: A Folk Song from the Old West.*** Illustrated by Maria Cristina Brusca. Holt, 1992. ISBN 0-8050-1712-7

This is an illustrated folk song about the trick some cowboys tried to play on a city slicker who proved to be a better cowboy than they. The illustrations show that the hero is a black man, and the afterword talks about the roles of minorities on the Prairie.

◆ Turner, Ann. ***Dakota Dugout.*** Illustrated by Ronald Himler. Macmillan, 1985. ISBN 0-02-78900-1

A woman, apparently Victorian, well-dressed, and walking a city street, tells a child what she remembers of her days in a sod house in Dakota territory. The pencil sketches reveal as much as the text does about a woman's role in that time and of the conditions within a Dakota dugout. The woman cries when she first sees the dugout, but when the crop comes in and better times and a better house come, the woman is nostalgic about life in that cramped, dark home.

Ackerman, Karen. ***Araminta's Paint Box.*** Illustrated by Betsy Lewin. Atheneum, 1990. ISBN 0-689-31462-0

This picture book tells the story of Araminta Darling's family who are bound for California by covered wagon. On the way, they stop in Pennsylvania where her uncle gives Araminta a special paint box. When the wagon breaks a wheel and everything is tossed about, the paint box is lost—lost to Araminta, that is. It travels through many hands in a much less direct route than the Darlings take, but it ends up in California and in Arabella's possession, although no one recognizes it.

Jeffers, Susan. ***Brother Eagle Sister Sky.*** Dial, 1991. ISBN 0-8037-0963-3

At the close of the last of the Indian Wars, it was said that Chief Seattle spoke eloquently while signing a paper consigning much of his people's land to the white men. Although the authenticity of the speech is questioned, this beautiful book, with excerpts from the speech, speaks to the future of the land.

Morrow, Barbara. ***Edward's Portrait.*** Macmillan, 1991. ISBN 0-02-767591-2

A traveling photographer is coming to town. The father and mother in this mid-eighteenth-century household are excited, but their young son Edward is not convinced that being photographed is something to be desired. In addition to giving us information about photography at the time, this book gives us glimpses of a household in a town that contrasts nicely with the households on the frontier.

Fiction

★ Conrad, Pam. ***Prairie Songs.*** HarperCollins, 1985. ISBN 0-06-021337-X

■■■■■■■□□□□□□□

Least Sophisticated   Most Sophisticated

Louisa and her father love the prairie. Her mother has accepted it. When Dr. and Mrs. Berryman arrive to set up a home nearby, Mrs. Berryman faints when she sees the sod hut she will live in. Louisa tries to get her to see the beauty of the prairie, but Mrs. Berryman misses the city and its refinements.

★ Turner, Ann. ***Grasshopper Summer.*** Macmillan, 1989. ISBN 0-02-789511-4

■■■■■■□□□□□□□□

This is a Focus Book; see page 279.

◆ Armstrong, Jennifer. ***Steal Away.*** Orchard, 1992. ISBN 0-531-08583-X

■■■■■■■□□□□□□□

See page 108.

◆ Byars, Betsy. ***Trouble River.*** Viking, 1969. ISBN 0-670-73257-5

■■■■■■■□□□□□□□

Twelve-year-old Dewey Martin is left at a remote cabin on the Prairie with his cranky grandmother while his parents go to a town when the baby is to be born. The Indians attack and Dewey's only hope is that his raft will carry him and his grandmother down Trouble River to safety. The river presents one challenge and Grandma presents another as, perched in the middle of the raft on her rocking chair, she complains and commands. The book has strong elements of adventure and comedy.

◆ Conrad, Pam. ***Stonewords.*** HarperCollins, 1990. ISBN 0-06-021315-9

■■■■■■■■■□□□□□

See page 37.

◆ Holland, Isabelle. ***The Journey Home.*** Scholastic, 1990. ISBN 0-590-43110-2

■■■■■■■■□□□□□□

This is a Focus Book; see page 282.

◆ Myers, Walter Dean. ***The Righteous Revenge of Artemis Bonner.***
HarperCollins, 1992. ISBN 0-06-020844-9

■■■■■■■□□□□□□□

It's 1880 and Artemis, an African-American New Yorker, travels to Tombstone to find gold, avenge a murder, and foil the Evil Catfish Grimes. Artemis has a friend, Frolic, but Catfish is aided by the formidable Lucy Featherdip. It's a wild and funny romp through the Old West.

Avi. ***The Man Who Was Poe.*** Orchard, 1989. ISBN 0-531-05833-6

■■■■■■■■■■■■□□

After Edmund's mother, aunt, and his sister disappear, the young boy is without funds and resources to survive, let alone locate his missing relatives. A mysterious alcoholic writer offers to help him, introducing himself as Auguste Dupin, in reality, the famous author Edgar Allan Poe. Poe is walking the thin line between madness and reality, but he manages to solve the mystery.

Brink, Carol Ryrie. ***Caddie Woodlawn.*** Macmillan, 1973. ISBN 0-02-713670-1

■■■■■■■■■□□□□□□

Based on the life of a pioneer family in 1864 Wisconsin, this novel brings to us one of the most memorable characters in literature—Caddie, a spunky eleven-year-old girl. Caddie is a tomboy, riding around on the Wisconsin frontier in search of adventure and challenge. Trouble with the Indians causes Caddie to rely on her friendship with one Indian to save the settlement.

Estern, Anne Graham. ***Letters from Philippa.*** Bantam, 1991.
ISBN 0-553-15941-0   ■■■■■■■■■□□□□□

See page 38.

Harvey, Brett. ***My Prairie Christmas.*** Holiday, 1990. ISBN 0-8234-0827-2

■■■■■□□□□□□□□□

Elenore fears that their first Christmas on the Prairie will be dreary, but Mama and the children make decorations and presents, and things are looking good until Papa is caught in a blizzard.

Howard, Ellen. ***The Chickenhouse House.*** Atheneum, 1991.
ISBN 0-689-31695-X   ■■■■■□□□□□□□□

Based on the story told by the author's aunt, this quiet book tells of young Alena, whose family moves into the chickenhouse while waiting for their Prairie home to be completed. Vexed by the lack of space and convenience, Alena hates the chickenhouse until they move into their completed home. Suddenly, the closeness of the chickenhouse seems warmer and less lonely.

Lasky, Kathryn. ***The Bone Wars.*** Morrow, 1988. ISBN 0-688-07433-2

■■■■■■□□□□□□□□

In the Badlands of Montana, there is a different kind of war than that between settlers and Indians. Here there are fierce battles among paleontologists, and into this battle come two orphans determined to thwart the scientists.

Loeper, John. ***The Golden Dragon: By Clipper Ship Around the Horn.*** Atheneum, 1978. ISBN 0-689-30658-X

■■■■■■□□□□□□□□

The trip is related through the eyes of Jeremy, a ten-year-old boy. While on the trip another boy is punished for washing his socks in fresh water and the weather turns wild off Cape Horn.

Magorian, Jim. ***Keeper of Fire.*** Council for Indian Education, 1984. ISBN 0-89992-088-8

■■■■■■■□□□□□□□

It's 1876. The Sioux Indians win the Battle of Little Big Horn under the leadership of Chief Sitting Bull, but they flee northwest to Canada hoping to escape the white man's wrath, which they know will be considerable. Shanni, a young hunter who is in training as a spiritual counselor for the tribe, lost his father in the battle, and he was wounded and separated from his tribe in a later skirmish. Using his considerable survival and tracking skills, Shanni is trying to evade white soldiers and find his ever-moving tribe. At one point, he is taken in by a white family who treats him kindly and he returns the kindness, but his place is with his tribe and he knows it. Shanni's values and skills contrast nicely with other survival stories such as **Sign of the Beaver** *(see page 191) and* **Hatchet** *by Gary Paulsen (Penguin, 1988. ISBN 0-14-032724-X).*

Moeri, Louise. ***Save Queen of Sheba.*** Avon, 1981. ISBN 0-380-71154-0

■■■■■■■■□□□□□□

Queen of Sheba is King David's little sister and the two children are the victims of an Indian attack while their wagon train is heading West. The boy is nearly scalped. Apparently the parents survived, but they must have thought the children were dead, so they are headed on by the time King David regains consciousness. The children must survive on their own long enough to catch up to the rest of the group.

Sandin, Joan. ***The Long Way to a New Land.*** HarperCollins, 1981. ISBN 0-06-444100-8

■■■□□□□□□□□□□□

This easy-to-read book tells of the immigration of one Swedish family in 1868, escaping the famine in Sweden and coming to America to join relatives already here. The voyage by steamship is long and many are sick on the trip. The book talks about the health checks by officials before boarding in Liverpool and before being allowed to leave the port of entry. Although brief and simple, the book does give us some idea of the concerns and motivations behind the great immigrations.

————. ***The Long Way Westward.*** HarperCollins, 1989. ISBN 0-06-444198-9

■■■□□□□□□□□□□□

This sequel to the preceding book follows Carl Erik's family from New York to Minnesota by train. Class difference is apparent in the late 1860s, and the immigrants' cars are far from comfortable, but sharing knowledge among the immigrants is helpful. The book gives a fundamental sense of the immigrant experience.

Stevens, Carol. ***Lily and Miss Liberty.*** Scholastic, 1992. ISBN 0-590-44919-2

■■■■■■□□□□□□□□

It's 1885 and the drive is on to pay for the pedestal for the Statue of Liberty. School children all over America are asked to contribute and Lily, in spite of her mother's disapproval, devises a money-making scheme.

Talbot, Charlene. ***An Orphan for Nebraska.*** Atheneum, 1979. ISBN 00-689-30698-9

■■■■■■■□□□□□□□

Orphans are taken from New York and shipped West where they are adopted by the settlers as workers. Kevin O'Rourke elects to go after trying life in New York. When all the farming families in Cottonwood City, Nebraska, reject him because he is too scrawny for hard work, he proves to the editor of the town's paper that he can read and is taken on as a printer's boy.

Wilder, Laura Ingalls. ***By the Shores of Silver Lake.*** HarperCollins, 1953. ISBN 0-06-026417-9

■■■■■■■□□□□□□□

The Dakota territory is the background for Pa's quest to move farther West.

————. ***Farmer Boy.*** HarperCollins, 1953. ISBN 0-06-026421-7

■■■■■■■□□□□□□□

This is the book about the boy who is to become Laura's husband. It covers his family's early years on their New York farm.

————. ***The First Four Years.*** HarperCollins, 1971. ISBN 0-06-026427-6

■■■■■■■□□□□□□□

The young family sets out on its own.

————. ***Little House in the Big Woods.*** HarperCollins, 1953. ISBN 0-06-026431-4

■■■■■■■□□□□□□□

In the beginning of the saga, Mary, Laura, and Carrie live with their mother and father in the Wisconsin forest. The china woman that Ma carries with her throughout the story is first introduced, as is Ma's amazing ability to make delicious meals with limited facilities and resources.

————. ***Little House on the Prairie.*** HarperCollins, 1953. ISBN 0-06-026446-2

■■■■■■■□□□□□□□

Wild Kansas country is the scene for the continuing adventures of the Ingalls.

————. ***Little Town on the Prairie.*** HarperCollins, 1953. ISBN 0-06-026451-9

■■■■■■■□□□□□□□□

Laura reaches adulthood and begins her teaching career.

————. ***The Long Winter.*** HarperCollins, 1953. ISBN 0-06-0226461-6

■■■■■■■□□□□□□□□

Living in town now, the Ingalls family experiences a mid-western blizzard so bad that even the railroads cease to run.

————. ***On the Banks of Plum Creek.*** HarperCollins, 1953. ISBN 0-06-026471-3

■■■■■■■□□□□□□□□

Pa moves the family to Minnesota next.

————. ***These Happy Golden Years.*** HarperCollins, 1953. ISBN 0-06-026481-0

■■■■■■■□□□□□□□□

Laura and Almanzo marry.

Nonfiction

★ Axelrod, Alan. ***Songs of the Wild West.*** Metropolitan Museum of Art, Simon & Schuster, 1991. ISBN 0-671-74775-4

■■■■■■■□□□□□□□□

Using paintings and statues from the museum and the words and music of popular songs from the cowboys, outlaws, prospectors, gunfighters, railroad workers, and sodbusters, this book is a valuable source of information about the days of the old West and a treasure of activities.

★ Conrad, Pam. ***Prairie Visions: The Life and Times of Solomon Butcher.*** HarperCollins, 1991. ISBN 0-06-021373-6

■■■■■■■■■■□□□□□

Solomon Butcher was an itinerant photographer in the late 1800s. He traveled the Prairie in Nebraska territory, taking photographs of pioneer families outside their sod homes. Many of his photographs are here, together with Pam Conrad's comments. It's an excellent source of information on Prairie life.

◆ ***Cobblestone Magazine***

The following issues of the magazine were devoted to topics of this era:
Transcontinental Railroad (May 1980)
Lewis and Clark (September 1980)
The Buffalo (August 1981)
Pony Express (October 1981)
Old Time Schools (November 1981)
Oregon Trail (December 1981)
The Alamo (March 1982)
The Beaver Trade (June 1982)
The Erie Canal (October 1982)
Laura Ingalls Wilder (February 1986)

The Santa Fe Trail (May 1990)
Joseph, a Chief of the Nez Percé (September 1990)
Back issues of the magazine can be obtained from Cobblestone Publishing, 30 Grove St., Peterborough, NH 03458.

◆ Force, Eden. ***John Muir.*** Silver Burdett, 1990. ISBN 0-382-09965-6

■■■■■■■■■■□□□□

An excellent biography, this book covers John Muir's life (1838-1914) from his birth in Scotland through his immigration to Wisconsin and his life's work at Yosemite. A crusader for the preservation of wilderness, Muir's life is a study in passion and nonconformity. His extensive traveling and his scientific studies of glaciers are fascinating. John Muir's life touched many, including famous people of the period, making it useful for role-playing or for concurrent biographies.

◆ Freedman, Russell. ***Cowboys of the Wild West.*** Clarion, 1985. ISBN 0-395-54800-4

■■■■■■■□□□□□□□

Amply illustrated with black-and-white photographs, this book attempts to dispel some of the myths about cowboys, while providing information about their lives, tools, and work. Concentrating on a thirty-year period from right after the Civil War to the invention of barbed wire, the author points out that many of the cowboys were Black (freed slaves) and Hispanic workers whose life was hard.

◆ Fritz, Jean. ***Make Way for Sam Houston.*** Putnam, 1986. ISBN 0-399-21303-1

■■■■■■■■■■□□□□□

Sam Houston felt that his destiny was Texas' destiny and, to a large degree, he was right. This colorful Texas hero did much to bring Texas into the Union and he argued with all his being that it should stay there. All his life, he had been a friend to the Indians, especially the Cherokees, and he worked to force the country to honor its agreements with them. This biography is done with Fritz's sure touch, and we end up learning a great deal of Texas' history as well.

◆ Levine, Ellen. ***If You Traveled West in a Covered Wagon.*** Scholastic, 1986. ISBN 0-590-42229-4

■■■□□□□□□□□□□□□

In simple text with a question-and-answer format, the author gives us a personal perspective on wagon travel. More than the other books on this topic, the focus is on the day-to-day aspects of travel. The fiction, because of a need for dramatic episodes, makes the trip seem like one harrowing escapade after another, but this book gives a more realistic look at the time, the road, the mechanics of travel.

◆ Weidt, Maryann. ***Wild Bill Hickok.*** Lothrop, 1992.

■■■■■■□□□□□□□□

This is a short biography of the well-known cowboy, starting with his death during a poker game holding what became known as a "dead man's hand" (two aces and two eights). The author then flashes back to James Butler Hickok's early years, his rise to fame as a gun-toting sheriff, and to his many feats both real and exaggerated. The book is uncomplicated but does show what seems to be a true picture of life in those days, at least from a cowboy's point of view.

◆ Wheeler, Leslie. *Jane Addams.* Silver Burdett, 1990. ISBN 0-382-09968-0

■■■■■■■■■■□□□□

See page 58.

Anderson, William. *Laura Ingalls Wilder Country.* HarperCollins, 1990. ISBN 0-06-055294-8

■■■■■■■□□□□□□□

Using old photographs and excerpts from the books and diaries of Laura Ingalls Wilder, the book evokes the time and the many scenarios of the stories, providing a nonfiction glimpse of the time and people.

Ashabranner, Brent. *A Memorial for Mr. Lincoln.* Putnam, 1992. ISBN 0-399-22273-1

■■■■■■□□□□□□□□

See page 45.

Clinton, Susan. *The Story of Seward's Folly.* Childrens, 1987. ISBN 0-516-04727-2

■■■■■■□□□□□□□□

This clear account starts with the exploration of Alaska by Vitus Bering and ends with a visit by Seward to Alaska in 1869. It is useful in its explanation of the political and economic reasons for the purchase.

Collins, James L. *Lawmen of the Old West.* Watts, 1990. ISBN 0-531-10893-7

■■■■■■■□□□□□□□

It was hard to tell the good guys from the bad guys in those days, and this book tells the good and bad of both sides.

Fleming, Alice. *The King of Prussia and a Peanut Butter Sandwich.* Scribner, 1988. ISBN 0-684-18880-5

■■■■■□□□□□□□□□

This book tells of a group of Mennonites who traveled from Prussia to the Crimea in the 1700s to escape service in the Prussian army, which would have violated their religious beliefs. In the Crimea, they were granted special dispensation from military service for one hundred years. During that time, they developed and planted winter wheat. When their dispensation expired, they were convinced by the US ambassador to settle in Kansas. President Grant assured them that they would not be forced to fight if it violated their religious principals. They brought with them the hardiest winter wheat seeds. When grasshoppers invaded the Plains, their wheat crop survived.

Green, Carl R. and Sanford, William. *Jesse James.* Enslow, 1992. ISBN 0-89490-365-9

■■■■■□□□□□□□□□

This simple biography is not simplistic and, although the writing is clear, the text is uneven. Readers are encouraged to evaluate the life of the outlaw to decide whether he was hero, villain, or both.

Landau, Elaine. ***Cowboys.*** Watts, 1990. ISBN 0-531-10866-X

■■■■■■■□□□□□□□□

Covering the period from the 1860s to the 1880s, this book shows the lifestyle and work of cowhands. Also discussed are the reasons for the decline of the cowboy culture. The book is amply illustrated with prints and photographs.

McGovern, Ann. ***If You Lived with the Sioux Indians.*** Scholastic, 1972. ISBN 0-590-41683-9

■■■■■□□□□□□□□□□

See page 138.

Morrison, Dorothy. ***Under a Strong Wind: The Adventures of Jessie Benton Fremont.*** Atheneum, 1983. ISBN 0-689-31004-8

■■■■■■■■■■■■□□□

This biography of John Fremont's wife gives extensive information about the lives of privileged families from 1824 through 1902 and about the exploration of the West, the Civil War, and the national politics of the times.

Stein, R. Conrad. ***The Story of the Homestead Act.*** Childrens, 1978. ISBN 0-516-04616-0

■■■■■□□□□□□□□□□

Abraham Lincoln pushed the Homestead Act in order to settle the Prairies. It was not until after his death, however, that the idea of land at eleven cents an acre took hold. The book details its provisions and tells of its effects on American farmers willing to settle and work the land and on people of other countries willing to emigrate.

Nonprint

Videos

Broken Treaties. Coronet, 1989.

In an imaginary trial of the US government against the Native American people of a century ago, Red Cloud and Chief Joseph tell of the massacre of their people and the loss of land. The goverment counters with the many attempts to get the Indians to adapt to the new ways. The decision is open-ended and the possibilities for further discussion are limitless.

The Turn of the Century: 1890–1920 *The Times at a Glance...*

Movers & Shakers

Susan B. Anthony
John Deere
Thomas Edison
Theodore Roosevelt
Sitting Bull
Wright Brothers

Headlines*

1890	Massacre at Wounded Knee, South Dakota
1891	Basketball invented
1894	Pullman Strike in Chicago causes violence
1896	Separate-but-equal doctrine established by Supreme Court
1897	Yukon Gold Rush
1898	Spanish-American War brings new territories under US control
1901	President McKinley assassinated
1906	Earthquake and fire in San Francisco kill 700
1914	US occupies Vera Cruz, Mexico

Meanwhile, In Other Parts of the World

1895	Japan gains Formosa and Korea
1900	Boxer Rebellion in China brings disruption
1902	Britain forms alliance with Japan
1907	Panama Canal started
1910	Union of South Africa formed

*Many of the dates are only estimates made by historians and scientists. We tried to verify each date with at least two reliable sources; in cases where we found disagreement, we checked several sources. It is reasonable to expect that in your research you will also find disagreement.

Inventions & Discoveries

c. 1890	Moving pictures developed
	Fingerprint system developed
1892	Diesel engine design patented
1895	X-rays invented
1898	Viruses discovered
1900	Paper clip invented
1901	Blood groups distinguished
	Radio invented
1903	Wright brothers fly first successful airplane
1906	Vitamins discovered
1906	Victrola invented
1908	Model T Ford produced on assembly line
1910	Chromosomes established as carriers of heredity
1911	Cellophane manufactured

Books

1899	Bannerman's *Story of Little Black Sambo*
1900	Baum's *The Wonderful Wizard of Oz*
1902	Potter's *The Tale of Peter Rabbit*
	Barrie's *Peter Pan*
1903	Wiggin's *Rebecca of Sunnybrook Farm*
1910	Burnett's *The Secret Garden*
1913	Porter's *Pollyanna*

Music

1889	Tchaikovsky's *Sleeping Beauty Ballet*
1891	Carnegie Hall opens
	Ta ra ra Boom der ay
1892	Tchaikovsky's *Nutcracker Suite*
	Bicycle Built for Two
	After the Ball
1894	*I've Been Working on the Railroad*
1895	*America the Beautiful*
1896	*Hot Time in the Old Town*
1897	*Stars and Stripes Forever*
1898	*When You Were Sweet Sixteen*
1899	*Maple Leaf Rag;* beginning of Ragtime era
	My Wild Irish Rose
1900	*A Bird in a Gilded Cage*
1901	*I'm Captain Jinx of the Horse Marines*
1902	*Bill Bailey*
1903	*Ida, Sweet as Apple Cider*
1904	*Give My Regards to Broadway*
1905	*In My Merry Oldsmobile*
1906	*China Town*
1907	*The Caissons Go Rolling Along*
1908	*Take Me Out to the Ballgame*
1909	*I Wonder Who's Kissing Her Now*
1910	*Come Josephine in My Flying Machine*

Fads & Customs

Taking snapshots with Brownie cameras

Bustles

Gibson Girls

The Turn of the Century: 1890–1920

Activities

- See The Native American Conflict on page 59, The Spanish-American War on page 85, World War I on page 87, Discovery and Invention on page 118, Transportation and Communication on page 123, and Cultures on page 128.
- Put on a Gay Nineties revue. Use costumes, props, and music.
- Make life-sized costumed torsos on posterboard with holes and spaces for limbs and faces. Take photos.
- Make a population map of the time showing where the major population centers were. Compare it to similar maps of today.
- Contrast city and country life of the time. What proportion of the population lived in the cities at the turn of the century?
- Where were Native Americans living at the turn of the century?
- Imagine that you lived in 1910. Make a list of the things you can't do or use after school because they haven't been discovered or invented yet.
- Find statistics about occupations at the turn of the century. How many people were in which jobs? Figure out what was considered a good salary at the time. Then figure out how many families got that kind of money.
- Find out about the Industrial Revolution. What major inventions led to it? What years do people usually use to encompass it? Did it occur in other countries? Was it at the same time? If not, why not?
- What did people do to celebrate the turn of the century? How will it be different at the turn of the next one?
- What was the life expectancy of people born at the turn of the century? What events would they live through?
- Describe an airplane to someone who knows nothing about manned flight.
- Interview your grandparents about stories they heard about the turn of the century.
- Put on costumes such as people wore at the time and try to do something like play badminton or just have recess.
- How much education did most people have? How much school was mandatory? Did boys and girls get the same education?
- Why were there so many orphanages and poor houses at the turn of the century and so few now?
- Write and put on a Victorian melodrama.
- Who were the sports heroes of the time? Conduct a mock interview with one of them.
- What did people do in the evening before radio was invented? Spend an evening at school doing some of those activities.
- Compare the life of the child in **The Best Town in the World** (page 34) to **Hattie and the Wild Waves** (page 217).

Picture Books   ★   Martin, Jacqueline Briggs. ***The Finest Horse in Town.*** Illustrated by Susan Gaber. HarperCollins, 1992. ISBN 0-06-024151-9

This delightful book is a series of suppositions about a horse that the author's two maiden aunts owned in Maine. In addition to giving us a good deal of information about small town life at the turn of the century, the author shows a way to make suppositions based on facts.

◆   Baylor, Byrd. ***The Best Town in the World.*** Illustrated by Ronald Himler. Scribner, 1982. ISBN 0-684-18035-9

See page 34.

◆   McPhail, David. ***Farm Boy's Year.*** Atheneum, 1992. ISBN 0-689-31679-8

See page 34.

◆   Stanley, Fay. ***The Last Princess: The Story of Princess Kaiulani of Hawaii.*** Four Winds, 1991. ISBN 0-02-786785-4

The brief life of a tragic real-life princess is touchingly told in this informative book. We are told of the betrayal by the haoles, white settlers, who took over the tiny kingdom of Hawaii and against the will of the native people, annexed it to the United States. Besides the brief history of the monarchy of Hawaii, we see the modes of travel and dress of the islanders and the British aristocracy at the turn of the century.

Coats, Laura Jane. ***The Almond Orchard.*** Macmillan, 1991. ISBN 0-02-719041-2

An old woman tells about a California almond orchard that her father planted and worked in the early 1900s. She tells about caring for the trees, gathering the nuts, and getting them ready for market then and now.

Cooney, Barbara. ***Hattie and the Wild Waves.*** Viking, 1991. ISBN 0-670-83056-9

A very privileged little girl and her family enjoy Brooklyn winters and Long Island summers in this picture book based on the author's own life.

Howard, Elizabeth. ***Chita's Christmas Tree.*** Bradbury, 1990. ISBN 0-02-744621-2

Christmas is celebrated by a middle-class Black family in Baltimore.

Fiction   ★   Estes, Eleanor. ***The Middle Moffats.*** Harcourt, 1942. ISBN 0-440-40180-1

————. ***The Moffat Museum.*** Harcourt, 1983. ISBN 0-150-255086-0

————. ***The Moffats.*** Harcourt, 1941. ISBN 0-15-255095-X

————. ***Rufus M.*** Harcourt, 1943. ISBN 0-15-269415-3

■■■■■■□□□□□□□□
Least Sophisticated   Most Sophisticated

These are Focus Books; see page 284.

★   Sebestyen, Ouida. ***Words By Heart.*** Little, 1979. ISBN 0-553-27179-2

■■■■■■■□□□□□□□

See page 57.

◆   Enright, Elizabeth. ***Gone-Away Lake.*** Harcourt, 1957. ISBN 0-15-231649-3

■■■■■■■□□□□□□□

In the 1950s, two children befriend an elderly brother and sister who are still living the lifestyle of the Victorian age. Portia and Julian are cousins. On one of their many excursions into the woods, they find some dilapidated Victorian summer homes near a swamp. They discover Mrs. Cheever and her brother Mr. Payton living in two of the homes. The couple dress in clothes that were left in these summer homes where they had spent their childhood summers. They have lived in the modern world and chose to retreat to this isolated spot. Mrs. Cheever never leaves the area and Mr. Payton drives into town in an old clunky car for supplies. Julian and Portia keep their discovery a secret and visit them daily.

◆   Karr, Kathleen. ***It Ain't Always Easy.*** Farrar, 1991. ISBN 0-374-33645-8

■■■■■■■□□□□□□□

Life on the street in the 1880s wasn't any easier then than it is now, and it takes the combined efforts of an unholy alliance of street kid and runaway girl to cope with survival. Eleven-year-old Jack is an orphan who is entrusted with the care of Mandy, a small runaway girl. Searching for a home, they spend a week laboring in a silk mill and then as apprentice servants. The historical background is authentic without being obtrusive.

◆   Leonard, Laura. ***Finding Papa.*** Atheneum, 1991. ISBN 0-689-31526-0

■■■■■■■□□□□□□□
See page 125.

◆   Peck, Richard. ***The Ghost Belonged to Me.*** Viking, 1975. ISBN 0-440-93075-8

■■■■■■■□□□□□□□

Living near St. Louis in 1913, Alexander Armsworth still hears a lot about the Louisiana Purchase Exposition and the World's Fair. Now there are automobiles and newly electrified street cars. His good friend is Blossom Culp, and her mother, who has Gypsy blood, is not surprised when Alexander sees a ghost in his barn.

◆   Robinet, Harriette Gillem. ***Children of the Fire.*** Atheneum, 1991.
ISBN 0-689-31655-0

■■■■■■■■□□□□□□

Although this book is set in 1871, a few years before this time, it revolves around the great Chicago fire and doesn't seem to fit into the Westward Movement as such. We see the fire through the eyes of Hallelujah, the orphaned child of freed slaves. There is a great deal of detail about the lives of African Americans of the time and about the fire, which serves as a catalyst for Hallelujah's acceptance of herself and of adult responsibilities.

◆   Voigt, Cynthia. ***The Callendar Papers.*** Atheneum, 1983. ISBN 0-689-30971-6

■■■■■■■■□□□□□□

Jean Wainwright, almost thirteen years old, spends the summer of 1894 at an estate in the Berkshire Mountains of Massachusetts. The owner, Mr. Thiel, has baskets of his dead wife's papers that he wants Jean to sort and catalog. The task leads to a mystery and to real danger for Jean. During the story, we are exposed to customs of the day: croquet, horse-driven carriages, women's roles, and proper attire.

◆ Weitzman, David. ***Thrashin' Time: Harvest Days in the Dakotas.*** Godine, 1991. ISBN 0-87923-910-7

See page 116. ■■■■■■■■□□□□□□□

Baum, L. Frank. ***The Wonderful Wizard of Oz.*** Many editions available.

————. ***El mago de Oz.*** Hispanic Book Distributors.

■■■■■■■■■■□□□□□□

This classic fantasy is included because it is said to be an allegory of the politics of the time. The Scarecrow represents the farmer whom politicians considered to be of little intelligence or sophistication. The Tin Man is the mechanization of America as industry overcame agriculture and took away the heart. The Cowardly Lion is thought to be William Jennings Bryant, a politician who supported free silver. Baum felt Bryant lacked the courage of his convictions. The gold standard is the yellow brick road that Baum felt would lead to nothing but a land of illusion and the silver slippers that Dorothy wears (they are ruby in the movie) represent the silver standard that Baum felt was the way back to a saner existence.

Beatty, Patricia. ***Eight Mules from Monterey.*** Morrow, 1982. ISBN 0-688-01047-4

■■■■■■■■□□□□□□□

A widow, her children, and a mule driver travel the mountains south of Monterey, California, in 1916 to take library books to the mountain people. The story is told by her daughter who has a keen eye for adventure and is something of a manipulator.

————. ***Sarah and Me and the Lady from the Sea.*** Morrow, 1989. ISBN 0-688-08045-6

■■■■■■■■□□□□□□□

When the Abbot family's fortune is lost, the children and their mother must learn new skills to survive a winter at their vacation home on the peninsula in Washington state without their usual servants. Not only do they survive, they thrive. When a mysterious lady is washed ashore tied to a mast and unable to speak any identifiable language, they have a mystery to occupy their thoughts and time.

Chandonnet, Ann. ***Chief Stephen's Parky: One Year in the Life of an Athapscan Girl.*** Council for Indian Education, 1989.

■■■■■■■■□□□□□□□

This story describes the steps Chief Stephen's wife must take to make the parka he will wear. Because the steps are laborious and time-consuming, the story of the parka is the story of one year in the life of an Alaskan woman at the turn of the century. Considerable detail is supplied about preparing the skins and other materials and about the Indians' life. Nomadic, they followed the food, returning to each area at a specific season and for a specific purpose each year, enjoying the area and the seasons. The book is a rich source of information.

De Trevino, Elizabeth Borton. ***El Guero.*** Sunburst, 1989. ISBN 0-374-31995-2

■■■■■■■□□□□□□□□

Although much of the action of this book takes place in Mexico, it concerns the border dispute with the United States over the territory of the Baja Peninsula during the time of Porfirio Diaz's dictatorship of Mexico (1876-1910). The politics of Mexico were a long way from the Baja, where Judge Cayetano Trevino and his family had been exiled, but they had a strong effect. El Guero, christened Porfirio Trevino, undertook a long and dangerous journey to San Diego and back to gain the release of his father, the judge, from prison and to assure his family's survival.

Fitzgerald, John D. **The Great Brain.** Dell, 1972. ISBN 0-440-43071-2

■■■■■■■□□□□□□□□

This is just the first in a series of books about a Catholic family in 1896 Utah. The books revolve around the exploits of Tom, a mischievous and enterprising young boy of, as observed by his younger brother J.D. In this volume indoor plumbing is the latest development and Tom manages to make money on its installation in their home. There are also some good ideas for conflict resolution, and we get a close-up look at the children's games and pastimes of the era.

Gross, Virginia. **The Day It Rained Forever: A Story of the Johnstown Flood.** Viking, 1990. ISBN 0-670-83552-8

■■■■■□□□□□□□□□□

Part of the Once Upon America series, this fictionalized account of the flood shows the devastation to one family of the time.

Hamilton, Virginia. **The Bells of Christmas.** Harcourt, 1989. ISBN 0-15-206450-8

■■■■■■■□□□□□□□□

An extended Black family living on the main road in Southern Ohio in 1890 celebrates Christmas together. The accent is on tradition, and the past and future are both considered by this loving family. The book jacket contains a map of the road, dating each extension as it grew from cow path to highway.

McKenzie, Ellen. **Stargone John.** Holt, 1990. ISBN 0-8050-1451-9

■■■■■■■□□□□□□□□

A special child endures ignorance and cruelty in a one-room school. We get a keen sense of life in a small Midwestern town at the turn of the century.

Naylor, Phyllis Reynolds. **Maudie in the Middle.** Atheneum, 1988. ISBN 0-689-31395-0

■■■■■■■□□□□□□□□

Replete with the pastimes, inventions, and customs of a turn-of-the-century farm, this novel is rich in detail although short on plot. Based on the memories of the author's grandmother growing up in the middle of a well-to-do family in Iowa, the book is worth reading for its atmosphere.

Nelson, Theresa. **Devil Storm.** Orchard, 1987. ISBN 0-531-08311-X

■■■■■■■■■■■□□□

Walter Carroll and his younger sister, Alice, dare to meet and talk with a spooky man who lives on the fringes of the town. Some say Old Tom the Tramp is the son of Pirate Lafitte and others say he's a chicken thief. After they've warned him about the angry farmers, he warns them of the oncoming hurricane that devastates Galveston, Texas, in 1900.

Stevens, Carla. ***Anna, Grandpa, and the Big Storm.*** Clarion, 1982.
ISBN 0-89919-066-9

*Eight-year-old Anna doesn't get along with her grandfather very well. Being
stranded together on an El train during the blizzard of 1888 forces them together
and they gain mutual respect.*

Taylor, Sydney. ***All-of-a-Kind Family.*** Taylor, 1951. ISBN 0-929093-00-3

*Everyday happenings of five sisters and their mother and father in a big house in
Manhattan come to life in this book. The family is Jewish and their traditions
color much of their existence at the turn of the century.*

Whelan, Gloria. ***Hannah.*** Knopf, 1990. ISBN 0-679-81397-7

*Set in Michigan in 1887, this brief novel tells of Hannah, a blind girl whose life is
changed when a teacher boards at her house.*

Williams, Ruth L. ***The Silver Tree.*** HarperCollins, 1992. ISBN 0-06-020296-3

See page 38.

Wyman, Andrea. ***Red Sky at Morning.*** Holiday, 1991. ISBN 0-8234-0903-1

*The story takes place in Indiana in 1910, which is pretty bleak for the two sisters,
Katherine and Callie, after their mother dies in childbirth. Their grandfather, a
German immigrant, copes as best he can, but times are hard. Their father has left
for Oregon and, after surviving a diphtheria epidemic, the family leaves the farm
and joins him there.*

Yep, Laurence. ***Dragonwings.*** HarperCollins, 1975. ISBN 0-06-026738-0

See page 113.

Nonfiction   ◆ ***Cobblestone Magazine***

The following issues of the magazine were devoted to turn of the century topics:
The Yukon Gold Rush (August 1980)
The Industrial Revolution (September 1981)
America's Cowboys (July 1982)
Immigrants: Part 1 (December 1982)
Immigrants: Part 2 (January 1983)
Helen Keller (May 1983)
Whaling (April 1984)
Chautauqua (July 1984)
Susan B. Anthony and the Women's Movement (March 1985)

222 Chronology of History

◆ Freedman, Russell. *The Wright Brothers: How They Invented the Airplane.* Holiday, 1991. ISBN 0-8234-0875-2

■■■■■■■□□□□□□□

See page 120.

Blos, Joan. *The Heroine of the Titanic: A Tale Both True and Otherwise of the Life of Molly Brown.* Morrow, 1991. ISBN 0-688-07546-0

■■■□□□□□□□□□□□

The inspiration for the Broadway play and film The Unsinkable Molly Brown is shown from her first days of mining in Leadville, Colorado, to her gallant behavior on the Titanic. This book succeeds in capturing her rambunctious personality.

Kent, Zachary. *The Story of Henry Ford and the Automobile.* Childrens, 1990. ISBN 0-516-04751-5

■■■■■■■□□□□□□□

See page 121.

———. *The Story of the Triangle Factory Fire.* Childrens, 1989. ISBN 0-516-04742-6

■■■■■■□□□□□□□□

The fire took place in 1911 and the horror of it is recorded here. Most of the victims were women, some no more than young girls, mostly immigrants, who worked in the factory. The owners of the factory were charged with manslaughter but found not guilty. The fire resulted in the establishment of a Bureau of Fire Prevention and a special Factory Investigating Commission to inspect other factories and they succeeded in getting thirty-three new labor laws passed by 1914. The book is not pleasant reading but does give insight into factory life at the time.

Levine, Ellen. *If You Lived at the Time of the Great San Francisco Earthquake.* Scholastic, 1987. ISBN 0-590-43798-4

■■■■■■□□□□□□□□

As the title implies, this book concentrates on the quake and its aftermath, giving details about acts of heroism, damage, and casualties as well as the resumption of daily life. The drawings provide information about clothing and styles of the era in addition to information about the disaster.

Rappaport, Doreen. *The Lizzie Borden Trial.* HarperCollins, 1992. ISBN 0-06-025114-X

■■■■■■■■■□□□□□

Part of the Be the Judge—Be the Jury series, this book asks readers to decide whether Lizzie should have been acquitted of the crime of murdering her mother and father in Fall River, Massachusetts, in 1892.

St. George, Judith. ***Panama Canal: Gateway to the World.*** Putnam, 1989. ISBN 0-399-21637-5

■■■■■■■□□□□□□□

In 1904, construction began that would transform a swamp into a fifty-mile-long waterway. The Panama Canal would connect the Atlantic and Pacific Oceans and change world trade. The personalities of Theodore Roosevelt and William Howard Taft had much to do with persuading the public that the cost in lives and equipment was worth it. The author tells of William Gorgas who succeeded in conquering yellow fever, the plague of the canal, and of the three chief engineers responsible for completing the work.

Stein, R. Conrad. ***The Story of Wounded Knee.*** Childrens, 1983. ISBN 0-516-04665-9

■■■■■□□□□□□□□□

Wovoka's vision of the white race being driven from the land led to the performance by many members of Paiute and Sioux tribes of the Ghost Dance. As plans for the dance grew bigger, white settlers became fearful of an uprising and determined to stop it. The awful massacre began. The details of the "battle" are gruesome and shameful, and the book records many of them. The book also talks about the use of the massacre as a rallying call during the 1973 uprising of Indian militants.

Steward, Gail B. ***Where Lies Butch Cassidy?*** Crestwood, 1992. ISBN 0-89686-618-1

■■■■■□□□□□□□□□

Part of the History's Mysteries series, this small book is a brief account of the life of the man known as Butch Cassidy and the mystery concerning his death. Readers are given the conflicting theories and asked for their opinion as to which is "true." In the process, readers are given a glimpse of the Wild West at the turn of the century. Although the book is not an outstanding piece of literature, it may well hook some of the less capable readers into doing further research.

Tames, Richard. ***Picture History of the 20th Century: 1900-1919.*** Watts, 1991. ISBN 0-531-14181-0

■■■■■■□□□□□□□

One of a series, this book uses many photographs and a small amount of text to cover the events and customs of the time. Even though the books are published in Britain, there is a surprising amount of information about life and events in the United States.

Nonprint

Videos

Words by Heart. Public Media Video, 1985.
A dramatization of the novel by Ouida Sebestyen, this is a story of a Black family living in the Midwest in 1920. The film sticks closely to the book and is well acted.

The Twenties and Thirties *The Times at a Glance...*

Movers & Shakers

Fred Astaire
William Jennings Bryan
Clarence Darrow
Amelia Earhart
Adolph Hitler
Herbert Hoover
Harry Houdini
Sinclair Lewis
Charles Lindbergh
Benito Mussolini
Jesse Owens
Franklin D. Roosevelt
Niccola Sacco
Margaret Sanger
Joseph Stalin
Shirley Temple
Leon Trotsky
Bartolomeo Vanzetti

Headlines*

1920 19th Amendment gives vote to women
1925 Scopes trial
1929 Stock Market Crash leads to unemployment and bank failures
      Great Depression begins
1932 Bonus Army of World War I marches on Washington to demand cash bonuses
1933 Franklin Roosevelt announces New Deal legislation
1935 Congress passes Social Security Act

Meanwhile, In Other Parts of the World

1922 Mussolini comes to power in Italy
1928 Chiang Kai Shek unifies China against Japanese expansion
1928 Stalin begins industrialization of Russia
1930 Gandhi begins civil disobedience campaign against British rule in India
1932 Japan occupies Manchuria and leaves League of Nations
1933 Adolph Hitler sets up Nazi dictatorship
1934 Civil war in China
1936 Civil war in Spain
1937 Japan attacks China
1938 Germany annexes Austria and Czechoslovakia
1939 Franco becomes dictator of Spain

*Many of the dates are only estimates made by historians and scientists. We tried to verify each date with at least two reliable sources; in cases where we found disagreement, we checked several sources. It is reasonable to expect that in your research you will also find disagreement.

Inventions & Discoveries

1920	Radio broadcasting on regular basis begins in US
1925	Birdseye markets first quick-frozen foods
	First electric recording
1927	Lindbergh's solo flight across Atlantic
1929	Penicillin discovered, but not ready for use until 1943
	First practical television system
1932	Electron microscope invented
1933	Vitamin C synthesized
	FM radio broadcasting begins
1937	Insulin used to treat diabetes
	Jet engine developed
1938	Nylon invented
	Ballpoint pen patented
	Photocopying machine developed
1939	DDT invented
	NBC begins first regular television broadcasts
	First helicopter developed
	Jet aircraft developed
	Microfilm camera developed

Fads & Customs

Rudolph Valentino movies
Talkies
Flappers
Speakeasies
Bobbed hair
Spats
Dance marathons
Monopoly
Comics
Art Deco

Music

Charleston
Tango
Black Bottom
Jazz
Big Band Sound

Popular Songs

1920	*I'll Be With You in Apple Blossom Time*
1921	*April Showers*
	California, Here I Come
1922	*Way Down Yonder in New Orleans*
1923	*Who's Sorry Now*
	It Ain't Gonna Rain No More
1924	*Somebody Loves Me*
1925	*Sweet Georgia Brown*
1926	*Muskrat Ramble*
1927	*Me and My Shadow*
	I'm Looking Over a Four-Leaf Clover
1928	*I'll Get By*
1929	*Stardust*
	Honeysuckle Rose
1930	*Georgia on My Mind*
1931	*I Love a Parade*
1932	*Say It Isn't So*
1933	*Only a Paper Moon*
	Stormy Weather
1935	*The Music Goes Round*
1936	*De Lovely*
1937	*Once In a While*
	Harbour Lights
1938	*You Go To My Head*
1939	*I'll Never Smile Again*
	South of the Border

Books

1920	Lofting's *Doctor Doolittle*
1927	Dixon's *Hardy Boys*
1932	Wilder's *Little House in the Big Woods*
1936	Streatfeild's *Ballet Shoes*

The Twenties and Thirties

Activities

- See Discovery and Invention on page 118, Transportation and Communication on page 123, Cultures on page 128, Politics and Government on page 140, and Racisim, Sexism, and Equality on page 146.

- Find someone who was alive during the twenties and/or thirties. Interview them about their lives when they were your age: What did they do for fun? What trips did they take? What were vacations like? What work did their adult family members do?

- Learn the dance steps for the Charleston or Black Bottom, and hold a Roaring Twenties dance.

- What happened to the financial structure of your community after the Stock Market Crash? Show the employment figures for your town. Plot the available figures from that time to this on a graph.

- Get a script or tape of a radio program from the thirties. Write a similar script based on one of the books in this section and perform it.

- Make a time line or flow chart of the events that led up to the economic crisis of this time. Draw lines to show relationships between events. Which of these events could have been changed to alter later events?

- Play and sing some of Woody Guthrie's songs about this period. Write skits that incorporate the songs.

- See all or parts of the movie The Grapes of Wrath. Find photographs of that period that expand some of the scenes in the movie. How does the movie relate to the book **Blue Willow/Sauce Azul** (page 228).

- Read **Child Star** (page 230). Then watch a silent movie. Notice the plot, the way captions are used, the flickering images. Put on a silent movie. Devise a plot that can be carried out mostly by pantomime with the addition of caption cards. Find some suitable music to accompany your movie. If you flick the lights on and off during the "movie," you can recreate the flickering motion of the silent film.

- Find out about the famous gangsters of this period. Why did they often become folk heroes? Do modern gangsters evoke the same feelings in us?

- What were the reasons for Prohibition? Could it have occurred at any other time in history? Why was it repealed? Is there a comparison with modern drugs? Would you outlaw anything currently legal? Would you legalize anything currently illegal? Explain your reasons. Decide what the results of your actions might be.

- Find out about the WPA (Works Progress Administration). Are there parks, works of art, or other evidence of the WPA in your area? Do we need a similar program today?

- Compare depressions and recessions before and after the Great Depression. Graph the information to show which times had the greatest percentage of unemployed.

- In **Ida Early Comes Over the Mountain** (see 288), Ida is an itinerant laborer. She goes where she hopes to find work. Find other characters, real and imaginary, who did the same. What sort of work are you apt to find that way? Would that be the way to get a high-paying, powerful job?

- When Ida comes in contact with Aunt Earnestine, there is more than a conflict of personalities; there is a conflict in class. Find conflicts in novels from any period in which what appears to be a personality clash could be attributed to a conflict in class values or customs.
- In *Grandpa's Mountain* (page 228), the rights of the group interfere with the rights of the individual. Can you find local examples of the same conflict? How could they be resolved? How were the local conflicts resolved?

Picture Books

◆ Burleigh, Robert. *Flight: The Journey of Charles Lindbergh.* Illustrated by Mike Wimmer. Putnam, 1991. ISBN 0-399-22272-3

With excellent illustrations, this book tells the story of Lindbergh's flight from New York to Paris in 1927. The book concentrates on his time alone in the air, fighting sleep and fear.

◆ Stevenson, James. *Higher on the Door.* Greenwillow, 1987. ISBN 0-688-06636-4

———. *July.* Greenwillow, 1990. ISBN 0-688-08822-8

———. *When I Was Nine.* Greenwillow, 1986. ISBN 0-688-05942-2

These three picture books give us glimpses of Stevenson's childhood in a small town not too far from New York City during the thirties and forties. The books are nostalgic but useful in identifying the fads and customs of the times.

Allen, Thomas. *On Granddaddy's Farm.* Knopf, 1989. ISBN 0-394-89613-0

Life on a Tennessee farm during the 1930s is shown with pastel drawings that evoke feelings of nostagia.

Bragg, Michael. *Betty's Wedding.* Macmillan, 1988. ISBN 0-02-711880-0

This picture book is designed to look like a photo album and covers a wedding from invitation to the wedding trip of a well-to-do couple from the twenties. The historical information, aside from the wedding customs, includes a look at several cars and, of course, some of the clothing of the period.

Fiction

★ Burch, Robert. *Ida Early Comes Over the Mountain.* Avon, 1980. ISBN 0-380-57091-2

■■■■■■■□□□□□□□□

Least Sophisticated   Most Sophisticated

This is a Focus Book; see page 288.

★ Fox, Paula. *One-Eyed Cat.* Dell, 1984. ISBN 0-440-46641-5

■■■■■■■■■□□□□□□

This story of guilt takes place in Tyler, New York, in the 1930s. Ned Wallis lives in a large, quiet house with his clergyman father and his invalid mother. The gift of a rifle from his Uncle Hilary changes him completely. His parents refuse to let him use the rifle and put it in the attic until they can decide what to do with it. Compelled to try it just once, Ned shoots at something in the night. Shortly thereafter, Ned sees a cat whose eye was shot out. Because of his guilt, Ned becomes obsessed with the cat.

★ Hamilton, Virginia. ***Willie Bea and the Time the Martians Landed.***
Greenwillow, 1983. ISBN 0-689-71328-2

■■■■■■■□□□□□□□

This is a Focus Book; see page 291.

◆ Gates, Doris. ***Blue Willow.*** Viking, 1940. ISBN 0-670-17557-9

———. ***Sauce Azul.*** Hispanic Book Distributors.

■■■■■■■□□□□□□□

Janey Larkin hangs on to the vision in a plate that came down to her from her great-great-grandmother. The heroes she finds in the few books she reads, especially King Arthur, also help. She needs that vision because life is tough: her mother is dead and her father lost the farm during the Depression. Now they live the life of migrant workers. Armed with little but dreams, she exposes the frauds perpetrated by the landowners and earns a home for her family and her willow tree plate.

◆ Reeder, Carolyn. ***Grandpa's Mountain.*** Macmillan, 1991. ISBN 0-02-775811-7

■■■■■■■■□□□□□□

The Great Depression has an effect on this story although it isn't its focus. Carrie's father is out of work, and CCC workers are part of the action. The main thrust of the story is the federal government's creation of Shenandoah National Park, using out-of-work young men in the CCC to build it. The government needs the land where Carrie's grandparents live and operate a store and restaurant. Her grandfather is determined to fight for the right to keep his land, and his fight deteriorates from a petition drive to an armed resistance. Many of his neighbors are anxious to sell out and take one of the government homesteads in the valley. Others are not so thrilled. One even kills himself rather than leave. Grandpa is the last holdout. During the summer, Carrie learns to talk about real feelings rather than hide them. She learns that her grandmother's feelings are just as strong as her grandfather's, but Grandma is a realist. This strong book can lead to a great deal of investigation and discussion.

◆ Taylor, Mildred. ***Mississippi Bridge.*** Dial, 1990. ISBN 0-8037-0426-7

■■■■■■■■□□□□□□

See page149.

◆ ———. ***Roll of Thunder, Hear My Cry.*** Dial, 1976. ISBN 0-8037-7473-7

■■■■■■■■■■□□□□

This is a Focus Book; see page 297.

◆ Uchida, Yoshiko. ***The Best Bad Thing.*** Aladdin, 1983. ISBN 0-689-71069-0

■■■■■■■■■■□□□□

See page 133.

◆ ———. ***A Jar of Dreams.*** Atheneum, 1981. ISBN 0-689-50210-9

■■■■■■■■■■□□□□

See page 149.

◆ Yep, Laurence. ***The Star Fisher.*** Morrow, 1991. ISBN 0-688-09365-5

■■■■■■■■■■□□□□□

This novel, set in a small West Virginia town in 1927, tells a story of racial prejudice and its effect on Joan Lee and her Chinese-American family. The prejudice, however, is not one-sided. Joan Lee's grandmother is as stubbornly unwilling to understand as the whites who are frightened and angered by her behavior. Racial slurs are painted on the family's front gate, and Mrs. Lee's characterization of her neighbors as stupid and lazy doesn't help.

Burch, Robert. ***Tyler, Wilkin and Skee.*** University of Georgia Press, 1990. ISBN 0-8203-1194-4

■■■■■■■□□□□□□□

The three Coley boys live in rural Georgia. Their father is lucky to have a job during the Depression years, but money is short and the family makes its own amusement. Skee can find a song for every occasion; Wilkin is better at talking to people. Tyler tries to hold the group together.

Clifford, Eth. ***The Summer of the Dancing Horse.*** Houghton, 1990. ISBN 0-395-50066-4

■■■■■□□□□□□□□□

The episodic story is set in 1923 and gives a nice glimpse into the time through the lives of three children: Bessie, Sam, and Ben.

Kherdian, David. ***A Song for Uncle Harry.*** Philomel, 1989. ISBN 0-399-21895-5

■■■■■■■□□□□□□□

Uncle Harry was gassed during World War I and cannot work. He has the time and the nature to spend time with his young nephew, listening and enjoying life, while quietly and good-naturedly teaching him about life. The boy's parents, although equally loving, are too busy to spend time with him. This loving memoir is set against the immigrant Armenian culture of the 1930s.

Koller, Jackie French. ***Nothing to Fear.*** Gulliver, 1990. ISBN 0-15-200544-7

■■■■■■■□□□□□□□

An immigrant family in New York City during the Great Depression struggles with the difficult times and the problems of adjusting to a new culture.

Oneal, Zibby. ***A Long Way to Go.*** Viking, 1990. ISBN 0-670-82532-8

■■■■■□□□□□□□□□

The Suffragette Movement is seen through the eyes of a young girl in New York City. The story is told simply but with a surprising amount of detail and characterization.

Peck, Robert Newton. ***Arly.*** Walker, 1989. ISBN 0-8027-6856-3

■■■■□□□□□□□□□□

In a migrant camp in Jailtown, Florida, Arly Poole lives with his father in Shack Row. Their lot is not happy, and Arly would surely have grown up as illiterate as his father and most of the other workers had it not been for Miss Binnie Hoe who, with her restraint, determination, and humor, decides to set up a school in the camp.

Taylor, Mildred D. ***The Friendship and The Gold Cadillac.*** Bantam, 1989. ISBN 0-553-15765-5

■■■■■■■□□□□□□□

See page 149.

Van Raven, Pieter. ***A Time of Troubles.*** Scribner, 1990. ISBN 0-684-19212-8

■■■■■■■■■■■■■□

See page 113.

Weaver, Lydia. ***Child Star: When Talkies Came to Hollywood.*** Viking, 1992. ISBN 0-670-84039-4

■■■■■■□□□□□□□□

Part of the Once Upon America series, this story is set in Hollywood in 1927. Even though the stock market crash is still two years away, times are tough for many people, including ten-year-old Joey's mother. She gets some work in films as an extra or as a pianist on the sets, helping to drown out background noise to set a mood for the actors in the silent films. It's a mixed blessing for Joey when he becomes a child star. Money is no longer a problem for his family, but the hours are long and the work cuts out most of his childhood. When talkies begin, many of his fellow actors with poor voices join the growing ranks of the unemployed, but Joey's star grows brighter. This is an interesting sideways glance at the time as well as a good look at movie making.

Nonfiction

◆ Stewart, Gail B. ***What Happened to Judge Crater?*** Crestwood, 1992. ISBN 0-89686-617-3

■■■■■■□□□□□□□□

See page 143.

◆ Uchida, Yoshiko. ***The Invisible Thread.*** Messner, 1992. ISBN 0-671-74164-0

■■■■■■■■■■■□□□

See page 136.

Glassman, Bruce. ***The Crash of '29 and the New Deal.*** Silver Burdett, 1986. ISBN 0-382-06978-1

■■■■■■■■■□□□□□

With many photographs, the author deals with the economics of the twenties and thirties, giving a well-balanced look at America's worst financial era.

Rappaport, Doreen. ***The Sacco-Vanzetti Trial.*** HarperCollins, 1992. ISBN 0-06-025116-6

■■■■■■■■■□□□□□

Part of the publisher's Be the Judge—Be the Jury series, this book asks readers to be the judge and jury in this famous case in which two Italian immigrants were executed for murder. Some say it was prejudice rather than guilt that caused their execution.

Sandak, Cass R. ***The Franklin Roosevelts.*** Crestwood, 1992. ISBN 0-89686-639-4

■■■■■■■■□□□□□□□

This slim book contains a surprising amount of information about the family and political life of the Roosevelts. Brief chapters with many black-and-white photographs tell of their childhood, courtship, and marriage. As in most accounts, much is made of Sara Roosevelt's domination of the couple until her death. Franklin's extra-marital affair is also mentioned matter of factly, but only as one of the factors in the distance between Franklin and Eleanor throughout most of their marriage. However, the contributions of both people are the focus of the frankly admiring book.

Stanley, Jerry. ***Children of the Dust Bowl.*** Crown, 1992. ISBN 0-517-58782-3

■■■■■■■■□□□□□□□

This is an account, amply illustrated with photographs, of people living in an emergency farm labor camp who devised a school for their children. The school was so good that their previously hostile neighbors demanded the right to send their children there.

Tames, Richard. ***Picture History of the 20th Century: The 1920s.*** Watts, 1991. ISBN 0-531-14182-9

———. ***Picture History of the 20th Century: The 1930s.*** Watts, 1991. ISBN 0-531-14059-8

■■■■■■■□□□□□□□□

These books are part of a set published in Britain that uses black-and-white photographs and brief text to portray the times. Major events in politics, as well as the arts and cultures, are covered. The books are rich sources of research topics and opportunities to observe clothing and styles of the times.

Nonprint

Video

In Coal Country. American School Publishers.

See page 117.

See page 117.

1929-1941: The Great Depression. National Geographic, 1990.

Black-and-white newsreel footage and other archive materials cover the 1929 Stock Market Crash and its effects through the beginning of World War II.

The World of the Thirties: America in the Thirties—Depression and Optimism. Films for the Humanities and Sciences.

This film starts with the Stock Market Crash of 1929 but concentrates on the poverty in the South and West.

The Forties *The Times at a Glance...*

Movers & Shakers

Lauren Bacall
Humphrey Bogart
Winston Churchill
Walt Disney
Dwight Eisenhower
Oscar Hammerstein
Adolf Hitler
Chiang Kai-Shek
Joe Louis
George Marshall
Benito Mussolini
George Patton
Jackie Robinson
Franklin Roosevelt
Richard Rodgers
Frank Sinatra
Joseph Stalin
Harry Truman
Hideki Tojo

*Headlines**

1941	Lend-Lease Act signed
1941	Japanese bomb Pearl Harbor
1941	US enters World War II
1942	Alaskan highway started
1945	US drops atomic bombs on Nagasaki and Hiroshima, Japan

Meanwhile, In Other Parts of the World

1940	Germany occupies France
1941	Germany invades Russia
1941	Japan attacks US at Pearl Harbor
1941	Hitler begins annihilating Jews
1942	Gandhi demands independence for India
1943	Allies take North Africa and invade Italy
1944	D-Day opens second front and drives wedge into Germany
1945	Stalin, Churchill, and Roosevelt split up Europe politically
1945	World War II ends
	United Nations Charter signed
1948	USSR blockades Berlin to isolate it from West
	Israel's independence declared
1949	Berlin airlift
	Mao Tse-tung sets up People's Republic of China

*Many of the dates are only estimates made by historians and scientists. We tried to verify each date with at least two reliable sources; in cases where we found disagreement, we checked several sources. It is reasonable to expect that in your research you will also find disagreement.

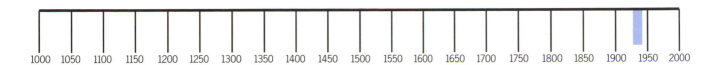

Inventions & Discoveries

1939	First jet-powered aircraft flown
1940	Plutonium made
	First electron microscope
1943	Penicillin used for medical treatment
1944	IBM produces an electronic calculating machine called ENIAC
	DDT used in agriculture
1945	Tupperware invented
1947	First atomic power station built in England
	Sound barrier broken
1948	Transistor invented
	Velcro invented

Fads & Customs

Jitterbug

Rationing

Loyalty oaths

Flying saucers

New Look

Swing bands

Andrews Sisters

Radios

Bubblegum

Casablanca

Bobby socks

Saddle shoes

Nylon stockings with dark seams

Upsweeps

Pompadours

Yo-yos

Music

Popular Songs

1946	*To Each His Own*
	Tenderly
	You Call Everybody Darlin'
	Old Buttermilk Sky
1947	*Golden Earrings*
	I'll Dance at Your Wedding
	Open the Door, Richard
1948	*Tennessee Waltz*
	On a Slow Boat to China
	Nature Boy
	A, You're Adorable
1949	*Bonaparte's Retreat*
	Dear Hearts and Gentle People
	I Don't Care If the Sun Don't Shine
	Scarlet Ribbons

Books

1943	McCloskey's *Homer Price*
1944	Lawson's *Rabbit Hill*

The Forties

Activities

- See World War II on page 90, The Cold War on page 101, Discovery and Invention on page 118, Transportation and Communication on page 123, and Cultures on page 128.

- Invent a rationing system for your classroom in order to save paper. Include all classroom members and the teacher. Make sure that need is taken into account when you are rationing the supply.

- Role-play being the leaders of the Allies dividing Europe politically at the end of World War II. Devise plans for the division and argue for the logic of your point. Compare the solution you devise with the actual one.

- Some people say that the Berlin Wall kept us from World War III. Others say that the Berlin Wall was a needless and cruel thing. Investigate both sides of that argument and draw your own conclusions.

- In Pine City, Minnesota, a few years ago the schools decided to do a system-wide study of World War II. They wanted to involve the whole community, so they invited anyone who was alive during those war years to come to the schools and tell their stories and hear the tales of others. They got people who had fought in the war in both the Pacific and Europe, survivors of the concentration camps, people who worked in the defense plants, and people whose families were less directly involved. One survivor of the German concentration camps electrified his audiences of all ages with stories of the people he met there and the ways they helped one another survive. With this rich background of personal memories, the study of this time took on a far more personal note than could otherwise have occurred. Your area is as rich as theirs in these and other memories. Try it!

- Assemble records and tapes of songs from this era. Research the songs and the bands and musicians who sang and played those songs. Plan a record hop, time for listening and dancing. Ask members of the community to participate by wearing clothing of the time or to come and just listen. Plan a time during the evening when there will be an open mike and people can tell their personal stories or add to the music.

- President Franklin Roosevelt had polio. He started the March of Dimes to collect money to fight the disease. Trace the history of polio, the two vaccines that were developed to fight it, and the state of the disease today. Are there other diseases that used to be scourges that have now become less of a threat? Investigate them.

Picture Books

Rosenblum, Richard. **Brooklyn Dodger Days.** Atheneum, 1991. ISBN 0-689-31512-0

Baseball fans haven't changed much since the 1940s setting of this picture book, but the teams and the players certainly have. Here are Peewee Reese, Leo Durocher, and Carl Furillo at a game being watched by their adoring fans. In addition to a bit of baseball history, viewers can see boys wearing knickers and some of the advertisements of the time.

Fiction

★ Wunderli, Stephen. ***The Blue Between the Clouds.*** Holt, 1992. ISBN 0-800-1772-0

Least Sophisticated   Most Sophisticated

This is a Focus Book; see page 293.

◆ Hahn, Mary Downing. ***Stepping on the Cracks.*** Clarion, 1991. ISBN 0-395-58707-4

This is a Focus Book; see page 295.

◆ Kinsey-Warnock, Natalie. ***The Canada Geese Quilt.*** Dutton, 1989. ISBN 0-525-65004-0

This is a touching story of Ariel, a young girl, and her loving family in Vermont during the late 1940s. Her grandmother is a quilter, and the Canadian goose quilt that she and Ariel work together becomes a symbol of a rich heritage.

◆ Little, Jean. ***Listen for the Singing.*** HarperCollins, 1991. ISBN 0-06-023910-7

Anna is about to enter her first mainstream high school after attending a school for the visually impaired. Her fears of and struggles in adapting to the new school and new classmates are set against the backdrop of her family's experience as Germans in Canada at the onset of World War II. The feeling of the era is effectively depicted in this story of determination and faith. Though set in Canada, this book is easily applicable to the United States' experience.

◆ Lord, Bette. ***In the Year of the Boar and Jackie Robinson.*** HarperCollins, 1984. ISBN 0-06-024004-0

The year was 1947, the Year of the Boar. The Brooklyn Dodgers lost the pennant, and Shirley Temple Wong finished her first year in America onstage with baseball great Jackie Robinson. She was a full-fledged student in the sixth grade. She had congenial classmates, good friends and neighbors, a loving family, and a year of double happiness.

◆ Paterson, Katherine. ***Jacob Have I Loved.*** Crowell, 1980. ISBN 0-690-04079-2

———. ***Ame a Jacob.*** Santillana.

Everyone loves Caroline, Louise's selfish younger sister. Isolated on a tiny Chesapeake Bay Island in the early forties, Louise feels that Caroline has robbed her of friends, her mother, and her dreams. Louise begins to learn the ways of the island and soon realizes that she must find her own identity.

◆ Uchida, Yoshiko. ***Journey Home.*** Macmillan, 1978. ISBN 0-689-50126-9

Although World War II is still raging, Yuki and her family have been released from the relocation camp where they had been forced to live since the beginning of the war. At the beginning of the book, they have found housing in Salt Lake

City and await permission to return to Berkeley, California. Adjusting to the prejudices and suspicions they face takes most of Yuki's energy. Her father is attempting to get other Japanese Americans released from the camp; her mother does housecleaning to earn money; and the whole family worries about Ken, the son who enlisted in the US Army. Even when the whole family is gathered in Berkeley and the war is over, their difficulties continue. Ken was disabled in battle and returns home withdrawn and depressed. The racism they experience is destructive both mentally and physically. The characters are well developed and the plot illustrates many concerns of the time.

Barrie, Barbara. ***Lone Star.*** Delacorte, 1990. ISBN 0-385-30156-1

■■■■■■■■■■■□□□□□

It's Christmas in 1944 and Jane and her immediate family have moved to Corpus Christi, Texas, far from their extended Jewish family in Chicago. Grandfather, however, has joined them and he seems determined to reject all that is not Jewish in their new community, even Jane's new friends. In an attempt to be like these friends, Jane puts up a Christmas tree that her grandfather throws out the window in rage. Jane's frustration and puzzlement are as profound as her grandfather's convictions. It isn't until news of the concentration camps and other horrors of the Holocaust reach her that Jane begins to understand.

Burch, Robert. ***Home Front Heroes.*** Puffin, 1974. ISBN 0-14-036030-1

■■■■■■■□□□□□□□□□

Here's a look at the time and the events of World War II from the point of view of Kate Coleman, a sixth grader in a small town in America. Flashbacks tell of the radio announcement of the air raid on Pearl Harbor, but most of the book talks about Kate's experiences when her temporary classroom is a one-room hut on the outskirts of town. Some of the customs and concerns of people of that time are revealed in the book.

Willis, Patricia. ***A Place to Claim as Home.*** Clarion, 1991. ISBN 0-395-55395-4

■■■■■■■■■■■□□□□□

Henry, an orphan, is hired to work on the farm of Miss Sarah Morrison during the summer of 1943. Their initial dislike and distrust of each other turns to grudging admiration as they share the chores of the farm. Gradually, Henry pieces together Sarah's tragic story. Sarah had given up a boy for adoption thirteen years earlier. Could it be Henry? The war that seems so distant through most of the novel reaches out to claim the life of a neighbor.

Nonfiction

◆ Houston, Jeanne Wakatsuki and Houston, James D. ***Farewell to Manzanar.*** Bantam, 1989. ISBN 0-553-23692-X

■■■■■■■■■■■□□□□□

The author was seven when she and her family were sent to the Manzanar internment camp for Japanese Americans. This story of her three-year experience there is not a bitter tirade against the injustices. It is a healing look at the truth about what really happened and the author's own reflections on its meaning and impact on her. From the tiny, drafty barracks to the high school yearbooks, from the guard towers and barbed wire to the large eating halls where she ate with her friends, we see the details of daily life. Because we see this through her family's experience, we see clearly the emotional impact on family structure, and we identify with the horrible hopelessness that faced them when they were finally released with nowhere to go and their assets confiscated or stolen.

◆ Uchida, Yoshiko. ***The Invisible Thread.*** Messner, 1992. ISBN 0-671-74164-0

■■■■■■■■■■■□□□

See page 136.

Freedman, Russell. ***Franklin Delano Roosevelt.*** Clarion, 1990. ISBN 0-89919-379-X

■■■■■■■■■■□□□□□

The focus of the book is on Roosevelt's personal crises and those of the United States during his leadership. Freedman is candid about the man, not capitalizing on his disability or his weaknesses, but giving them the weight they deserve. As in all of Freedman's books, the photographs are at least as important as the text, and extensive information about the man and his times is available from the photographs alone.

Tames, Richard. ***Picture History of the 20th Century: The 1940s.*** Watts, 1991. ISBN 0-531-14035-0

■■■■■■□□□□□□□□□

This book is part of a set published in Britain that uses black-and-white photographs and brief text to portray the times. Major events in politics, the arts, and cultures are covered. The books are rich sources for research topics and opportunities to observe clothing and styles of the times.

Nonprint

Videos
Jacob Have I Loved. American School Publishers.
Meet the Newbery Author: Russell Freedman. American School Publishers.

Audios
Jacob Have I Loved. American School Publishers.

The Fifties *The Times at a Glance...*

Movers & Shakers

Dwight Eisenhower

John Foster Dulles

Joseph McCarthy

Pope John XXIII

Elvis Presley

Benjamin Spock

J. D. Salinger

Harry Truman

Headlines*

1950	Korean War begins
1950	Truman authorizes production of hydrogen bomb
1950	First military advisors sent to Vietnam
1951	Truman relieves MacArthur of command in Korea
1954	Senate censures Joseph McCarthy
1954	Brown v. Board of Education; Supreme Court rules against segregation
1955	AFL merges with CIO
1955	Bus boycott in Montgomery, Alabama
1958	John Birch Society founded
1959	Alaska becomes 49th state
	Hawaii becomes 50th state

Meanwhile, In Other Parts of the World

1950	War between North and South Korea begins
1955	Vietnam divided into North and South after French withdrawal
1956	Soviet Union crushes Hungarian uprising
1957	European Common Market established
1958	John XXIII becomes Pope
1959	Fidel Castro takes power in Cuba

*Many of the dates are only estimates made by historians and scientists. We tried to verify each date with at least two reliable sources; in cases where we found disagreement, we checked several sources. It is reasonable to expect that in your research you will also find disagreement.

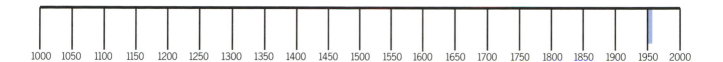

| 1000 | 1050 | 1100 | 1150 | 1200 | 1250 | 1300 | 1350 | 1400 | 1450 | 1500 | 1550 | 1600 | 1650 | 1700 | 1750 | 1800 | 1850 | 1900 | 1950 | 2000 |

Inventions & Discoveries

1951	First commercial manufacture of computers
1953	Hillary and Tenzing climb Everest
1953	First music synthesizer
1954	Link established between smoking and cancer
1956	First video recorder developed
1958	Jet airline service begins
1959	St. Lawrence Seaway opens

Fads & Customs

I Love Lucy
Mickey Mouse Club
Milton Berle
Cinerama
Credit cards
Hula hoops
Frisbees
Drive-in movies

Dial telephones
Station wagons
Dungarees
Bermuda shorts
Ducktail hairdos on men
Flip hairdos on women

Full skirts

Books

1950	Cleary's *Henry Huggins*
1952	White's *Charlotte's Web*
1959	George's *My Side of the Mountain*

Music

Popular Songs

1950	*Dearie*
	If I Knew You Were Comin'
	It's So Nice to Have a Man Around the House
	Music, Music, Music
	Rag Mop
1951	*In the Cool Cool of the Evening*
	Kisses Sweeter Than Wine
	Unforgetable
	Mockingbird Hill
1952	*Takes Two to Tango*
	Do Not Forsake Me
	Till I Waltz Again with You
	Don't Let the Stars Get in Your Eyes
1953	*I'm Walking Behind You*
	Crying in the Chapel
	Rags to Riches
	Oh, My Papa
1954	*Three Coins in the Fountain*
	Mister Sandman
	The Naughty Lady of Shady Lane
	Sh Boom
1955	*Rock Around the Clock*
	Maybelline
	Memories Are Made of This
	Love and Marriage
1956	*Love Me Tender*
	Hound Dog
	I Walk the Line
	Qué Sera, Sera
1957	*All the Way*
	April Love
	Young Love
	A White Sports Coat
1958	*Satin Doll*
	Volaré
	Everybody Loves a Lover
	Sugartime
	Catch a Falling Star
1959	*High Hopes*
	I'm Just a Lonely Boy
	Put Your Head on My Shoulder

The Fifties

Activities

- See The Civil Rights Movement on page 97, The Cold War on page 101, The Vietnam War on page 103, and Racism, Sexism, and Equality on page 146.

- What do you think about loyalty oaths? How are they different from the Pledge of Allegiance, or are they? Why was there all the fuss about them during this period? Would you sign one?

- The McCarthy hearings were called a "Witch Hunt." Make a chart showing similarities between the events of this time and the Salem witch trials. (See page 258 for a Focus Book about the Salem witch trials.)

- Why were people so afraid of Communism? Is there any evidence to support their fears?

- Find excerpts from the McCarthy hearings that you think are particularly eloquent. Find statements by Joseph Welch and Lillian Hellman, among others. Find out how their testimony, or lack thereof, changed people's careers. Write a short play about one person who was affected by the hearings.

- The desegregation law for schools was set forth during this time. Find out how it affected your community.

- Research Elvis Presley. Talk to people who loved him and his music. Find out what he meant to them and what they did about it. Why do you think people keep insisting that he's alive?

- People refer to the fifties as a peaceful time, especially if they compare it to the next decade. What factors can you find to support the idea or contradict the idea that not much tension was connected with this decade?

- Research the United Nations. Was it the first time nations had banded together to prevent war? What powers does it have? How did it function during the fifties? How has it functioned since that time? Do you think it contributed to the collapse of the Cold War? What do you think could be done to make it stronger?

- The fifties saw the beginning of Rock and Roll. Talk to people who hated it and to people who loved it. What effects can you see in today's music?

Picture Books

Smucker, Anna Egan. *No Star Nights.* Knopf, 1990. ISBN 0-394-89925-3
See page 112.

Fiction

◆ Enright, Elizabeth. *Gone-Away Lake.* Harcourt, 1957. ISBN 0-15-231649-3

■■■■■■□□□□□□□

Least Sophisticated   Most Sophisticated

See page 218.

Gondosch, Linda. **The Best Bet Gazette.** Lodestar, 1989. ISBN 0-525-67287-7

■■■■■□□□□□□□□□

Being the editor of a neighborhood newspaper in 1954 turns out to be more of a challenge than these sixth graders expect. When little Ralph Wallace contracts polio, the newspaper assumes a more serious role.

Taylor, Mildred D. **The Friendship and The Gold Cadillac.** Bantam, 1989. ISBN 0-553-15765-5

■■■■■■■□□□□□□□

See page 149.

Nonfiction

◆ Levine, Ellen. **If You Lived at the Time of Martin Luther King.** Scholastic, 1990. ISBN 0-590-42582-X

■■■■■□□□□□□□□□

See page 98.

◆ Parks, Rosa. **Rosa Parks: My Story.** Dial, 1992. ISBN 0-8037-0673-1

■■■■■■■■■□□□□□

See page 99.

Larsen, Anita. **The Rosenbergs.** Crestwood, 1992. ISBN 0-89686-612-2

■■■■■■□□□□□□□□

With a style approaching that of the television series Unsolved Mysteries, this book is one of a series called History's Mysteries. In this one, we start with rather grisly details of the execution of the Rosenbergs. The rest of the book is devoted to the facts of the case. The question, of course, is whether the Rosenbergs were guilty of the crimes for which they were executed. Some of the paranoia of the time is conveyed in this rather sensationalized account.

Tames, Richard. **Picture History of the 20th Century: The 1950s.** Watts, 1991. ISBN 0-531-14034-2

■■■■■■□□□□□□□□

This book is part of a set published in Britain that uses black-and-white photographs and brief text to portray the times. The books are rich sources for research topics and opportunities to observe clothing and styles of the times.

Nonprint

Videos

Democracy and Rights: One Citizen's Challenge. Close Up Foundation, 1989.

Narrated in part by Sandra Day O'Connor, the film deals with the 1957 integration of a school in Little Rock, Arkansas. Ernest Green, now a business executive, tells of his experiences as one of eight Black students who broke the color barrier.

Unknown Secrets: Art and the Rosenberg Era. Green Mountain Post Films, 1990.

The trial and execution of the Rosenbergs are interwoven with the art of the times. Its creators were inspired by the Rosenbergs and the early 1950s.

The Sixties *The Times at a Glance...*

Movers & Shakers

Neil Armstrong

Muhammed Ali

Rachel Carson

Fidel Castro

Cesar Chavez

Medgar Evers

Lyndon Johnson

John F. Kennedy

Robert Kennedy

Martin Luther King, Jr.

Nikita Khrushchev

Ho Chi Minh

Malcolm X

Mao Tse-tung

Headlines*

1961	US invades Cuba in Bay of Pigs
	Peace Corps founded
1962	Cuban Missile Crisis
	Cesar Chavez organizes farm workers
1963	President Kennedy assassinated
	Medgar Evers assassinated
1964	Civil Rights Act passed
1965	US Armed Forces increase in Vietnam
	Watts riots
1966	Black Panther party formed
1968	Martin Luther King, Jr., assassinated
	Riots at Democratic National Convention
1969	Woodstock Festival
	Astronaut walks on the moon

Meanwhile, In Other Parts of the World

1961	Russia constructs Berlin Wall
1967	Six Days War between Egypt and Israel
1968	Vietnam peace talks open

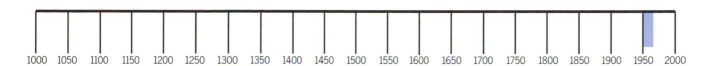

| 1000 | 1050 | 1100 | 1150 | 1200 | 1250 | 1300 | 1350 | 1400 | 1450 | 1500 | 1550 | 1600 | 1650 | 1700 | 1750 | 1800 | 1850 | 1900 | 1950 | 2000 |

Inventions & Discoveries

1960	Laser built in US
1960	First weather satellite launched
1961	Yuri Gagarin is first man in space
1962	First communications satellite launched
1963	First hologram produced
1964	Verrazano Narrows bridge opens
1966	Fiber optic telephone cables devised
1969	Astronauts walk on the moon
1969	SST makes test flight
1969	Microprocessor developed

Fads & Customs

Surfing

Stereo

Recreational drug use increases

Hippies

Transcendental meditation

Mini skirts

Long hair on men

Afros

Love beads

Books

1961	Lee's *To Kill a Mockingbird*
	O'Dell's *Island of the Blue Dolphins*
1962	Carson's *Silent Spring*
1963	Sendak's *Where the Wild Things Are*
	L'Engle's *A Wrinkle in Time*
1964	Fitzhugh's *Harriet the Spy*
1966	Burch's *Queenie Peavy*
1969	Taylor's *The Cay*
	Armstrong's *Sounder*
	Byar's *Trouble River*

Music and Art

The Beatles

Pop Art

Andy Warhol

Op Art

Folk Songs

Popular Songs

1960	*The Twist*
1961	*Moon River*
	Those Lazy Hazy Days of Summer
	Ramblin' Rose
1963	*I Want to Hold Your Hand*
1964	*She Loves You*
	I Get Around
	Mr. Tambourine Man
1965	*Yesterday*
	Sounds of Silence
	What the World Needs Now
1966	*Yellow Submarine*
	Eleanor Rigby
	Monday, Monday
1967	*Ode to Billy Joe*
	Up, Up, and Away
	Can't Take My Eyes Off of You
1968	*Hey, Jude*
	Little Green Apples
1969	*Honky Tonk Woman*
	Come Saturday Morning

The Sixties

Activities

- See The Civil Rights Movement on page 97, The Cold War on page 101, The Vietnam War on page 103, and Racism, Sexism, and Equality on page 146.

- Watch a video of the first trip to the moon. If you were the first person to walk on the moon and knew that people all over the world could hear what you were saying, what would your first words be?

- Why did we want to go to the moon? Should we have spent all that money and should we continue to spend money on the space program? How much money did we spend getting a person to the moon the first time? What else could have been done with the money? Develop arguments for and against space research and space missions. Present your arguments visually with posters, charts, brochures, and letters.

- Make a time line of the sixties, showing major events. Talk to people who were adults at the time to see which of those events they think were most important. Make a graph showing the relationship of their age at the time to the importance they place on the events.

- Do protests work? Talk to people who have participated in protests to see how they feel about them. Are they still involved in protest marches or demonstrations? Why?

- Find newspaper articles from the time. Which do you think are impartial recordings of events and which show the feelings of the editors or writers?

- How did television affect the events of the time? Find news clips or videos of the time to bolster your argument.

- What issues of today are provoking demonstrations? What and when was the largest demonstration in Washington?

- What was the "counterculture" of the time? What were they rebelling against? Which of those things have changed? What did the counterculture accomplish? How was it different or the same as the rebellion most young people of every generation experience?

- Talk to people who used illegal drugs during the sixties or had close contact with people who did. Why did they become involved? What effect did the involvement have? What price did they pay? What were their feelings about illegal drugs at the time? How do they feel about them now?

- Make a list of the assassinations of this time. Interview people who were alive during the sixties and find out what effect the assassinations had on their lives. Where were they when they heard the news? Who helped them through the grief?

- Investigate the assassination of one of those people. Who killed him? Why was he killed? What happened to the killer? Was there a conspiracy involved? Find people or read about people who think there were conspiracies. What evidence do they give for this?

- Why were there so many assassinations during this decade? What events do you think led up to them?

- The picture book ***Drummer Hoff*** by Barbara and Ed Emberley (Prentice, 1967. ISBN 0-13-220822-9) was a Caldecott Award book that caused a great deal of controversy at the time. It shows soldiers building a cannon that explodes when they try to fire it. Rhythmic text and rhyme with striking woodcuts tell the story.

Some people objected to the story because they said it glorified war. Others said, because of the exploding cannon and the appropriation by birds and flowers, that it was pro-peace and objected to that. Read it. What do you think about its message? Find out what the authors said the message was.

- Did the sixties era last more than a decade? When do you think the sixties ended? What events brought an end or a transition to that era?
- Johnson's War on Poverty and Great Society programs were attacked during the 1992 presidential campaign. Find out about those programs. What were their goals? What did they cost? What programs can you find the most support for? Which still exist? What did they accomplish? While you're investigating, find out about the number of people living below the poverty line in the sixties and the number today.

Picture Books ★ Bunting, Eve. ***The Wall.*** Illustrated by Ronald Himler. Clarion, 1990. ISBN 0-395-51588-2

See page 103.

Fiction ◆ Boyd, Candy D. ***Charlie Pippin.*** Macmillan, 1987. ISBN 0-02-726350-9

■■■■■■■■■■□□□□□

Least Sophisticated   Most Sophisticated

See page 104.

◆ Byars, Betsy. ***The Two-Thousand-Pound Goldfish.*** HarperCollins, 1982. ISBN 0-06-020890-2

■■■■■■■■□□□□□□□

Warren's mother has been a fugitive, wanted by the FBI, since she joined a revolutionary movement in the 1960s. Warren and his sister, Weezie, are living with their grandmother. Warren dreams of a life reunited with his mother, but Weezie realizes that their mother's commitment to causes doesn't extend to her children. Meanwhile, Warren delights in horror movies and in inventing plots for new ones. His current plot concerns a two-thousand-pound goldfish loose in the sewers of New York. When his grandmother dies and his mother doesn't show up, Warren admits that Weezie is right and regretfully lets go of all his fantasies, including the goldfish.

◆ Moore, Yvette. ***Freedom Songs.*** Orchard, 1990. ISBN 0-531-08412-4

■■■■■■■■■■■□□□

See page 98.

◆ Paterson, Katherine. ***Park's Quest.*** Lodestar, 1988. ISBN 0-525-67258-3

■■■■■■■■■■□□□□

See page 104.

Davis, Ossie. ***Just Like Martin.*** Simon and Schuster, 1992. ISBN 0-671-73202-1

■■■■■■■□□□□□□□□

See page 57.

Marino, Jan. ***The Day That Elvis Came to Town.*** Little, 1990.
ISBN 0-316-54618-6

■■■■■■■■■■■■□□□

See page 149.

Nonfiction   ◆ ***Cobblestone Magazine***
The July 1981 issue of the magazine was devoted to Our Voyage to the Moon. Back issues of the magazine can be obtained from Cobblestone Publishing, 30 Grove St., Peterborough, NH 03458.

◆ Levine, Ellen. ***If You Lived at the Time of Martin Luther King.*** Scholastic, 1990. ISBN 0-590-42582-X

■■■■■□□□□□□□□□

See page 98.

Foster, Leila. ***The Story of the Great Society.*** Childrens, 1991.
ISBN 0-516-04755-8

■■■■■■□□□□□□□□

Lyndon Johnson's plan for a continuation of the ideals and programs of the Roosevelt administration eventually lead to legislation for voting and Civil Rights, Headstart, VISTA volunteers, aid to Appalachia, and many community action programs throughout the country. The book shows how Johnson used his Senate experience to encourage legislators to pass his programs. In addition to Johnson's political squabbles, motivations, and accomplishments, the book covers the march on Selma, the rioting in Watts, the assassination of Martin Luther King, Jr., the appointment of Thurgood Marshall to the Supreme Court, and Johnson's surprise decision not to run for re-election.

Harrison, Barbara and Terris, Daniel. ***A Twilight Struggle: The Life of John Fitzgerald Kennedy.*** Lothrop, 1992. ISBN 0-688-08830-9

■■■■■■■■■□□□□□

See page 144.

Kent, Zachary. ***The Story of the Peace Corps.*** Childrens, 1990.
ISBN 0-516-04752-3

■■■■■■□□□□□□□□

From Kennedy's proposal to use United States' know-how to help underdeveloped nations to the present work of the Peace Corps and the work done by the volunteers after their return to the United States, the book is clear and quite realistic in detailing what the Peace Corps attempted and achieved.

Sullivan, George. ***The Day We Walked on the Moon: A Photo History of Space Exploration.*** Scholastic, 1990. ISBN 0-590-43632-5

■■■■■■■□□□□□□□

Using primary sources such as newspaper clippings and NASA photographs, Sullivan shows US and Soviet achievements in space.

Tames, Richard. ***Picture History of the 20th Century: The 1960s.*** Watts, 1991. ISBN 0-531-14035-0

■■■■■■□□□□□□□□□

This book is part of a set published in Britain that uses black-and-white photographs and brief text to portray the times. The books are rich sources for research topics and opportunities to observe clothing and styles of the times.

Nonprint

Videos

And the Children Shall Lead. Public Media Video, 1984.

This is a dramatization of events in 1964 in Catesville, Mississippi, a fully segregated town until the drive for Black voter registration begins. Using music of the sixties and TV coverage as background, the film brings the reality of that time into effective focus.

The March on Washington Remembered. Encyclopedia Britannica, 1990.

Eleanor Norton, a Civil Rights activist, recalls the march of 200,000 people against the ravages of racism. The film covers the times and the events leading up to the 1963 march.

Meet the Newbery Author: Katherine Paterson. American School Publishers.

The Seventies and Eighties *The Times at a Glance...*

Movers & Shakers

Spiro Agnew
Alvin Ailey, Jr.
George Bush
Jimmy Carter
Mikhail Gorbachev
Florence Griffith Joyner
Sadam Hussein
Ayatollah Khomeini
Ralph Nader
Richard Nixon
Deng XiaoPing
Ronald Reagan
Margaret Thatcher
Donald Trump
Ted Turner
Lech Walesa
George Wallace

Headlines*

1970	Four students killed at Kent State
1971	Supreme Court upholds forced busing
1972	Watergate break in
	President Nixon visits China
	George Wallace shot
1973	US troops leave Vietnam
	American Indian Movement occupies Wounded Knee
1973	Senate investigates activities in Nixon campaign
	Vice President Agnew resigns
1974	President Nixon resigns
	Patty Hearst kidnapped
1977	President Carter pardons Vietnam draft dodgers
1980	Mt. St. Helens erupts
1981	Vietnam War Memorial completed
1981	First reports of AIDS virus
1983	US invades Grenada
1986	*Challenger* explodes
1988	Two whales trapped in ice capture world-wide interest
	Widespread forest fires decimate Yellowstone
1989	US invades Panama
	The Exxon *Valdez* oil spill

*Many of the dates are only estimates made by historians and scientists. We tried to verify each date with at least two reliable sources; in cases where we found disagreement, we checked several sources. It is reasonable to expect that in your research you will also find disagreement.

1000	1050	1100	1150	1200	1250	1300	1350	1400	1450	1500	1550	1600	1650	1700	1750	1800	1850	1900	1950	2000

Meanwhile, In Other Parts of the World

1970	Rhodesia declares itself a segregated independent country
1972	Eleven Israelis killed by terrorists at Olympic Games in Munich
1973	US ends bombing in Cambodia, marking end of Vietnam War
1978	Begin and Sadat sign "Framework for Peace" treaty
1979	Ayatollah Khomeini takes over government of Iran after Shah flees
1981	Anwar Sadat assassinated
1984	Indira Gandhi assassinated
1986	Meltdown at Chernobyl
	Corazon Aquino takes power in Philippines
1987	Work begins on Channel Tunnel
1988	Iran-Iraq eight-year war ends
1989	Berlin Wall demolished
	Uprising in Tiananmen Square, China

Inventions & Discoveries

1982	First artificial heart transplant
1989	*Voyager* sends back images of Neptune

Fads & Customs

Environmental awareness
Yuppies
Satellite dishes
Portable telephones
Car telephones

Music

1970	*Bridge Over Troubled Waters*
	I'll Never Fall in Love Again
	Your Song
1971	*You've Got a Friend*
	Take Me Home, Country Roads
	Lonely Days
1972	*American Pie*
	Operator
1973	*Goodbye, Yellow Brick Road*
	Give Me Love
	Bad, Bad Leroy Brown
	You Are the Sunshine of My Life
1977	*I'll Never Love This Way Again*
1980	*Hill Street Blues Theme*
1982	*On the Wings of Love*
1984	*I Just Called to Say I Love You*
1989	*After All*

Books

1974	Adam's *Watership Down*
1979	Peck's *Secrets of the Shopping Mall*
1981	Van Allsburg's *Jumanji*
1985	Bank's *Indian in the Cupboard*
1987	Paulsen's *Hatchet*

The Seventies and Eighties

Activities

- See The Cold War on page 101, Politics and Government on page 140, and Racism, Sexism, and Equality on page 146.

- Very little of the literature that gives a sense of this period is labeled historical literature because the seventies and eighties are so recent. Find some books written during the seventies and early eighties that show life during that time.

- Gather statistics for this period. Start generating data based on the statistics you find: How many households were and are below the poverty level? What are the unemployment figures for times during and since this period? What portion of income is spent on child care? Health care? Housing?

- Find out about the accomplishments of Ralph Nader and others who worked to increase consumer awareness during this period.

- Find out about Rachel Carson's book *Silent Spring.* What effect did it have on your community? To what extent did it influence the environmental movement of today?

- Find newspaper clippings about the oil embargo and resulting gas shortage of 1973. What caused it? What were the results? What changes did it make in use or supply of oil in America? What else might have changed if oil had continued in short supply?

- Find statistics to show average or typical family structures of the last six decades. What changes occurred? What do these changes show?

- Find accounts of women's efforts to gain rights: the right to vote, the right to work, the right to equal pay, the right to benefits, the right to child care, the right to abortion. What legislation covered or covers these rights? What strategies did Women's Rights groups use to pass this legislation? Who opposed it and why?

- What effects did the women's movement have on the lives of women and their expectations of themselves? How did new opportunities affect their lives?

- How is the men's movement similar to and different from the early years of the women's movement?

- Watch the scene in *Mary Poppins* when Mrs. Banks sings and talks about the women's suffrage movement. Although the lyrics to the song give the appearance of being pro-suffrage, Mrs. Banks and her co-demonstrators are ridiculed in the film. Find other examples where the agents of change are seen as ludicrous even though their beliefs eventually become widely accepted.

- These are the years in which the first generation of people raised with television were becoming adults. What effect did this have on society? Make charts showing its effect on consumerism, communication within the home, entertainment, violence, and news sources. How many television advertisements did the average person see by the time he/she was twenty?

- What was happening in cities at this time concerning housing, crime, drugs, economic stability, power in federal government, and tax structure.

- Make a time line showing political events from the 1968 demonstration at the Democratic National Convention in Chicago to Nixon's resignation. Show how or whether each of these events was related to Watergate.

- Make a gallery using enlarged photographs from the news media showing the main figures in the Watergate scandal. Under the photos tell what each person did and what they are doing now. How did Watergate change their lives?

- List as many political crimes as you can find in the twentieth century. Why did Watergate cause a president's resignation? What other crimes on your list do you feel should have lead to removal from office?

- What are the long-term effects of Watergate?

Picture Books

★ Bunting, Eve. ***The Wall.*** Illustrated by Ronald Himler. Clarion, 1990. ISBN 0-395-51588-2
See page 103.

Blaine, Marge. ***The Terrible Thing That Happened at Our House.*** Macmillan, 1975. ISBN 0-02-710720-5
The terrible thing is that mommy went to work.

Ehrlich, Amy. ***Zeek Silver Moon.*** Dial, 1972. ISBN 0-8037-9826-1
This counterculture family brims over with love and joy in one another.

Hazen, Barbara. ***Why Couldn't I Be an Only Kid Like You, Wigger.*** Macmillan, 1979. ISBN 0-689-70460-7
An only child and a child who is one of many in a family compare lifestyles.

Keats, Ezra Jack. ***Louie's Search.*** Macmillan, 1980. ISBN 0-02-749700-3
Louie searches for a father.

Merriam, Eve. ***Mommies at Work.*** Simon, 1989. ISBN 0-671-64386-X
Jobs, white collar and blue, are performed by mothers in and outside the home.

Thomas, Marlo. ***Free to Be a Family.*** Bantam, 1987. ISBN 0-553-5235-7
This is a book of short stories, poems, and songs celebrating choices of lifestyles and different women's roles in society.

Zolotow, Charlotte. ***A Father Like That.*** HarperCollins, 1971. ISBN 0-06-026949-9
A boy who doesn't have a father tells his mother what his ideal father would be like.

Fiction

Clymer, Eleanor. ***The Spider, the Cave and the Pottery Bowl.*** Dell, 1971. ISBN 0-440-40166-6

■■■■■□□□□□□□□□

Least Sophisticated   Most Sophisticated

Kate, a Native American girl, narrates a story of life in a Hopi village on the mesa where she lives with her grandmother every summer. Grandmother, who is a master potter, is becoming too old and frail to continue her craft. After Kate's brother inadvertently breaks a special clay pot, he runs away and discovers a cache of clay that inspires Grandmother to pass on her craft and skill.

Prather, Ray. ***Fish and Bones.*** HarperCollins, 1992. ISBN 0-06-025121-2

■■■■■■■□□□□□□□□

Bones is a thirteen-year-old African American in the 1970s in a racially divided town. He becomes involved in a bank robbery and uncovers the secret of a lynching that took place in the area years before.

Nonfiction

◆   Kilian, Pamela. ***What Was Watergate?*** St. Martins, 1990. ISBN 0-312-04446-1

■■■■■■■■□□□□□□□

This is a lively and well-illustrated account of the events leading up to Watergate, the crime and its aftermath. The book is balanced and easy to read.

◆   ***Cobblestone Magazine***

The following issues of the magazine were devoted to the eighties:
Mount St. Helens (May 1981)
Environmentalism (August 1989)
Tuning In to Television (October 1989)
Energy: Powering Our Nation (October 1990)
Back issues of the magazine can be obtained from Cobblestone Publishing, 30 Grove St., Peterborough, NH 03458.

◆   Carr, Terry. ***Spill! The Story of the Exxon Valdez.*** Watts, 1991. ISBN 0-531-10998-4

■■■■■■■□□□□□□□□

Starting with a history of the Alaskan pipeline and its economic benefits to the region, but without talking about the environmental impact of the pipeline itself, Carr gives a minute by minute account of the accident. The rest of the book is devoted to the cleanup efforts. Although it scarcely touches on the controversy, the book does provide a chance to talk about environmental disasters.

Lauber, Patricia. ***Summer of Fire: Yellowstone 1988.*** Watts, 1991. ISBN 0-531-05943-X

■■■■■■□□□□□□□□□

With abundant color photographs of the fire and its aftermath, Lauber brings an immediacy to the text and the event itself. In addition to this specific fire, the book covers the nature of forest fires, the questions concerning which fires to fight and how to fight them, and the short- and long-term effects on wildlife.

Nadel, Laurie. ***The Great Stream of History.*** Atheneum, 1991. ISBN 0-689-31559-7

■■■■■■■■□□□□□□□

Concentrating on Richard Nixon's life after Watergate, the book provides an interesting look at the seventies and at Nixon's life since his resignation.

Pious, Richard M. ***Richard Nixon: A Political Life.*** Messner, 1991. ISBN 0-671-72852-0

■■■■■■■□□□□□□□□

Nixon's achievements, his motivations, and his flaws are covered fairly evenly in this straightforward book that attempts to explore the character of the man

through his actions. Nixon's belief that the end justified the means was, of course, his downfall and the author refrains from being too judgmental.

Probosz, Kathilyn Solomon. ***Alvin Ailey, Jr.*** Bantam, 1991. ISBN 0-553-15930-5

■■■■■■■□□□□□□□

Part of the Changing Our World series, this brief biography tells the story of the dancer and choreographer who became the founder of one of the world's foremost dance companies. From his company's 1958 debut, his triumphant presentation of Revelations in 1960, to the founding of a permanent home for the Alvin Alley American Dance Theater in 1989, Alvin Ailey used his art and skill to celebrate the African-American experience. The biography is simply told with obvious enthusiasm for his work .

Sandak, Cass R. ***The Nixons.*** Crestwood, 1992. ISBN 0-89686-638-6

■■■■■■■□□□□□□□

As with other books in the First Families series, this is a brief but informative look at the personalities and achievements of Pat and Richard Nixon. Although the author tries to put the best face on most events, he does show the contradictions in Nixon's personality, his ambitions, and the distrust that many had of him. The author recounts Nixon's achievements in ending the Vietnam War and in reestablishing trade with China. The bulk of the book is about the Nixons's political career.

Smith, Samantha. ***Samantha Smith: Journey to the Soviet Union.*** Little, 1985. ISBN 0-316-80175-5

■■■■■■■□□□□□□□

See page 102.

Tames, Richard. ***Picture History of the 20th Century: The 1980s.*** Watts, 1991. ISBN 0-531-14079-2

■■■■■■□□□□□□□□

This book is part of a set published in Britain that uses black-and-white photographs and brief text to portray the times. The books are rich sources for research topics and opportunities to observe clothing and styles of the times.

Nonprint

Videos

The Big Spill. Coronet Film & Video, 1990.

The impact of the Exxon Valdez spill is the focus of this film that offers several perspectives on the tragedy, questions the effectiveness of the clean-up operation, and discusses technology that may prevent a recurrence.

Part
4

Focus Books

Squanto

Squanto

By Feenie Ziner. Linnet, 1988.
ISBN 0-208-02274-0

■■■■■■□□□□□□□□

Genre: Fictionalized Biography

Setting: New England, Early 1600s

Summary: Almost every American has heard the story of how Squanto helped the Pilgrims survive that first winter in Plymouth, but few know any details of his life. This book is based primarily on historical fact with conversations and some sketchy details filled in by the author's imagination. It supplies considerable information on this amazing man and on the people with whom he came in contact.

Twice captured through treachery and transported to Europe (once to England and later as a slave to Spain), Squanto led a life that would have broken most people many times over. Most of the book is devoted to Squanto's life before he met the Pilgrims.

Background Information

• Tasquantum, a Patuxet Indian, known as Squanto, was kidnapped as a young man and taken to England by explorers of the New England coast.

• He stayed in England for many years trying to find passage back to his people.

• He spent some time in Newfoundland before he got back to New England where he was recaptured and sold into slavery in Spain.

• By the time he got back to what is now Massachusetts, he found that his people had been wiped out by diseases brought by the Europeans.

• He was a friend of Massasoit and Samoset and was chosen by Massasoit to help the settlers at Plymouth.

• He felt it was his destiny to help the Pilgrims thrive in a land once inhabited by his people.

Things to Talk About and Notice

• Make a list of the many people who betrayed Squanto. What might Squanto have become without this betrayal?

• Discuss Squanto's ability to hold on to who he was in spite of his great misfortunes. Where did he get the strength to survive?

• Look at the role Squanto played in US History and compare it to the roles of Sacajawea and Pocahontas. In what ways might Indian people today regard those three: as heroes, villains, victims, or traitors?

• Like the other Native Americans mentioned above, Squanto was a person caught between cultures. Find other people, real and fictional, who shared this position. What did they do about it? Did they choose that role deliberately or have it thrust upon them?

• What if Squanto had not existed? Could the Pilgrims have survived without him? Would another Indian have done the same?

Things to Do

• Squanto is sold into slavery in Spain. Find out as much as you can about what happened to other Indians taken to Europe by early settlers.

• Find out what other countries of Squanto's time allowed slavery.

• Trace Squanto's journeys on a map. What would he see if he traveled the same route today? Figure out the miles he traveled during those years.

• To explore the motivations of the various people in this book, make a chart such as the one on the next page.

Name of Character	John Smith	Captain Waymouth
What He Did	Brought Squanto back to Cape Cod	Shanghied Squanto at Pemaquid
Why He Did It	To gain favor with the other Indians	Wanted information about a Northwest passage and favor with King James
Other Factors	Wanted to have a part in the settlement and exploration of "Northern Virginia"	Had no feeling for Indians as people

Picture Books

★Sewall, Marcia. *People of the Breaking Day.* Atheneum, 1990. ISBN 0-689-31407-8

See page 177.

★———. *Pilgrims of Plimoth.* Macmillan, 1986. ISBN 0-689-31250-4

See page 177.

Fiction

◆Clapp, Patricia. *Constance: A Story of Early Plymouth.* Morrow, 1991. ISBN 0-688-10976-4

■■■■■■□□□□□□□□

Least Sophisticated   Most Sophisticated

See page 178.

◆Monjo, F. N. *The House on Stink Alley.* Dell, 1977. ISBN 0-440-43376-2

■■■■■■■■■□□□□□

See page 179.

Nonfiction

★Fritz, Jean. *The Double Life of Pocahontas.* Putnam, 1983. ISBN 0-399-21016-4

■■■■■■■■■□□□□□

See page 180.

◆Bradford, William et al. *Homes in the Wilderness: A Pilgrim's Journal of Plymouth Plantation in 1620.* Linnet, 1988. ISBN 0-208-02269-4

■■■■■■□□□□□□□□

See page 180.

◆Fritz, Jean. *Who's That Stepping on Plymouth Rock?* Putnam, 1975. ISBN 0-698-20325-9

■■■□□□□□□□□□□□

See page 180.

Barth, Edith. *Turkeys, Pilgrims and Indian Corn.* Clarion, 1975. ISBN 0-395-28846-0

■■■■■■□□□□□□□□

The book deals with harvest festivals and customs in many cultures but has quite a bit of material about the Pilgrims and their dealings with the Indians, particularly Squanto.

Dalgliesh, Alice. *The Thanksgiving Story.* Aladdin, 1954. ISBN 0-689-71053-4

■■■■■■■□□□□□□□

See page 178.

San Souci, Robert. *N. C. Wyeth's Pilgrims.* Chronicle, 1991. ISBN 0-87701-806-5

■■■■□□□□□□□□□□

See page 181.

The Salem Witchcraft Trials

The Salem Witchcraft Trials

By Karen Zeinert. Watts, 1989.
  ISBN 0-531-10673-X

■■■■■■■■□□□□□□□

Genre: Nonfiction

Setting: Salem, Massachusetts, 1692

Summary: One of a series of books called Venture, this book deals with the roots of the fear of witches that spurred on the hysteria in Salem in 1692. It does so clearly and interestingly, succeeding where many adult books have failed because it provides a context for what seems to have been a bizarre occurrence. We find out about life in Salem at the time as well as a bit about the lives of the accused and the accusers. The trials themselves are recounted, of course, but even more interesting are the accounts of what happened to some of the girls who started the whole thing. The book is fascinating reading for adults and younger audiences.

Things to Talk About and Notice

- Notice how small events led to big ones.

- Why do you think it all happened? What evidence can you find to support your hypothesis?

- Who benefited?

- What do you think about the fact that the accused were mostly from one side of town and the accusers from the other?

- Do you think the girls were sincere?

- What could have happened to stop it? Who had the power to stop it?

- Has anything like this ever happened since? Could it?

Things to Do

- Find ways to show the causes and effects of the events in the book. Explain your methods.

- Find out about the McCarthy Communist "witch hunts." Do you see similarities?

- Tell the story from Goody Nurse's point of view or from that of some other character in the book.

- Send for information from the Chamber of Commerce in Salem, Massachusetts, or from the Massachusetts Historical Society about the Witch House and other points of interest in Salem today.

- Imagine that you are living in Salem at the time of the trials and find "real" evidence of witchcraft around you.

- Make a chart such as the one below organizing information about people tried for witchcraft in 1692. You will have to consult other resources for information.

Accused	Accuser(s)	Charges or Evidence	Outcome of Trial
Rebecca Nurse	Abigail Williams	Saw her shape and it caused her (Abigail) to have fits. Her appearance at court caused girls to have fits.	First declared not guilty, then declared guilty and hung.
Bridget Bishop	5 girls and 23 townspeople	Saw her shape in their dreams Saw her at witches' sabbath. Found puppets with pins in them in her cellar.	Declared guilty and hung.

Fiction

◆ Clapp, Patricia. ***Witches' Children: A Story of Salem.*** Lothrop, 1982. ISBN 0-14-032407-0

Least Sophisticated   Most Sophisticated

See page 178.

◆ Cross, Gilbert B. ***A Witch Across Time.*** Atheneum, 1990. ISBN 0-689-31602-X

■■■■■■■■■■□□□

See page 38.

◆ Petry, Ann. ***Tituba of Salem Village.*** HarperCollins, 1964. ISBN 0-06-440403-X

■■■■■■■□□□□□□

See page 179.

◆ Speare, Elizabeth. ***The Witch of Blackbird Pond.*** Houghton, 1968. ISBN 0-440-49596-2

■■■■■■■■□□□□□

See page 179.

Bawden, Nina. ***The Witch's Daughter.*** Lippincott, 1966. ISBN 0-7451-0654-4

■■■■■□□□□□□□□

Perdita, a lonely orphan, is rejected by others when she claims to be able to see into the future. Eventually, she realizes that her powers are not witchcraft but a special and useful talent.

Dunlop, Eileen. ***The Valley of Deer.*** Holiday, 1989. ISBN 0-8234-0766-7

■■■■■■■■■□□□

See page 273.

Miller, Arthur. ***The Crucible.*** Available in many collections.

■■■■■■■■■□□□□

A play concerning the witch trials of Salem, or is it about McCarthyism?

Nonfiction

Cohen, Daniel. ***Curses, Hexes and Spells.*** HarperCollins, 1974. ISBN 0-397-31494-9

■■■■■■□□□□□□□

Witches and the tools of their trade.

Harrison, Michael. ***Scolding Tongues: The Persecution of Witches.*** Dufour, 1987. ISBN 0-685-19631-3

■■■■■■■□□□□□

Fear of witchcraft was not confined to Salem. Here the author places those trials in a larger context.

Jackson, Shirley. ***Witchcraft of Salem Village.*** Random, 1963. ISBN 0-394-90369-2

■■■■■■■□□□□□

Another view of the same period with more suspense.

Kent, Zachary. ***The Story of the Salem Witch Trials.*** Childrens, 1986. ISBN 0-516-04704-3

■■■■■■□□□□□□

This, too, is a clear account of the events in Salem.

Kurland, Gerald. ***Communism and the Red Scare.*** SamHar Press, 1982. ISBN 0-87157-319-9

■■■■■■■■■□□□

What made the McCarthy attitude successful? Who stopped it? The witch hunting of that era is covered from the politcial, financial, and emotional points of view.

Scot, Reginald. ***Discoveries of Witchcraft.*** Dover, 1989. ISBN 0-486-26030-5

■■■■■■□□□□□□

Like the Harrison book above, this book cites witchcraft accusations throughout history.

Starkey, Marion. ***The Visionary Girls: Witchcraft in Salem Village.*** Little, 1973. ISBN 0-316-81087-8

■■■■■■□□□□□□

Starkey concentrates on the lives of the "victims" before, during, and after the trials.

The Courage of Sarah Noble

The Courage of Sarah Noble

By Alice Dalgliesh. Illustrated by Leonard Weisgard. Aladdin, 1954. ISBN 0-689-71057-7

■ ■ ■ ■ □ □ □ □ □ □ □ □ □ □

Genre: Fact-based fiction

Setting: New England, 1707

Summary: This short novel is based on a true incident. John Noble, of Westfield, Massachusetts, takes his eight-year-old daughter, Sarah, with him to build a house in New Milford, Connecticut, a new settlement in the wilderness of 1707. Sara is fearful during the trip to the new land; however, she is proud of the trust her father places in her. The cloak her mother gave her is a source of security, and she treasures it. After the house is built, John leaves Sarah with a trusted Indian family while he returns to Westfield for the rest of the family. Sarah has many opportunities to call on her courage before their return.

Background Information

- During this time of Westward expansion, many Indians dealt with the white settlers and became their friends.

- The attitudes of Indians and settlers were different toward many things including clothing.

- Young children were often given responsibilities that today's children would not be given.

Things to Notice and Talk About

- Talk about the clothing in the illustrations.

- Talk about Sarah's statement in reference to the Robinsons' house: "There is no love in that house."

- Talk about Sarah's fears: the wolves, the trees, and the Indians. Were they reasonable?

- Discuss the fears the Robinson children had about the Indians: "They will eat you." "They will chop off your head." "They will skin you alive." Were they reasonable? What might Indian children have thought about the white settlers?

- Discuss the land deal the settlers made with the Indians: "They gave them a fair price and promised they might keep their right to fish in the Great River." Find out about deals for Manhattan Island and for your area. Did the Indians get fair value?

- The book says, "Men had come over from Milford, on the coast, to buy the land from the Indians. They had cleared it and divided it into plots for the houses." Why would it have been necessary to divide the land into plots? Why couldn't each new settler build anywhere?

- Discuss Sarah's attachment to the cloak.

- Sarah mentioned the Indians' bark-covered houses. What did those houses look like? What were they made of?

- Discuss Sarah's use of the Bible for reading material. What other books were available in America at that time?

- Notice Sarah's lack of toys. Plan a morning of free time in which you can use only things that were available to Sarah for amusement.

- Think about what you were like and what you did when you were Sarah's age. Could you have done what she did?

- Compare the Indians' use of clothing to Sarah's and her father's. Discuss the change in Sarah's feelings about clothes after she had stayed with the Indians.

- Sarah and her father did not learn to say the Indians' real names, but the Indians learned theirs. Sarah's father referred to "Tall John's" wife as "his squaw." What does this show about the settlers' attitudes toward the Indians? Sarah referred to the woman as Tall John's wife. Didn't she have a name? Didn't she at least deserve the kind of name Mr. Noble gave Tall John? What does this show about attitudes toward women?

- Discuss Sarah's concerns when her father left her with the Indians.
- Talk about Sarah's doubts that God might care for the Indians as He cared for her.

Things to Do

- Locate New Milford on the map. What might the "Great River" be?
- Trace the route the first settlers of New Milford might have used from Milford, Connecticut. Use a topographical map so you don't route their trail over the highest peaks or through rivers.
- Map routes John and Sarah might have taken from Westfield, Massachusetts, to New Milford? Which route covers the longest distance? Which route would have been easier?
- The Indians Sarah stayed with feared an attack from the Indians of the North. Which tribe might that have been and what tribe was Sarah probably living with?

Fiction

★Speare, Elizabeth George. *The Sign of the Beaver.* Dell, 1984. ISBN 0-440-47900-2

■■■■■■■■□□□□□□□

Least Sophisticated   Most Sophisticated

See page 191.

◆Fritz, Jean. *The Cabin Faced West.* Putnam, 1958. ISBN 0-14-032256-6

■■■■■■□□□□□□□□

See page 185.

Nonfiction

◆Fradin, Dennis. *The Connecticut Colony.* Childrens, 1990. ISBN 0-516-00393-3

■■■■■■□□□□□□□□

See page186.

◆————. *The Massachusetts Colony.* Childrens, 1990. ISBN 0-516-00386-0

■■■■■■□□□□□□□□

See page 186.

◆Perl, Lila. *Slumps, Grunts, and Snickerdoodles: What Colonial America Ate and Why.* Clarion, 1975. ISBN 0-395-28923-8

■■■■■■■□□□□□□

See page 187.

◆Smith, Carter. *Daily Life: A Sourcebook on Colonial America.* Millbrook, 1991. ISBN 0-1-56294-038-4

■■■■■■■□□□□□□

See page 187.

Calico Bush

Calico Bush

by Rachel Field. Dell, 1931. ISBN 0-440-40368-5

■■■■■■■□□□□□□□

Genre: Fact-based novel

Setting: New England, 1743

Summary: This book was written in 1931 and received the Newbery Award. It's amazing that the book is so timely and could have been written last year. It is the story of Marguerite Ledoux, a French orphan, who in 1743 became a bound servant in the household of Joel and Dolly Sargeant. Joel bought land in Penosbcot Bay off the Maine coast and is determined to move his wife and children there from Marblehead, Massachusetts, in spite of dire warnings from other settlers who claim that the Sargeants' land is cursed and that settling on it will only further enrage the Indians who consider it sacred ground. Marguerite, being French and Catholic, often finds her ways incompatible with the English Protestants who will own her until she is eighteen. It is these very ways, however, that save the family when the Indians do come.

Background Information

- The French and Indian War occurred during this time.

- Many settlers in that part of Maine were attacked and killed by the Indians.

- The French and English were often at odds with each other.

- Bound servants had few rights and were often orphaned or poor.

- Ballads reflected heroic deeds and it is possible that there was one about Marguerite.

Things to Notice and Talk About

- Do you think Marguerite and Caleb will marry? What makes you think that?

- Discuss the prejudice shown against Marguerite. Have you ever been the victim of prejudice?

- Think about the weapons we have today to fight prejudice and contrast these with the help Marguerite had.

- Would you like to have lived in Marguerite's day? Would you choose her life or someone else's life from the book to live if you could?

Things to Do

- Choose a character other than Marguerite. Pretend you are that character and describe Marguerite from your point of view. How does Dolly see her? The children? Aunt Hepsa? Caleb?

- Marguerite and the Sargeant family have many fears as they approach Maine. Write about your own experiences moving to a new town, visiting a new place, or starting at a new school. What was scary? What was different? What reminded you of familiar places? How did your feelings change over time?

- Calculate how much seed the Sargeant family needed to plant or how much they needed to save. Calculate what you could eat each day during winter.

- Figure out how to put together the pieces of a log cabin.

- Make a stick calendar like the one Uncle Ira used.

- The people in the story treasured cloth and used every piece of it. How many things can you make with a piece of cloth?

- As a group, make a quilt of leftover pieces of cloth. What else can you do with worn out clothing?

- Prepare the essentials for a winter in the wilderness. Choose something that is necessary for survival and that interests you, such as sewing, weaving, knitting, leather work, preserving food, growing winter vegetables, carving spoons or plates, making toys for kids, gathering kindling, making a model shelter, gathering fuel, fishing, hunting. Do it or find out as much information as possible about doing it.

- Write a letter from Marguerite to the nuns in France, describing her situation at various points in the story.

- Create a diary of the year in which the book takes place. Choose a character as the author.

Fiction

◆ Gilman, Dorothy. *Girl in Buckskin.* Ballantine, 1956. ISBN 0-449-70380-0

Least Sophisticated   Most Sophisticated

See page 65.

◆ Speare, Elizabeth George. *Calico Captive.* Houghton, 1985. ISBN 0-395-07112-7

This story deals with a young girl from New Hampshire, captured by the Indians and taken to Montreal where her Puritan views are rejected by the French settlers. See page 65.

Longfellow, Henry Wadsworth. *Evangeline and Other Poems.* Airmont, 1985. ISBN 0-8049-0094-9

This classic poem tells of an Acadian couple who are separated during the British takeover of Canada.

Nonfiction

★ Marrin, Albert. *Struggle for a Continent: The French and Indian Wars 1690-1760.* Atheneum, 1987. ISBN 0-689-31313-6

See page 65.

Anderson, Joan. *Pioneer Settlers of New France.* Lodestar, 1990. ISBN 0-525-67291-5

See page 66.

Fradin, Dennis. *The Massachusetts Colony.* Childrens, 1990. ISBN 0- 516-00386-0

See page 186.

Smith, Carter. *Battles in a New Land: A Sourcebook on Colonial America.* Millbrook, 1991. ISBN 1-56294-034-1

This fact-filled resource book uses drawings, paintings, and other illustrations to cover early skirmishes among the Colonists, the French, and the Indians.

Early Thunder

Early Thunder

By Jean Fritz. Puffin, 1967. ISBN 0-14-032259-0

■■■■■■■■■■□□□□□

Genre: Fiction

Setting: New England, 1775

Summary: Daniel West's household is in turmoil: His mother recently died after giving birth to his brother, Jonathan. Since then, Daniel's physician father has been away frequently on "business" and Daniel has been cared for by a housekeeper. The West family are Tories and they are being increasingly ostracized and isolated as relations between the American Colonies and England deteriorate. However, as the plot makes clear, most people are still loyal to the king; their anger is toward Parliament. What is so striking about the book is the portrayal of Daniel's inner development in a town moving quickly toward violence. He'd rather work on solving the problems but is forced to choose a side. His torment is particularly well portrayed.

Background Information

- Samuel Adams was a powerful force toward revolution, but his appearance was not that of a major figure. According to one observer in this book he "looks like a bum."

- King George was revered by many Colonists before and during the Revolution.

- Some Colonists dumped tea into Boston Harbor to protest taxes. This was called the Boston Tea Party.

- The location of the book is Salem, Massachusetts, and the book refers to the Witch Trials of Salem.

- The Stamp Act and the so-called Intolerable Acts caused increasing protest among many Colonists.

- A meeting of the Provincial Congress was held in Salem.

- The "Affair at North Bridge in Salem" was probably the first confrontation in the Revolution.

Things to Notice and Talk About

- Talk about Daniel's need for his father and his father's indifference or inability to respond. Do you know any other books in which a parent and child have trouble communicating?

- Discuss the role Daniel's friends Jeremy and Tillie play in his life. Would any of your friendships be similar?

- Compare the treatment of Tories before, during, and after the Revolution to our treatment of Japanese during World War II. See page 90.

Things to Do

- Read a novel about the Revolutionary War in which the main character sympathizes with the Rebels. Which side do you think your family would have been on?

- Read a nonfiction source about the treatment and view of the Tories during the Revolution. Is the information in this book consistent with the facts?

- Read **Sarah Bishop** (see page 266). In what ways are Daniel and Sarah similar? Would you have been more like Daniel or more like Sarah in your reaction to the war?

- Make a diagram that shows each character from the book and what he or she wants. If their wants conflict, make the arrows cross. How would you show Daniel's wants? If his are fulfilled, what happens to all the others you have so diagrammed?

- Make a diagram, such as the one on the next page, that shows all the people and things pulling and pushing at Daniel's political beliefs. Use pictures from the book or draw them to illustrate each of the characters who influenced or tried to influence Daniel.

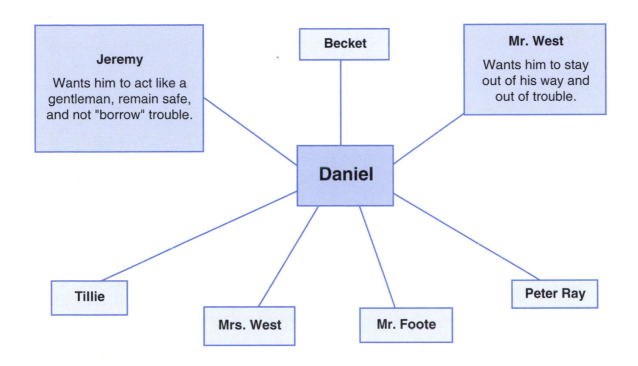

Fiction

★ Reeder, Carolyn. ***Shades of Gray.*** Macmillan, 1989. ISBN 0-02-775810-9

Least Sophisticated   Most Sophisticated

Although the action of this book takes place about a century later, the dilemma is similar.

◆ O'Dell, Scott. ***Sarah Bishop.*** Houghton, 1980. ISBN 0-395-29185-2

This is a Focus Book; see page 266.

Wibberly, Leonard.***John Treegate's Musket.*** Farrar, 1959. ISBN 0-374-43788-2

See page 72.

Nonfiction

See page 67 for more books and activities about the American Revolution.

Sarah Bishop

Sarah Bishop

By Scott O'Dell. Houghton, 1980.
  ISBN 0-395-29185-2

■■■■■■■■■■■■■□

Genre: Fiction

Setting: New England, 1775

Summary: Sarah Bishop's father is a staunch Tory. When the trouble begins, some of the Rebels in their New England town begin to focus their hatred on the Bishop family even after Chad, Sarah's brother, joins the Colonists' army. After they burn the farm and tar and feather Mr. Bishop, who dies, Sarah runs from the town. Her treatment by the British and Hessian soldiers is no better than she received from the Colonists. After hearing of her brother's death on a British prison ship, she retreats from people entirely, taking refuge in a cave, miles from the nearest town. Rejecting human company and even the Bible's words of love, Sarah survives with the help of a young Indian couple. An albino bat and a maimed muskrat become her only constant companions. Eventually, she is accused of witchcraft and narrowly escapes a harsh judgment, but she does not reject the outstretched hand of a young Quaker man who offers her friendship and, we suspect, an eventual romance.

Background Information

- Before and during the Revolution, people were forced to declare their loyalties and many who chose to remain loyal to the King suffered considerable violence and prejudice.

- The Hessians who fought with the British were thought by many to be the most fearsome soldiers.

- Witches were thought to be real and capable of causing a great deal of damage.

- Quakers were and still are generally pacifists.

Things to Notice and Talk About

- Notice the attachments Sarah forms: first to the Bible, then to the musket, the cave, the bat, and the muskrat. When does she form these attachments and when does she let them go? Find similar talismans or objects of attachment used by characters in other books.

- Discuss the views of witchcraft in the past and in the present. Do people still believe in witchcraft?

- Compare Sarah's survival techniques to those of other characters in survival stories. See ***Long Ago and Far Away*** (DLM, 1991. ISBN 1-55924-556-5) for a list of books and suggested activities based on a survival theme.

- Compare the hardships suffered by Sarah's family to those experienced by the West family in ***Early Thunder*** (see page 264).

- Why was Isaac Morton so anxious for Sarah to attend the meeting? Was it wise?

- Why was she put in jail by the constable? Was it wise?

- Compare Sarah Bishop's use of the Bible with Sarah Noble's use in ***The Courage of Sarah Noble*** (see page 260).

Things to Do

- As a indication of repentance during the Quaker meeting, Mr. Morton frees his slaves. Research the amount of slavery that existed in New England at that time. Why was it abandoned in the North long before it was in the South? What role did Quakers play in the abolition of slavery in the United States?

- Find out more about the Quaker religion.

- Use clues from the book to locate the action of the story.

- Sarah is a strong character. Make a list of the things she did that showed her strength of body and soul.

- Find out about the witchcraft trials of Salem in the 1600s. Were the accusations against those people similar to those made against Sarah? Would she have been declared guilty of witchcraft? When was the last trial of a witch in North America? See page 258 for a Focus Book about witchcraft.

Fiction

★ Speare, Elizabeth George. ***The Sign of the Beaver.*** Dell, 1984. ISBN 0-440-47900-2

■■■■■■■□□□□□□□

Least Sophisticated   **Most Sophisticated**

See page 191.

◆ Dalgliesh, Alice. ***The Courage of Sarah Noble.*** Aladdin, 1954. ISBN 0-689-71057-7

■■■■□□□□□□□□□□

This is a Focus Book; see page 260.

◆ Fritz, Jean. ***Early Thunder.*** Puffin, 1967. ISBN 0-14-032259-0

■■■■■■■■■■□□□□

This is a Focus Book; see page 264.

◆ Petry, Ann. ***Tituba of Salem Village.*** HarperCollins, 1964. ISBN 0-06-440403-X

■■■■■■■■■□□□□□

See page 179.

◆ Speare, Elizabeth. ***The Witch of Blackbird Pond.*** Houghton, 1968. ISBN 0-440-49596-2

■■■■■■■■■□□□□□

See page 179.

Nonfiction

See page 67 for fiction and nonfiction books and activities about the American Revolution.

★ Zeinert, Karen. ***The Salem Witchcraft Trials.*** Watts, 1989. ISBN 0-531-10673-X

■■■■■■■□□□□□□□

See page 258.

Nonprint

Meet the Newbery Author: Scott O'Dell. American School Publishers.

The Great Little Madison

> ## The Great Little Madison
>
> By Jean Fritz. Putnam, 1989. ISBN 0-0-399-21768-1
>
> ■■■■■■■■■■□□□□□
>
> **Genre:** Biography
>
> **Setting:** Virginia, 1751-1836
>
> **Summary:** Madison was an unprepossessing figure to have such a major effect on his time. He was sickly and thin with a very weak voice, but he was a figure to be reckoned with. His voice was that of reason, and he was devoted to the establishment and preservation of the Union. His love for Dolley made his life complete, and his friendship and respect for and from the greatest people in the young nation gave him a vast influence. In this book, we begin to understand the personality as well as the effect on United States history of this "little" man.

Things to Talk About and Notice

- Discuss the way that slow communication affected the War of 1812.

- The book quotes Captain Oliver Perry: "We have met the enemy and they are ours." What are some other famous quotes from wars? Why do people remember them?

- Compare Madison to other presidents, including our current one. What do you think Madison's position would be on our current problems? Would he agree or disagree with our president today?

- Dolley Madison played an important role in her husband's career, but she was not as visible as more recent first ladies have been. What role do you think she would play in today's politics and society? Would she be pro-women's rights? Would she run for office herself?

Things to Do

- Make a chart of the well-known people of history who are mentioned in the book and show their relationship to Madison.

- Add other names to the chart such as the Marquis de Lafayette, Aaron Burr, John Adams, Andrew Jackson, and John C. Calhoun.

- Make a time line of Madison's life, showing some of the things he accomplished while he was president and his role in such events as the Revolution, the Continental Congress, and the Constitutional Convention.

- James Madison was, apparently, not a very imposing figure. His voice was sort of weak and he disliked public speaking. Would we elect him today? What would his television appearances be like? Could he survive a presidential debate?

- Find out about our presidents. How many short men have been elected to the office? What's the average height of our presidents? Who was the shortest? Tallest? Youngest? Oldest? Who had the most children? Make a display of the information you find.

- Make a chart showing Madison's point of view.

Fiction

◆ Collier, James Lincoln and Collier, Christopher. ***Jump Ship to Freedom.*** Dell, 1987. ISBN 0-440-44323-7

■■■■■■■■■■■■□□

Least Sophisticated   Most Sophisticated

See page 192.

Monjo, F. N. ***Grand Papa and Ellen Aroon.*** Dell, 1974. ISBN 0-440-43004-6

■■■■□□□□□□□□□□

See page 199.

Nonfiction

◆ Fritz, Jean. ***Shhh! We're Writing the Constitution.*** Putnam, 1987. ISBN 0-399-21403-8

■■■■■□□□□□□□□□

*Only Fritz can make the construction of a historic document into such good reading. Here, on a much less sophisticated level than she addresses in **The Great Little Madison,** Fritz reveals the quirks and foibles of the many personalities that came, most of them grudgingly and with vastly different agendas, to write the document.*

Lewis and Clark, Leading America West

Lewis and Clark, Leading America West

By Steven Otfinoski. Fawcett, 1992.
ISBN 0-449-90398-2

■■■■■■■■□□□□□□□

Genre: Nonfiction Narrative

Setting: Western region, 1804-1838

Summary: This account of the exploration of land acquired through the Louisiana Purchase by Lewis and Clark is the most interesting one we read. There is more personal detail in this book, not only about Meriwether Lewis and William Clark but also about the other members of their crew. The role of Sacajawea is less prominent in this account although the author talks about the variations in the role historians think she played. In many ways this nonfiction work reads like a good survival novel. There is, however, some subtle condescension in the author's treatment of Native Americans, but that can serve as a teaching tool in and of itself.

Things to Notice and Talk About

- Compare this factual account of the journey with Scott O'Dell's **Streams to the River, River to the Sea** (see page 199). Where do the accounts diverge? Which book contains dialogue? Why doesn't the other book use dialogue?

- How do you think today's Native Americans would view Sacajawea? In what ways is she like Squanto?

- What do you think was the cause of Meriwether Lewis's death?

- Two of the men on the expedition were flogged for misbehavior. What would be done today for the same behavior?

- Could you eat dogmeat?

- Although most of the expedition's treatment of the Indians was non-violent, there was some killing and mistreatment. Could it have been avoided?

- The book says: "After one powwow with Indians, Cruzatte brought out his fiddle and the men danced to the happy music. The Indians, who had no musical instruments of their own, were as delighted watching and listening as children." Is that a demeaning or derogatory statement? Why? Are there other places in this book where the author leaves the impression that Indians were childish or not very smart?

- What if there had never been a Lewis and Clark expedition?

Things to Do

- The map at the beginning of the book is not very clear. Make a large map of Lewis and Clark's journey, using symbols to mark the places the book talks about.

- Use an Indian map to find the names of all the tribes who were in the land the expedition explored.

- Find towns and landmarks named for or by Lewis and Clark and locate them on a map.

- Find out what some of the places mentioned in the book are like today.

- Figure out the miles traveled by the expedition and how long it would take to travel that route today, using ground transportation.

- Make a chart like the one on the next page, showing information about the members of the expedition.

Name	Reason for Coming	Skills and Contributions	What Happened to Him/Her Afterward
Meriwether Lewis	Friendship with Jefferson, curiosity and love of adventure and nature.	Some knowledge of the western areas; knew some herbal medicines; kept a journal.	Died from gunshot wounds—murder or suicide.
William Clark	Knew and liked Lewis.	Good map maker and navigator; knew something about Indian culture; kept a journal.	Married twice and had five children; Superintendent of Indian Affairs.
York	Slave; had no choice.	Great strength; good sense of humor.	Given freedom by Clark; ran a freight business; died of cholera in Tennessee.
Sacajawea			
George Drouillard			

- Describe a moose to someone who has never seen anything like it before. Do the same for a grizzly bear.

- Read a page from the journals of one of the travelers. Why is their spelling so poor by today's standards? Is this the sort of entry you would make if you were a member of the expedition?

- This book is a nonfiction book. Are there any opinions given in it? Are they the author's opinions or is he reporting factually on the opinions of various historic figures?

Fiction

◆ Bohner, Charles. ***Bold Journey: West with Lewis and Clark.*** Houghton, 1985. ISBN 0-395-36691-7

■■■■■■■□□□□□□□

Least Sophisticated   Most Sophisticated

This fictional account of the journey is supposedly given by Hugh McNeal, a private in the Corps of Discovery. The author stays close to the known information about the expedition while embroidering the role of McNeal who is only listed as a private in the journals and about who little is actually known. Bohner personalizes the journey by seeing it from McNeal's point of view.

O'Dell, Scott. ***Streams to the River, River to the Sea.*** Houghton, 1986. ISBN 0-449-70244-8

■■■■■■■□□□□□□□

See page 199.

Nonfiction

★ Fisher, Leonard Everett. ***The Oregon Trail.*** Holiday, 1990. ISBN 0-02-719020-X

■■■■■■□□□□□□□□

See page 200.

Morrison, Dorothy. ***Under a Strong Wind: The Adventures of Jessie Benton Fremont.*** Atheneum, 1983. ISBN 0-689-31004-8

■■■■■■■■■■■□□□

See page 213.

Rowland, Della. ***Sacajawea, Guide to Lewis and Clark.*** Dell, 1989. ISBN 0-440-40215-8

■■■■■■□□□□□□□□

See page 200.

The Journeyman

The Journeyman

By Elizabeth Yates. Bob Jones University Press, 1990. ISBN 0-89084-535-2

■■■■■■■■■■□□□□□

Genre: Historical Fiction

Setting: New Hampshire, 1816

Summary: Jared Austin has just finished his apprenticeship as a painter of household interiors. His stenciling and other creative treatment of Colonial homes is gaining him a worthy reputation in early nineteenth-century New Hampshire and his future seems bright. Then in 1816, the year without a summer, crops freeze and the cold never leaves. Frightened farm families look for a scapegoat and there is Jared, a boy whose mother froze to death at his birth, but who appears not to mind the cold in spite of his spare frame. Rumors of witchcraft soon begin and, for a while, people turn on Jared. His life has never been easy, but he is not one to run from unpleasantness. With the help of his childhood sweetheart and a little luck, Jared turns aside their wrath.

Background Information

- The volcanic ash created by the eruption of Mount Tambora caused a climactic change in 1816, a year in which snow fell in many places every month of the year.

- During the first part of the nineteenth century, many people were ready to beautify their homes and often hired journeyman painters to decorate them.

- The War of 1812 was short and had little effect on the lives of people in New England.

- Painters of that day sometimes used soured milk as a base for their paints.

- Stenciling is still used as a decorating technique.

Things to Notice and Talk About

- Notice the way society in this story treats people who are different. Are we more tolerant today? What facts can you use to support your opinion?

- Discuss how Jared's achievements changed him and how he stayed the same.

- What is spotted fever?

- Notice the care the horses got. Was this typical? Why?

- Explain why Jared's father hated him.

- Discuss the way Mr. Toppan, and later Jared, studied the people they painted for and then designed their paintings. Do decorators today take time to know their customers before they design or furnish their homes?

- Talk about the way fear about the weather turned to suspicion and superstition. Discuss similar scapegoats.

Things to Do

- Create a panel from the descriptions of Jared's or Mr. Toppan's artwork.

- Find out more about journeyman painters. Were there any in your area? Is there any surviving work?

- Find pictures of stencil work like that described in the book. Make a stencil and use it to decorate a bulletin board, notebook, or piece of wood.

- Figure out how much corn Jared could possibly get from his bag of kernels. How many people would it feed?

- Read about other people accused of witchcraft. See page 258.

- Compare the persecution of Jared with that of **Tituba in *Tituba of Salem Village*** (see page 179).

- Read the transcripts of one of the real witch trials. (You can usually get a transcript by writing to a historical society in Massachusetts or Connecticut or by finding probate court records in those or other early states.)

Picture Books

Rylant, Cynthia. **All That I See.** Orchard, 1988. ISBN 0-531-08377-2

An artist paints whales day after day, even though his view as he paints is a small mountain lake. The book furnishes some feeling for the artist's need to paint his or her inner vision.

Van Allsburg, Chris. **The Stranger.** Houghton, 1986. ISBN 0-395-42331-7

A stranger is taken in by a family, and he seems puzzled and amazed by the technology in the home. While he is there, the weather fails to change.

Fiction

Dunlop, Eileen. **The Valley of Deer.** Holiday, 1989. ISBN 0-8234 0766-7

■■■■■■■■■■■□□□

Least Sophisticated   Most Sophisticated

A young girl, Anne Farrar, establishes a connection, real or imagined, with Alice Jardyne, a young woman accused of witchcraft who lived in the same house centuries before. See **Long Ago and Far Away** *for more information and activities about this book.*

Henry, Marguerite. **Benjamin West and His Cat Grimalkin.** Macmillan, 1947. ISBN 0-02-743660-8

■■■■■■■□□□□□□□

See page 154.

Nonfiction

Esterman, M. M. **A Fish That's a Box: Folk Art from the National Museum of American Art.** Great Ocean, 1990. ISBN 0-925556-21-9

■■■■■■■□□□□□□□

Folk art from America's past.

Smith, Carter. **The Arts and Sciences: A Sourcebook on Colonial America.** Millbrook, 1991. ISBN 0-56294-037-6

■■■■■■■■■□□□□□

See page 157.

The Borning Room

The Borning Room

By Paul Fleischman. HarperCollins, 1991.
ISBN 0-06-023785-6

🟦🟦🟦🟦🟦🟦🟦🟦🟦⬜⬜⬜⬜

Genre: Historical Fiction

Setting: Ohio, 1820–turn of the century

Summary: One room in the house her grandfather built is the focal point of birth and death in Georgina's life. In that room she was born and she witnesses the birth of a sibling. Eventually, Georgina has her own babies there. There her mother dies giving birth to another baby. The room is also where Georgina's beloved grandfather dies after refusing to change his free-thinking ways.

Background Information

• Superstition played a big role in many people's lives in the nineteenth century.

• There was an Underground Railroad at work in Ohio during the years preceding the Civil War.

Things to Notice and Talk About

• Make a list of the risks everyone in that household took.

• Discuss Cory's feelings about being sold away from her children. Was her fear justified? What might have become of Cory?

• Discuss Grandfather's religious beliefs.

• Notice the change in Hattie and Georgina's friendship and when it happened.

• Georgina's family plants trees to commemorate the dead and records births and deaths in the family Bible. What does your family do?

Things to Do

• Read other books about runaway slaves. See page 108.

• Draw a family tree of Georgina's family.

• Find other books in which a building or a part of a building plays an important role, such as **The House of Dies Drear** (below) and **The Root Cellar** (see page 277).

• Compare Georgina to Catherine in **A Gathering of Days** (page 197).

• Find a character from another book, set in another time, who would be a better friend for Georgina than Hattie.

• Find a picture of a house you would use for the location of **The Borning Room** if you were making a movie or television show. Whom would you cast as the characters? Write one scene from the book as a screenplay.

Picture Books

★ Dragonwagon, Crescent. **Home Place.** Macmillan, 1990. ISBN 0--02-733190-3

See page 40.

Johnston, Tony. **The Quilt Story.** Putnam, 1985. ISBN 0-399-21008-3

This quilt of memories will witness many more events.

Fiction

Hamilton, Virgina. **The House of Dies Drear.** Macmillan, 1984. ISBN 0-02-742500-2

🟦🟦🟦🟦🟦🟦⬜⬜⬜⬜⬜⬜⬜

Least Sophisticated   Most Sophisticated

An old house on the Ohio River was the scene of drama during the days of the Underground Railroad.

Reiss, Johanna. **The Upstairs Room.** HarperCollins, 1990. ISBN 0-06-4440370-X

🟦🟦🟦🟦🟦🟦🟦⬜⬜⬜⬜⬜⬜

During World War II, the upstairs room becomes the hideout and refuge for a Jewish girl.

The Perilous Road

The Perilous Road

By William O. Steele. Scholastic, 1990.
ISBN 0-590-45128-6

■■■■■■■■□□□□□□□□

Genre: Historical Fiction

Setting: Tennessee, 1860s

Summary: Chris Brabson hates the Yankees and is determined to do whatever he can to thwart them when they come to his mountain ridge in Tennessee. When they take away most of his family's winter provisions, his hatred is doubled. Even his brother's enlisting on the Yankee side doesn't change his mind. He manages to do some damage to their cause by sending out word through a man he thinks is a spy for the Confederacy that a large Yankee supply wagon train is camped in the valley. When he realizes that his brother may well be a part of that wagon train, Chris attempts to warn him of the coming attack. In the process, Chris gets to know some of the Yankee soldiers and the humanity of the enemy comes as a real shock. When the battle begins, Chris is in the middle of it. Death and dying are all around him and Chris's horror is overwhelming. When he returns home, Chris and his father put words to the feelings and the realization that wars are destructive and horrible and that there has to be a better way to resolve disputes. This is an exciting story and a powerful anti-war book.

Background Information

- Particularly in the border states, family members had conflicting loyalties and sometimes fought on opposite sides.

- The Union army needed food and often took what they needed from families' supplies.

- Some people felt neither side was right in the Civil War.

Things to Notice and Talk About

- After the battle, Chris makes the statement: "I reckon even if I couldn't smell this smoke . . . even if there wasn't a leaf changed from what it was when I left here yesterday, it would look different to me. I'm different from what I was yesterday. Won't nothing look just like it used to, not to me it won't." What does he mean? How is he changed?

- Pappy Brabson has strong feelings about war. How might he have come to feel that way?

- What is Silas's motivation? Was he a spy?

- Notice the diet of the mountain people. Did they have a good diet?

- Which characters from other books have come to the same conclusions Chris did?

- If you could introduce Pappy Brabson to the Foxman (see page 88), what do you think they'd talk about? Who else would you bring into the conversation?

- Compare Chris's feelings at the beginning of the story to those he had at the end. Did anybody else change?

- What would be different if the setting of the book were changed to a place north of the Mason-Dixon line?

- Early in the book, Pappy says, "We're the kind of folks always gets the short end of things in wartime." What does he mean?

Things to Do

- Find out what a dogtrot is and draw a picture of the Brabson cabin from the scattered descriptions you get of it in the book.

- Using clues from the book, locate Walden's Ridge.

- Make a list of the unfamiliar words you found in this story and the ways you used to figure out what they meant.

- Make a list of the events that changed Chris, first in chronological order and then in order of their importance to Chris. Would they have been the same for you?

- Use that same list of events to make a graphic showing how Chris reacted to each event.

- Find out which generals might have been leading the armies in Tennessee at the time of this story.

- Find out how old Chris is in the book and then figure out how many other wars he might have seen if he lived to be eighty years old. Would he have fought in any of them?

Fiction

See the Civil War on page 78 for additional book and activity suggestions.

★Lunn, Janet. ***The Root Cellar.*** Scribner, 1983. ISBN 0-684-17855-9

Least Sophisticated   **Most Sophisticated**

This is a Focus Book; see page 277.

Nonfiction

See the Civil War on page 78 for additional book and activity suggestions.

The Root Cellar

The Root Cellar

By Janet Lunn. Scribner, 1983.
ISBN 0-684-17855-9

■■■■■■■■□□□□□□□

Genre: Time Fantasy

Setting: Canada and Washington, DC., the present and the 1860s

Summary: Rose, an unloved though well-cared-for child, is deposited with relatives just over the border in Canada. The ramshackle house and exuberant family of her Aunt Nan are in sharp contrast to the carefully controlled life with her grandmother. The family is as wary of her as she is of them and, in her loneliness, Rose discovers a way into the past through an abandoned root cellar. There she befriends and is befriended by Susan and Will. When Will fails to return from the Civil War, Rose and Susan set out to find him. Rose's previous and present-day world travel with her grandmother has not prepared her for the hardships of the trip to Washington of 1864, but she is better prepared than Susan. The fantasy is well done and offers an insight into the motivations behind the Civil War and its tragic results.

Background Information

- Many Canadians enlisted in the Civil War.

- Many young boys were used as drummers, flag bearers, and fife players during battles.

- Some of the worst battles of the Civil War were at Cold Harbor, Petersburg, Chaffin's Bluff, and the siege of Richmond.

- Deserters were called "Skedaddlers."

- Regiments usually stayed together throughout the war.

- Troops were "mustered" when they were paid, on sick call, and when they were disbanded.

- Medical care for Civil War casualties was very limited.

- Travel during the period was uncomfortable and slow.

Things to Notice and Talk About

- Notice evidence of Rose's changing relationship with the Henry family.

- Compare the method of time travel in this book with that in other time travel books. See page 36.

- What became of Will and Susan?

- What did this experience in time travel teach Rose?

- Why did Will and Susan first suspect and later believe that Rose came from another time?

- What were the biggest adjustments Rose had to make when she went back in time?

- Talk about why the change in Grand Central station made such a big difference to Rose.

- What place could be your "root cellar"?

- Why did Janet Lunn have to make time pass at a different speed in one time or the other?

- What does Janet Lunn want us to know?

Things to Do

- Research the real events and places mentioned in the book.

- Draw a map of the action, starting with the Canadian home and going to Washington, DC, and back.

- Find photographs by Civil War photographers that could be used to illustrate part of this story.

- Make a chart that contrasts events in the present with events in the past for this book. Is there a way to show the difference in the time these events took?

Fiction

See page 78 for additional books and activities about the Civil War period.

See page 36 for additional time fantasies.

Nonfiction

See page 78 for additional books and activities about the Civil War period.

◆ Fisher, Leonard Everett. ***Tracks Across America: The Story of the American Railroad, 1825-1900.*** Holiday, 1992. ISBN 0-8234-0945-7

■■■■■■■□□□□□□□

Least Sophisticated   Most Sophisticated

See page 126.

Grasshopper Summer

Grasshopper Summer

By Ann Turner. Macmillan, 1989.
ISBN 0-02-789511-4

■■■■■■■□□□□□□□

Genre: Historical Fiction

Setting: Kentucky and Dakota Territory, 1874

Summary: Sam White likes living with his grandmother and grandfather in their big house in Kentucky. He likes the rules there and adores his grandparents. So does his mother. His father and younger brother are frustrated by the very things he loves. Sam sees no reason for his father's decision to strike out on their own for Dakota Territory. However, all too soon the covered wagon is equipped and loaded and they're off. The prairie both thrills and frightens Sam. When the sod house is ready, however, it quickly becomes home and Sam's fear and resentment turn to pride in their home and their family. Just when things look bright, the plague of grasshoppers arrives. In a few painful weeks, everything they've worked for is gone and the rest of the family just about gives up. It's Sam and his father who find ways to start again, and the book ends with the family determined to stick it out.

Background Information

- The Dakota Territory was opened up and the railroads and federal government encouraged settlement.

- People started West with all kinds of destinations and goals in mind. Many gave up and went back East or South.

- Sod houses were often used on the Plains and the book gives detailed information on how those houses were built.

- A plague of grasshoppers hit the Plains and devoured everything in sight.

Things to Notice and Talk About

- Discuss the differences between Sam's and Billy's personality. Which person would you like for a friend?

- Talk about the effects of the Civil War on Pa and Grandpa. Why are their memories so different?

- Notice the role Mrs. White plays in the story. Is it like the role Mrs. Ingalls played in the Little House books?

- Notice the foods the settlers ate.

- What would it be like to live in a sod house? Which of your present living conditions would you miss most if you moved to a sod house?

Things to Do

- Find out about the grasshopper plague. How far did it reach? What stopped it? Why don't we have such plagues anymore? What is the effect?

- Mrs. White talks about making vinegarade. Experiment with vinegar, water, and sugar and see if you can make a drink that tastes good.

- Look at photographs of sod houses, especially in *Prairie Visions: The Life and Times of Solomon Butcher* (page 210). Read the information and notice the photograph on page 26 of *Prairie Visions* for another look at the grasshopper plague.

- Read the picture book *Dakota Dugout* (page 205) by the author of *Grasshopper Summer.* How do you think Ann Turner got the information to write both books?

Picture Books

◆ Brenner, Barbara. **Wagon Wheels.** HarperCollins, 1978. ISBN 0-06-020669-1

See page 147.

◆ Goble, Paul. **Death of the Iron Horse.** Bradbury, 1987. ISBN 0-02-737830-6

See page 124.

◆ Harvey, Brett. **Cassie's Journey: Going West in the 1860s.** Holiday, 1988. ISBN 0-8234-0684-9

See page 124.

◆ Turner, Ann. **Dakota Dugout.** Illustrated by Ronald Himler. Aladdin, 1985. ISBN 0-689-71296-0

See page 205.

Fiction

★ Conrad, Pam. **Prairie Songs.** HarperCollins, 1985. ISBN 0-06-021337-X

■■■■■■■□□□□□□□

Least Sophisticated   Most Sophisticated

See page 206.

◆ Byars, Betsy. **Trouble River.** Viking, 1969. ISBN 0-670-73257-5

■■■■■■□□□□□□□□

See page 206.

◆ Holland, Isabelle. **The Journey Home.** Scholastic, 1990. ISBN 0-590-43110-2

■■■■■■■□□□□□□□

This is a Focus Book; see page 282.

◆ Levine, Ellen. **If You Traveled West in a Covered Wagon.** Scholastic, 1986. ISBN 0-590-42229-4

■■■□□□□□□□□□□□

See page 211.

Brink, Carol Ryrie. **Caddie Woodlawn.** Macmillan, 1973. ISBN 0-02-713670-1

■■■■■■■■□□□□□□

See page 207.

Harvey, Brett. **My Prairie Christmas.** Holiday, 1990. ISBN 0-8234-0827-2

■■■■■□□□□□□□□□

See page 207.

Howard, Ellen. **The Chickenhouse House.** Atheneum, 1991. ISBN 0-689-31695-X

■■■■■■□□□□□□□□

See page 207.

Magorian, Jim. **Keeper of Fire.** Council for Indian Education, 1984. ISBN 0-89992-088-8

■■■■■■■□□□□□□□

See page 208.

Moeri, Louise. **Save Queen of Sheba.** Avon, 1981. ISBN 0-380-71154-0

■■■■■■■■□□□□□□

See page 209.

Sandin, Joan. **The Long Way Westward.** HarperCollins, 1989. ISBN 0-06-444198-9

■■■□□□□□□□□□□□

See page 209.

Wilder, Laura Ingalls. **The Little House series.**

■■■■■■□□□□□□□□

See page 209.

Nonfiction

★Conrad, Pam. ***Prairie Visions: The Life and Times of Solomon Butcher.*** HarperCollins, 1991. ISBN 0-06-021373-6

■■■■■■■■■□□□□□

See page 210.

Anderson, William. ***Laura Ingalls Wilder Country.*** HarperCollins, 1990. ISBN 0-06-055294-8

■■■■■■□□□□□□□□

See page 212.

Fleming, Alice. ***The King of Prussia and a Peanut Butter Sandwich.*** Illustrated by Ronald Himler. Scribner, 1988. ISBN 0-684-18880-5

■■■■■□□□□□□□□□

See page 212.

Stein, R. Conrad. ***The Story of the Homestead Act.*** Childrens, 1978. ISBN 0-516-04616-0

■■■■■□□□□□□□□□

See page 213.

The Journey Home

The Journey Home

By Isabelle Holland. Scholastic, 1990. ISBN 0-590-43110-2

■■■■■■■■□□□□□□

Genre: Historical Fiction

Setting: Kansas, after the Civil War

Summary: Life was not pleasant for Maggie and her younger sister, Annie, even before their mother died of tuberculosis in Bellevue Hospital. They had been burned out of their home in Ireland, immigrated to New York, and were living in a cramped tenement room. Their father had been killed in an accident on the docks. Still they were with people like themselves, mostly Irish immigrants, and they had their Catholic faith to sustain them. Before her death and over the objections of their priest, their mother arranged for them to board the Orphan Train with the hope of finding a family on the Plains. After a heartbreaking trip, the girls are taken in by a childless couple, the Russells. Mrs. Russell surrounds the girls with warmth and love. It's harder for Mr. Russell, because of his stern Protestant beliefs, to reach out to them and harder still for Mrs. Russell's mother, the formidable Mrs. Vanderpool. School presents its own difficulties and the religious bigotry of some of the townspeople almost overwhelms them.

Background Information

- Some children were transported by train to farms in the West and Midwest to be adopted by families living there during the late 1800s and early 1900s.

- Life for many immigrants in New York City was difficult and many died of tuberculosis and other diseases.

- There was often a strong spirit of community among the farmers on the Plains who often held the same religious beliefs.

- At that time there were few Catholics on the Plains.

Things to Notice and Talk About

- Talk about the strengths that each girl had.

- Notice the sensitivity on the part of Mr. and Mrs. Russell and Mrs. Vanderpool.

- Why was Mrs. Vanderpool so angry?

- What do you think about Mrs. Vanderpool's talk with Maggie about bitterness and what it does to people? Do you agree?

- Talk about Annie's near-death experience and how it changed things in the Russell household.

- Was that effect the same as that caused by Mrs. Russell's nearly dying?

Things to Do

- The book doesn't say how long the trip from New York to Kansas took. How long would it take now? How long might it have taken then?

- Compare the religious prejudice in this book to that in **Calico Bush** (see page 262).

- Find out about orphan trains. How many children found homes this way? Read other books about them. Which experiences sound most realistic to you?

- What other choices were open to orphans at that time? Which choice would you have made?

- Talk to members of your family about prejudice they may have experienced because of their religious views. How did they handle it?

- Read the newspaper tonight for evidence of conflict somewhere in the world due to people's religions.

- Investigate religious freedom in America. Find out which groups of people came here to escape religious persecution in other countries. Then find out how much religious freedom those people gave to others.

- What do you think Isabelle Holland wants us to know after reading this book?

Fiction

★Cohen, Barbara. ***Molly's Pilgrim.*** Bantam, 1983. ISBN 0-5532-15833-3

■■■■■□□□□□□□□

Least Sophisticated   Most Sophisticated

See page 179.

Kherdian, David. ***A Song for Uncle Harry.*** Philomel, 1989. ISBN 0-399-21895-5

■■■■■■□□□□□□□

See page 229.

Koller, Jackie French. ***Nothing To Fear.*** Gulliver, 1990. ISBN 0-15-200544-7

■■■■■■□□□□□□□

See page 229.

Sandin, Joan. ***The Long Way Westward.*** HarperCollins, 1989. ISBN 0-06-444198-9

■■■□□□□□□□□□□□□

See page 209.

Nonfiction

◆ Freedman, Russell. ***Immigrant Kids.*** Dutton, 1980. ISBN 0-525-32538-7

■■■■■■■□□□□□□

See page 135.

Ashabranner, Brent. ***The New Americans: Changing Patterns in U. S. Immigration.*** Putnam, 1983. ISBN 0-396-08140-1

■■■■■■■■■□□□□□

See page 114.

Herda, D. J. ***Ethnic America: The North Central States.*** Millbrook, 1991. ISBN 1-56294-016-3

————. ***Ethnic America: The Northeastern States.*** Millbrook, 1991. ISBN 1-56294-014-7

————. ***Ethnic America: The Northwestern States.*** Millbrook, 1991. ISBN 1-56294-018-X

————. ***Ethnic America: The South Central States.*** Millbrook, 1991. ISBN 1-56294-017-1

————. ***Ethnic America: The Southeastern States.*** Millbrook, 1991. ISBN 1-56294-015-5

————. ***Ethnic America: The Southwestern States.*** Millbrook, 1991. ISBN 1-56294-019-8

■■■■■■■■■■□□□□□

See page 137.

Stein, R. Conrad. ***The Story of the Erie Canal.*** Childrens, 1985. ISBN 0-516-0482-9

■■■■■■■■□□□□□□

See page 201.

The Moffats Series

The Moffats. Harcourt, 1941.
The Middle Moffats. Harcourt, 1942.
Rufus M. Harcourt, 1943.
The Moffat Museum. Harcourt, 1983.

By Eleanor Estes.

■■■■■■□□□□□□□□□

Genre: Fiction Series

Setting: Connecticut, 1916-1918

Note: There are several books about the Moffats by Eleanor Estes. Each of them is special and, in addition to being good, episodic stories, they provide information about small town life in the years from 1916 to 1918. They make excellent family read-alouds with a wide range of age appeal.

Summary: The Moffat family has been just making ends meet since Mr. Moffat died when the youngest Moffat, Rufus, was a baby. Mrs. Moffat is a loving and hard-working woman who cares for her family while earning a living as a dressmaker. The family has little money but lots of spirit. Each member of the family is presented as a distinct individual with talents and trials of his or her own. Two family members, Jane and Rufus, are the principal characters in two of the books. The series is not really intended to be historical novels but, in portraying the lives of these very realistic children, the incidental history is extensive. The books have a lot of humor and the Moffat family becomes very real to most readers.

Background Information
Technology

- The Moffats use oil lamps and gas jets for light although some wealthier families of the time have electricity. Most people burn coal or wood for heat.

- Motor cars are available but rare and most transport is by horse or trolley car. Occasionally the Moffats see an airplane.

- Radio is new and the record player is a wind-up Victrola.

- People write with a straight pen dipped into ink or with a pencil or chalk.

- Scarlet fever is a serious disease. Home remedies for illness include mustard plasters, chamomile tea, and castor oil.

- Streets are lit by a lamplighter.

Economics

- There is no financial help from the government for this underprivileged, fatherless family.

- Sugar is five pounds for a quarter.

- The family's gas is metered with a quarter meter. Coal is sold by the bushel bag or by the truck load.

- Most women do not work outside the home.

Customs

- At school everyone stands in unison and marches out.

- Halloween is celebrated by costumes and scaring people and some children do minor damage.

- The doctor makes house calls and stays all night if the patient is seriously ill.

- Children's games and activities include: rollerskating, walking on stilts, playing hide and seek, digging a hole to peek at China, taking dance lessons, spinning tops, flying kites, whittling, making whistles, going on picnics, crocheting and knitting, playing the pump organ, looking through a stereoscope, going to the moving pictures, watching lantern slides, playing double solitaire, playing croquet, playing basketball.

Geography and History

- The First World War is going on and there are frequent references to it.

- Cranberry is near New Haven, Connecticut. Sleeping Giant Mountain is nearby.

- Veterans of the Civil War are alive and honored.

Things to Notice and Talk About

- Notice the way the children have some responsibilities for the operation of the household. What jobs might these same children have in today's households?

- Make a list of the things the Moffats would have called improvements in technology during their lifetime.

- Look for signs that the Moffat family is poorer than most of their friends and neighbors.

- Talk about the Moffats' feelings about the yellow house being sold out from under them.

- If you were making a film showing the fight between the trolley car drivers, what would you show? What details would you make sure were included? What musical accompaniment would you choose?

- Why would Ms. Estes have written a book in 1941 that takes place in 1916? What does she want us to know?

Things to Do

- Compare the life of the Moffats to life in wealthier homes such as in **Hattie and the Wild Waves** (see page 217).

Find pictures or real examples of some of the things the children used, such as stereopticons and wind-up Victrolas.

Find the rest of the words to "The Lost Chord," the song that they quote: "Seated one day at the organ."

Find out what moving pictures the children might have seen. Could Charlie Chaplin have been in them?

Find a current map of the area where the book takes place. Is there a Sleeping Giant Mountain?

Make a map of Cranberry.

Compare the bully, Peter Frost, to bullies in other books you've read.

Make character sketches of each of the characters in the books, including the minor ones.

Make a list of the occupations mentioned in the books and mark those women do. Compare the list to one of today's jobs for women.

Picture Books

Cooney, Barbara. **Hattie and the Wild Waves.** Viking, 1991. ISBN 0-670-83056-9

The contrast between the life Hattie lives and that of the Moffats is almost diametric but should provide many discussion topics.

Fiction

◆ Kinsey-Warnock, Natalie. **The Night the Bells Rang.** Dutton, 1991. ISBN 0-525-65074-1

Least Sophisticated   Most Sophisticated

See page 88.

Houston, Gloria. **Littlejim.** Philomel, 1990. ISBN 0-399-2220-0

See page 88.

Kudlinski, Kathleen. **Hero Over Here.** Viking, 1990. ISBN 0-670-83050-X

See page 88.

Nonfiction

Lewis, Claudia. **Long Ago in Oregon.** HarperCollins, 1987. ISBN 0-06-023839-9

See page 89.

Tames, Richard. **Picture History of the 20th Century: 1900-1919.** Watts, 1991. ISBN 0-531-14181-0

See page 223.

Nonprint

Meet the Newbery Author: Eleanor Estes. American School Publishers.

Letters from Rifka

Letters from Rifka

By Karen Hesse. Holt, 1992. ISBN 8050-1964-2

■■■■■■■□□□□□□□

Genre: Historical Fiction

Setting: Russia and New York, after World War I

Summary: Based on the memories of the author's aunt, this small book is a series of letters never sent. The letters are from Rifka to her cousin whom she left behind in Russia. Rifka's family has suffered much during the times of upheaval in Russia; not only are they poor peasants, they also are Jews. Her two older brothers have already immigrated to America and now the remainder of the family is forced to flee or suffer further hardships. During the trip to America, Rifka contracts ringworm and has to remain behind in Belgium while the family goes on to New York. There she finds a welcoming society and her ringworm is cured, leaving her bald. Cleared to come to America at last, she is nearly killed during a storm at sea. Arriving at Ellis Island, her troubles are not over. There too she is retained because of what they fear is ringworm because her hair has not grown in. On Ellis Island she becomes a substitute mother for a frightened Russian peasant boy and a little baby. Reunited with her own family at last, the book ends with a new beginning for the family.

Background Information

- Immigrants to America had to be in perfect health to be admitted and were often turned back for arbitrary reasons.

- The Jews have been persecuted frequently and terribly in many countries throughout history.

- In 1919, motor cars were appearing in Europe.

- The factory work that was open to immigrants was poorly paid and arduous.

Things to Notice and Talk About

- Notice the health requirements for admission to the United States. Are the requirements still the same?

- Why is it remarkable that Rifka should become friendly with and eventually rescue Ilya?

- Discuss the rigors of travel in that day and age. How long would the same journey take today?

- Why were the Russians so angry with Rifka's family?

- Talk about Rifka's need to write letters she would probably never send.

- Talk about the role poetry played in Rifka's and Ilya's life.

- How would you describe Rifka's character?

- Talk about the role her hair played in her life.

- Talk about the expectation of a female's life then and Rifka's need to have her own Bat Mitzvah. What is she saying about herself then?

Things to Do

- List the people who helped Rifka and the reasons they did.

- Read aloud the poem Rifka wrote. Why do you think it affected people so strongly?

- Find and read other stories of immigrants. Are their stories similar in any way to Rifka's?

- Make a chart showing the reasons for immigration to this country since its beginning.

Picture Books

◆ Bunting, Eve. ***How Many Days to America: A Thanksgiving Story.*** Clarion, 1988. ISBN 0-89919-521-0

See page 112.

Fiction

◆ Caseley, Judith. ***Apple Pie and Onions.*** Greenwillow, 1987. ISBN 0-688-06763-8

■■■■■☐☐☐☐☐☐☐☐☐

Least Sophisticated   Most Sophisticated

Although Rebecca loves her grandmother's stories about her life in Russia, she is mortified when her grandma meets an old friend from Russia on the street and the two old friends begin a loud Yiddish conversation, but her mortification only reminds Grandma of another story.

◆ Kidd, Diana. ***Onion Tears.*** Orchard, 1989. ISBN 0-531-08470-1

■■■■■■■☐☐☐☐☐☐☐

See page 113.

Yep, Laurence. ***Dragonwings.*** HarperCollins, 1975. ISBN 0-06-026738-0

■■■■■■■■■■■☐☐☐

See page 113.

Nonfiction

Ashabranner, Brent. ***The New Americans: Changing Patterns in U. S. Immigration.*** Putnam, 1983. ISBN 0-396-08140-1

■■■■■■■■■☐☐☐☐☐

See page 114.

Hitchcox, Linda. ***Refugees.*** Gloucester, 1990. ISBN 0-531-17242-2

■■■■■■■■■☐☐☐☐☐

The problems of refugees escaping the devastation of war and persecution are recounted as well as information about the organizations endeavoring to help.

Jacobs, William Jay. ***Ellis Island: New Hope in a New Land.*** Scribner, 1989. ISBN 0-684-19171-7

■■■■■■■■☐☐☐☐☐☐

*Using many photographs, the author tells the history of immigration to America from Europe. There is information about the medical examinations immigrants had to pass, lending background to **Letters from Rifka.***

Kurelek, William and Englehart, Margaret S. ***They Sought a New World: The Story of European Immigration to North America, 1850-1950.*** Tundra, 1985. ISBN 0-88776-172-0

■■■■■■■■■☐☐☐☐☐

Although the focus of this book is the immigrants to Canada, it has information that applies to Rifka's ordeal.

Ida Early Comes Over the Mountain

Ida Early Comes Over the Mountain

By Robert Burch. Avon, 1980.
   ISBN 0-380-57091-2

■■■■■■■□□□□□□□

Genre: Historical Fiction

Setting: Georgia, late 1920s

Summary: Ida is a free spirit who, according to her, has been everywhere, done everything, and done it well before turning up at the door of the Sutton family in rural Georgia during the Depression, looking for work. She is wearing a baggy brown sweater, overalls, and clodhoppers with a buckeye dangling from one of the laces. The motherless Sutton family needs her as much as she needs them and Ida's presence is soon felt everywhere. When children at school make fun of Ida, the Sutton children don't stand up for their friend and lose her, almost for good.

Background Information

- During the Depression, many people who were out of work traveled to find work somewhere else. Some people made money during the Depression.

- Attitudes on smoking have changed since this book was written.

- Ice boxes were used for refrigeration.

Things to Notice and Talk About

- Figure out the point of view of the book. Although it's told in the third person, we do see the action through one character's experience.

- Notice Ida's self-confidence. How do you think she got it?

- Compare Ida with other non-conformists in literature such as Mary Poppins.

- Talk about Ida's reaction when her family doesn't stick up for her. What does the incident tell about all concerned?

- Notice the role Ida creates for herself within the Sutton family. How does she do it?

- Talk about Aunt Earnestine's feelings when Ida takes over.

- Ida and Aunt Earnestine belong to different "classes" or positions in society. How does this difference become apparent? What feelings does it generate?

- Notice the way Ida handles Earnestine.

- Which of the jobs Ida claims to have had do you think she actually had?

- When does exaggeration become lying?

- Ida rolls her own cigarettes. What does that say about Ida? If this book were written today, do you think the author would have found another way to say that?

- Notice how what Ida wears defines what she is and what she thinks is important.

Things to Do

- List the comparisons Randall makes in the book.

- Make a list of what Ida claims to be true and what the story proves to be true about Ida.

- When Ida makes stew, the children do all the work. In that way she's like Tom Sawyer whitewashing the fence. Find other characters who con others into doing their work.

- Cooking plays an important part in the story. Find and try recipes for such things as fried chicken, sawmill gravy, grits, cornbread, boiled custard, turnip greens, candied yams, country bacon, sweet potato pie, and raisin pie.

- The action of the story is very much influenced by its setting. Find out about the Twenties and Thirties. Find out how the Depression affected members of your family.

- Find pictures of such Depression era items mentioned in the book, such as ice boxes, washtubs (big enough for bathing), Progressive Farmer Magazine (or similar titles), freak shows.

- Ida wasn't the only one traveling the road looking for work at that time. Look in nonfiction books about that time for other "Knights of the Road."

- Research the locale of the book as it was then and as it is now. Do people in the Blue Ridge Mountains of Georgia still live the way the Sutton family did?

- Locate the Blue Ridge Mountains and name the states they stretch across.

- Compare Ida to the tramps in Helen Cresswell's **Night Watchmen** (Aladdin, 1989. ISBN 0-689-71292-8).

- The children and Ida play many games. List them and play them.

- Ida reads the children the comic strips and then the children color them. Find out which of those they mention are still in the newspapers today.

- Ida isn't the only character in literature who is prone to exaggerate a bit. Find others who exaggerate and others whose feats you are sure are exaggerated, such as Davy Crockett, Iva Dunnitt, Shirley in the Shirley and Claude books, and Pecos Bill.

- Find other motherless families in literature and compare their situations and solutions to those of the Sutton family.

- Charlotte Huck said, "Burch's characters have warmth and sympathy which is lacking in those created by Robert Newton Peck." Do you agree?

- Compare Ida to the main character in Eleanor Estes' **The Hundred Dresses.** She too is the brunt of jokes because of her clothing.

Fiction

★Hamilton, Virginia. **Willie Bea and the Time the Martians Landed.** Greenwillow, 1983. ISBN 0-689-71328-2

■■■■■■■□□□□□□□

Least Sophisticated   Most Sophisticated

This is a Focus Book; see page 291.

◆Gates, Doris. **Blue Willow.** Viking, 1940. ISBN 0-670-17557-9

———. **Sauce Azul.** Hispanic Book Distributors.

■■■■■■■□□□□□□□

See page 228.

◆MacLachlan, Patricia. **Sarah, Plain and Tall.** HarperCollins, 1985. ISBN 0-06-024101-2

■■■■■■■■■□□□□□

A lonely, motherless family on the prairie places an ad in the newspaper. Sarah Elisabeth Wheaton of Maine, describing herself as "plain and tall," arrives and answers the family's needs. See **Once Upon a Time** *(DLM, 1990. ISBN 1-55924-324-4) for more activities with this book.*

Burch, Robert. **Christmas with Ida Early.** Viking, 1983. ISBN 0-670-22131-7

■■■■■■■□□□□□□□

This sequel to **Ida Early Comes Over the Mountain** *finds Ida still with the Sutton family as housekeeper and friend. Twelve-year-old Randall tells us about Ida's effect on the Christmas pageant .*

———. ***Tyler, Wilkin and Skee.*** University of Georgia Press, 1990. ISBN 0-8203-1194-4

■■■■■■■□□□□□□□

The three Coley boys live in rural Georgia. Their father is lucky to have a job during the Depression years, but money is short and the family makes its own amusement. Skee can find a song for every occasion. Wilkin is better at talking to people. Tyler tries to hold the group together.

Clifford, Eth. ***The Summer of the Dancing Horse.*** Houghton, 1990. ISBN 0-395-50066-4

■■■■■□□□□□□□□□

See page 229.

Estes, Eleanor. ***The Hundred Dresses.*** Harcourt, 1974. ISBN 0-642350-2

■■■■■□□□□□□□□□

A poor girl, goaded and ridiculed by her classmates, claims to have one hundred dresses.

Koller, Jackie French. ***Nothing to Fear.*** Gulliver, 1990. ISBN 0-15-200544-7

■■■■■■■■□□□□□□

See page 229.

Oneal, Zibby. ***A Long Way to Go.*** Viking, 1990. ISBN 0-670-82532-8

■■■■■□□□□□□□□□

See page 229.

Peck, Robert Newton. ***Arly.*** Walker, 1989. ISBN 0-8027-6856-3

■■■■□□□□□□□□□□

See page 229.

Nonfiction

Glassman, Bruce. ***The Crash of '29 and the New Deal.*** Silver Burdett, 1986. ISBN 0-382-06978-1

■■■■■■■■■□□□□□

See page 230.

Stanley, Jerry. ***Children of the Dust Bowl.*** Crown, 1992. ISBN 0-517-58782-3

■■■■■■■□□□□□□□

See page 231.

Tames, Richard. ***Picture History of the 20th Century: The 1920s.*** Watts, 1991. ISBN 0-531-14182-9

■■■■■■□□□□□□□□

See page 231.

Nonprint

Videos

Roll of Thunder, Hear My Cry. American School Publishers.

Meet the Newbery Author: Mildred Taylor. American School Publishers.

Willie Bea and the Time the Martians Landed

Willie Bea and the Time the Martians Landed

By Virginia Hamilton. Greenwillow, 1983.
  ISBN 0-689-71328-2

■■■■■■■■□□□□□□□

Genre: Historical Fiction

Setting: Ohio, 1938

Summary: Willie Bea loves her extended family and is deeply loved in return. The book revolves around Halloween Eve, in 1938. Almost all her extended family has gathered for a traditional family dinner at Grand's house in rural Ohio. Their immediate neighborhood consists mostly of her relatives, most of whom are struggling financially and who rely on each other for emotional support. After the dinner, everyone goes home, including glamorous Aunt Leah who lives far away but drives an automobile. It is she who hears the broadcast, and with her equally glamorous escort, flees back to her family and gets most of them as hysterical as she is. Willie Bea dashes across the countryside on stilts to a nearby farm where more Martians have landed. There in the pitch dark she sees what she thinks are Martians, but what turns out to be the first harvesting machines at work.

Background Information

- Many people had a hard time finding work and making a living in 1938.

- Many families lived close to their relatives in rural areas and could share in the raising of their families.

- Orson Welles directed a radio program based on H. G. Wells' book **The War of the Worlds** about a landing of Martians in New Jersey. Because the program was acted as if it were a news broadcast, many people believed it to be actual news and became hysterical.

- Farm machines such as combines were new, noisy, and might be frightening to someone seeing them for the first time in the dark.

Things to Notice and Talk About

- Many of the names of the characters in this story are unusual: children named Big and Little, Willie Beatrime, Bay Sister and Bay Brother. How do people with unusual names feel about them?

- Notice the way each of the characters reacted to the news that the Martians had landed. How would members of your own family react? Who would become hysterical? Who would be skeptical?

- Why did people believe the broadcast?

- If she had not believed the broadcast were true, would Willie Bea have been as frightened by the farm machines?

- If you hadn't read this book and you saw a television broadcast that seemed to be a news flash about flying saucers landing in New Jersey, would you believe it? Why? Which of your friends and relatives do you think would be most apt to believe it?

Things to Do

- You can get audio tapes of that broadcast through some public radio stations. Listen to the broadcast to see how and why it was so believable.

- Get tapes of some of the other radio programs mentioned in the book. Listen to them and then take them to a person who listened to those radio programs when they were young. Listen to the tapes together. Ask the person about his or her favorite characters, episodes, theme songs, and commercials. Ask them about their favorite television shows now. Is there any similarity?

- Use a microfilm reader at a library to read newspaper accounts from the day after the broadcast. Compare them with the newspapers quoted in the story.

- Find out what people believed about Mars and Martians at the time.

- Willie Bea and Toughy rush over to the Kelly farm on stilts. Try walking on stilts yourself. Could you rush? How could they?

• Make a chart like the one below showing how each character reacted to the broadcast.

Name of Character	Character Traits	Reaction to Broadcast
Willie Bea	Feisty, daring, jealous of others getting attention.	Jumps on stilts to get to Kelly farm to see the Martians.
Aunt Leah	Generous, believes in numerology and fortune-telling.	Faints.
Willie's father, Jason	Reasonable, hard-working, kind, loving	Thinks the Nazis have invaded

Picture Books

Allen, Thomas. **On Granddaddy's Farm.** Knopf, 1989. ISBN 0-394-89613-5

See page 227.

Fiction

◆ Taylor, Mildred. **Roll of Thunder, Hear My Cry.** Dial, 1976. ISBN 0-8037-7473-7

■■■■■■■■■□□□□□

Least Sophisticated   Most Sophisticated

This is a Focus Book; see page 297.

———. **The Friendship and The Gold Cadillac.** Bantam, 1989. ISBN 0-553-15765-5

See page 149.

Nonfiction

Tames, Richard. **Picture History of the 20th Century: The 1930s.** Watts, 1991. ISBN 0-531-14059-8

■■■■■■□□□□□□□□

See page 231.

The Blue Between the Clouds

The Blue Between the Clouds

By Stephen Wunderli. Holt, 1992. ISBN 0-8050-1772-0

■■■■■■■□□□□□□□

Genre: Historical Fiction

Setting: Utah, 1940s

Summary: Matt and Two Moons are best friends and this book is a celebration of their friendship. Two Moons's parents are dead and his sister wants him to live with her in Bozeman, Montana, but his grandfather who lives on the reservation has decreed that Two Moons can stay with Matt and his family for a while. Perhaps because both boys know their living arrangement is temporary, they thoroughly enjoy and understand each other. Both are determined to fly and manage, amazingly, with the help of a disturbed World War I veteran, to do so.

Background Information

- The following are often part of some Indian ceremonies and rituals: sweat lodges, sand painting, eagle feathers, amulets and necklaces, name-giving, sacrifice, and chanting.

- Many people who fight in wars are psychologically affected by what they have done and seen.

- Many of the veterans of World War I were alive during World War II.

- Neither of those wars took place on American soil.

- Early airplanes were fairly unsophisticated and fragile machines.

- There is a Greek myth about Icarus who flew too close to the sun.

Things to Notice and Talk About

- Talk about the psychological similarities between Emmett and Mr. Simmons and the way people treated both men.

- Notice the way the boys showed their friendship and the feelings between them and Esther.

- Was Miss Alexander a good teacher? What evidence can you find to defend your position?

- Notice the way the clan treated the death of Two Moons's grandfather. Are there any similarities to the way other religions deal with a death?

- What do you think is going on in Emmett's head?

- When do you think Mr. Simmons knew that Matt was not his son?

- Notice the way Matt's parents treat him and Two Moons. Are they realistically portrayed?

- Do you think the boys will ever see each other again? How and when?

- Find examples in the book of a character showing or gaining wisdom.

- Find the parts of the story that show Emmett's and Mr. Simmons's crazy behavior and parts that show their bravery.

- What do you think of Matt's Indian name? What would you have chosen for him?

- The plane the boys flew is a World War I plane. What planes were being used in the war that was being fought at the same time of this story?

- What do you find out about World War I in this book? What do you find out about World War II? Why do you think the author chose to present the wars that way?

Things to Do

- Find out about early aircraft and find a picture that you think is closest to what the boys' airplane looked like.

- Find pictures of sand paintings. Can you do one?

- Figure out what tribe Two Moons was from.

- Find out if the town of Thistle, Utah, exists.

- Find and read the story of Icarus.

- Read the wordless novel ***The Silver Pony*** by Lynd Ward (Houghton, 1973. ISBN 0-395-14753-0). How does that book relate to ***The Blue Between the Clouds?*** Would the boys like it?

Picture Books

◆ Burleigh, Robert. *Flight: The Journey of Charles Lindbergh.* Illustrated by Mike Wimmer. Putnam, 1991. ISBN 0-399-22272-3

See page 227.

Bantock, Nick. *Wings: A Pop-up Book of Things That Fly.* Random, 1991. ISBN 0-679-81041-2

An interesting and cleverly engineered pop-up book.

Provensen, Alice and Provensen, Martin. *The Glorious Flight: Across the Channel with Louis Bleriot.* Viking, 1983. ISBN 0-670-34259-9

This is a picture book account of the flight of the Bleriot XI, which crossed the English Channel in the early 1900s.

Yolen, Jane. *Wings.* Illustrated by Dennis Nolan. Harcourt, 1991. ISBN 0-15-297850-X

The myth of Icarus is retold with sensitivity and with luminous illustrations.

Fiction

★ Twain, Mark. *The Adventures of Tom Sawyer.* Many editions available.

■■■■■■■■■□□□□□

Least Sophisticated   Most Sophisticated

See page 197.

Fitzgerald, John D. *The Great Brain.* Dell, 1972. ISBN 0-440-43071-2

■■■■■■■□□□□□□□

This is one of a series of books about J.D. and his brother, growing up in Utah in the nineteenth century. The boys have a similar capacity for getting into wild and often disastrous adventures.

Nonfiction

◆ Freedman, Russell. *The Wright Brothers: How They Invented the Airplane.* Holiday, 1991. ISBN 0-8234-0875-2

■■■■■■■■□□□□□□

See page 120.

Maynard, Christopher. *The Aces: Pilots and Planes of World War I.* Watts, 1987. ISBN 0-531-10367-6

■■■■■□□□□□□□□□

See page 89.

Tessendorf, K. C. *Wings Around the World: The American World Flight of 1924.* Atheneum, 1991. ISBN 0-689-31550-3

■■■■■□□□□□□□□□

See page 127.

Stepping on the Cracks

Stepping on the Cracks

By Mary Downing Hahn. Clarion, 1991.
ISBN 0-395-58507-4

■■■■■■■□□□□□□□

Genre: Historical Fiction

Setting: 1944

Summary: Margaret and Elizabeth are next-door neighbors and best friends with strikingly different personalities. Both have brothers who are in the service, and they, like the rest of their families are worried about them. At the beginning of the story, each girl is convinced that the war is necessary and a little bit glamorous. When they are confronted with a sick deserter, they are horrified and convinced he's a traitor. They become aware that there are some people whose ethics are violated by any kind of warfare, no matter how just the cause may seem.

Background Information

- World War II was fought far away from where most Americans lived.

- The penalties for desertion could include execution.

- Pneumonia was a more life-threatening disease then than now.

Things to Notice and Talk About

- Why do people hang blue and gold stars in the windows of homes where family members were in the service or had been killed in the war?

- Notice the clothing styles the author mentions. Do you like the look?

- Talk about the role the radio played in people's lives then.

- Why is Gordy angry and afraid? Do you blame him?

- Look at the role of the teacher. Why didn't they ask her for help? What might she have done?

- Notice the way each adult in the book handles his or her concerns about the war.

- What do you think of the attitude of the people who knew that Mr. Smith was abusing his family? Would people today be apt to have the same attitudes toward family violence?

- Gordy frightens the girls by telling them there is a crazy man in the woods. Is he telling the truth?

Things to Do

- Make a map of your neighborhood like the one in the front of the book.

- Mark the places on your map where someone could be hidden for a few days without anyone finding him or her.

- Find out as much as you can about each radio program that is mentioned in the book.

- Compare Gordy to other bullies such as the ones in Spinelli's ***Maniac Magee*** (Little, 1990. ISBN 0-316-80722-295), Kinsey-Warnock's ***The Night the Bells Rang*** (see page 88), Byars' ***The Eighteenth Emergency*** (Puffin, 1981. ISBN 0-8161-4432-X), and Henkes' "older boys" in ***Chester's Way*** (Greenwillow, 1988. ISBN 0-688-07608-4).

- In some books, we never know what made the bully act the way he or she did. In other books, such as this one, the reasons are clear. Make a chart such as the one below about books you've read.

Bully	Book Title	Reason for Behavior

- Find out about the number and treatment of deserters in American wars.

- Role-play a meeting between Elizabeth and Margaret years later when they have grown sons of their own. What will they advise their sons to do in the event of war? What would you do?

- Compare this book to books about families in other wars. What is similar and what is different about their actions and feelings?

Picture Books

Hest, Amy. ***The Ring and the Window Seat.***
Scholastic, 1990. ISBN 0-590-41350-3

See page 92.

Fiction

◆ Lowry, Lois. ***Autumn Street.*** Houghton, 1980.
ISBN 0-395-27812-0

■■■■■■□□□□□□□□

Least Sophisticated   Most Sophisticated

See page 93.

◆ Hest, Amy. **Love You, Soldier.** Four Winds,
1991. ISBN 0-02-743635-7

■■■□□□□□□□□□□□

See page 93.

Burch, Robert. ***Home Front Heroes.*** Puffin,
1974. ISBN 0-14-036030-1

■■■■■■■□□□□□□□

See page 236.

Chaikin, Miriam. ***Lower! Higher! You're a Liar.***
HarperCollins, 1984. ISBN 0-06-021186-5

■■■■■■■■■□□□□□

See page 93.

Hotze, Sollace. ***Summer Endings.*** Clarion, 1990.
ISBN 0-395-56197-3

■■■■■■■□□□□□□□

See page 94.

Nonfiction

Dolan, Edward F. ***America in World War II:
1941.*** Millbrook, 1991. ISBN 1-878841-05-X

■■■■■■□□□□□□□□

See page 95.

Freedman, Russell. ***Franklin Delano Roosevelt.***
Clarion, 1990. ISBN 0-89919-379-X

■■■■■■■■■□□□□□

See page 237.

Tames, Richard. ***Picture History of the 20th
Century: The 1940s.*** Watts, 1991. ISBN 0-531-
14035-0

■■■■■□□□□□□□□□

See page 237.

Roll of Thunder, Hear My Cry
Let the Circle Be Unbroken
The Road to Memphis

Roll of Thunder, Hear My Cry

By Mildred Taylor. Dial, 1976. ISBN 0-8037-7473-7

■■■■■■■■■■■□□□□□

Let the Circle Be Unbroken

By Mildred Taylor. Dial, 1981. ISBN 0-8037-4748-9

■■■■■■■■■■■■■□□□

The Road to Memphis

By Mildred Taylor. Dial, 1990. ISBN 0-8037-0340-6

■■■■■■■■■■■■■■■□

Genre: Historical Fiction

Setting: Mississippi, 1933–1941

Note: We've grouped these three books as a single Focus Book because as a group they allow us to learn about a Southern Black family's experiences during the Depression. Because they are of increasingly more difficult reading levels, it may be appropriate to use multiple copies and have the entire class read **Roll of Thunder, Hear My Cry.** Then read aloud **Let the Circle Be Unbroken** and **The Road to Memphis.**

Summary: The three novels are about the Logans, who are Black landowners in a small town in Mississippi. The other Black families around them are sharecroppers. Through the eyes of this family, particularly Cassie, the author is attempting to show the changes that preceded the Civil Rights Movement. In **Roll of Thunder, Hear My Cry,** there is great hostility toward Blacks from nearby white landowners and business people. Cassie is spunky and grows from childhood innocence to an awareness of segregation. Shocked by her first visit to town and her rude treatment from white store owners and a white child her own age who demands submissive behavior, Cassie is humiliated when her grandmother must force her to obey the white child. By the end of the first book, T.J., a Black friend, is in deep trouble and is nearly lynched.

In the second book, **Let the Circle be Unbroken,** Cassie and her brothers listen outside the window to T.J.'s murder trial. Through this experience and her family's friendship with T.J.'s white lawyer, Cassie becomes fascinated by the legal process and learns, for instance, that juries are made from the pool of registered voters and are, therefore, all white. When Mrs. Lee Annie, a sixty-four-year-old Black woman, decides to register to vote, Cassie's family supports her by helping her study the state constitution. Meanwhile, sharecroppers and day laborers have been trying to form a racially-mixed union, which is broken, in part, by the white landowners who use Mrs. Annie's registration to show how uppity Blacks are becoming.

The Road to Memphis shows Cassie and her brother as young adults, defending themselves as they shoulder the burden of being Black in a climate that requires courage and suffering. The acquisition of a car and the slightly improved job situation for Blacks expand their opportunities, but segregation and racism continue to denigrate and limit options.

Background Information

- The sharecropping system was widespread in the South at this time.

- Black schools were vastly inferior to white schools and higher education was severely limited for Blacks.

- The legal system was run by whites only.

- During the Depression, the cost of cotton plummeted, so government programs attempted to limit production. White landowners used these programs to swindle white and Black sharecroppers.

- Attempts to unionize were fought by white landowners with threats and violence.

- In spite of all the segregation and fear, many Black families maintained strength and hope for change and a sense of community.

Things to Notice and Talk About

- Look at the titles of the books. Why did the author choose those titles? What do they mean? What would you have chosen?

- Look at the cover art. Would you have chosen those scenes or items to represent the book?

- While reading one of these books, what surprised you most? What did you feel most uncomfortable about? How does your own background affect your feelings as you read this?

Roll of Thunder, Hear My Cry

- Cassie describes her brother as an "always meticulously neat, six-year-old Little Man [who] never allowed dirt or tears or stains to mar anything he owned." Why did she use the word *tears* and how does it affect the meaning of the sentence?

- Follow the family from slavery during the Civil War, through World War I, and to World War II. Decide how such events might have affected them.

- Why didn't the family move to the North? What was happening during Chicago's race problems in 1933?

- Read aloud the last section of Chapter Five of **Roll of Thunder, Hear My Cry**, ending with "No day in all my life had ever been as cruel as this one."

- Find the poem "Incident in Baltimore" by Countee Cullen (it is in many anthologies). Compare it to Cassie's feelings on her trip to Strawberry.

Let the Circle Be Unbroken

- Russell joins the army because it is "better than starving." How prevalent was enlisting for this reason then and now?

- Discuss the situation of the cane workers and compare their lot to that of slaves'.

- **Let the Circle Be Unbroken** brings up the subject of racially-mixed marriage and its attendant problems at the time. Who opposed it and why?

- Discuss the choice Suzella must make after her parents divorce. Should she live as colored with her father or pass as white with her mother? What factors do you think she considered?

- Compare and contrast racial harassment in these books and racial harassment now.

The Road to Memphis

- The author's note at the beginning of this book gives a clue to some of the research she did. Make a list of the things this section shows she did. What else did she have to know or find out about?

- Why does Cassie's mother correct Cassie's speech? How do you think Cassie feels about dialect? How do you feel about it? Read some of the conversation from the book to an adult in your home. What is his/her reaction to the dialect? If possible, talk with southern African Americans about it. What are their reactions?

- Compare the teasing that goes on within the group of Black friends with the teasing that Statler and the others inflict on Harris and other Blacks. Who laughs? Who suffers? Who is in control? What recourse does the person being teased have? What are the consequences of not being a good sport about being teased? What are the intentions of the person doing the teasing?

- Explore the role of Jeremy. What choices does he make? What price does he pay? What options does he have after he must leave town contrasted to those that Moe has once he leaves town?

Things to Do

- After reading **Roll of Thunder, Hear My Cry,** research what happened to families like the Granger family during and after the Civil War. How would some of the rich families of today react to losing their riches over a moral issue?

- Chart landowning Blacks, sharecroppers, and day laborers showing relative income, freedom of choice, dependence on whites, and likelihood of change.

- Make a list of historical information from these books. How did Mildred Taylor manage to convey all that information without sounding like a textbook? What information was most startling to you? Is there anything you'd like to know more about?

- List and try to position on a spectrum from mild to severe as many of the racial incidents from one of these stories as possible. List the causes and consequences, if known, of those incidents. Can you find a piece of writing on current racism and prepare a similar chart?

Picture Books

◆ Hoffman, Mary. ***Amazing Grace.*** Illustrated by Caroline Binch. Dial, 1991. ISBN 0-8037-1040-2

See page 147.

◆ Medearis, Angela. ***Dancing with the Indians.*** Illustrated by Samuel Byrd. Holiday, 1991. ISBN 0-8234-0893-0

See page 34.

◆ Golenbock, Peter. ***Teammates.*** Harcourt, 1990. ISBN 0-15-200603-6

See page 147.

Fiction

★ Hamilton, Virginia. ***Willie Bea and the Time the Martians Landed.*** Greenwillow, 1983. ISBN 0-689-71328-2

■■■■■■■□□□□□□□

Least Sophisticated   Most Sophisticated

This is a Focus Book; see page 291.

◆ Armstrong, William H. ***Sounder.*** HarperCollins, 1969. ISBN 0-06-020144-4

■■■■■■■■■□□□□□

See page 148.

◆ Hooks, William. ***Circle of Fire.*** Atheneum, 1982. ISBN 0-689-50241-9

■■■■■■■□□□□□□□

See page 148.

◆ Moore, Yvette. ***Freedom Songs.*** Orchard, 1990. ISBN 0-531-05812-3

■■■■■■■■■■□□□

See page 98.

Taylor, Mildred D. ***The Friendship and The Gold Cadillac.*** Bantam, 1989. ISBN 0-553-15765-5

■■■■■■■□□□□□□□

See page 149.

Van Raven, Pieter. ***A Time of Troubles.*** Scribner, 1990. ISBN 0-684-19212-8

■■■■■■■■■■■□

See page 113.

Nonfiction

★ Myers, Walter Dean. ***Now Is Your Time: The African-American Struggle for Freedom.*** HarperCollins, 1992. ISBN 0-06-024370-8

■■■■■■■■■□□□□

See page 98.

◆ Adoff, Arnold. ***Malcolm X.*** Crowell, 1970. ISBN 0-06-446015-0

■■■■■■□□□□□□□

See page 98.

◆ Parks, Rosa. ***Rosa Parks: My Story.*** Dial, 1992. ISBN 0-8037-0673-1

■■■■■■■■■□□□□

See page 99.

◆ Rubel, David. ***Fanny Lou Hamer: From Share Cropping to Politics.*** Silver Burdett, 1990. ISBN 0-382-09923-0

■■■■■■■■■□□□□

See page 99.

Haskins, James. ***Thurgood Marshall: A Life for Justice.*** Holt, 1992. ISBN 0-8050-2095-0

■■■■■■■■■□□□□

See page 99.

Turner, Glennette Tilley. ***Take a Walk in Their Shoes.*** Cobblehill, 1989. ISBN 0-525-65006-7

■■■■■■■□□□□□□

See page 100.

Appendix

Index

*Boldfaced type indicates a book summary.